The Camps of the
Death Railway

The Camps of the Death Railway

Stories of Suffering and Survival on the Burma-Thailand Railway

John Grehan and Ben Luto

FRONTLINE BOOKS

First published in Great Britain in 2025 by
Frontline Books
An imprint of Pen & Sword Books Limited
Yorkshire – Philadelphia

Copyright © John Grehan and Ben Luto 2025

ISBN 978 1 52672 476 2

The right of John Grehan and Ben Luto to be identified as
Authors of this work has been asserted by them in accordance
with the Copyright, Designs and Patents Act 1988.

A CIP catalogue record for this book is
available from the British Library.

All rights reserved. No part of this book may be reproduced, transmitted, downloaded, decompiled or reverse engineered in any form or by any means, electronic or mechanical including photocopying, recording or by any information storage and retrieval system, without permission from the Publisher in writing. NO AI TRAINING: Without in any way limiting the Author's and Publisher's exclusive rights under copyright, any use of this publication to "train" generative artificial intelligence (AI) technologies to generate text is expressly prohibited. The Author and Publisher reserve all rights to license uses of this work for generative AI training and development of machine learning language models.

Typeset by Mac Style
Printed in the UK by CPI Group (UK) Ltd, Croydon, CR0 4YY.

The Publisher's authorised representative in the EU for product safety is Authorised Rep Compliance Ltd., Ground Floor, 71 Lower Baggot Street, Dublin D02 P593, Ireland.
www.arccompliance.com

For a complete list of Pen & Sword titles please contact

PEN & SWORD BOOKS LIMITED
47 Church Street, Barnsley, South Yorkshire, S70 2AS, England
E-mail: enquiries@pen-and-sword.co.uk
Website: www.pen-and-sword.co.uk
or
PEN AND SWORD BOOKS
1950 Lawrence Road, Havertown, PA 19083, USA
E-mail: uspen-and-sword@casematepublishers.com
Website: www.penandswordbooks.com

Contents

Introduction		vii
Part I: Japanese Official Report on the Burma-Thailand Railway		1
Chapter 1	General Outlook	3
Chapter 2	General Outline of Construction Programme	5
	Allotment of Duties Concerning the Railway Construction	6
	State of Affairs in the Early Stage	8
	State of Affairs in the Period When Construction Was Urged On	8
	Period of Delay in Construction Work	12
	Conditions After Completion of Construction	13
Chapter 3	Factors Impeding Construction	14
	Technical Obstacles	14
	Natural Obstacles	14
Chapter 4	Supervising the Pows	16
	Supply and Maintenance	17
	Billeting	21
	Sanitary Arrangements	22
Chapter 5	Outbreak of Disease	25
	How Cholera Broke Out	25
	How Cases of Malaria Occurred	27
	Tropical Ulcer	28
	Other Prevailing Diseases	28
	Medical Supplies	28

vi   The Camps of the Death Railway

Chapter 6	Supervision and Employment of Prisoners	30
	Relations between the Supervising party and the Employing Party	31
	Outline of supervision and service	32
	Conclusion	34

Part II: The Movement of POWs from Holding Camps to Thailand and Burma   37

Part III: Camps of the Thai-Burma Railway   43

Postscript   273
Source Information   275
Index   280

Introduction

Shortly after the Japanese surrender in September 1945, news of the shocking conditions endured by Allied prisoners of war in the building of the Thailand to Burma railway, and the brutal treatment they suffered at the hands of the Japanese during that time, became known to the wider world.

It was clear that an investigation into what were potentially war crimes, would be undertaken by the Allies and, it would seem, the Japanese sought to get their side of the story out first. In February 1946, as the South East Asia Translation and Interrogation Centre was compiling its report on the railway, John Edward Padfield, who was a captain in the Intelligence Corps attached to the Supreme Allied Commander, South East Asia Command, was handed a letter from the United Kingdom Liaison Mission in Japan. With the letter were two copies of a document entitled 'Report on Employment of War Prisoners in the Siam-Burma Railway', purporting to have been issued by the Japanese Government. The report had initially been sent to the Swiss Legation in Tokyo before being forwarded to the British Embassy.[1]

As there was no other information available from Tokyo, the Japanese report was presented in evidence at the War Crimes Trials. It is reproduced in Part I almost in its entirety and with only minor corrections or modifications for clarification, though some of the wording is a little incomprehensible in parts.

What the Japanese report attempts to show is that the many deaths and privations suffered by the POWs were due to factors largely beyond their control and that they attempted to do all they could to mitigate the hardships the prisoners endured. The reality was quite different, as we shall read. But the report does provide us with a good introduction to the story of the of the railway, the reasons for its construction and how the work was organised.

Many affidavits were submitted by the Allied prisoners to the War Crimes Trials relating to the ill treatment they had received. These, in large numbers, are to be found in The National Archives at Kew in London and with the Australian War Memorial in Canberra. Over time, more details have emerged of that bleak episode of the Second World War in the form of diaries and memoires,

---

1. The National Archives (TNA), WO 325/90, Japanese Official Report.

published and unpublished, so that, taken together, today we can construct a more comprehensive assessment of life in the various camps.

What very quickly became obvious in attempting to compile this collection of reports and statements was that there was no universal agreement on either the location or names of every single camp. It is known that the camp sites in Burma were chosen by Major Yabe, the Commander of the 4th Battalion, 9th Railway Regiment, who ordered that the prisoners of war must clear the sites in the jungle and build their own huts. Camp sites were chosen for their access to flat land and water, be it a stream or the Khwae Noi river.

According to one of the defendants at the War Crimes Trials, the commander of 60 Company of the Building Unit which built many of the early camps on the Burma side of the railway, the first consideration with regards to the location of the camps was that they were sited where there was running water and that it was on ground high enough 'so that water can be disposed of during the rainy season'. The only other consideration was that, as far as practical, the camp could not be seen from above by aircraft.

It was stated that the siting of the cookhouses was determined by access to the river (meaning generally the Khwae Noi) to enable the easy transportation of food supplies. Latrines were dug away from the river or at 'the lower part of the slope where it was a certain distance from the huts'. That distance was given as 50 to 100 metres. It was also stated that latrines were dug at a ratio of one for every twenty men. Urinals were attached to each latrine. The Japanese also claimed that the huts used for accommodation were the same for the Japanese as they were for the native labourers and the POWs. When asked about hospital or medical facilities, the Japanese representative claimed that, 'We usually built a hut apart from the other huts with a size to take in about 10 to 20 per cent of the entire population of the camp'.[2]

When asked if the POW camps were fenced in, it was said that this was determined locally. Regarding the nature of the POW accommodation, it was stated that each man was allocated 2.5 metres in length and 75 to 80 cm in width. The prisoners slept on bamboo boards which, it was asserted, 'is rather comfortable'. The huts were built to last just four months, by which time the roof and the floor would need to be repaired or replaced.

It is interesting to note that when high-ranking Japanese officers were due to visit a camp, the respective camp commanders allowed the prisoners to improve buildings and sanitation. In at least one instance, some of the hospital patients were hidden in the jungle during such a visit to conceal the true sickness levels.

---

2. Information from the War Crimes Trials can be found in the Australian War Memorial's (AWM) 54 series of files.

By contrast, depending which officer from which branch of the Japanese Army was visiting, the percentage of working men to hospital cases had to be increased. Any man who could move had to undertake some task, however light, during the visit. All this demonstrates how badly coordinated and poorly organised the whole railway project really was.

What we have attempted to achieve is to provide both a general view of the construction of the railway through the Japanese official account, as well as describe, through the words of the internees, as precisely as possible, what each camp was like and the conditions the prisoners endured within it. While we have researched widely, we realise there are many published and unpublished accounts we have not been able to consult. A list of the books and documents that have been used can be found at the end of this book, and those seeking more details of particular camps or individuals are advised to read these remarkable, if at times harrowing, stories. All have their own unique tales to tell.

Readers may also note contradictions between one prisoner's experience and that of others. Much of the differences are explained by the fact that conditions varied enormously from the terrible effects of the monsoon rains, and the corresponding rushed construction of the 'speedo' period, to the dry season after the completion of the railway when conditions became much more benign.

It must also be noted that the Asians who worked on the railway were referred to at the time as 'coolies' or Asiatics. These were known to the Japanese as *rōmusha*, which is a Japanese word for a 'paid conscripted labourer'. Other than in direct quotes, this is the term we have adopted in most cases to categorise these workers.

Our first requirement was that of identifying the various camps, but this proved to be no simple task. As Kazuo Tamayama explains, the names were 'taken from the nearest village or physical feature'.[3] That was fine for the larger towns whose names were known, but in the depths of the jungle there were no signposts or village signs. Added to this was that both the Japanese soldiers and the Allied prisoners were generally incapable of reading Sanskrit Thai, so places were known only by the names given by the locals in their multi-tonal spoken form. This led to a multiplicity of interpretations as individuals wrote down their understanding of the names they had heard, particularly as the Allied soldiers often only heard the name given to a camp third hand from the Japanese.

'You have to remember,' one survivor, Reg Twigg, explained, 'that these camps were hacked out of the undergrowth by us, the British, the Aussies and the

---

3. Kazuo Tamayama, *Building the Burma-Thailand Railway 1942-43, An Epic of World War II* (The World War II Remembrance Group, Japan, 2004), p.IX.

Dutch. They had no names before we got there because they had no existence and you won't find them on any map today.'[4]

Many of the camps were only known to the prisoners by their distance from the railway's starting point, be that from Bam Pong in Thailand or from Thanbyuzayat in Burma; this is a convention which we have followed. Frequently, however, these distances do not comply with known or actual locations. An example of this is what was initially named 211 Kilo camp. It was later found to be seventeen kilometres further on. It then became 228 Kilo camp! Sadly, numerous books have been published with different names on the maps to those in the text, with no attempt made at reconciling these differences. Placing individual accounts, often very interesting and valuable, in the correct camp is, therefore, highly challenging. Indeed, some stories could not be included because the camp the prisoners were in simply could not be identified.[5]

Nothing could illustrate all of this better than Chungkai camp. No native village or local landmark bears that name. However, there is a hill near where the original road from Kanchanaburi crosses the Khwae Yai called Khao Chungkai. There is speculation that this was the intended path of the railway, which is why the Japanese expected the camp after the river crossing to be called Chungkai. This makes much sense as this alternative route crosses a narrower stretch of the river than the famous, though possibly not the correct, bridge on the River Kwai[6], and the open flat land beyond would have been far more suitable for the laying of a railway than the difficult route actually taken which necessitated cutting through hills (such as the Hellfire Pass) and building of viaducts (for example Wampo) high above the Khwae Noi. It could be that crossing the river near Kanchanaburi was an error which meant the railway took longer to build and resulted in many more POW deaths.[7]

It is also the case that so many of the camps have all but, or completely, disappeared. This was something Lieutenant Colonel 'Weary' Dunlop was conscious of as far back as 1943 as he pondered on the fate of those who had died at Konyu camp: 'How long will it be before the relentless jungle obliterates

---

4. Reg Twigg, *Survivor on the River Kwai, The Incredible Story of Life on the Burma Railway* (Viking, London, 2013), pp.221-2.
5. For instance, Captain Adrian Curlewis refers to a camp by the name of Middle Tementap in a diary he kept. There is no known camp of that name nor anything similar, see TNA WO 235/1034.
6. Kwai, or more accurately, Khwae, actually means river or tributary in Thai, so there never was a River Kwai. What is generally referred to is the Khwae Noi, or little river. Equally confusing is that the famous bridge in question is not on the Khwae Noi at all, but spans what was formally called the Mae Klong River, though is now known as the Khwae Yai or big river.
7. Clifford Kinvig, *River Kwai Railway, The Story of the Burma-Siam Railroad* (Brassey's, London, 1992), pp.69-70 and Imperial War Museum (IWM), Ewart Escritt, *Beyond The Three Pagodas Pass*, pp.18-19, Escritt Collection, Catalogue No. 2267.

all trace of their coming and departure.' This was confirmed in an official Dutch survey prepared by the Rijksinstituut voor Oorlogsdocumentatie (National Institute for War Documentation). The survey looked at POW diaries and formal statements from known official reports and tried to marry the two. The report's authors had to concede that there were at least fourteen camps referred to by POWs which could not be located.[8]

Equally, information from the larger camps is often found in abundance, while with some of the smaller secondary and transitory camps there is little detail to be readily found. There are some camps where we have been unable to find any information whatsoever and, therefore, the list of camps recorded here should not be considered in any way as being definitive. While we have been able to uncover information on more than seventy camps, we are acutely conscious that there are others for which we have found nothing. This should not be taken as meaning such information does not exist, merely that in the course of our investigation we have not come across it.

In those camps where there is a great deal of information, deciding what not to include was the most challenging task given publishing constraints. The diaries and memoirs of such men as Edward Dunlop and Robert Hardie are large books in their own right and for those who wish a more detailed picture of life and death on the railway, these, and many of the books listed at the end of this monograph, are essential reading. The end notes will help as a guide for those seeking to explore further this tragic, though often uplifting, episode in the history of the nations involved.

All that has been possible within the parameters set for this volume, is a brief overview of the layout, life and conditions in the camps, where this is available, along with some of the stories of notable events. In general, we have not written about the work the prisoners had to undertake or the construction of the railway in relation to the camps, as that is covered in the Japanese account which sets the scene for what follows. However, some comments by Dunlop as he walked along the track in August 1943 give an indication of the nature of the railway: 'At times the rails are up in the air above the sleepers, sometimes the sleepers are up in the air attached to the rails!' He wrote that, apart from being parallel, just about everything was wrong with the track. 'The sleepers are not even faintly laid – just like so many matches tossed down by a giant hand.'[9]

By way of a prelude to the suffering endured by the prisoners in the camps, we have included extracts from a report by the commanding officer of one of the groups of prisoners – 'F' Force – sent from Singapore to Thailand. This report

---

8. IWM, Escritt Collection.
9. E.E. Dunlop, *The War Diaries of Weary Dunlop* (Penguin, Harmondsworth, 1986), p.310.

makes clear the terrible circumstances in which the men were transported and then force-marched into the jungle to the work camps. Equally challenging were the conditions numbers of Australian, American and Dutch prisoners endured on the ships in which they were moved to Burma. All that subsequently happened to the prisoners began on those punishing journeys.

While accepting that there is no unanimity on the location or names of the camps, the list so painstakingly drawn up by Rod Beattie of the Thailand-Burma Railway Centre (TBRC) in Kanchanaburi is generally the one we have followed, coupled with a map compiled from Japanese sources, and which is reproduced in this book, and other original versions found in the files of The National Archives. Precise locations of the known camps can be found Rod Beattie's book, *The Thai-Burma Railway: The True Story of The Bridge On The River Kwai*. The guidance and information provided by TBRC's Andrew Snow, whose knowledge of the railway is phenomenal, has been invaluable.

Also, of great help have been Caitlin James of the Research Centre of the Australian War Memorial, Cheryl Mellor, 2/4th Machine Gun Battalion ex-Members Association, and Lieutenant Colonel Peter Winstanley who granted me access to the material on his Prisoners of War of the Japanese website, as did Will at Anzac Portal. Robert Mitchell provided help with photographs and, sketches and maps.

Part I

Japanese Official Report on the Burma-Thailand Railway

Chapter 1

General Outlook

1. By order of the Imperial General Headquarters, the preparations for the construction of this railway were commenced in June 1942 by the South Army with the view of using it as a ground supply route and a trade and traffic one between Thailand and Burma, being urged on by the proposal of the South Army and the construction work was virtually begun in November 1942 in hopes of completing it by the end of 1943. But while counterattacks, particularly bombing, of the British Indian Army rapidly became fierce and the situations in this area considerably serious since the end of the rainy season of 1942, our sea-transportation from Malaya to Burma gradually became hard.

   As there could be found no ground transport route for its substitute, it was closely estimated that, if the situations were left as they were till the end of the next rainy season, transportation to Burma would be almost entirely interrupted and even the defence of the area, not to mention positive actions, impossible and furthermore the work itself quite difficult. For these reasons the Imperial General Headquarters ordered early in Feb. 1943 to shorten the term of the work, taking the best possible measures and the working troops also did their best, so that the work made favourable progress for the time being. However, as the rainy season earlier than usual set in, in addition to the bad conditions in jungles since April or March of 1943 which the Japanese Army had never encountered before, victims of the work gradually increased, not to speak of the delay or scheduled work.

   Confronted with these bad conditions, the Imperial General Headquarters, ordered at last to postpone the period of the work by two months in spite of the fact that this order had a grave influence the operations in Burma, considering the general situations of the Burma front at that time, and that the prospect of communication with Burma was becoming clear with the partial completion of the railway and local employment of newly constructed roads and water-ways paralleled with the railway.

2. It is not unnatural that a great many persons should be employed in such construction work in order to strengthen operation capacity. Although the South Army levied labourers on the spot and employed them in the work

beside Japanese troops, it was so difficult to gather a great many labourers immediately that the South Army asked permission to employ POWs in the work of the Imperial General Headquarters.

Considering that the work would be carried on in the rear far away from the first front, and search would be for a trade route between Thailand and Burma, the Imperial General headquarters complied with the request and sanctioned the employment or POWs. Then the forced construction work was carried out in precipitous jungles spreading over 400 kilometres conquering natural hindrances such as the influence of bad weather, particularly that of the rainy season, and the environment injurious to health etc. and surmounting technical hindrances – such as time limit due to operational needs and the imperfect preparation due to it, inadequate accommodation along the lines of communication, and the inferior technical skill of the Japanese Army.

3. Although the Japanese Army did its best in taking the best possible measures conceivable at that time in order to improve the treatment of the POWs co-operating with the Japanese troops, laying stress on billeting, ration and health, many POWs fell victim of the work at last much to our regret. We should like to declare the Japanese troops participated in the joys and sorrows of the POWs and native labourers in the construction work, and by no means completed or intended to complete the work only at the sacrifice of POWs.

NOTE: The director of construction cherished the motto: 'POWs and labourers are Fathers of Construction', and constantly endeavoured at improving the treatment of POWs.

Chapter 2

General Outline of Construction Programme

1. With the development of the North Burma operation, to construct a railway connecting Thailand and Burma as an operational supply route and for trade and traffic, had become so urgent that the South Army proposed its construction to the Imperial General Headquarters. Therefore, the latter directed its preparation to the former in June of the same year.
2. The preparations of the constructions are summarized as follows:
   (1) Route: about 400 km, from Nonpradoc to Thambisaya along the River Kaonoi.
   (2) Transportation capacity: about 3,000 tons a day in each direction.
   (3) Period: scheduled to complete by the end of 1943.
   (4) Materials: mainly to use the materials on the spot with a part being transferred from the home islands.
   (5) Military strength: The Railway Inspection Office, two railway regiments, the Railway Material Depot and some other auxiliary troops.
   (6) Labour: (auxiliary personnel): labourers levied on the spot and POWs.
3. In conformity with the above preparation items, the South Army began conducting a survey along the route of the proposed railway, and undertook negotiations with Thailand for the establishment of construction bases, the preparation of construction materials, arrangements for labourers, a survey of military geography and sanitary arrangements, and moved the railway units in Burma to the construction bases one after another, where they were then deployed.

    As the negotiations with Thailand were concluded at the beginning of November of the same year, the order of the Imperial General Headquarters concerning execution of the railway construction was issued and soon after, in accordance with the above items the order concerning the construction, was issued by the South Army.
4. The chief inspector of the Second Railway Inspection Office (staying in Bangkok) took command of the following units of which the South Army Railway Corps was composed. The 5th Railway Regiment, with its base in Thambisaya [Thanbyuzayat] was allotted the duty of construction on the Thailand-side, and the 9th Railway Regiment (its base was in Kanchanaburi)

that on the Burma-side. The main part of the 1st Railway Material Depot was deployed in Nonpradoc and the other part in Rangoon. Thus, the preparations made progress step by step, and virtual construction work was started in December, complying with the above-mentioned orders.

The South Army Railway Corps was commanded by The Chief Inspector of the Second Railway Inspection Office, Major General Shinoda. It comprised the following units:

> The Second Railway Inspection office.
> The Fifth Railway Regiment.
> The Ninth Railway Regiment. The First Material Depot.
> Two units serving on land.
> Two building units.
> Two field well-drilling units.
> The Field Epidemic prevention and Water-supply Depot co-operators.

Co-operators:
The Thailand Interment Camp
The Field Supply Park.

5. The Thailand Interment Camp, having finished preparations, co-operated in the construction work from the beginning by order of the South Army.

Allotment of Duties Concerning the Railway Construction

Imperial General Headquarters – Directions Concerning the Railway Construction:

1. Negotiations with the Ministry of war concerning estimate and materials.
2. Diplomatic negotiations through the Ministry of War.
3. Orders concerning the railway construction (directives of the Imperial General Headquarters).
4. To help supply of materials necessary for the construction.
5. Directions of the construction complying with the operational needs.
6. To decide whether the employment of POWs is appropriate.

South Army General – Chief Supervisor of Railway Construction:

1. To estimate and concentrate military strength and labour necessary for the railway construction. Supply, maintenance and sanitary arrangements for them.

2. To make POWs co-operate with the construction units or to allot them to the units.
3. Directions concerning the employment of POWs.
4. Planning of the railway construction.
5. To keep harmony between the railway construction units & co-operating attached units.
6. Maintenance of traffic routes and waterways necessary for the construction.

Railway Inspection Office – Commander in Charge of Railways Construction:

1. Inspection survey and construction of the route according to the railway construction plan.
2. Employment of the railway units and attached units.
3. To make POWs and labourers co-operate with the railway units or to allot them to the unit.
4. Directions concerning the employment of POWs.
5. Negotiations with the Internment Camp concerning the employment of POWs.
6. To take care of billeting, maintenance & health of POWs.

Railway Regiment: Commander in Charge of Railway in the Allotted District:

1. Construction of railway in the allotted district.
2. Employment of the allotted and co-operating POWs according to the directives of the Commander in charge of Railways construction.
3. Negotiations with persons in charge of supervising POWs.
4. To take care of billeting, maintenance and health of POWs.

Internment Camp, to assist and control the railway construction in the capacity of the supervisor of POWs:

1. To make POWs co-operate with the railway construction units or to allot them to the units by order of the South General Army.
2. Negotiations with railway construction units concerning the employment of POWs.
3. Chiefly to take care of billet maintenance and health of POWs and to request assistance to the units concerned.
4. Execution of the business of supervising POWs.

State of Affairs in the Early Stage

From June 1942 to the Middle of February 1943

1. In accordance with the above details, the prepared works such as survey work, collection of materials necessary for the maintenance of the bases and a part of ground-construction etc. were begun. The construction was commenced from both sides, Thailand and Burma, and the supply in the rear was assisted by the Army stationing in Thailand in the case of the former and by the Burma B Army Group in the case of the latter.
2. Virtual construction work was commenced in November 1942; an order to put it into practice being given.
3. However, the areas where the railway was to be constructed were covered with great jungles and if we had waited for the completion of the survey of the whole route, the construction period would have been so prolonged that the work was carried out keeping pace with the survey. Therefore, as to estimation of quantity of labour and materials, sufficient measures could not be prearranged.
4. In January 1943 when the work was progressing smoothly, Major General Shinoda, the commander of the construction, while patrolling over the construction area in an airplane in order to inspect the work was killed by crashing against a border mountain between Thailand and Burma, Major Irie, the chief staff of the construction, riding with him in the same plane was also killed at the same time.
5. In this period the number of POWs increased by degrees and POWs in Java and Singapore were transferred to the construction areas. The Thailand Internment Camp gradually enlarged itself and assisted the construction work on the Thailand-side with main strength while that on the Burma-side with the other strength.

State of Affairs in the Period When Construction Was Urged On

From the Middle of February 1943 to the Middle of July 1943

How and why the construction period was cut short:

1. Since the end of the rainy season of 1942, the counter-attack on Burma of the British Indian Army became so rapidly violent and the situations in this area so serious; the British Army being steadily reinforced with military strength and goods. Besides, the only transport route by sea became so dangerous as

was almost interrupted by the enemy's disturbance both from the sea and air. Hence the Japanese Imperial General Headquarters keenly felt the necessity of completing the railway connecting Thailand and Burma and intended to urge the construction on.

Namely at that time transportation of military strength and goods with which the Burma Army Group was being greatly reinforced to cope with the critical situations in Burma caused by the counter-attack of the British Indian Army, relied on the sea route from Singapore alone. But in addition to the shortage of shipping this route was extremely threatened both by the enemy planes and submarines and thus the prospects of transportation became increasingly dark. Although we tried to cut a road from Raheng to Moulmein via Mesot, it was unsuccessful as too many trucks were required, and the labour was out of proportion to the effect. At last, we faced such plight as we had to rely upon forced supply executed by small boats.

This transportation by force could be barely executed by taking advantage of the rainy season and was expected to be available only until September 1943. Under the circumstance that suspension of the sea transport and general counter-attack of the British Indian Army were expected immediately after the rainy season, a ground transport route for its substitute was absolutely necessary for the Japanese Army. Moreover, it was expected that unless it was completed by the end of the next rainy season, the Army Group operating in Burma would come to a crisis and at the same time the construction of the railway connecting Thailand and Burma would become quite difficult.

The Imperial General Headquarters, not to mention the South Army, were very anxious about the circumstance and discussed the counter-measures and tried to find a break in the deadlock. Finally, they could not but conclude that there was no other way than to complete by the end of the rainy season the railway connecting Thailand and Burma under construction at that time, and intended to cut short the construction period, having been driven to the last extremity.

2. Then, the Imperial General Headquarters consulted with the South Army, and being aware of many difficulties such as shortage of military strength, labour and materials, great amount of the work, destructive influence of the rainy season and unhealthy surroundings, yet both agreeing upon speeding up of the work by all possible means and shortening of the work, took necessary measures respectively. Viz., estimating the whole amount of the earth-work from the result of the survey executed at that time and prudently examining the military strength, labour and materials the Headquarters lowered the construction gauge (from 3,000 tons a day to each direction to 1,000 tons) and as to military strength, labour and material, took every measure possible

in the capacity of the Central office, expecting to shorten the construction period by four months and to complete the work by the end of August 1943.

They can be summarized as follows:

(1) To restore the 4th battalion, the 5th Railway Regiment in Kwantung to the home regiment. To alter the demobilization schedule of the 4th Auxiliary Railway Unit and to prepare for allotment to the railway construction units.

(2) To deliver 150 K. rails which are under charge of the central office and reserved in the South area, many rock-drills and a large quantity of explosives.

(3) To dispatch medical veterans in order to intensify measures against malaria.

3. As the tactical situations in East New Guinea were critical at that time, and the breakdown of the fighting front in this area expected imminently, quick reinforcement to the front of West New Guinea and Banda Sea areas was being carried out; transportation units, supply depots and airfield construction units which could be diverted to this purpose, were dispatched or were on route to these areas. As for labourers, they were insufficient to a certain degree, owing to the necessity of building up self-support industry on the spot caused by insufficient supply to the South Army, airfield construction for defence and dispatching labourers to the above diverted units: shortage of labour was arising even in the over-populated Java.

Then the South Amy, according to the order to cut short the construction period of the Thailand-Burma railway, diverted the following units which had been by that time employed in urgent operational duties to the railway construction, and at the same time ordered that each sector commander of Burma, Thailand, French Indo-China, Malaya and Java districts should give assistance to the railway construction, and took appropriate measures especially in the systematic supply and maintenance of labourers. As for POWs, they were transferred there all the way from French Indo-China and Java, taking into consideration the above mentioned situation.

Thus we tried to increase labour capacity by these means:

(1) The 4th Auxiliary Railway Unit, the 41st Independence Garrison Infantry Battalion, the Imperial Guards Railway Regiment, the 54th Engineer Regiment, the 42nd Line of Communication Area Unit, the Field Construction Service Unit of the 14th Division main part of the Epidemic Prevention and Water-supply Depot of the South Army and the Field Hospital of the 21st Division.

(2) Two internment branch camps in Malaya (about 10,000 POWs).

(3) A motor-car company and 300 trucks.

General Outline of Construction Programme 11

Transition of situations:
1. Because of the arrival at the construction spot of the military strength, labour, POWs and construction materials reinforced according to the above measures, the work further progressed since the end of March.
2. After Major General Shimoda's death Major General Takasaki succeeded him as the commander of the railway construction, and arrived at the spot in the middle of February of the same year, and the work was being eagerly carried on as before.
3. Contrary to our expectations the rainy season set in one month earlier than usual, i.e., it began towards the end of April in Thailand and in the middle of April in Burma, which influence upon the work and supply were tremendous.
4. At the same time, cholera which had been prevalent in some areas of Burma, was spread over the border line between Thailand and Burma and simultaneously with the setting-in of the rainy season, became increasingly prevalent. June was its most prevalent time when there broke out about 6,000 cases (of which 1,200 were the POWs) or of which about 4,000 proved fatal (of which about 500 or so were the POWs). Thus, many fell victim to the work in a short time. As this fact inspired fear in the labourers on the spot, many fled away and even some cases stole out of a hospital. The situations, dangerous both from the point of view of epidemic prevention and the work itself were brought about.
5. If cholera was prevailing, the Headquarters not only despatched medical authorities there, but sent some staff officers in order to make them take necessary steps, and the South Army, also often despatched principal medical officers and some staff officers in order to cope with the situation: the construction units fulfilled their duties, overcoming unfavourable circumstances: the prisoners of war earnestly co-operated with them.
6. On the other hand, as an emergency road for automobiles and the newly constructed railway were often destroyed and the bridges often washed away because of the long heavy rain, the ground transport was apt to be tied up, and as it was impossible to sail up the Keonoi [Khwae Noi] to the upper reaches for one month, its rising being slow, we were frequently faced with a crisis.

   Particularly, the construction unit on the Burma-side, having no parallel waterways, toiled and toiled at the construction of a rain-proof road, by which it could transport necessary materials. For this reason, the railway construction work was inevitably suspended for a while. The construction unit on the Thailand side, waiting for the rising of the Keonoi, made use of it and narrowly escaped starvation. At that time though ration to units in the innermost regions was below the standard owing to such circumstances, yet

considering the characteristics of POWs food, scores of cattle were driven by land in order to supply them with meat.
7. The above-mentioned difficulty of transportation caused delay of supply and gave rise to malaria epidemic, and gastro-enteric disorder, together with malnutrition. Coupled with difficulty in medicine supply, the number of the patients increased in spite of the toil of medical units. It is clear that the prisoners of war who were not used to outdoor life, would greatly suffer.
8. Towards the end of April, Major General Takasaki, the commander of the railway construction, caught malaria, and yet he continued to fulfil his duty until he fell down on his bed. The situations came to the worst.
9. The working units, however, endeavoured to fulfil their duty, overcoming. all difficulties.

Period of Delay in Construction Work

From the Middle of July to October 1943

1. Confronted with the state of affairs above-mentioned, the Imperial General Headquarters dispatched the Director of Transportation and Communication and members of the General Staff to the scene of construction work to observe the state of affairs there, and came to the conclusion that if the forced work were to be continued with the aim of completing the plan by the end of August, nothing but unnecessary sacrifice would follow; and considering the general situations of the Burma front at that time, the prospect of communication with Burna becoming clear with the partial completion of the railway, and local employment of newly constructed roads and waterways parallel with the railway, order was at last given to delay the completion of the construction work by two months in order to reduce victims, in spite of the fact that this order had a grave influence upon the operations in Burma area. Major General Ishida was newly appointed to the director of construction for perfect realization of this scheme.
2. Major General Ishida, the new director of construction, arrived at his post on the sixteenth of August 1943. He aimed at the completion of the work by the end of October, renewed the organization of the staff, endeavoured to stimulate the morale, and was always in the van of the party, the main object of reorganization being in the innovation and improvement of the supervision of working conditions.

    He cherished the slogan, 'prisoners of war and labourers are fathers of construction', corrected the erroneous idea of 'mastership', prevailing among the officers and men, and was foremost in making personal inspection and improvement of the normal life of the prisoners of war.

3. The rainy season which culminated in August, gradually reduced the amount of rainfall, and the working party did their best for the completion of the work, surmounting ever increasing difficulties in the innermost regions. The activities of the water line of communications making use of the River Keonoi and the strenuous efforts of the working troops and the cooperating units in carrying on forced labour favoured the co-ordination between the preservation of military strength and labour (completion of supply work at the beginning at the end of the rainy season in September at the ends in the inner regions) and the execution of tasks.

Conditions After Completion of Construction

From November 1943 to August 1945

1. With the completion of the construction work, the South General Army, in accordance with the general situation at that time, took greatest care in restoring the health of the prisoners of war, enlarged and improved the sanitary arrangement at the Thai Internment Camp and endeavoured to concentrate prisoners of war at salubrious quarters where billeting and supplies were easily accessible, two branch camps of the Malay Internment Camps being merged to the Main Internment Camp in Shonan (Singapore).
2. The railway working troops co-operated in the concentration activities, rendered services in sending back invalid prisoners, in accommodating billet facilities, and employed no more than one thousand healthy prisoners in urgent and indispensable supplementary construction work, the rest being left with lessoned labour. By special order of the Director of Construction, a monument was erected each in Thailand and Burma to console those departed spirits of the prisoners of war and ordinary labourers engaged in this construction work, a mass was held and their souls were deeply venerated in the fashion of Imperial Japanese ceremony.
3. The railway working troops also wheeled round successively into Burma, and from March 1945 on, the remaining work was carried out entirely by a party mainly composed of the 4th Special Railway Unit, and part of the staffs of the Thai Internment Camp who co-operated in the remaining work while the main body tried to regain their physical strength, only making preparations for returning prisoners back to Japan.
4. From that time on, thousands of prisoners of war were employed for maintaining railway services until the end of war, being taken special care of the preservation and improvement of their health.

    During this period, there were no small casualties suffered by the Allied air bombing.

Chapter 3

Factors Impeding Construction

1. Operational demands restricted the term of construction work, (N.B. to be completed in about ten months after it was started in earnest). This was forced construction and there followed many unreasonable demands in various quarters.

Technical Obstacles

2. The inexperience of the Japanese Army in great construction work in the jungle made it especially difficult for them to make fair estimation of their work there, which was the great cause of miscarrying the program and hampering the execution of construction work, and they found it is very difficult to make scrupulous and appropriate preparations beforehand.
3. The Japanese Army were poor in mechanized tools and materials and in the equipment of supply. They had to accomplish this work with manpower, instead of mechanical power, with no small waste of physical strength which followed.

Natural Obstacles

1. The construction was a hazardous one which had to be carried out through the geographical hindrance of a great jungle belt extending on the border of Thailand and Burma untrodden before, there epidemics and pestilence are prevalent. This construction work was 415 kilometres in length, the total amount of earthwork 4,000,000 cubic meters, rock-clearing about 300,000 cubic meters, the total length of bridging about 15 kilometres.

    On the Thai side, there were rather too many spots on the line where rock-clearing had to be done the River Mecron [Mekong] had to be crossed near the base, and excavation of cliffs was necessary in order to go along the Keonoi Valley.

    On the Burma side, the two rivers, Shittan and Salvin [presumably the Sittaung and the Salween], hindered supply from the base in Rangoon. (N.B. the iron railway bridge on the Shittan had been destroyed, and the working troops hurriedly constructed a wooden railway bridge 2 kilometres in length, and ran locomotives brought from Burma).

Roads were the only routes of supply, there were no waterways running in parallel, many rivers intersecting the line of construction.

2. Generally speaking, the temperature is high with high levels of humidity, but among the mountains, it is chilly in January, and, during the rainy season, the temperature sometimes falls. In this district, we suffer a good deal from the influence of the rainy season, especially on the Burma side. During the rainy season, hastily constructed motor-roads and newly built railroads were very difficult to maintain and were a great cause of hindering supply. On the Thai side, since the middle of May, a through motor car communication was suspended, on the Burma side, with difficulty kept up by every available means.

When the waters of the Keonoi rose, it could be utilized for navigation, serving as line of communications, but when in flood, was rather a hindrance to communication.

Immediately after the rainy season sets in, no navigation is possible bar about twenty days when the waters rise slowly. During this period, there lurks the danger of suspension of through communication both on land and on water. On the Burma side, both railway bridges and road bridges on the Mezari and Winyau (both rapids, with driftwoods in them) were swept away and the supply was in crisis.

3. Bad sanitary conditions. Malignant malaria is prevalent in those regions where the construction work was carried on. Moreover, such epidemics as cholera, pests, smallpox etc., are raging all the year round. The influence of the rainy season and the native labourers brought into these regions made worse the sanitary conditions there.

Another hindrance to be especially noticed is the fact that the rainy season set in one month earlier than usual. For this reason, various counter-measures against the rainy season had not yet been completed, when we were taken by surprise, with the consequence that most of our utmost endeavour came to nothing. The effect was decisive and fatal to our work, supply and maintenance, to the sanitary arrangements etc., and coupled with the simultaneous sudden prevalence of cholera, the construction work and the superintendence of prisoners became much more difficult, and the number of victims increased.

Chapter 4

Supervising the Pows

1. The success of this construction solely depended upon the preparedness in the rearward area. Therefore, the South General Army fully acknowledged the necessity of:

    (1) Preparation for supply.
    (2) Measures for sanitary arrangements.
    (3) Securing and maintaining labour.
    (4) Securing and pooling of materials of construction, and every endeavour was made for the realization of this plan.

2. In June 1942, at the time when order was going to be given for the preparation of this construction work, the South Army had dispatched line of communication troops, especially transport troops to other fronts (mainly in Burma) and owing to the scarcity of transportation capacity to send for these troops to the scene, the construction work made no rapid progress. Moreover, there was a great flood in the Autumn of 1942 in the basin of the river Mae Nam Khong [today known as the Mekong] in the central plain of Thailand, and Bangkok, one of the base depots on the line of communications was under water, became like an isolated island, and greatly hampered the preparations for construction.
3. On the other hand, these preparations in the rear were being made through diplomatic negotiations with the Thai Government, and no speedy solution could be hoped for. Under these circumstances various preparations could not be made satisfactorily, and we were obliged to start the construction work step by step.
4. In February 1943, two months after the construction was started in earnest, the necessity of operations due to the circumstances above-mentioned suddenly demanded curtailment by four months of the period of construction, and every measure was taken to cope with the situation. The Imperial General Headquarters and the South Army did their best in lowering the gauge of construction, and in increasing fighting strength and material, the working party was no less active in making desperate efforts for the realization of the plan.

But these counter-measures of shortening the period of construction were not quickly put into execution for various reasons: especially the road for concentrating troops was stretching too far and the transportation capacity too low.

The concentration of fighting troops, labour and supply was at its height during the rainy season (the earlier setting-in of the rainy season cannot be overlooked), and it was our greatest regret that we could not fully display our fighting strength.

Supply and Maintenance

1. With the curtailment of construction period, establishment of supply system became a pressing question for securing and maintaining the increased military strength and labour. But in this period, there was a serious lack in the line of communication troops (which were the main force this is area) especially in motor trucks, and it was not before the earlier part of April 1943 that the deployment was over of the line of communication troops (which had by every means been extracted and allotted to this area) and that systematic supply in the construction area was started. The delay in making preparations for line of communication system, coupled with the early setting-in of the rainy season made the general counter measures for rainy season discordant, followed by the difficulties of supply during that season.
2. Measures taken for the establishment of supply and transportation systems were as follows:

    (a) Emphasis was laid on the counter-measures for the rainy season, and considering the topographical characteristic, on the Burmese side, preparations were made, from the outset, for the construction of rain-tight roads, and on the side of Thailand, hurried construction of motor-roads parallel with the railway was urged. At the same time, we were ready for utilizing water-line of communication along the river Keonos [Khwae], and negotiations were made for the procurement of barges in large quantities.

    (b) As the construction work progressed, the South Army sent two motor car companies and 300 supply motor-trucks and increased motor repair corps (two corps of five sections).

    (N. B. There were no considerable reserve units at that time, and measures were taken for employing war materials in stores for use by groups operating in isolated islands.)

(c) Plans were made for pushing forward the head of heavy construction train, and on the Thai side, efforts were centred round the spot 90 kilometres from the starting point for cutting through cliffs, and plans were made for the preparation of pushing a supply base as far forward as Wanyai (125 kilometres from the starting point). In the Burma area, the head of the heavy construction train was pushed forward 12 kilometres from the starting point).

(d) Pushing supply point forward. On the Thai side, a branch office of the freight depot was pushed forward from the Ban Pong area to Kanchanaburi; which was a march of 50 km, into the construction area. On the Burma side, supply points were pushed forward from Rangoon area to Moulmein area.

3. The above mentioned counter-measures were put into execution as follows, accompanied by such results as are stated below and influenced by the rainy season:

(a) The hurriedly constructed parallel motor road was completed on 5th April 1943, but on the Thai side, it was nothing more than an improvement of a pack-horse way with many curves, upon which notorious trucks ran at an average speed of about 10 km. per hour with an average maximum loading capacity of 1 ton (average – about 500g.)

The main part of the newly delivered supply motor trucks (200 cars) was put into active use for only about twenty days before the rainy season set in, and only 40 of these cars were fit for service, many of them often breaking down. Therefore, every effort was made for the supply of fixed rations, and attempts were made to pile up reserve stocks of provision and forage for use in the inner regions during the rainy season but were not successful. During this period there was no great difficulty in the supply of staple rations, although a certain quantity of supplementary rations was lacking in the inner regions.

The notorious trucks were sent there too late; the constructions of the motor road was not completed within the appointed time; during the dry season, the road was in active use only for a short time and there was a shortage in transport capacity; those were the main causes for the lack of rations above-mentioned.

On the Burma side, the road constructed parallel with the railway was comparatively well prepared, and as a whole, there was no difficulty for supply during the dry season,

(b) On the side of Thailand, the head of the heavy construction train reached Wanyai (125 km. from the starting point) about the middle of May, but the rainy season set in May, and the roadbed was broken in many places. In July the River Keonoi overflowed its banks, the railway was flooded between Kanchanaburi and Ban Pon and trains on the newly constructed line were held up for about twenty days. The stretching of work further than Wanyai made but little progress hindered by the difficulty of rock-clearing. On the Burma side, the head of the heavy construction train reached the spot about 40 km. from the starting point by the middle of April, but during the rainy season, it was difficult to stretch the railway of the heavy construction train on account of the soft and weak roadbed.

(c) Thus, the supply was comparatively easy during the dry season, but as soon as the rainy season set in, the roads both in Thailand and Burma were full of mud with marshy places here and there, which permitted no motor-car traffic while the waters in the rivers did not rise rapidly. For a month (in May), through traffic, both on land and water, was held up, the supply was cut short, and those stationed in the inner regions – 100 kilometres along the line – had to be content with half or one third of the supply of fixed rations.

But with the rising of waters in the River Keonoi since June, land traffic was superseded by water traffic, the water line of communications was extended, and by the end of July establishment of the water line of communications was completed between Ban Pon and Niike (270 km.); on the other hand, the Government of Thailand was urged to offer boats; from March on, boats were gradually gathered together and by the end of July more than 700 tugboats and 1200 lighters were secured, by which critical situation of supply could be entirely swept away.

During this period, the activities in the upper rapids of the Water Transportation Corps of the Imperial Guard Engineer Regiment, the activities on the water of the personnel from the company serving on land and from the motor car company, the efforts of the line of communication troops in the unified employment of these activities, together with the water transportation supply carried out by the internment camp itself, enabled them to discharge the duties of supply work during the rainy season.

(d) During the time when transportation and communication both on land and on water had been suspended, shortage of supply was locally covered by sending and receiving stocks accumulated in various parts of the inner regions. Special consideration was given to the daily food especially the side dishes, of the prisoners of war, and from the middle of May on, herds of cattle were driven by land into the inner regions every several days. This was successful and nearly one thousand head of cattle were secured on the Thai side alone.

(e) On the Burma side, where there were no waterways available, supply had been going on smoothly until the middle of April, but in the rainy season setting in about that time, its influence was considerable, and in June, railway bridges and road bridges on the Mezari and Wanyai were swept away. The working troops concentrated their efforts on relay intercommunication and maintenance of the road, and could barely continue supply, and near Niike in the inner regions motor trucks broke down one after another, the supply was suspended and some of the troops were withdrawn from that region. But with the rising of waters, water-line of communications was extended from the side of Thailand and in July supply could be made as far as Niike.

(f) As is evident from the above-mentioned circumstances, difficulty of transportation in supply arose from the influence of the rainy season, and distress existed in various parts of the inner regions. All the Japanese working troops and a little less than one third of the prisoners of war were suffering from the influence.

(g) The Japanese army stationed in Thailand and Burma Amy Group were responsible for supplying to the internment camps, but since the establishment of line of communications early in April 1943, the task of supplying provisions was assigned to the railway unit.

In supplying provisions to the prisoners of war, special attention was paid for allotting fixed rations in accordance with various prescriptions of the law, and at the beginning of 1943 an addition of 50 grams in the supply of both staple food and supplementary rations was decided upon by the South Army. Furthermore, provisions were revised and several times the amount of the fixed rations for the POWs was increased on account of their being engaged in heavy labour.

(h) As is mentioned above, the branch internment camps situated in the innermost regions suffered from shortage of rations to the same degree as the Japanese soldiers, during the rainy season. In order to facilitate the supply work at the ends executed by the internees themselves, the construction party delivered 30 motor trucks and scores of boats successively from the latter part of March 1943.

Besides this, the internment camps had about 60 motor trucks and about the same number of boats and was actively engaged in transporting supplies.

(i) Acquisition in large quantities of supplementary rations, especially vegetables, was difficult, and during the dry season they were liable to be spoiled while they were being carried a long distance; while during the rainy season, they were always lacking owing to the difficulty of transportation. To cope with these situations, a great effort was made to encourage growing of vegetables so as to be able to do without the supply of supplementary rations, and considerable results were obtained in this way. Fishing in the River Keonoi had to be prohibited for a long time (from May to September) as cholera was prevailing along its banks, which was a great hindrance to better nutrition.

(j) Articles of luxury for internees (butter, cheese, sugar, coffee, black tea, etc.) were specially supplied by the South Army.

(k) Spare suits of clothes were supplied by the South Army but were not by any means enough.

(l) The difficulties of supply work during the rainy season were as stated above. Enemy counter-attacks in Burma with the end of the rainy season could clearly be foreseen. Therefore, an army group en route to Burna (two divisions, part of troops under direct control of the Army, individual soldier and civilian employees) marched along the railway under construction from April to September 1943. It was quite natural that the construction troops assisted them with munitions and there occurred no small shortage in the stores or provisions.

To sum up, under the circumstances in that period, billeting and supply could not be anything but unsatisfactory, and both Japanese army and prisoners of war were obliged to endure hardships and privations.

Billeting

1. Billeting facilities in Thailand were somewhat different from those in Burma. On the Thai side, the working party had the advantage of utilizing the water course for supply in the rainy season, and employed the method of deploying on the whole line and of working all along the line simultaneously; curtailment of the construction period, however, necessitated quick deployment in the inner regions, and there was no time to build enough cottages (a kind of hut made of bamboo poles and 'chaku' roof plant-called 'nipper' house) to billet the working party. Tents were generally used, only key points of construction having billeting facilities. The South Army, therefore issued almost all campaign tents on hand to the construction party, to accommodate nearly fifty thousand men, and afterwards ten odd thousand for supplementary use.

2. On the Burma side, consideration had from the outset been given to the supply of work during the rainy season, and method of working from the ends had been taken in order to steadily push forward working sectors by gradually establishing supply from the starting point. Groups of billeting huts (nipper houses) were built at intervals of from 5 to 10 km., tents being sometimes used for carrying during movements.
3. The P.O.W.s in the Internment Camp, following the example of the construction party, built huts by themselves, and the construction party cooperated with them when necessary. Considerable working personnel were allotted for the work of the Internment Camp itself and for the improvement and for supervision and maintenance.
4. Since May, after the setting-in of the rainy season, camp-life proved defective; a wet pit was especially unwholesome; every effort was made to raise floors, and spoiled beddings were exchanged for new ones. At the same time, nipper-houses gradually took the place of tents. Only bamboo poles could be obtained on the spot, a predator plant (*chatu*) being imported, from other districts.

    But the supply of *chaku* was not sufficient owing to the difficulties of securing and transporting them in large quantities. Thus, nipper-houses were built almost everywhere except the inner regions about 100 km. along the line of construction. But even those nipper-houses were not complete to bear the heavy rain coming down every day.
5. In order to accommodate the marching troops, (into Burma) preparations were made for arranging resting places with tents, (standard capacity 250 men) and billeting area (standard capacity 500 men) were almost completed early in May.

    These facilities were used by the working party and the prisoners while they were shifting places within the construction arena.

Sanitary Arrangements

Outline of medical services

1. Taking into consideration the characteristics of this construction work area, preservation of health of the working party was a matter of greatest concern, success of this railway construction depending upon it. The South Army, therefore, attached greatest importance to the service of sanitation, and, following the example of building a canal at Panama, made re-enforcement in sanitary organization. The main body of the South Army Epidemic Prevention and Water Supply Corps, which was the only standing epidemic prevention water supply corps throughout the South area was allotted the duties of

service of sanitation; at the same time almost all the sanitary organizations under the direct control of the Director of Railway Construction.

Moreover, necessary medical service corps were extracted from the army corps engaged in first line operations and were allocated to the medical organization. Considering the situation of the general operations at that time, this effort can never be under-estimated.

2. In taking care of the health of the prisoners of war, the system of the supervising the organization of prisoners of war was mainly followed and about 900 medical personnel of the Allied captives and some of the Japanese medical personnel engaged in the service. About fifty-five invalids were in the charge of one medical personnel, and this ratio was high compared with those of the Japanese army (100 cases to one medical personnel attached to a unit) and an ordinary working party (200-300 cases to one medical personnel). But the composition of sanitary corps belonging to the Internee camp was not suited to field manoeuvrability and could not be made to display its ability to the full.
3. At the outset, the Thai Internment Camp was in co-operating relationship with the construction party, and the service of sanitation was being carried out by the corps itself, Japanese medical corps going to its assistance when necessary. But there arose the necessity of intensifying the general control of the medical service and, in July 1943, this camp was placed under the control of the Director of Construction, after which unification of medical service was realized, resulting in the innovation of medical activities.
4. On the Burma side, medical services were carried out by the medical organs belonging to the Burma Area Army under the superintendence of the Railway Medical Corps, South Army.
5. Why there was a difference in the number of casualties between the POWs and Japanese Army:

    (a) Japanese army, especially railway units, were only about 4,000 in number, even when two regiments were put together. Naturally enough they were employed mainly for supervision of construction work and in the delicate technical work, POWs being mostly engaged in manual tasks. The result was that the decline of physical strength on the part of the Japanese army was not as remarkable as in the case of the prisoners of war; this is why some difference is noticed in the figures indicating the results of medical activities under the same condition.
    (b) Compared with the Japanese, prisoners of war, were less accustomed to the primitive life and had less powers of resistance.
    (c) Many cases of tropical ulcer occurred on account of their dress (knee breeches), which accelerated the decline of their physical strength.

6. The number of deaths among the POWs, Japanese Army, and labourers are approximately as follows:

	Total	Deaths
POWs	about 50,000	about 10,000 (20%)
Japanese Army	about 15,000	about 1,000 (7%)
Labourers (fugitives included)	about 100,000	about 30,00 (30%)

7. Colonel Kitagawa, Chief of the South Army Railway Medical Camp, was killed by an airplane accident while actively engaged in making arrangements for the supply of medical materials.

Chapter 5

Outbreak of Disease

In November 1942, after the prisoners of war had begun their work, members of the South Army Medical Corps were dispatched to the scene of their activity in order to inspect and further improve their treatment in respect of supply and maintenance. Increase of fixed rations was made (50 grams both in staple food and meat) and additional mosquito nets and blankets were delivered. But since the setting-in of the rainy season, in May 1943, traffic was sometimes suspended, and in the inner regions fixed rations had to be reduced by half, while the construction work was forcibly carried on. The work made such rapid progress that the workers had no leisure; neither time or material was found enough to complete billeting facilities, and sanitary conditions were anything but satisfactory.

Under such unfavourable conditions, and as a result of forced work since the middle of 1943, decline in the physical strength of the POWs was conspicuous, many cases of malnutrition appeared, and the number of deaths increased. Therefore, serious cases were gradually transferred to the vicinity of Bangkok to receive treatment. Those who were in a stage of convalescence were assembled near Kanchanaburi, given small work, and were allowed to recover there. For the rest, less amount of work was allotted, as much ration as possible was provided and every effort was made to restore their physical strength. Thus in 1944, they gradually regained their physical strength and the number of deaths dwindled.

How Cholera Broke Out

Prevention of acute infectious diseases, together with precautions against malaria, was a most painstaking task, and in order to prevent infection through water all the sanitation water filters available by the South Army were assembled in this construction area and they numbered 454 (including 7 motorcar filters).

Epidemic Prevention Water Supply section composed of one Allied medical officer and four non-commissioned medical officers and privates equipped with a set of sanitation water filters, and considerable amount of epidemic prevention and emergency sanitary materials, were allotted to every working company of the Prisoners of War and every necessary measure was taken for prevention, medical examination and attendance. The headquarters of the medical corps was at Kanchanaburi and was active in coaching the prevention in the examination and disinfection of bacteria and in other precautions. Every one of those who were going to the construction area, was inoculated against cholera.

Cases of cholera first broke out among the local labourers on the side of Burma in November 1942, and in spite of desperate efforts to check it, cases spread into Thailand across the border in April 1943.

At the time of its outbreak, the number of cases among the natives swelled and shrunk with alternating intervals until at last, from May, there broke out cases among the Japanese and POWs. Therefore, the South Army often dispatched medical personnel to the scene to coach prevention. Every working party and sanitary organ did its best in prevention activities, sometimes entirely suspending construction work. At last, at the end of July, the plague quieted down except in some quarters. Although more cases broke out afterwards, they gradually dwindled away and in October completely died down. In June staff of the medical Bureau in the War Department were dispatched to the scene.

Out breaks of cases at the end of June 1943 are as follows:

1st Period	Nov–Dec 1942	43
2nd Period	Feb–March 1943	48
3rd Period	April–May 1943	586
4th Period	3 June–30 June 1943	2046
Total		*2723*

The grand total by 10 August was about 6,000 of which about 4,000 died. Among these figures, about 1,200 are the cases of prisoners and it is our greatest regret that about half of these never survived.

The main causes of such raging were:

(1) Fugitives of the native labourers suffering from cholera dispersed bacteria.
(2) Cases broke out on the upper reaches of the Rivor Keonoi and infected the construction work area.
(3) Imperfect prevention instruction on the part of a civilian employee in charge of the POWs who was poor in the knowledge and ability and inferior in the quality.
(4) Difficulty of applying epidemic prevention materials due to pressed transportation. It was largely due to the activities of the Sanitary Organs that the epidemic died down in a comparatively short period and that great bursting out could be prevented, in spite of the unfavourable conditions under which they had been placed.

How Cases of Malaria Occurred

Greatest emphasis was laid on the prevention of malaria in the service of sanitation. A malaria prevention party was organized (composed of 341 officers and men, allotted at the ratio of one party to 5,000 labourers) and allotted to each unit, and was controlled by the South Army Epidemic Prevention Water Supply Corps; every possible science and technique was put into active use by them.

The following five items were measures of prevention:

(a) To give complete knowledge and training of malaria prevention.
(b) To prevent biting of mosquitoes; to prepare mosquito nets and clothing to fumigate.
(c) To prevent the brooding of mosquitoes and to exterminate them by drainage, oil-sprinkling, cleaning etc.
(d) To take 45 doses of sulphur-quinine and 3 doses of 'Plasmohin' internally per capita per month; Every Japanese, prisoner and native labourer is required to take the same quantity.
(e) Early discovery and separation of the case and keeper of 'malaria protozoan'.

Doctor Kimura, Professor in the Research Institution of Tropical Medicine, an authority on malaria prevention, came to the assistance of this service as a non-regular member of the staff of the South Army. The ration per month of malaria cases occurring during this construction is as follows:

Japanese Army 1-7%
Prisoners of War 0-11%
Local labourers 10-20%
N.B. The ration per month of malaria cases occurring in New Guinea area rose to about 20%.

As is shown above, the ratio of malaria cases occurring among Japanese array is comparatively low, but at the end of the construction period, the ratio of the keepers of malaria protozoan among the Japanese had risen to nearly 100% and only by internal use of doses could some of the units prevent the attacks of malaria. Generally speaking, the ratio of cases per month was about 4% throughout the Japanese and prisoners of war, which was a rather favourable indication compared with those of other theatres of war, and we may conclude that national results are obtained from the preventive measures.

Tropical Ulcer

Tropical ulcer which was prevalent among prisoners of war was incurable and we found difficulty in its remedy. As a precaution measure, we made war prisoners put on leggings made of bamboo and had them wear boots. As a remedy permanganic acid salvarsan were used. In addition to these measures, each unit made ointment from lard by itself, and used it.

Inert skin, bare legs and insufficient auxiliary medicine such as disinfectant due to inexperience of the Japanese Army etc. were the reasons why this disease was prevalent especially among prisoners of war. Although we dispatched medical veterans to the infected districts and made them study it, a complete remedy could not be found because of the inexperience of the Japanese army.

Other Prevailing Diseases

Generally speaking, coupled with malnutrition, many cases of dysentery beriberi and gastroenteric disorder occurred. Pestilence and smallpox against which great precautions were taken broke out fortunately only a little at the beginning of 1943.

As mentioned above, various diseases were so prevalent that the percentage of the war prisoners in service was from sixty to seventy per cent on average. But it rolls to forty percent in the innermost and most unhealthy area. On the contrary about eighty percent were maintained in well controlled and healthy area of about fifty thousand war prisoners, about three thousand were in hospital on 8 July 1943.

Medical Supplies

The South Army laid great stress on the supply of medical supplies to these construction units and tried to prepare abundant malaria medicine and materials for epidemic prevention. Although quinine which was produced in Java was sufficiently supplied and materials for epidemic prevention, especially sanitary water-filters, were nearly sufficient, the South Army suffered from a shortage of medical supplies in general, as the other medical supplies were all transported from the home islands and a quantity of supplies from the central office to the South Army was about 50,000 boxes (about 1,700 tons) in 1943 and about a half of 1943 in 1944, of which 20 percent were lost as a result of sinkings.

The Bangkok Field Goods Depot endeavoured to supply the construction units; nevertheless, it could not supply in such a large quantity as was expected because of insufficient stocks and difficulty of transportation. The South Army ordered that the ratio of supply to the war prisoners and to the Japanese troops should be equal.

To sum up, we took every measure possible under these circumstances and did our best to maintain the health of the prisoners of war. The main reasons why such a miserable result brought about in spite of our efforts are as follows:

1. As a result of the forced construction work, various defects accrued. Especially, the work was commenced without sufficient sanitary arrangements.
2. Unhealthy conditions in the construction areas.
3. In addition to bad conditions of the roads, traffic during the rainy season was tied up, so that supply was very difficult and the standard of ration fell down.
4. Mixing of the native labourers who had no knowledge of sanitation disturbed sanitary tasks.
5. The main body of foremen were Koreans, and their supervision was not proper. Accordingly, hygiene could not be thorough.

It is quite regretful that in spite of all the sanitary measures many defects accrued and many invalids and deaths occurred.

Chapter 6

Supervision and Employment of Prisoners

1. It is natural that the labour which is primary constituent of the building requires an enormous number of the assistant workers, in addition to the troops. Therefore, although the local labourers (Thailanders, Malayans, Burmese, Chinese, Javanese, Annamese) were raised it was very difficult to get a large number of labourers without delay, on account of various circumstances, and moreover, those natives who are inferior in their physical conditions and ability would not be made the leading part of the labour for this construction which ought to be plotted in a short time.
2. Hereupon the South General Army requested the sanction of the General Headquarters concerning the employment of the war prisoners. The General Headquarters sanctioned the employment of the war prisoners, because this construction was partly work to be done far from the front, and partly bore the mission of the trade route between Thailand and Burma.

    At that time the army, as a whole, had a view that it is not against the Geneva Treaty on the War Prisoners to employ the prisoners of war in such work.
3. Consequent to the sanction, in the beginning of the preparation for construction, the South Army ordered the railway troops to supervise as part of prisoners of war and to engage them in the preparation work. After that, subsequent to the organization of the Thailand Camp, the South General Army made those of the camp be engaged in the construction work under their control.
4. And after the considerable progress of the construction, especially as it became more and more indispensable to increase the labour, because the term for the construction was shortened, a great number of war prisoners in Java, Borneo, Singapore and Indo-China were transmitted to the Thailand Camp and newly two branches of the Malay Camp was attached to the commander of the construction troops.
5. The prisoners of war in the above paragraphs were transported, those on Thailand side by railway, those on Burma by ships, respectively to the construction area, while their removals within the construction area were done on foot. The details about this transport will be shown in Chapter V, 'Explanation for the Protests'.

Relations between the Supervising party and the Employing Party

1. After the Thailand camp was organized, (August 1942), it was designated to co-operate with the construction troops about for a year to July 1943.
2. The delay in the progress of the work owing to the increase of patients due to the influence of the weather and climate made necessary still closer relation between the working troops and the camp regarding the improvement of supply and sanitation, as well as the working capacity, until at last in July 1943, the Thailand camp was put under the command of the construction commander. However, a part of war prisoners located on the Burma side, (two branches, with about 15,000 prisoners) were from July 1943 put under the care of the commander of the 5th Railway Regiment, who was concurrently the commander of the construction work in that area, by the reason of the difficulty of liaison, the remoteness, and the inconvenience of supply.

    But as to the supervision of the war prisoners in the proper sense, were under the control of the head of the Thailand camp, except in the Burma area, the camps were under the direct management of the construction commanders but were never put under the direct control of the working troops.
3. The fact that two branches of the Malay camp were set up in May 1943 and put under the control of the construction commander described in the above paragraphs.
4. On the employment of prisoners of war, they were not attached separately to working troops on the spot. As regards employing then on the spot, the branch leaders of the camps and the commanders of battalions and companies negotiated together and regulated the working hours of employed members. That means that, after the camps were put under the control of construction commanders, the camps delivered the required number of persons to the required places in accordance with the orders of the constriction commanders, who were not entitled to interfere in the business of supervisions itself, according to the above-mentioned method of employment, and the construction troops co-operated in improvement of the supervisions as far as their circumstances permitted.
5. When some of prisoners of war who have a special ability were to be temporarily detached, they were attached along with the supervising personnel after the negotiation between the camps and the employing parties. For instance, some were employed as chauffeurs for the commissary troops or as a technical men for the material depots.
6. Subsequent to the progress of the work, special attention was paid at the time of the moving forward of the camps, their removals were limited only within a small range so that the time waste and the unnecessary establishments might be saved as far as possible. From August, they were ordered to remove only when the accommodation and food stuffs had been completely prepared.

7. As is mentioned above, the close relation was kept on between the supervision party and the employing party, and much attention was paid to the prisoners' health, and a special effort was made to improve the situation of supervision on the basis of their customs and manners. This can be seen from many instructions rendered by the commanders of the camps to their men, those rendered on the part of embarkation to the prisoners to be transported, and on the occasion of their transportation to the homeland.

Outline of supervision and service

1. The Thailand Camp completed its organization at Bangkok in the middle of August 1942. At its opening, the number of the prisoners of war was about 3,000, and they were put into service in the preparation work of each troop located at the bases for the railway construction. After that from October of the same year to March 1943, the war prisoners, 50,637 in all (including the dead) were transferred several times to Bangkok and Moulmein from the Malaya and Java Camps, and most of them (38,000) were obliged to cooperate with the 9th Railway Regiment whose mission was to work on the Thailand side, while some of them co-operated with the 5th Regiment whose mission was to work on the Burma side.
2. Subsequently in April 1943, to accelerate the construction work, more two branches of the Malay camp (about 10,000 war prisoners) were despatched and co-operated in this work, deploying near Niike and Kinsaiyok.
3. At the beginning, the equipment of the camps was in so poor a state that they had no vehicles, and the lorries for the construction troops were used at the same time for the purpose of supplying. For that reason, the war prisoners to be transferred were obliged to march on foot, and to deploy in the remote places, walking a long distance under the burning sunshine.

    On their arrival at the destination, little more than 30% fell ill, and in addition to that, the insufficient accommodation and the unsteady supplies by reason of the bad condition of the transportation route, accelerated the increase of patients.
4. In May 1943, the track was opened to Wanyai, Thailand (at 120 kilometres from the starting point) while in Burma, the head of the upper construction of the track was towards the vicinity of Anakwin (at 40 kilometres from the starting point[1]). However, as mentioned above, as the rainy season set in

---

1. Beketaung camp was at the 40 kilometres mark, or very close to it, while Anakwin camp is at the 45 kilometres mark; see Rod Beattie, Rod, *The Thai-Burma Railway: The True Story of The Bridge On The River Kwai* (T.B.R.C., Kanchanaburi, 2015),

about one month earlier, and because of the enormousness of rainfall, the transportation of supply did not go as intended.

As in remote places, the ration of food stuff was sometimes reduced to a half or one third by the above reason and the temperature was low, there broke out a sudden consumption of energy. But the work was still continued in accordance with the order which commanded that the work would finish by the end of August (though it was ceased temporarily when cholera broke out) and owing to working in the rain, the supervision of the war prisoners fell unproper as a result, and many patients came out; above all, as unexpectedly cholera became prevalent and onset of tropic ulcers increased, the service rate was extremely lowered.

5. At the end of June, cholera broke out in some working troops and, as it threatened to spread over, still more surgeons, medical non-commissioned officers and privates of the war prisoners, 230 in all, were attached to the railway troops from the Malay camp and charged to check the disease.

6. In September, when the rainy season was over, the condition of roads became better, and also in addition to the advance of the head of the upper construction of tracks, the concurrent employment of the water-route of the Keonoi River became possible. Therefore, as the transportation of supply got better, the regular ration could be given with the aid of the commissary troops and by the great effort of the transportation section of the troops. Moreover, owing to the fatigue accumulated within more than one year past, and the deployment in the remote places being insufficiently equipped with the sanitary arrangements, the number of patients and the deceased did not shrink.

7. After the completion of the work in October 1945, the Thailand camp dispatched 1,000 healthy prisoners alternatively from the flat country to the remote places and caused them to engage in the reinforcement work of the railway; and at the same time, successively transferred and collected this main body over the level ground, and endeavoured especially to recover the health of the prisoners. The supervision, too, became normal.

Especially many camps were established in the rendezvous, such as Ban Pong, and Kanchanaburi, and a camp hospital was built at the cost of 1,500,000 yen at Nakonpaton. Besides making such a great effort to give medical treatment to the patients, the supplies were given beyond the regular ration.

So, the health condition of the prisoners got better step by step and the number of patients and dead dwindled. The two branches of the Malay camp were restored successively to their proper positions by the end of that year and their health condition also recovered.

34 The Camps of the Death Railway

General Diagram of Railway Between Thai and Burma and Brief List Showing Prisoners of War Camps (about Oct 1943)

Note.

1. 司 Headquarters of Prisoners of War
2. ● " Branch (Figure shows No of Branch)
3. 病 " Hospital
4. ++++ Lines in operation
5. ——— Lines newly established
6. ----- Parallel Routes by Thai and Burma.

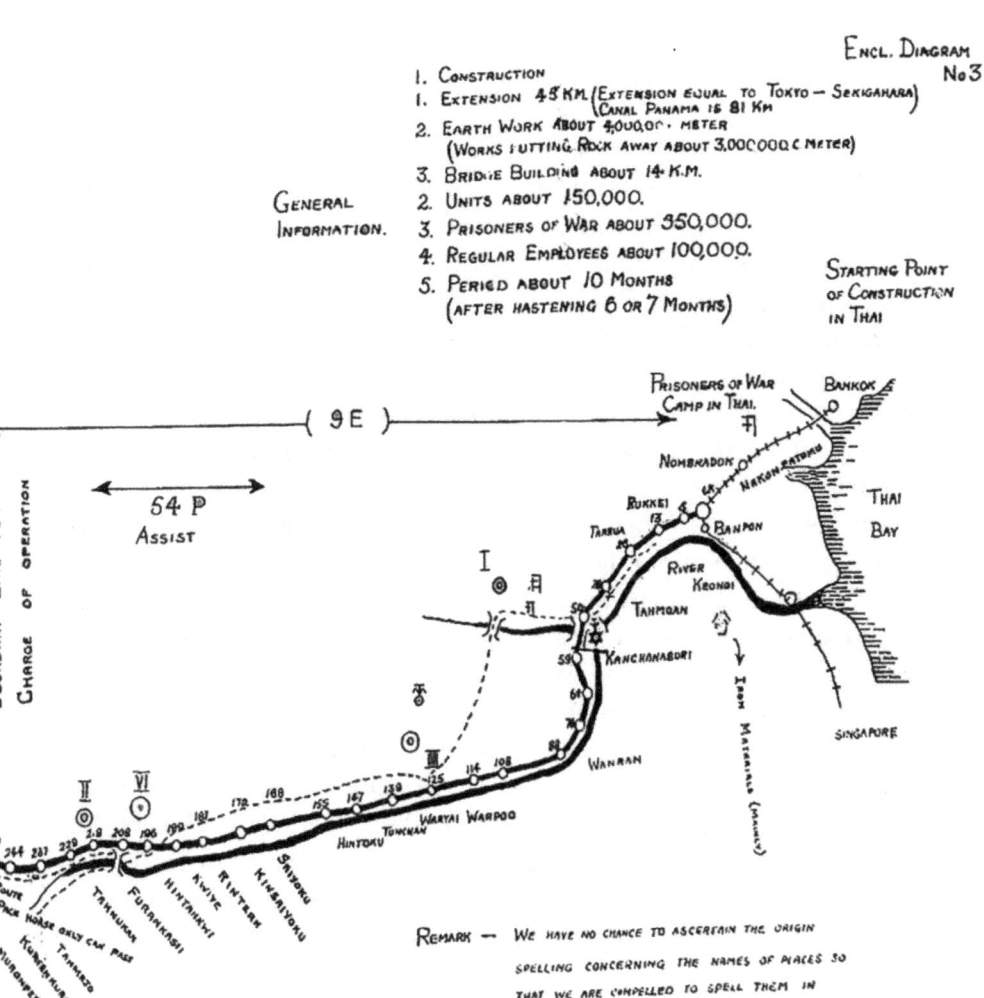

To improve the supervision, the camps organized transportation and supply sections and accommodation, building, and special medical sections and so on; and made efforts to eliminate inadequate circumstances, allotting considerable personnel to these functions.

Conclusion

The foregoing is an explanation of the circumstances which compelled a heavy toll of life during the progress of the construction work. In the final analysis, causes of the tragedy may be traced principally to the placement of a time limit on the construction, the immense difficulty in making thorough preparation and to the precipitancy with which the Japanese soldiers, despite their lack of experience in such large-scale construction work and meagre scientific equipment, dared to carry on their work in strict obedience to orders which they characteristically regarded an imperative. Thus, the occurrence of the casualties, it should be declared, was by no means due to any deliberate intention on the part of the Army authorities.

As regards the employment of prisoners of war in the above construction work, it may be stated that at the time the Japanese Army as a whole entertained the ideas that the employment of prisoners of war in any work other than military operations was not a breach of the Geneva Convention. Further, it is to be insisted that the incident was of a radically different character from the so-called maltreatment of prisoners of war.

The incidents, already stated was an inevitable outcome of the situation then prevailing, and, if anyone is to be called to account for the dreadful death rate, the responsibility ought to be placed on the then chief of the General Staff (General Sugiyama) who ordered the construction, the War Minister (General Tojo) who sanctioned the employment of prisoners and the Commander-in-Chief of the South Area Corps (General Terauchi) who was entrusted with the construction on the spot.

As regards individual cases of maltreatment of prisoners of war, it is desired that investigation be started upon the further receipt from the Allied Powers of a report of the details, particularly the ranks and names of the suspected offenders, and if, as a result they should be found guilty severe measures should be meted out to them.

Part II

The Movement of POWs from Holding Camps to Thailand and Burma

Altogether ten groups were established from POWs held in Singapore by the Japanese to work on construction projects and, in general, they were composed of the healthier, fitter men. These were 'A' Force of 3,000 men, sent to Burma, initially to construct airfields and then to work on the railway, under the command of Brigadier Varley. It was organised into three battalions known by the name of their respective commanders – Major C.E Green of the 2/4th Machine Gun Battalion, Lieutenant Colonel George Ramsay, and Lieutenant Colonel C. M. Black.

'B' Force of 1,487, sent to Borneo to construct airfields. 'C' of Force, 551, sent to Japan to work in shipyards, factories and mines. 'D' Force, of 2,218, sent to Eastern Thailand to work on the railway, and 'E' Force, of 500, sent to Borneo also to construct airfields. Other groups were formed to work on the railway, including, in May 1943, 'F' Force and 'H' Force which were sent to work on the railway line, and these included a large number of men who were in poor physical shape. The 3,000-plus men of 'H' Force had been put together from POW holding camps in Singapore and Java, while 'F' Force was composed of prisoners held in Singapore's Changi goal many of whom had been considered too old or unwell to undertake heavy manual labour.

Lieutenant Colonel S.W. Harris, the Officer Commanding 'F' Force, received the following orders from the Imperial Japanese Army to prepare to move from Changi goal to a new area. Harris was told that the AIF contingent was to total 3,600 and the British 3,400.

In his 'history' of 'F' Force, Harris described the journey which took the prisoners by train from Changi to Thailand: 'The force travelled to Bampong in 13 freight trains, leaving Singapore on successive nights in parties of 500-600. The accommodation was one steel box-car for approx. 27 men. The journey lasted 4-5 days. Cooked rations of rice and vegetable stew, provided at various stations, were generally inadequate; drinking water was never supplied in sufficient quantities, and this caused unnecessary hardship to men travelling in such crowded conditions during the heat of the day. In particular, most train parties received no food or water during the last 24 hours of the journey.'[1]

---

1. TNA, WO 203/5823, South-East Asia Translation and Interrogation Centre Bulletins: 246 Burma-Siam Railway.

Others painted a far bleaker picture of that train journey, such as British prisoner, John Barnard, described what he said was the worst journey he had ever undertaken: 'The days were worse than the nights. The heat blazed down on the steel roofs and sides of the trucks, making the interior like ovens. We had to sit there hour after hour, naked except for a loin cloth or a pair of shorts, the perspiration pouring off us.'

Colonel Harris continued his narrative from the railhead in Thailand at Bam Pong: 'On arrival at Bampong the train parties were marched to the first staging camp, about one mile from the station. The camp was in a filthy state having previously been used by native labour gangs. An I.J.A. notice posted at the entrance in English was entitled "Camp Orders for Coolies and Prisoners of War". Accommodation consisted of large attap (or atap) roofs resting on the ground, without floors. Latrines, which were merely open trenches about six feet deep, were filthy beyond description and the whole area was as insanitary as it could be. There was no water for washing and a bare sufficiency for cooking.

'The "*gunzoku*"[2] guards at Bampong were in an even more excitable state than is usual among them when a move is in progress. Detrainment was carried out to the accompaniment of blows and the usual stream of conflicting orders. In the Camp itself, a *gunzoku* called "Toyama" on several occasions thrashed prisoners, for no apparent cause, with the steel shaft of a golf club, inflicting more or less serious injuries on a number of officers and men.

'As each train load arrived, it learned for the first time that the rest of the journey was to be made on foot, starting on the evening following arrival.'

The only water available was from roadside wells and could not be boiled or chlorinated. 'During the latter stages of our march,' wrote Dr Stanley Pavillard with 'D' Battalion, 'men drank from stagnant pools which were often full of mosquito larvae.'[3]

RASC Adjutant Richard Laird was on that march: 'We were on unmade-up track and in the dark it was impossible to avoid the roughness of the track, which resulted in many cuts and bruises which later developed into tropical ulcers. Some nights it was so dark that we resorted to tying a piece of white cloth or towel onto our packs so that the man behind could have something to follow. We normally started our march at dusk and would arrive soon after daylight at the next staging camp (bivouac). All too often we were kept on parade all morning, sometimes up to twelve noon and frequently in full sun, to allow stragglers to catch up and for the Nips to get their figures right. At the

---

2. 'Gunsoku' were civilians, often foreign civilians, employed by the Imperial Japanese Army.
3. TNA, WO 235/963.

end of that we had no more than a few hours before we were due to move out again in the evening, and during this time we had to get what food we could.'[4]

'No man was permitted to fall out,' reported Major John Parsons of the 2nd Battalion, Garhwal Rifles. 'Men who collapsed on the track were beaten with rifle butts or kicked until they crawled on.'[5]

'F' Force had the furthest to march of all the groups, being given the task of constructing some fifty kilometres of track leading up to the Thai-Burma border at the Three Pagodas Pass: 'The march lasted for about 2½ weeks, over a distance of roughly 300 kilometres, covered in 15 stages of about 20 kilometres each,' continued Harris. 'Marching was invariably done by night, between 2000 hrs and 0800 hrs. Except for the first two stages the road was merely a rough jungle track, capable of taking wheeled traffic in dry weather only. Long stretches of it were corduroyed, which, with snags and holes, made marching in the dark difficult and dangerous. Falls, resulting in sprains and even broken legs, were frequent. Control on the march was virtually impossible as all torches had been confiscated during a military search at Bampong. At the same time, the fate of stragglers was uncertain, as Thais armed with knives hung on the tail of the column in certain areas, ready to strip off the equipment of any man who fell behind. It is probable that some at least of the 20 men still missing from the force met their end at the hands of these bandits.'

'Daily thunderstorms started on 30 April and the monsoon proper broke just after the earlier parties reached their destination. The later parties thus had to contend with even worse marching conditions. The road surface became slippery and treacherous and long stretches were flooded and even totally washed away. The night march now frequently lasted for 14 or 15 hours instead of 12, and during the day's rest exhausted men had nowhere to shelter from the rain except on sodden ground under trees and bushes. It was unfortunately the less fit British parties which had to contend with these worsened conditions, and this undoubtedly accentuated their already inferior physical state on reaching their final camps …

'The staging camps were jungle clearings at the side of the road, at about 20 kilometres distance from each other, generally (but not always) near water. Accommodation consisted of a cookhouse and open trench latrines, and flies abounded: but of shelter there was none, except in two of the fifteen camps where tents were available for about a hundred men only … Food, which consisted of rice and vegetable stew, was supplied in insufficient quantities to maintain

---

4. Rory Laird, *From Shanghai to the Burma Railway: The Memoirs & Letters of Richard Laird, A Japanese Prisoner of War* (Pen & Sword, Barnsley, 2020), p.88.
5. TNA, WO 235/963.

the strength of men engaged on such a march, and water was often short. At Kanburi staging camp drinking water had to be bought by the prisoners from a privately owned well.'

The strain fell particularly heavily on the medical officers and orderlies Harris, explained, 'as they had to attend to casualties on the line of march and hold sick parades during the day's halt, not only for their own sick but also for the steadily increasing numbers left behind by previous parties. Also, at every camp the day ended and the march began with an argument with the Japanese N.C.O. as to the number of sick men to be left. The end of this was always that seriously sick men, with blistered and ulcerated feet, and such illnesses as dysentery, beri-beri and malaria, were driven out of the camp to join the marching party, often with blows.

'Similar scenes were being enacted daily at every staging camp along the road. Hundreds of unfit were being rendered seriously ill by this treatment, and the whole force was being rapidly infected with malaria, dysentery and diarrhoea. In addition, the health and physique of the fit men also was deteriorating under the strain, so that they also were rendered more liable to infection.

'Finally, at Konkoita staging camp, after a fortnight's marching, every party was quartered in immediate proximity to hundreds of coolies, who were suffering from some intestinal disease, of which numbers died daily. The whole area was heavily fouled and infested with a plague of flies. The I.J.A. pretended that the deaths were due to dysentery; it soon became certain that it was, in fact, cholera.'

'A' Force had experienced similar conditions when transported on the little coastal tramp steamer, *Celebes Maru*, to work from the Burma end of the railway, as Brigadier Varley noted in his diary: 'So ended a 12-day journey which will always remain vivid in the minds of all. The congestion of the men in holds; diarrhoea, dysentery, bad latrines etc … As we had rain daily and nightly we had to sit up in our capes to keep bodies dry. Little sleep obtained, all things getting wet.'[6] Those latrines, just six in total, were merely formed of an iron trough with several small cubicles built over it.

The men in the holds of the ships found themselves crouching on temporary decks with head room of only about 1.2 metres and when an acute form of amoebic dysentery broke out there was no chance of halting its spread in the filthy and crowded conditions spaces. Adding to the prisoners' discomfort was that almost all sunlight was blocked by two landing barges which were placed across the top of the hold.

To make the situation even worse 350 Japanese troops were later embarked, pushing the POWs further into the bottom of the hold where, Lieutenant

---

6. Transcript of the diary of Arthur Leslie Varley, 1942-1944, AWM 2019.22.101.

The Movement of POWs from Holding Camps to Thailand and Burma 41

Colonel Ramsay reported, 'the conditions were appalling'.[7] It was suffocatingly hot in the holds with temperatures never dropping below 100 degrees Fahrenheit so some of the prisoners slept amid the coal, but there they were exposed without shelter to the incessant rain. Those who remained in the hold suffered from prickly heat.

A number of Dutch POWs, mostly captured in Batavia and Java, were shipped to Burma via Singapore on the rusty old Japanese cargo ship, *Tacoma Maru*. The ship's cargo hold was fitted with an additional platform to squeeze more men in. The prisoners were driven like cattle, wrote Otto Kreeff, with rifle butts, and 'packed together with their knees drawn up', making it impossible for the men to straighten their legs.[8]

All of this meant that the prisoners were in poor shape before they even reached what would be the areas where they would build their work camps, where conditions rapidly deteriorated even further.

---

7. Report by Lieutenant Colonel G.E. Ramsay, AWM, 2018.8.163, p.6.
8. Otto Kreefft (Trans. John Webb and Netteke Crombie), *Burma Railway, A Visual Recollection* (Museum Bronbeck, 2008), p.18.

Part III

Camps of the Thai-Burma Railway

Nong Pladuk   0 Kilo
Also known as Nompladuk, Nom Pladuc, and Hnong Pladuk

Nong Pladuk was where the railway workshops were based and where there were three camps. It was located about five kilometres from the main railway station of Ban Pong near a junction station on the Southern Line to Bangkok. Work on the camp started in June 1942, with the arrival of 600 British prisoners from the First Mainland Party lead by Major R.S. Sykes of the 18th Infantry Division.

The first groups were tasked to clear the forest, built the shelters, and a Japanese workshop, as Fred Hoskins recalled: 'Each day we had to march from Ban Pong to Nong Pladuc to construct the huts we were to live in and then back again. Gradually it emerged that we were to build a railway line from this point to Burma … Our education in a new life was beginning. The huts were wood framed with bamboo matting sides and holes cut out for windows. The roof was made of attap, which made it looked as though it was thatched. The whole was raised off the ground two feet. Railway sleepers were used to make steps up to the entrance. Each hut was intended to hold two or three hundred men. There were six [huts] forming a U shape and a cookhouse, Japanese headquarters and guardroom situated near the gate. All were of similar construction and the camp was enclosed by a high bamboo fence. Each man was again allowed only two feet of space.'[1]

Bamboo was often the prisoners' only resource, and as well as living in bamboo huts, often surrounded by bamboo, fences the POWs throughout the camps had bamboo water carriers, bamboo wash bowls, bamboo furniture and, in some of the camps, bamboo water pipes.

Major W.E Gill of the 137 (A) Field Artillery, R.A., was in charge of a party of 600 men from his own unit as well as the 80th Anti-Tank Regiment, Royal Artillery and a detachment from the RASC which moved up from Ban Pong to Nong Pladuc on or around 23 July 1942. Of the camp, he wrote that the huts were cool, light and, being 10 metres by 48 metres were 'not too bad' for the allotted 240. But, as only three were partially built, and the remainder

---
1. britain-at-war.org.uk/WW2/Death_Railway.

hardly started, large numbers of men had to sleep in the open or under the huts. The camp strength eventually reached 600 officers and 4,200 other ranks and, as the ranks of the prisoners swelled, some men were again left to sleep in the open. Major Gill was noted for running a well-ordered camp and for standing up to the Japanese, earning the respect of his troops the same way that Colonel Toosey did at Tamarkan, as we will shortly learn.

The hospital at Nong Pladuk was heavily infested with lice and all manner of insects. The infestation became so bad that the Japanese agreed to the floorboards being taken up and the bugs being smoked out. Major Gill reported that at one point more than 3,000 of the 4,800 men at the camp were sick.[2]

In September 1942 Lance Corporal R.G. Payton of the Royal Army Service Corps on a ration collection trip from Ban Pong to Nong Pladuc, was handed a note which stated that civilian internees in Bangkok had heard disturbing reports about conditions in the POW camps in the interior. The note asked for more information. It was simply signed 'V', the widely recognised two-finger sign employed by Winston Churchill.

A reply was sent from the officer in charge of the RASC detachment at Ban Pong and Nong Pladuk, Major Sykes, describing conditions there as well as what was known about other camps brought down the line in secret notes by the RASC drivers. This was the start of a regular exchange of information and the monthly supply of small packets of medicines and money to the POWs.

The organisation that developed was run by K.G. Gairdner, who was one of around 200 British subjects interned by the Japanese in Bangkok. Gairdner's wife was a Thai lady who was able to move around freely. Over time, Gairdner sought to extend his organisation's reach to the camps further north that were served by one Boonpong Sirivejjabhandu – usually referred as Boon Pong. Sirivejjabhandu, of whom we shall read of later, had a thriving general store at Kanchanaburi, as well as interests in motor haulage and other enterprises.[3] Initially, Boon Pong was contracted by the Japanese to supply the camp canteens along the river with such items as duck's eggs, tobacco, and canned pilchards, from which they took their cut of the profits. Little could they have realised that he would become one of the prisoners' greatest helpers. His barges travelled as far as Takanun in the dry season and all the way to Nieke during the monsoon.

After all available camp funds had been spent, the manner in which Boon Pong was to be paid was by cheque. A Bank of New South Wales cheque book was found in the haversack of Sergeant John French of 2/20th Battalion AIF. Captain Reg Newton of 2/19th Battalion crossed out the Wahroonga Branch on

---

2. TNA, WO 235/963.
3. IWM, C.E. Escritt, "Note on the 'V' Organisation", Escritt Collection.

each cheque and re-labelled them 'Head Office Sydney' where Newton had an account. Boon Pong agreed to keep the cheques and redeem them after the war.[4]

At one point during the increased work demands when the period for the construction of the railway was shortened, or 'urged on' as the Japanese official report referred to it but was known to the prisoners as the 'speedo' period – from mid-spring to mid-October 1943 – the individuals in Bangkok raised the considerable sum of 12,000 ticals for the prisoners. This was all in 20 tical notes which was the highest denomination issued to the prisoners by the Japanese. The money was smuggled into the camp in a bag of tapioca which was handed over to Sykes by Gairdner's wife directly in front of a Japanese guard. All those involved in the 'V' organisation risked their lives with their actions. Had the Japanese discovered the illicit trade, torture at the hands of the dreaded Japanese Military Police, the *Kempeitai* would have been followed by execution.

Ill treatment of the POWs at almost all the camps became commonplace and beatings with rifle butts and sticks by some of the Japanese guards increased in severity and frequency as the months passed. This was the case at Nong Pladuk and repeated promises were made by the commandant that he would put a stop to this practise, but not kept. Eventually, this reached such a level that Gill informed the camp commandant on 7 September at that unless the Japanese soldier responsible for the last 'senseless' beating was punished and warnings issued to the guards against ill-treating the prisoners, the men would not go to work the next day. The incident in question concerned Sergeant Joseph Bhumgara, of 'C' Company, 137th Field Regiment, who was beaten unconscious with a heavy bamboo stick. When he was informed about this, Major Gill called his fellow officers and told them, 'the moment of truth' had arrived.

Gill and Sykes (who was later killed in an Allied air raid on 3 December 1944) ordered the men not to go to work that day, 8 September. In response the Japanese brought up two machine guns and informed Gill and Sykes they would be shot. To save their officers around a fifth of the prisoners immediately went to work. Those that didn't, along with the officers, were made to stand from 10.00 hours until midnight at attention without rest and with Japanese guards watching to make sure the men did not slouch.

The only movement permitted was a walk of two paces to the rear to urinate. The officers were kept at attention for a further two hours. Eventually, a compromise was reached whereby the officers apologised to the then camp commander, Lieutenant Tanaka, allowing him to save face, which, in turn enabled him to let the officers stand down.

---

4. Peter Brune, *Descent into Hell, The Fall of Singapore – Pudu and Changi – The Thai-Burma Railway* (Allen & Unwin, London, 2014), p.621.

The determination of the prisoners to refuse to work had the desired effect, however, and after that the men were treated more fairly, though it did not stop face-slapping by the IJA engineers.

Not all the officers were present in the camp at the time of the stand taken by Gill and Sykes. One of those was Captain Ewart Escritt, who was on an (abortive) six-weeks Japanese language course. Another was Chaplain Christopher Ross. He was hauled up in front of Tanaka who demanded to know why he had not paraded with the other officers. Ross replied that he neither obeyed Gill or Tanaka, only 'His Master in Heaven'. Astonishing, the Japanese lieutenant seemed to accept this, and Ross went unpunished.[5] 'Whilst Tanaka could be an absolute swine,' Colonel Knights observed, 'he did have his rational moments, when he was quite human and understanding.'[6]

As one of the Master in Heaven's earthly representatives, Chaplain Ross did much for the morale of the men in the camp. There was no provision for padres to accompany the prisoners when they left Changi for Thailand and he had to 'wangle' his way into one of the battalions. During the above-mentioned strike he repeatedly appealed with the Japanese to let the men stand down. He was, of course, beaten for his efforts and threatened with a sword.

He established a little bamboo church for all denominations – built by the prisoners in their spare time – which was well attended. The conditions the men had to endure turned many to religion and, in addition to the permitted one service a week (where the prisoners were not allowed to pray for an Allied victory), little groups met secretly each night at great risk with lookouts posted to warn of any approaching Japanese.

Ross also trained around fifty other men to be lay preachers to conduct services for when they were moved up to the jungle camps. Ross regarded this as his greatest contribution to the welfare of the POWs, bringing spiritual support to many hundreds of men.[7] The chaplains throughout the camps were not granted any special status and were forced to work along with the other prisoners.

The Japanese and Koreans, the latter being recruited to act as camp guards to free up Japanese soldiers, regarded the behaviour of the likes of Ross with some degree of wariness. Anyone who seemed to be mad was given a wide berth. This included two men of the Argyll and Sutherland Highlanders who created a 'phantom' dog. They took the dog everywhere with them, throwing

---

5. IWM, Escritt Collection.
6. Alfred E. Knights (Ed. Reginald Harland), *Singapore and the Thailand-Burma Railway* (Arena, Bury St. Edmunds, 2013) p.103.
7. IWM, Escritt Collection, Christopher Ross, *A Methodist Chaplain's Experiences in Japanese Camps*, p.5.

it sticks to catch, giving it food and water and waited while it urinated against trees. The guards kept well away from the two 'madmen'.[8]

Nong Pladuk was usually a hive of activity, with trains arriving with the materials required for constructing the railway. When a train arrived, the prisoners would have to unload drums of oil, sleepers and heavy steel sections of rail in double quick time, and transfer them, along with items manufactured in the adjacent workshops, to the waiting trucks of the train which would take them up the line.

The camp hospital, run by British medical staff with the assistance of Dutch doctors, was also visited by the Japanese guards needing treatment, usually for venereal disease. Because of their greater knowledge of diseases in the region, the Dutch took care of all the laboratory work. The hospital was adequate for the original number of prisoners but, as mentioned previously, at one time there were 3,000 sick out of the total 4,800 POW population and bamboo and attap extensions had to be hurriedly made.[9]

With food more abundant than in the jungle camps, there were separate Dutch, Chinese and British canteens. The camp canteen was able to provide coffee, bananas, fried eggs, omelettes, fudge, roasted peanuts, jam tarts and meat pies.[10] There was also a concert party, and a cycling club.

There were, though, internal disciplinary problems. In December 1943, a bombardier employed in making soup was found to be producing more than he was supposed to, selling the surplus and pocketing the money. In another incident, two Australian cooks were caught stealing eggs and soap from the canteen at night.[11]

In January 1944, Lieutenant Colonel Philip Toosey was placed in overall command of Nong Pladuk. When he arrived, the camp held around 4,000 British, Australian, Dutch and a few American prisoners. The numbers at the camp varied throughout the following months from 2,500 to 8,000. The work at Nong Pladuk at this later stage consisted of maintenance duties in the railway workshops, moving stores and digging local defences and air raid shelters. This was because the camp was situated right in the centre of sidings on which petrol and ammunition trains were parked, and where there were Japanese stores and an anti-aircraft post.

From the moment that he arrived, Toosey saw that Nong Pladuk would be targeted by the Allied bombers and he made this point to the Japanese. The

---

8. IWM, Escritt Collection, *Beyond The Three Pagodas Pass*, p.44.
9. TNA, WO 235/963.
10. TNA, WO 235/963.
11. Brian Best (Ed.), *Secret Letters from the Railway, The Remarkable Record of Charles Steel – a Japanese POW* (Pen & Sword, Barnsley, 2004), pp.94 & 98.

reply he received was that 'You British have no aircraft left; you have no need to worry.' However, after repeated representations, the Japanese permitted the prisoners to dig slit trenches around the base of the huts. This was 'a most stupid measure,' Toosey wrote, 'since in the rainy season these trenches would fall in and undermine the huts, which were on stilts.' This, of course, is exactly what happened, and the prisoners were ordered to refill the trenches and dig new ones in the ground between the huts.

Reconnaissance aircraft were heard, and occasionally seen over the railway, from September 1943 but it was a year later when these installations were attacked by Allied bombers on the night of 6/7 September 1944. The raid lasted for three hours during which the prisoners were held in their flimsy huts at the point of the bayonet. One bomb fell within four feet of one of the huts, completely demolishing it. It was part of a 'stick' of bombs which was dropped right across the camp, killing ninety-five and wounding more than 300.

In the raid some petrol wagons in the sidings had been set on fire. A party of around fifty prisoners was taken by the Japanese to salvage all the undamaged wagons. There was a real chance of unexploded bombs igniting in the heat and the guards stood well back while the POWs recovered the wagons.[12]

Immediately after the raid the then camp commandant, Lieutenant Colonel Sugasawa, visited the hospital where the wounded were lying on the floor. The Japanese officer was immediately confronted by Major Gill: 'I protested vehemently and told him the camp must be moved to a safer area.' Sugasawa responded equally forcibly: 'You must remain in this camp and there will be many more similar raids. You are soldiers and must expect to die.' The main problem for the prisoners was the overcrowded nature of the huts. One bomb striking a single hut could cause an enormous number of casualties.

There were further attacks, including one three months later: 'On 3 December 1944, while eating the evening meal, we saw a bomber formation approaching the camp,' wrote Toosey. 'There was just enough time to take cover before it pattern-bombed the Station and sidings. The outside bomb of the pattern killed 9 P.O.W. in the centre of a slit trench area, and another bomb destroyed the Cookhouse. While rescue work was in progress two more formations approached from the opposite direction. Of these ... the outside stick in the pattern fired 2 huts and burned out a large part of the P.O.W. Hospital.'

As a result, Toosey renewed his protests and he wrote to the Japanese headquarters, pointing out, quite sensibly, that if the Japanese wanted to continue using POWs to maintain the railway then they had better do all they could to keep the prisoners safe. This had the desired effect, and the camp was moved 200

---

12. TNA, WO 235/963.

yards away from the railway and two months later was abandoned altogether.[13] Total casualties from air raids at Non Pladuk were 104 killed and more than 400 wounded.

Colonel Toosey wrote of two incidents of 'extreme brutality' at Nong Pladuk during his time there. The first concerned Company Sergeant Major Dooley who was struck so savagely on the back of his neck that his spinal cord was nearly broken. Dooley had to spend two months in hospital as a result.

In the other incident Sergeant C.W.J. Pratt who, while holding a concert in one of the huts in June 1944, was ordered to attend the Guard Room to explain what the concert was about. There he was 'kicked in both legs and beaten about the face at least a dozen times'. Another Japanese soldier entered the Guard Room and joined in, 'and immediately started kicking me in the privates,' reported Pratt, 'just above the bladder and all over the abdomen and hitting me in the face. I fell to my knees, and he still kept on kicking me. He kicked me all around the Guard Room.'

Nevertheless, Toosey was willing to give the Japanese credit where it was merited. He noted that at Nong Pladuk the Japanese always supplied, at least twice a year, vaccinations against typhoid, paratyphoid A, and paratyphoid B, cholera, dysentery and plague. By comparison, Toosey reported that Red Cross parcels intended for individuals had to be shared among ten or twenty men, with the Japanese helping themselves 'openly and shamelessly'.

As the tide of the war was clearly turning against the Japanese by this time, the prisoners were told they would no longer permitted to sing in their huts or at church services and Chaplain Ross had his sermon notes, papers and even his bible taken from him. These were later returned when the camp adjutant, at great personal risk, broke into the Japanese storeroom and recovered them.[14]

Bam Pong 3 Kilo
Also Known as Bhan Pong or Ban Pong

Bam Pong was the last stop for the prisoners on their gruelling five-day train journey from Singapore to Thailand. They disembarked here to begin their tortuous march north through the jungles of Thailand to the work camps.

The first prisoners, numbering 650 men, arrived at Bam Pong in June 1942. They were housed in huts, with 100 men in each one, the floors of which were awash with stagnant water.

---

13. AWM, 54 554/2/1C.
14. Ross, pp.6-7.

The prisoners' days were spent digging latrines and performing other construction work around the camp. They also helped build a camp and railway workshop for the Japanese. The prisoners were warned that they would be executed if they talked to any of the local civilians, but there are few records of ill treatment at this camp, thanks in no small measure again to Major Gill who continued his firm stance here against the Japanese.[15]

Gill's party was sent to work at Nong Pladuk in July 1942. He wrote that the camp: 'Lay on the outskirts of the village and consisted of four huts (each for 500 troops) … These huts were merely crude attap and bamboo roofs reaching to within 3 or 4 feet of the ground with no sides and bamboo sleeping platforms. They were dark and the earth floor muddy and flooded at times during rainstorms. A small cookhouse was built on the opposite side of the road and again consisted merely of an attap roof with iron cauldrons held in mud supports. Water supply consisted of a well in the camp and later permission was granted to use a petrol pump on the other side of the road. Bathing was in full view and within 10 feet of the main road running between the camp and the cookhouse and much frequented by the Thais.'

Major Gill considered the latrines at Bam Pong to be 'appalling' and when they flooded during heavy rain excreta was scattered over a large area of the camp 'making it a mass of human faeces and bluebottles.'[16] The latrines at Bam Pong also made a lasting impression on Lieutenant Colonel Lionel Manning, who described them as ghastly: 'insofar as it consisted of one enormous open trench filled to within eighteen inches of the top with excreta and which was crawling and seething with white maggots, which were the larvae of flies, and which crawled over one's boots while the latrine was in use and was undoubtedly the cause of the spreading of various tropical diseases.'[17] Part of the problem with Bam Pong was that it was largely a staging post for the groups of prisoners moving up the line and the composition of the camp was never stable long enough for the camp to be properly maintained.

Captain M.K. Winchester, of the Australian Army Medical Corps who was the 'H' Force Dental Officer, called the latrines 'startling'. He also wrote: 'As one used the latrines, men and women attempted to purchase the shirt from one's back, paying cash; or in the case of the women, a shirt for a few moments of their Thailand charm.' Through force of circumstances, the prisoners were also compelled to bathe in full view of the Thai women. The women, though, looked on 'unconcernedly'.

---

15. Report on camps by John Slaughter (Royal Norfolk Regiment), www.mansell.com/POW_resources.
16. TNA, WO 325/157.
17. TNA, WO 311/547.

The officers had been told at Singapore they could take with them all the personal belongings they wished. These items were offloaded from the trains at Bam Pong. But the Japanese placed no guards over the baggage, and it was looted, with some officers losing everything they possessed.

Throughout the camps, the Japanese, and later Korean, guards were repeatedly conducting rollcalls, or *tenko*. These were rarely carried out effectively, often leading to repeated re-counts until the correct figure was achieved. In one instance at Bam Pong, when Major Roderick Anderson was staging through the camp with his party of 400 prisoners a *tenko* was demanded by the Korean guard Toyoyama Kise. Anderson gave his count to Toyoyama. As this figure, though correct, did not correspond to Toyoyama's, he struck Anderson over the head with a steel-shafted golf club.[18]

Toyoyama carried this golf club around with him to administer punishment whenever he felt like it.

His attacks were spasmodic. On one afternoon he might hit four or five prisoners and then not strike anyone for a week.

According to Captain Barry Custance Baker of 27 Line Section, Royal Corps of Signals, Bam Pong was a 'very disgusting place.' As it was a transit camp, there was no Allied officer in command to keep it in good order. The running of the camp was in the hands of a 'particularly idle and brutal Japanese major who deputed everything to his second in command who was equally idle.'[19]

As we have read, the prisoners were sent down the line to help build sidings, a Japanese camp, workshops and the POW camp at Nong Pladuk. Only the Adjutant, one clerk, six cooks and the doctor accompanied by a medical orderly were allowed to remain at the camp. All the rest, including the padre as we have learned, had to work. The men marched out of the camp at 08.00 hours, returning after work had finished at 19.00.

The Japanese camp commander was Lieutenant Otanyi who, again according to Major Gill, did all he could to improve conditions at the camp within the limitations imposed by the need to complete the railway in the shortest time possible. After much persuasion, Gill was able obtain five or six lamps for the huts and a small canteen of fruit, other foodstuffs and tobacco, and even to allow the British officers to merely command their troops instead of working.

While there might have been few recorded incidents at Bam Pong, this was not the case when the men went out to work. Corporal Roy Pearce of the Royal Army Service Corps submitted an affidavit regarding the actions of Lieutenant

---

18. TNA, WO 235/1034.
19. Hilary Custance Green (Ed.), *Surviving the Death Railway: A POW's Memoir and Letters from Home* (Pen & Sword, Barnsley, 2016), p.81.

Jugi Tarumoto during the building of an embankment about twenty kilometres from Bam Pong: 'As we each proceeded to our work Tarumoto kicked us in the back to start off ... When any of us started to tire Tarumoto would beat us with a bamboo stick, usually the first piece he could lay his hands on. He would always hit us where we had an injury or a sore, or on any part of the body, usually the head or the back. For another punishment if we lagged behind Tarumoto would make any offender hold a heavy piece of wood, which weighed 40 or 50 pounds, above his head for sometimes as long as an hour, in the blazing sun. Some of the men could not do this and were beaten with a bamboo stick by Tarumoto.'[20] Tarumoto was quite open about his feelings towards the prisoners: 'I loathe and detest all English people,' he once told a Staff Sergeant Leech of the Royal Army Ordnance Corps, 'and will make their bodies sleepers for my railway.'[21] Tarumoto was proud of his ability to speak English and if any of the prisoners failed to understand him, which happened quite often, he would hit them with his bamboo stick.[22]

Eric Lomax – *The Railway Man* – was in the Japanese workshops about a mile to the west of the camp at Bam Pong. He was sent to work for the Japanese railway fitters, turners and welders, most of whom were 'humane', interested only in getting their jobs done. As long as the prisoners cooperated with them, they treated the POWs fairly.

Lieutenant Colonel Owtram arrived at Bam Pong in July 1942. At that time there were twelve huts in a line with about four feet between each one. At one end were the latrines placed just three feet away at right angles to the accommodation huts, the stench from which was, as others have remarked, was dreadful.

In August 1943, the Japanese ordered the prisoners to rebuild the camp but a sudden deluge of monsoon rain one night in September softened the ground and the huts began to lean at 'crazy' angles and several collapsed altogether.

When Sergeant H. Jones arrived at Bam Pong on 4 November 1942, he found the camp completely under water 'with no sanitary arrangements or conveniences whatsoever ... The whole area was one vast breeding ground for mosquitos. The food ration was three-quarters of a pint of rice per meal per man, made slightly palatable with vegetable water. When two Thai women and three small children tried to give some fruit to the prisoners they were hung by their thumbs from a fence for an hour and then taken down and tied up in front of the Korean guard hut in the 'boiling' heat for two days without food

---

20. TNA, WO 235/857.
21. TNA, WO 235/857.
22. TNA, WO 235/857.

Camps of the Thai-Burma Railway

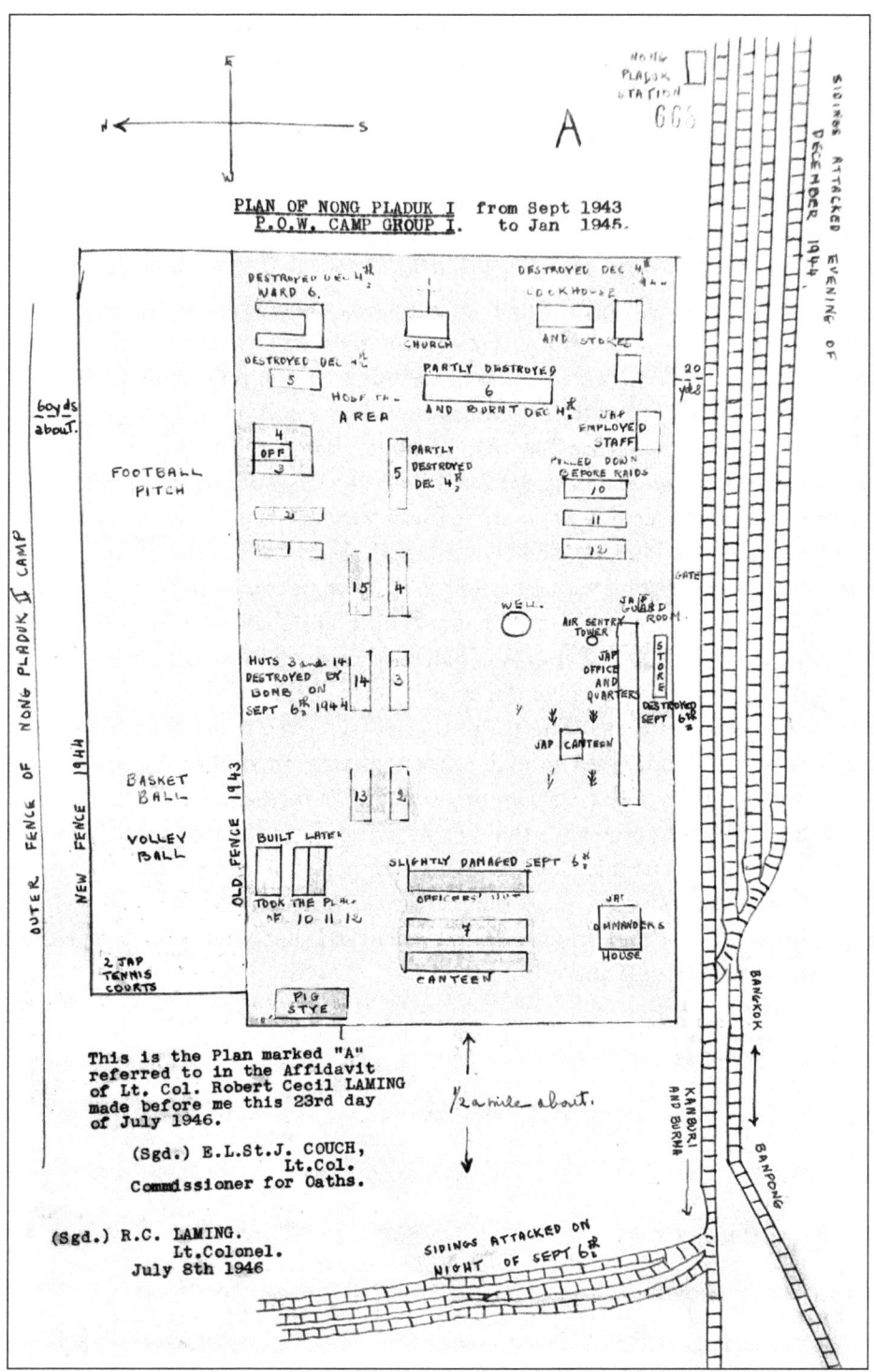

Nong Pladuk camp.

or water.²³ The Koreans, described as 'purely amoral coolie vermin', had arrived in November to take over many of the guard functions.

Lance Corporal John Wyatt of the 2nd East Surrey Regiment said that Ban Pong 'stank to high heaven and was a complete hell-hole, just a huge morass of mud ... The huts were alive with bugs and insects of all shapes and sizes. The floor was just a sea of mud and maggots, and cockroaches, ants and spiders crawled out from the cess pits used as latrines into the huts.' The only fresh water supply available was drawn from a well, served by a single bucket on a rope.²⁴

The situation at Bam Pong had not improved when 'H' Force arrived at there in early May 1943: 'Conditions were appalling,' wrote Lieutenant Colonel H.R. Humphries in his report on 'H' Force, 'the only source of water supply being one well in the forecourt and the latrines consisted of two slit trenches with bamboo footrests. These trenches, which had obviously been used by preceding Forces passing through, were indescribably filthy, being already 2/3rds full of excreta, rubbish, swill, surface water and urine. Fly larvae to the number of millions were in the trenches and here, as well as over the whole area of the establishment, flies and numerous other insect pests abound.'²⁵ Lieutenant Colonel Charles Kappe of 'F' Force agreed, complaining that at Bam Pong 'chaos reigned supreme'.

Bam Pong Hospital Camp was half-a-mile away from Bam Pong transit camp. There was no perimeter fence surrounding the Hospital Camp and no Japanese guards present. The medical staff were free to roam into the local village to buy food. Even though it was situated on slightly higher ground than the main camp, during the rainy season, the medics had to 'slosh' around in knee-high, filthy water to attend to the patients on their raised platforms.²⁶ The water was generally only six inches from the sleeping platforms and in some cases the water rose over the platforms. When Colonel Toosey saw the hospital at the end of October 1942, he believed that conditions were so bad the staff had 'lost grip and given up hope'.²⁷

---

23. TNA, WO 325/157.
24. John Wyatt & Cecil Lowry, *No Mercy from the Japanese: A Survivor's Account of the Burma Railway and the Hell Ships* (Pen & Sword, Barnsley, 2008), p.76.
25. ibid.
26. Kenneth Adams, *Healing in Hell: The Memoirs of a Far Eastern POW Medic* (Pen & Sword, Barnsley, 2011), p.53.
27. Toosey Report.

Tha Rua   26 Kilo
Also known as To Reoa Noi, Talua or Taruanoi

Private Glen Skewes painted a surprisingly favourable image of Tha Rua as he passed through this transit camp on 27 April 1943: 'This was the first of the river camps. The river wound in and out of the hills and dales with pretty mountains – a very beautiful sight was this peaceful river, fish jumping out of its waters, canoes and Native barges moving and gliding along its surface. However, I felt too sleepy and exhausted to enjoy it – and no money. It was indeed a lovely and most picturesque site.'[28]

It was as the prisoners were clearing the ground for the railway line to reach Rukke and then onto Tha Rua, that one of the Japanese engineers, Norihiko Futamatu, noticed that the workers were not clearing a straight line through the jungle. Even though the man overseeing the work, the surveyor Mouri, asked the prisoners to correct what he thought was an error, the line they were clearing still veered to the right. This was ignored and the path cleared by the POWs continued to deviate until the reason for this was realised by Futamatu – the hungry prisoners had seen a large banana tree which they were hoping to cut down.

Tha Muang   39 Kilo
Also known as Tamuang or Tamoan

Tha Muang (Tamuang or Tamoan) was one of the main camps for the prisoners after work on the railway had finished. The camp held around 12,000 Australian, British, Dutch and American prisoners. The camp was divided into two parts, Hospital and Fit. As with the other base camps, accommodation, food and sanitary arrangements were far better than they had been in the work camps further up the line and the work was not punishing. Discipline, though, was severe, as exemplified by this description of the Roll Call in Tamuan: 'Battalions (or what was left of them) paraded, at 9 am and 7 pm, on a large field. (This used to be a Tobacco Plantation), in groups of ten, Sergeant Majors called the Roll and dressed the ranks. After waiting about an hour, a Nip Officer accompanied by Korean Guards would arrive on the scene. The Nip Officer would mount a raised dais, so that he could see the whole parade, or should I say, "That he would be higher up so that white men had to looked up to him" (Nippon Creed). The Senior P.O.W Officers would call the parade to "attention" and give the order "Eyes Centre". All P.O.Ws would look directly at the Nip Officer, who

---

28. britain-at-war.org.uk/WW2/Death_Railway.

would salute. Then "Eyes Front". The Korean Guards would then check each Battalion in turn. When checked and correct, the same saluting procedure would be carried out and the parade dismissed, sometimes at 8 pm or at 9-30 am. Sometimes at 9.0 pm, but never later than 9.30 am in the morning. Night time, our time, did not matter.'[29]

C.S.P. J.A. Harrell of the U.S. Navy was at what he called Tamwan, and in his post-war report wrote that there were a number of latrines ranging from ten to fifty feet away from the accommodation huts. They were about fifteen feet deep, ten feet wide and thirty feet long. Water for washing was restricted to one bucketful per day drawn from a well. Washing was done anywhere there was space to pour the bucket over oneself.[30]

There was an infrequent daily meat ration, and it was the responsibility of Bombardier G.R. Lancaster of the 4th Anti-Tank Regiment to go to the ration store to find out the number (if any) of the cattle which were to be killed that day.

When Gunner George Kemp arrived in November 1943, 'the camp was in a filthy condition. The swill pits were open holes in the ground, full up to the top with old swill, with flies swarming all around. The huts were not rain-proof, nor was the so-called hospital hut, which was in no way different from any of the living huts in the camp.'[31]

Lance Bombardier E.S. Benford was among those transferred to Tamuang in June 1944. After all he had witnessed at Kanu camp, he believed he was inured to scenes of suffering and death, but he was 'sickened' with what he saw in the dysentery hut at Tamuang. With 200 men fouling themselves up to forty times a day and just a handful of orderlies to try and clean up the mess, the place had become just a heap of unwashed, ragged bodies. No time was wasted on men who were obviously dying, and they were left lying in their own excreta. Benford offered his services and was invited to join the staff in the ulcer ward where the Australian doctor was having to perform up to forty amputations a day.[32]

Hundreds of war crime complaints ('Q' forms) were raised concerning the conduct of the Japanese at Tamuang, including an incident regarding Major Mizutani on 31 December 1944. That night, shortly after 'lights out' (approximately 23.45 hours), Fusilier Len Wanty was stopped by a Korean guard when he was trying to cross from the work camp to the hospital. After being interrogated by the Koreans it was agreed Wanty should be released. At this point Major Mizutani appeared on the scene and asked what was happening. When the major learned that Wanty had been trying to reach the hospital after

---

29. far-eastern-heroes.org.uk/Freeing_the_demons/html/nakom_paton.
30. Center for Research Allied POWS Under the Japanese, mansell.com/POW_resources/camplists.
31. TNA, WO 235/918.
32. IWM, E.S. Benford, *The Rising Sun on my Back: A Personal Account of War, 1939-1945*, LBY K. 95/2303.

lights out, he immediately said: 'There is no need for further enquiry, this man must be shot.' He ordered one of the Koreans to kill Wanty. The guard refused, so Mizutani slapped him in the face three times, took his rifle from him. He told Wanty to walk towards the fence surrounding the camp. Mizutani walked up behind the fusilier and shot him in the back. Wanty fell down and died.[33] Many others witnessed this murder.

One of the Korean guards, Kinzo Motoyama, referred to by the prisoners as 'The Black Prince' because of his dark complexion and his haughty, swaggering manner, featured in many of these complaints. According to one statement, he 'took great delight in hitting and kicking us at every possible chance' and when he was in charge of the ration barges there was not a day when, during loading and unloading 'men were not either pushed into the river, kicked, or severely beaten.'[34]

One of his punishments handed out to prisoners caught stealing from the Japanese food store was for the culprit to be staked out on the ground with his ankles and wrists tied down with wet rattan. As the rattan dried out it would shrink and slowly cut into the skin and sinews of the poor victims as his limbs were pulled out of their sockets. The number of beatings carried out by Motoyama are far too many to record.

Possibly the most egregious of his tortures was carried out by his deputy, Sergeant Seiichi Okada. His victim would be pinned down by other guards as water was poured down the prisoner's throat. 'The man's stomach would swell up from the huge volumes of water,' recalled Alistair Urquhart. 'Okada would then jump up and down gleefully on the prisoner's stomach. Sometimes guards would tie barbed wire around the poor soul's stomach.' Not every victim of this torture survived.[35]

The death of prisoners also gave the ever-enterprising POWs a chance to record the crimes committed against them. The burying of bodies gave the men the opportunity to bury diaries and other evidence of their ill treatment at the hands of the Japanese in the hope that these items would later be discovered and the atrocities they were subjected to would be revealed to the world.

Even in the midst of the death and squalor lived through by the prisoners, there were emotional and touching scenes. One such occasion took place at Tamuang in 1944. Private William Mackie of the Gordon Highlanders received a silver wedding anniversary card made by his camp comrades. He managed to keep the card throughout the remainder of his captivity and took it home with him after his release.

---

33. TNA, WO 311/547.
34. TNA, WO 325/157.
35. Alistair Urquhart, *The Forgotten Highlander: My Incredible Story of Survival During the War in the Far East* (Abacus, London, 2011), pp.62-3.

When Stuart Young of the 85th Anti-Tank Regiment, Royal Artillery, arrived at Tamuang after leaving Tonchan (see below) following the completion of the railway, C Work Battalion to which he belonged, was ordered to build fifty huts for the expected arrival of more men from the northern camps. The men quickly developed an almost production line manufacture of the huts, cutting the bamboo into measured parts which could be slipped together during construction. The prefabricated huts were assembled quickly, but almost as soon as a hut had been erected it was filled with the latest intake of returning prisoners.[36]

When the officers were separated from the Other Ranks in January 1945, Tamuang was one of the camps into which the Other Ranks were concentrated. The only officers left with the men were padres and medical officers. One of those medical officers, Lieutenant Colonel W.G. Harvey, R.A.M.C., was impressed at how well the men managed without their officers: 'After seven months' experience of WO and NCO administration, I am convinced the camps benefitted by the removal of the officers. This was due … Firstly, the removal of a source of irritation to the Nips; secondly, the excellent behaviour of the men themselves and thirdly, the first-class work of all the WOs and NCOs who had the administrative jobs in the camp.'[37]

As a hospital base camp, it was occupied by IV Group between August 1944 and June 1945 with II Group taking over until the end of the war. There were still Dutch prisoners here until 1947.[38]

Kanchanaburi   51 Kilo
Also known as Kanburi, Kamburi and Kan'buri

Kanchanaburi camp, often shortened to Kanburi, was established in October 1942. Kanburi became the Japanese headquarters for the construction of the southern part of the railway in Thailand and the most important base station for them. In the area of Kanchanaburi was a large locomotive shed station and as well as a Base Hospital Camp, a Working Camp and Aerodrome Camps No. 1 and No. 2. Later all the officers were placed in one large camp. It was referred to, mockingly, as the 'Imperial War Museum'.[39]

---

36. Stuart Young, *Life on the Death Railway, The Memoirs of a British POW* (Pen & Sword, Barnsley, 2013), pp.102-3.
37. Paul H. Kratoska, *The Thailand-Burma Railway, 1942-1946: Documents, and Selected Writings* (Routledge, New York, 2006), p.86.
38. britain-at-war.org.uk/ww2/Death_Railway/html/tha_muang.
39. Cecil Lowry, *Last Post Over the River Kwai: The 2nd East Surreys in the Far East 1938-1945* (Pen & Sword, Barnsley, 2018), p.127.

The railway head offices were located just two kilometres away which included the centre from which all train movements south of the Burmese border were arranged. Appropriately, a number of locomotives used on the railway have been preserved there which can be seen today.

The camp was described by Private Fred Cox of the East Surrey Regiment at the end of March 1943: 'The camp was situated on the edge of what had previously been a landing field for aircraft. There were eight long huts, each constructed of bamboo with a thatched roof of dried palm trees, or attap. Each of the huts held roughly two hundred men but, even with a few more squeezed in, the majority of our party were still left without accommodation and had to use groundsheets to improvise some sort of shelter for themselves on the few patches of dry ground available. We soon discovered that camp conditions were very basic but by this time we had learned to expect nothing else from the Japanese. It quickly became obvious that there were not enough latrine trenches to cope with such a large influx of men and that more would have to be dug. However, just as there were not enough huts for everyone to sleep in, such matters were not considered a priority by our captors.'[40]

After the privations the prisoners had experienced in Singapore's Changi goal, Kanchanaburi was, to the men of 2/19 Battalion A.I.F., 'our dream of the land of plenty'. Thai traders lined the road as the new arrivals detrained, who offered eggs, bananas, melons, paw-paws, guavas, mangoes, tomatoes, onions, ducks, fish and steaks, the stalls resembling an 'eastern bazaar'.[41]

When Captain Reg Newton's 'U' Battalion of 'D' Force arrived at Kanchanaburi in March 1943, it was placed in Aerodrome Camp for a week. Left unsupervised for those 'blissful' seven days, the prisoners who still possessed many valuable personal items, sold their watches, rings and clothing to the locals, in return buying 'all manner' of fruits and vegetables, eggs, ducks and fish.[42]

The first task of the prisoners, under Colonel Toosey, based at nearby Tamarkan, was to build a bridge the over the Khwae Yai near where it joins the Khwae Noi to form the Mae Klong. From Kanchanaburi the Mae Klong flows on to enter the Gulf of Thailand. Before this substantial iron and concrete bridge could be built (see below), a temporary wooden bridge was constructed nearby to enable supplies to be moved further up the line. Battery Sergeant Major Charles Steel saw the work on the main bridge being 'something at which a man can take an interest in,' being responsible for a team of ten gunners engaged on driving the bridge's concrete pillars into the riverbed.[43]

---

40. Ellie Taylor, *Faith, Hope and Rice: Private Cox's Account of Captivity and the Death Railway* (Pen & Sword, Barnsley, 2015), p.42.
41. Reginald W.J. Newton and Peter E.M. McGuinness, *The Grim Glory of the 2/19 Battalion A.I.F.* (2/19 Battalion Association, Sydney, 1975), p.577.
42. Brune, p.619.
43. Brian Best, pp.68-9.

It was those previously mentioned latrines which were most vividly recalled by Arthur Godman: 'When the rains came the latrines started to fill up with water and very soon the contents approached the top of the trench. The sewage was a seething mass of maggots which did not cause much concern during the dry weather because the level was a good five feet below the surface. But with the rains the maggots started to crawl over your feet as you squatted on the bamboo poles laid across the trench on which we had to squat ... The horrors of those latrines stayed in everyone's minds for a long time and was one of the lasting impressions of the camp at Kanburi.'[44]

'H' Force passed through Kanburi on its way north in the second week of May 1943. There was an acute water shortage at the camp at that time as there was only one well in the camp, which the local Thais took advantage of by selling buckets of water to the prisoners for 5 cents. There was a constant queue of a dozen or more prisoners with their pails or kerosene tins, with the happy Thai owner making a small fortune.

All water had to boiled or chlorinated under medical supervision before it was fit for drinking. Nevertheless, bathing in the river was permitted and once a day a party was assembled and marched there, a distance of about two miles, under IJA guards.

Many of the parties which passed through Kanburi on their way to camps further north were inoculated against typhoid and cholera. They were also tested for dysentery and inoculated against smallpox.[45]

One day a Thai woman threw a fowl to a small group of prisoners. She was spotted by the Japanese and strung up outside the camp for all the prisoners to see her slowly dying as they passed by her on their way to work. It took her one and a half days to die.[46]

Lieutenant Eric Lomax was sent to Kanburi from Ban Pong where he found there was nothing to stop men walking out of the camp and the prisoners were able to walk freely into the town. Lomax explored the area, finding such an abundance of mangos, durians and pawpaw he 'hardly knew what to do with the fruit.'[47] Lomax worked with a number of other prisoners in the railway workshops a short distance away from the main camp.

An almost essential element in the prisoners' will to survive was the belief that one day their suffering would come to an end. This was fostered by news from the outside world of the progress of the war. Wireless enthusiasts and

---

44. Arthur Godman, *The Will to Survive: Three and a Half Years as a Prisoner of the Japanese* (History Press, Stroud, 2002), p.115.
45. TNA, WO 325/17.
46. Pattie Wright, *The Men of the Line: Stories of the Thai-Burma Railway Survivors* (Miegunyah Press, Melbourne, 2008), p.275.
47. Eric Lomax, *The Railway Man* (Vantage, London, 1996), p.99.

members of the Royal Corps of Signals had dismantled sets in Singapore before being interned. To avoid being found by the Japanese, the parts were distributed among many other men, and a number of sets were secretly rebuilt in Thailand. Eric Lomax was involved in the operation of a set in Kanburi. With power from an old battery, the prisoners were able to tune into the BBC in the evenings.

Snippets of key items of news were passed along the line to the other work camps. A 'trusted' man – a Gunner Tomlinson – was placed on the rations train going up country and he was briefed on what information was to be relayed to the prisoners. With the Axis powers in retreat throughout 1943 the news was almost universally uplifting.

Unfortunately, the wireless set at Kanburi was discovered by the Japanese. On 29 August 1943 after an early morning roll call, instead of dismissing the prisoners, they were kept standing at attention, being surrounded by guards with fixed bayonets while the huts were searched. After three hours, the prisoners were stood down, but the radio had been discovered at the bed of Sergeant Major Lance Threw of the Royal Army Ordnance Corps. The Japanese also found three other sets in the process of being built as well as items stolen from the Japanese stores.

The inevitable punishments began early the following morning. Threw and one other soldier who, in the opinion of the Japanese had stolen the most stores, were made to stand to attention in the 100 degrees heat all day. During the afternoon, Threw was also made to swing a heavy iron sledgehammer against a wooden block. He was not released until late in the night. This, though, was not the end of the treatment.

A week later, Threw was sent to the post of the much-feared Japanese *Kempeitai*, where he was interrogated, beaten, and made to stand for two days. The next to be sent there was Sergeant Fred Smith who was made to stand to attention continually for four days. Every time he fell asleep and collapsed to the ground, he was kicked awake and dragged to his feet.

On 21 September five of the nine officers in the hut where the radio had been found, including Lomax, were also taken to the main camp, and forced to stand at attention for a day before the beatings began. The Japanese and Korean guards used pickaxe handles as, one by one, all five men were severely beaten and kicked. Collectively, they were struck 900 times.

Finally on 23 September they were taken to the camp hospital. That night they heard that four more officers were to be punished. In the assault that followed, lieutenants Armitage and Hawley were beaten to death; their bodies were thrown into a deep latrine in the Japanese section of the camp.[48]

---

48. Much of Eric Lomax's stirring book from page 109 onwards is devoted to his treatment following the discovery of the wireless.

The Japanese believed Thais had facilitated the acquisition of the batteries and parts needed for the assembly of the radios and from this point onwards, contact between prisoners and natives was further restricted throughout the camps.

Kanchanaburi Hospital Camp was opened in late 1942 by Lieutenant Colonel John Malcolm RAMC. As well as the large ward huts, there was a central complex for the medical officers where there was also an operating theatre, a laboratory for analysing blood and faecal samples, an operating theatre and a dental surgery.

The conversion of Kanchanaburi to that of a Base Hospital began in the summer of 1943 after the completion of the bridges and the departure of most of the fit prisoners for the camps further up the line.

Prior to that, the hospital intake from the camps up country had already pushed up patient numbers from around 600 in March 1943 to more than 1,000 by June. 'The men arrived in a dreadful state,' remembered Kenneth Adams, 'a picture of utter misery and desperation on a scale I'd not seen before. In one memorable trainload carrying about 100 wretches, a few were dead; some had ulcers stretching from ankle to knee revealing the structure of bones and joints and could have been living exhibits on human anatomy; some had bones sticking out of feet in place of toes ... They were soaked in excrement, covered in lice and stank of gangrene.'[49]

As a result of so many desperately sick men being herded together at Kanchanaburi Hospital Camp, it became, one patient said, 'the vilest place that was ever created on earth'.[50]

The Japanese attitude to the sick prisoners was summed up Colonel S. Nakamura, Commander of the Prisoners of War Organisation in Thailand. On 26 June he issued a General Order from Kanchanaburi, which stated: 'Those who fail to reach objective in charge by lack of health or spirit is considered in the Japanese Army as most shameful deed.'[51]

Nevertheless, evacuation of sick personnel from the camps of 'H' Force to what would become became 'F' and H' Force Hospital Camp, began on 20 July where the only medical staff available were one medical officer, one nursing orderly, and two non-medical NCOs.

On 27 August, Major E.A. Marsden, 'H' Force's Senior Medical Officer, along with Captain W.R. Jackson, with a small fatigue party, escorted by an IJA sergeant major, arrived to help at the hospital, which was still in the process of being extended to accommodate the expected influx from up country. Being

---

49. Kenneth Adams, pp.59-60 & 72.
50. Wright, p.169.
51. TNA, WO 325/35, Report by Lt. Col. P.J.D. Toosey on Malay and Thailand Prisoner of War Camps.

by a large town, native labour was available to build the huts and building materials were plentiful.

The hospital was still under construction as parties of patients arrived, being placed in attap huts which had only been finished twelve hours before. At first, each hut held sixty men, but this quickly increased to 100 and the huts became too crowded to permit any satisfactory hygiene to be practised. To assisted in the running of the hospital, volunteer orderlies, such as cooks or some of the less sick patients, helped as much as they could.

Captain Donald Dyer was seconded to Kanburi 'F' and 'H' Hospital Camp from 'F' Force at Shimo Sonkurai in August 1943 to assist with the handling of the parties arriving from the jungle camps. Feeding the arrivals was a major problem as the kitchen was merely an open space with trench fires and no overhead cover, which meant keeping the fires going during the monsoon rains was almost impossible. The parties coming down from the north arrived mostly at night with no advance warning. The men were usually in very poor condition and had not been fed since they left their respective camps. Fukuda, promoted from lieutenant to captain, was in charge of the camp. He would not permit the cooks to retain a floating ration which meant that when the unexpected and unplanned for parties arrived, they would have to wait until rations had been drawn from the Japanese storeman before any meals could be prepared for them.

Dyer wrote that the camp was so overcrowded the vast majority of men had to sleep in the open. Most of the arrivals had dysentery and, due to their weakness and lack of adequate latrines in the camp, it meant that the ground soon became 'fouled with ordure'.

The medical staff often found themselves overwhelmed with the number of patients and the multiple diseases from which they suffered. There were times when there were so many critically ill, that some men died alone. Yet astonishing efforts made to help patients recover, with artificial limbs being made for amputees out of bamboo and therapeutic massage being carried out to help strengthen under-used muscles. For those who had lost eyes, highly polished wooden eyes were made by a skilled Dutch prisoner. These kept the sockets from shrinking so that glass eyes could be fitted when the men returned home.[52]

The usual lack of medicines led to all manner of inventive alternatives. Possibly one of the most outstanding examples of this was with a patient who was dying from wet beriberi. The patient in question was bloated with the disease from head to toe and was experiencing repeated fits as the swelling reached his brain. He was fed the hospital's last jar of Marmite. It saved his life.

---

52. Kenneth Adams, pp.73-4.

When cholera struck in 1943 the response from the medical team here was to immediately erect a tent for the first, single patient, about fifty yards from the main part of the hospital and surround it with a barbed wire fence.

On 6 September 1943, Colonel Humphries was ordered to go to Kanchanaburi and 'organise a camp on British lines, run it anyway you please to your own satisfaction but please stop the prisoners from buying and selling things and talking to the natives.'

Meanwhile, parties arrived from up-country in an exhausted condition and the staffing situation was acute with some 800 patients being care for by just one medical officer, one nursing orderly and two non-medical N.C.O.s.

But this improved considerably with the arrival of Lieutenant Colonel Benson's 'L' Force medical party which included nine medical officers and sixty fit medical orderlies. The staffing situation improved further when Humphries arrived after his three-day journey from Tampi with a medical party from 'H' Force. This party included ten officers and 154 fit other ranks, who later built a 'Fit' camp some four kilometres away.

By this time there were some 3,000 men in the hospital camp filling twenty-eight wards. Humphries found the hospital functioning well under Benson's guidance, but he saw that every hut was full and as soon as another one was built it was soon occupied by new arrivals. Food, which initially had been quite plentiful, became an increasing problem as the hospital population grew. There was, though, food to be bought from the local Thais for those that had the cash. While this was not officially permitted by the Japanese, where there is money to be made, a way will always be found, and items were passed through the bamboo fence.

The most serious disadvantage from which this establishment suffered as an hospital was the continuing shortage of water during the dry season, and constant battles were fought with the IJA authorities in an effort to overcome this difficulty. Finally, it was agreed that 'carrying parties' could leave the camp to draw water from a nearby well. Yet even though thousands of sick men depended upon this water for survival, some of the carrying party took advantage of the situation and, in strict contravention of the Japanese rules, began to fraternise with the locals, and it took all of Colonel Humphries persuasive powers to allow this privilege to continue.

However, at around 21.30 hours on 20 October 1943, Humphries was arrested by the *Kempeitai*, and together with two other officers, Reverend L. V. Headley and Captain J. Driver, was handcuffed and taken away. They were interrogated initially at the *Kempeitai* headquarters in Kanchanaburi and then moved to another *Kempeitai* headquarters at Wanyai. They were held and repeatedly interrogated for a full month before being released.

During the period of 28 September to 12 December a total of 406 men died at Kanchanaburi 'F' and 'H' Hospital camp, of which 265 were from 'H' Force and 142 from 'F' Force. All those of 'H' Force who had survived, less sixty-two seriously ill, were evacuated from Kanchanaburi to Singapore between 19 November to 23 December 1943. Those that remained were transferred to 'F' Force and it is known that at least one half of them later died. Because there were so many deaths plus the limited number of fit men available, it was not always possible to dig individual graves and the bodies were interred collectively.

In the midst of this tragedy, On New Year's Eve 1944, men of the Argyll and Sutherland Highlanders managed to obtain some Thai whiskey and marked the passing of the terrible year of 1943 in true Hogmanay fashion. The IJA officer in charge also made a playing field available to the prisoners, and electric lighting was provided for No.2 Hospital. After the jungle camps, Kanburi seemed like 'Buckingham Palace' to Major Jeffrey English of the 3rd Indian Corps Signals Regiment, and he was astounded to find that even the latrines had attap roofs.[53]

Kanchanaburi was the target of numerous Allied bombing raids. During one particularly heavy attack on 15 December, when the Japanese commandant, Kokuba, saw the POWs running for the slit trenches, he 'excitedly' charged out of his office waving his sword shouting, in Japanese, 'Keep calm! Keep calm! Or I will kill you!'[54]

Towards the end of 1944, with the tide of war turning against them, the Japanese became worried that the tens of thousands of Allied prisoners under their supervision could be organised against them. So, in February 1945 all the Allied officers from the Thailand camps, with the exception of some medical officers, were separated from the other ranks and the majority were placed in very crowded conditions in Kanburi. Altogether approximately 3,000 officers were housed in the Officers' Camp under, as Lieutenant Colonel George Ramsay wrote, 'a particularly brutal and unpleasant Japanese Camp Commander', Captain Nagouchi.[55] Major John Parsons believed that Nagouchi was quite obviously doing everything in his power to make the camp as bad as he could.[56]

Unlike the open jungle camps, the Officers' Camp was surrounded by a deep ditch (which the Japanese made the officers dig) and a high barbed wire fence with machine gun positions posted at intervals along the perimeter. The officers were later made to build a bamboo stockade around the camp for added security.

---

53. Jeffery English, *One For Every Sleeper: The Japanese Death Railway through Thailand* (Robert Hale, London, 1989), p.169.
54. Albert Coates and Newman Rosenthal, *The Albert Coates Story: The Will that Found the Way* (Hyland House, Melbourne, 1977), p.154.
55. George Ernest Ramsay papers, AWM PR00079.
56. TNA, WO 235/963.

With only a handful of other ranks in the Officers' Camp who were used by the Japanese guards as their orderlies, the officers had to perform all the usual camp tasks themselves as well as digging latrines and air raid shelters for the Japanese. The officers sorted themselves out into whatever tasks they could perform. The older and more senior officers, for example, became vegetable peelers or peanut 'bashers' to produce a form of peanut butter.

The camp had a large cookhouse with the usual *quallis* set in mud under improvised shelters. Its water supply came from one of two wells, the second well being used for washing. Dried mud bricks were also produced from which, among other items, was built a 'magnificent' bakery with 40-gallon oil drums used as the ovens. From these, bread was baked using rice flour.

The ingenuity of the prisoners also led to the building of a paper 'factory' which produced valuable sheets of toilet paper.

Due to the cramped location, the only exercise available to the officers was to walk up and down the parade ground which was just 150 yards long. Later, though, some of the younger officers 'rigged up' a basketball pitch and an inter-hut league was formed with regular games.[57]

There is a well-known story of the dreadful treatment received by the camp's interpreter Captain W.M. Drower. It is told here by Ensign C.D. Smith of the U.S. ship *Houston*: 'An incident arose between Jap guards British and British officers acting as a pump team. The British officers had refused to do more than pump water – they would not carry it to the Jap kitchen. As a result several of them were bashed … About 1 hour later a Jap Sergeant passed by and was not seen, so the usual salute was not given. On this excuse the entire pump team of 25 were stood at attention bareheaded in the sun before the Jap guard house from 11 to 3. Several fainted from sunstroke and were left there where they fell.' Colonel Toosey, who was the liaison officer at the Officers' Camp, went to see Nagouchi to protest at this treatment, taking with him Captain 'Bill' Drower, to interpret.

The issue with the officers of the pump team and the Japanese guards had been going on for a couple of days. The officers were refusing to take orders from Japanese privates. They accepted that Noguchi had ordered them to pump water, but it was the privates who had demanded the Allied officers carry the water to them – which they were determined not to do.

We have Drower's full, if somewhat confusing, account of the incident. The previous day when discussing the carrying of water to the Japanese guards, Drower, instead of just translating, had offered his own opinion, saying that

---

57. Colonel Cary Owtram OBE, *1000 Days on the River Kwai: The Secret Diary of a British Camp Commandant* (Pen & Sword, Barnsley, 2017), pp.122-4 & 128.

he believed the Allied officers should take orders only from the Japanese administration not from privates. Noguchi asked Drower if indeed he had offered his own opinion rather than just translating the words of the other officers. When Drower said he did, and that he had said he did not believe the POW officers should carry water for Japanese privates, Noguchi shouted: 'I arrange things as I like, its damned insolence.' The Japanese adjutant, Lieutenant Takazaki (the 'Frog' to the prisoners), leapt up and punched Drower in the face three or four times. He then tried to throw Drower to the ground 'ju-jitsu fashion' but Drower resisted. After Takazaki had tried to throw Drower to the ground and failed, Drower thought it wise to no longer resist and he went limp. 'We both fell together against Takazaki's table, the legs of which collapsed. I got up and Noguchi started applying a ju-jitsu hold,' Drower later reported to the War Crimes trial. 'Noguchi was even less dextrous than his adjutant, so I let myself be thrown and was kicked in the face by Noguchi's booted foot. I then got up and again and Takazaki hit me once on one side of the face, once on the other side and once on the top of the head with a wooden sword.'

Drower was then taken to the guard house where he was beaten again by one of the guards before being placed in a small cell. Two days later he was confined to a Japanese air raid shelter in front of the guardhouse and later an underground pillbox for eighty-six days, being fed on one bowl of rice and one mug of water twice a day. His comrades did manage to smuggle in extra items occasionally but when the Japanese discovered this, they reduced Drower's ration to just one ball of rice a day. He was not allowed to wash, shave or speak to anyone. 'As the bottom was wet I had to sit on one of the two steps leading down to it,' continued Drower. 'There was not room for me to sit upright, but if I leaned my head out I could get some relief from the cramped position.'

Rumours spread through the camp that there was a hidden radio in the camp and as Drower had kept notes to remind himself of facts, he believed he was under suspicion for involvement in passing on news received from the radio. Fearing he would be handed over to the *Kempeitai*, he decided to commit suicide rather than face the inevitable torture. He tried to make a rope out of the threads of a jute bag and hang himself on a spike, but there was not enough room, as his legs trailed on the floor. He also tried to cut an artery with the spoon he had been provided to eat his rice, but this proved impracticable.

It is said by others that Drower, stuck in such terrible circumstances had 'lost his mind' and he stopped taking food believing then that Noguchi wanted to poison him. For days on end, he received little or no water and had to resort to holding out his mess tin through a gap in the cell planking when it was raining to catch a few drops from the attap roof. During this time, the guards placed a bucket of iced water near his cell and would drink from it 'ostentatiously smacking their lips and sucking through their teeth and the cold drops would spatter tantalisingly over my naked body owing to the intense heat of the afternoon sun'. During his final weeks he was taunted with threats of torture described in chilling detail as he passed in and out of malaria-induced delirium.[58]

Further general punishments followed. Officers were made to stand outside the Japanese guard hut in the full glare of the sun for forty-eight hours without a hat, and with no food or water for the first twenty-four hours for minor infringements of entirely arbitrary rules. When cigarette ends were found on the floor of one of the huts during an inspection by a Japanese guard the entire camp was placed under a two-week lock down, the officers only being allowed to leave their huts to wash and use the latrine. The prisoners were not allowed to lie down between the hours of 08.00 and 18.00 hours regardless of their physical condition, or to read or talk in groups of more than five or six.

Further restrictions were imposed on the officers by Noguchi. Only three lights were allowed in each 100-metre-long hut and there was to be no talking at all after lights out. Officers were not permitted to sing, whistle, or play a musical instrument. They were only allowed to visit the sick in hospital one afternoon each week. They were not allowed to read or play games indoors or outdoors until 18.00 hours. 'It was a serious offence to have pencil or paper,' recalled Major John Lloyd, 'to smoke outside the huts excepting for a short period after evening meal at marked places [and] to have water buckets in the huts.'[59]

Despite such oppressive measures, morale in the officers' camp remained high as a secret wireless, operated by Captain Weber of the Malay Regiment, kept the prisoners informed of the progress of the war and the continuing successes of the Allied forces. As mentioned above, the officers were later permitted to play basketball and volleyball (within the designated time period), but the camp was too small for a football pitch.

As well as an officers' camp at Kanchanaburi another camp was formed near the aerodrome in December 1943. The camp generally accommodated 'fit' prisoners evacuated from the jungle camps. The men were still required to work, even though the railway had been completed in October, being put on various projects by the Japanese, but these tasks were far less gruelling than the ones they had previously endured on the railway. Often the work was merely something to keep the POWs busy.

The small Aerodrome Camp hospital held about 100 light sick. It was run by Major de Soldinoff. Life was not unpleasant for the men at the Aerodrome Camp, with food being comparatively plentiful and varied. The attitude of some

---

58. TNA, WO 235/867.
59. TNA, WO 235/867.

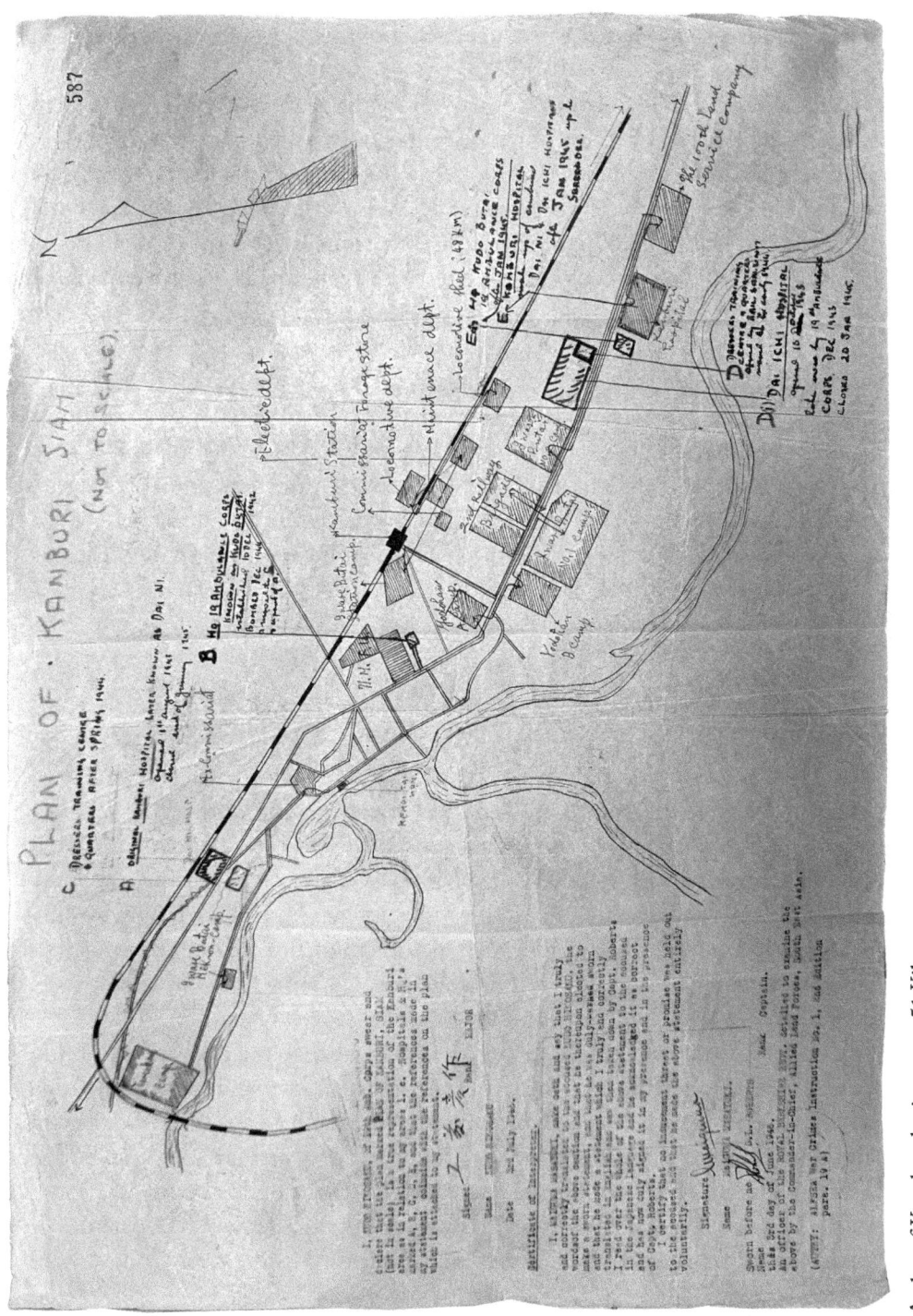

A plan of Kanchanaburi camp at 51 Kilo.

of the guards also lightened with the pressure of the railway construction lifted from their shoulders.

On 22 March 1945, locomotives parked on the line close to the camp were attacked by Allied bombers. Three prisoners were killed and six others were wounded as the slit trenches that had been dug by the prisoners were wholly inadequate. The Japanese ordered the POWs to dig deep trenches for the Japanese, but the camp commander refused permission to dig new or improve existing slit trenches for the prisoners and, when other raids occurred, machine guns were trained on the prisoners to stop them seeking shelter in the trenches.[60]

On 23 August, eight days after Emperor Hirohito had announced Japan's surrender, Allied aircraft were once again over Kanchanaburi. This time it was a Spitfire, the first one most of the prisoners had ever seen, which did an exuberant victory roll. It was followed by two Dakotas, which dropped containers. These contained cigarettes, Red Cross supplies, tins of preserves and clothing. A message was also dropped saying the aircraft would return again in two days.[61]

The end of the war meant that Bill Drower, who was only semi-conscious and barely alive, was finally released.

Tha Makhan   55 Kilo
Also known as Tamarkan, and even Termacam to the Japanese

Tha Makhan camp was built by a party of 200 all ranks under the command of Major Roberts of the 80th Anti-Tank Regiment in early October 1942. They were joined by 110 men of the Argyll and Sutherland Highlanders in March 1943. Their arrival was watched by Probationary Officer Masaru Tsuruta of the 6th Company, 3rd Battalion, 9th Railway Regiment: 'I heard the faint whistling of a march tune far away, at the other side of the palm forest. The whistling gradually came closer to us with the sound of the army boots of a big group. The tune they were whistling was the "Colonel Bogey March"'[62]

The men were told the day after their arrival that their job was to build two bridges over a stretch of the river that was then known as part of the Mae Klong River. These, it is usually presumed, were the bases of the famous book and film *The Bridge on the River Kwai*, though it may be that it was the bridge near Songkurai which was the inspiration for Pierre Boulle's novel.

The first of these bridges at Tamarkan, would be a temporary structure of wood to carry construction vehicles and supplies across the river while a more

---

60. AWM, 54 554/2/1C.
61. Taylor, pp.127-8.
62. Tamayama, p.6.

Camps of the Thai-Burma Railway 71

substantial concrete and steel bridge was being erected. In addition, they would also have to build around two kilometres of embankment on either side of the main bridge. They were also told that the work was likely to last for nine to twelve months.

The camp was situated on the Mae Klong river about three miles from Kanchanaburi. It consisted of five attap huts plus a cookhouse and Japanese quarters surrounded by a fence. The Japanese camp commandant at that time was a Lieutenant Kosakata, described by the man who became the camp's Allied commander, Colonel Toosey, as 'a stupid man who made himself awkward whenever possible'. The camp Sergeant Major was Sōchō Szito whom Toosey regarded as being very strict but honest.[63] Tamarkan was an all British camp until the arrival of 1,000 Dutch prisoners of war commanded by Captain Hendrik Anthonie Tillema in late January 1943, which necessitated the building of five more huts. In the early months, the camp 'hospital' was a screened off area in one of the huts. Later, a separate hospital hut was built which opened at the beginning of January 1943. The Japanese engineers who supervised the bridge construction work were accommodated in their own camp which was adjacent to the POW camp.

Toosey maintained a clean and well-ordered camp, with new arrivals being driven into the river to wash themselves before being permitted to take up their berths. Dr Rowley Richards wrote that Tamarkan was known for its cleanliness, its well-ordered kitchens, canteens and gardens. It even had proper compounds for ducks and cattle. With its military police and strict enforcement of discipline, it was run like a peace-time barracks.[64]

What Toosey managed to achieve was that instead of the Japanese organising the work parties, it would be handled by the POW officers, thus reducing friction between the prisoners and the Japanese or Korean guards. The Japanese engineers were persuaded to provide a list of men they would require each evening for the following day. That way, the officers were able to organise the men efficiently, saving a great deal of unnecessary confusion and arguing, and lessened the strain on the men.[65]

Toosey was willing to give the Japanese credit where it was merited. He noted that the Japanese always supplied, at least twice a year, vaccinations against typhoid, paratyphoid A, and paratyphoid B.

The prisoners were also able to buy fruit, eggs and tobacco from elderly Thai women vendors, as well as cheap cakes which Toosey called 'Dysentery Cakes'.

---
63. Toosey Report.
64. Rowley Richards and Marcia McEwan, *The Survival Factor* (Costello, Tunbridge Wells, 1989), p.166.
65. Peter N. Davies, *The Man behind the Bridge: Colonel Toosey and the River Kwai* (Athlone, London, 1991), p.151.

Duck eggs were considered to be the most valuable supplement which could be bought, and many men owed their survival to the ducks of Thailand.

Toosey, as with many of the officers in the camps, earned the respect of the other ranks with his courageous conduct. Private Carlton of the 2nd East Surreys witnessed this at first hand, describing Toosey as 'A brave officer and good camp commander, who was often slapped in the face and made to stand to attention for hours outside the guardroom when he tried to save a man from getting flogged.'[66]

Toosey's determined approach earned him the respect of the Japanese as well, as shown in an incident on 27 October 1943. A Japanese soldier went into the cookhouse and demanded men to go and work for him. Major Roberts refused to allow this and was struck across his face with a stick. So Roberts punched the Japanese soldier and knocked him down. The incident was reported to the camp commander and, surprisingly, it was the Japanese soldier who was made to apologise to Major Roberts.

Toosey managed to persuade the Japanese to allow the prisoners' own administration to handle discipline in the camp and for many of the tasks carried out by the guards to be undertaken by the prisoners themselves. He also reached agreement for the daily rollcall, *tenko*, to be carried out in English instead of Japanese. These measures helped maintain reasonable relationships between the prisoners and their captors.

Unlike at many camps where the other ranks were often resentful of their officers who lived comparatively leisurely lives with ample food, Toosey did not allow the officers to have their own mess, and he made the officers sleep in the same huts with the men. Toosey also insisted that officers should go out with the working parties, not to work on the railway but to intervene in case of trouble. He also, in his own words, 'milked' his officers. They received pay of thirty ticals a months, of which Toosey took twenty to add to camp funds. He even made those prisoners who had sold stolen Japanese property hand over a percentage of their gains to the camp hospital.

Though these measures greatly helped morale, they led to an unforeseen consequence. Seeing the officers watching over their men working on the railway, the Japanese demanded that the officers worked as well. This was sparked by an incident when a Lieutenant Black was ordered by Kosakata to work instead of merely supervising his men. Black refused and was taken and placed under arrest in the camp's guard house.

This brought matters to a head, with Kosakata demanding that all officers must work. Toosey called a meeting at which he said that officers would still be able to protect their men and that they should agree to work. He did say,

---

66. Lowry, *Last Post*, p.116.

however, that the decision was up to individuals, and he would not order officers to work and 'If you refuse, I will stand and get shot with you.'[67] The meeting ended with a unanimous decision to work with their men.

The next day, the officers went out with their men fully prepared to work, and indeed they were just as able to help defend their men from the worst of the Japanese maliciousness as before. Having demonstrated his position of authority over the Allied officers, Kosakata soon lost interest in them working and gradually they returned to a purely supervisory role.

Toosey made those officers who remained in camp work beyond the hours of those men who went out to work on the bridge and he always ensured that when the prisoners returned each evening they came back to a hot meal.

Before the onset of the 'speedo' period A ration scale was established per man per day of 700 grams of rice, 600 grams of vegetables, 100 grams of meat, twenty grams of salt, twenty grams of sugar and twenty grams of oil. The working day was from 09.00 hours until 18.30, with 1.5 to 2 hours' break during the day.

Tamarkan had its first death on 15 November 1942. The thirty-five-year-old Colour Sergeant Valentine Thomas Osborn 2nd Battalion, The East Surrey Regiment, was buried in a graveyard close to Tha Makhan's Buddhist temple about a kilometre from the camp. Toosey attended the funeral as he did for every one of the more than 200 which took place at Tamarkan during his time there. He even led the service on occasion when a padre was unavailable.[68]

Among the Dutch prisoners who worked on the bridges was Sergeant Fred Seiker, who described the work of piledriving into the bed of the river: 'Work was carried out from early morning to late evening. Every phase of this cooperation was executed by manpower only. A Japanese guard would stand on the embankment and dictate through a loudhailer the rhythm of the "pull" and "release" operations. POWs were standing waist deep in water all day. The counting from the riverbank was relentless whatever the problems. Tree trunks and other debris was a constant hazard. With a fast-flowing river they caused many accidents, sometimes fatal, to the amusement of the guards.'[69]

One of the men sent to work on the bridge was Lance Corporal William Bilyard: 'One day while working I was accused of not working hard enough and was made to stand with a sack containing mould above my head for 30 minutes. If I dropped the sack through strain I was beaten about the face by whichever Jap was near me ... I dropped the sack several times and was beaten up each time.'[70]

---

67. Davies, p.108.
68. Davies, p.150.
69. Fred Seiker, *Lest We Forget, The Railroad of Death* (Bevere Vivis Books, Worcester, 1996), p.39.
70. TNA, WO 235/922.

When out working on the bridge and the railway, the prisoners were able to buy fruit, cakes and tobacco from old Thai female vendors who hung around near the working parties – but the men had to wait until the guards' backs were turned.

The outbreak of cholera saw an immediate response from the Japanese, recalled Fred Seiker: 'Overnight the huts were filled with the dead and the dying. The Japs were terrified of this disease and hastily retreated to a safe distance up the road after barricading the entrance to the camp with X-shaped barricades and rolls of razor wire.' For a period of time Fred was part of the team whose job was to incinerate the bodies of the cholera victims, which became a twenty-four-hour operation at the height of the epidemic.

With a limited diet and heavy labour and long hours, sickness rates began to rapidly increase, as was the case in all the camps. But unlike most other camps, Toosey managed to persuade Kosakata and the Japanese railway engineers that they would get their bridge built far quicker if the men received better treatment. The result was that rations were increased, the working day was limited to 09.00 to 18.30 hours with a one-and-a-half to two-hour break in the middle of the day, and the men got one day's rest – a *yasume* – at least every ten days. On such days, the men (and officers) who had the energy were permitted to play sports. This included football, with a league being formed.

This paid almost immediate dividends for both sides with sickness rates dropping rapidly, and more work being accomplished on the bridge. This in no way meant the prisoners worked willingly in the construction of the bridge, as is portrayed in the famous film. As Captain Ernest Gordon made clear, 'We worked at bayonet point and under the bamboo lash, taking any risk to sabotage the operation whenever the opportunity arose.'[71]

Even during the 'Speedo' period, when working hours reached eighteen out of every twenty-four, the closeness of the camp to the working area and the better food meant that the men at Tamarkan suffered far less than their counterparts in many of the jungle camps further north.

Nevertheless, two officers and four other ranks escaped on 28 January 1943. Toosey had initially wished to join the escape party but was reminded that he could not leave his men leaderless. He was able to conceal the escapers absence from the Japanese roll calls for two days. Sadly, after ten days the four other ranks were captured and returned under armed escort to the camp where they were locked up in the Guard Room. Two days later they were driven into the jungle and never seen again. Reports of shots being fired were received from locals. On 20 February the two officers, Captain E.C. Pomeroy and Lieutenant

---

71. Ernest Gordon, *Through the Valley of the Kwai* (Harper & Row, London, 1962), p.70

Howard, were also brought back into the camp. On 23 February these two were also driven into the jungle where, again according to the Thais, they were bayonetted to death.[72]

After the great bridge had been built in May 1943, those still capable of work were disposed to other camps while Tamarkan changed from being a work camp to that of a hospital. Toosey remained at Tamarkan with just a few men to organise the camp to accept the large numbers of sick which were moved from camps further up country.

These sick arrivals, Toosey reported, 'were in appalling condition, approximately 75 per cent of the parties were stretcher cases and the men frequently arrived dead.' During this time, he wrote, 'we saw scenes of misery that will live for ever in the memories of all of us.'[73]

The patients for the new base hospital began arriving in batches of around 100 being received each night. They came in cattle trucks or loaded thirty or forty at a time into railway wagons. The majority of these men were stretcher cases: 'It is impossible to adequately describe the condition of these men,' wrote Toosey. 'As a typical example, I remember one man who was so thin he could easily be lifted by one hand. His hair was growing down his back and was full of maggots; his clothes consisted of a ragged pair of shorts soaked with dysentery excreta; he was lousy and covered with flies all the time. He was so weak that he was unable to lift his hand to brush away the flies which were clustered on his eyes and on the sore places on his body.'

Of the approximately 3,000 men in the camp only around 400 were working. These were the only ones who were paid by the Japanese. None of the sick received any money as failing to work was regarded as an insult to the Emperor. Yet, when those prisoners arrived at Tamarkan from the jungle camps they were amazed at how different conditions were. One of those new arrivals was Jim Bolero who remarked, in particular, about the food at Tamarkan. He noted that the cooks baked bread and rice cakes in their mud and brick ovens. The Dutch prisoners introduced a new baked dish called *nasi goring* which was made of rice, fish, onions, chillies, lentils, bean sprouts, eschalots and any other greens they could obtain.[74] This was only because of the 'V' Organisation which was able to smuggle money into the camp.

Facilitated by the Thai trader mentioned earlier, Boon Pong Sirivejjabhandu, but just known to the prisoners as Boon Pong, this remarkable group supplied Toosey with 5,000 Ticals (as the Thai baht was referred to by Westerners) a

---

72. Toosey Report.
73. Toosey report.
74. Jim Brigginshaw, *Survival on the Railway of Death* (Pen & Sword, Barnsley, 2018), p.76.

month, on a regular basis, along with some medicines obtained from Bangkok. As well as providing money, medicines and foodstuffs, Boon Pong also nourished the morale of the prisoners, slipping copies of the *Bangkok Chronicle* – a liberally-minded newspaper with pronounced pro-Allied sympathies – into the stacks of canteen goods.[75] Colonel Toosey claimed, as did many others, that Boon Pong's actions saved hundreds of lives. As Tamarkan was a large camp, the accounts of the POW canteen had to be shown to the Japanese. Fortunately, there were a few chartered accountants among the prisoners, and they were able to 'hoodwink' the Japanese as to the true state of the camp's finances.

The ingenuity of the prisoners was notable throughout the camps and at Tamarkan the medical staff were able to solve the problem of potentially lethal blood clots when giving blood transfusions. It was known that this danger was eliminated if the clots were removed before transfusion. For this, the medics made a 'egg whisk' out of bamboo. The blood was placed in a vessel and stirred gently with the whisk. The clots would gather on the whisk leaving the blood clear and safe for use.[76]

One of the treatments for ulcers in the hospital camp was for patients to wade into the river up to their waists. There they would stand while fish ate away the pus and the rotting flesh.[77] During the dry season, the water level in the river fell so low that men could sit on the pebbles on the bottom with their heads above the water.

This was not always as benign as it sounds. There was one species of fish which did more than just nibble at affected skin but took chunks out of prisoners' private parts. Concerned that upon return to home after the war, wives might become highly suspicious of their husbands' wounds, one doctor compiled and signed brief certificates attesting to the cause of the injury. As paper was in extremely short supply, these certificates were written on any available scrap. What credence was given to these by suspicious spouses one can only wonder.[78]

In February 1944, the Japanese unveiled a memorial at Tamarkan to the POWs and Japanese who had died on the railway project. The prisoners were invited to attend the ceremony, which War Correspondent, Rohan Deakin Rivett called an insult, and each man was given a tin of biscuits after the unveiling. The centrepiece of the memorial was in memory of the '990-odd' Japanese who had died. There were four other posts representing the British, Dutch

---

75. John Durnford, *Branch Line to Burma* (Four Square, London, 1966), pp.77-8.
76. Geoff Gill and Meg Parkes, *Burma Railway Medicine: Disease, Death and Survival on the Thai-Burma Railway 1942-1945* (Palatine, Lancaster, 2017), p.175.
77. Bill Reed with Mitch Peeke, *Lost Souls of the River Kwai: Experiences of a British Soldier on the Railway of Death* (Pen & Sword, Barnsley, 2004), p.84.
78. Stanley S. Pavillard, p.115.

and Australian dead.[79] Brigadier Varley, the senior POW, read out a statement emphasising that the conditions under which the prisoners had worked on the railway would be investigated after the war – as indeed it was.

On 24 March 1944, at the morning *tenko*, it was discovered that in a party of the British Sumatra Battalion one man was missing. Major Dudley Apthorpe decided to take a chance, and he announced to the Japanese that the man was in the '*benjo*', the latrine. As it happened the missing man had been caught trying to get through the camp fence during the night and was already in detention. For Apthorpe's evident untruthfulness, all 189 men present were given a stroke across the buttocks with a bamboo.

For trying to break out of the camp, the individual in question was to be shot. However, the guard had been told to send a certain number of men to Kanchanaburi and if the prisoners was shot he would be held accountable for failing to produce the specified number. The guard was 'in a frenzy of indecision', until Apthorpe offered him a way out of his dilemma. Apthorpe would take a note to the Japanese commander at Kanchanaburi saying that the man was to be shot on arrival. The relieved Japanese guard readily agreed. Needless to say, the note was lost en route.[80]

In June of 1944, the camp commander demanded that all POW officers, other than those that were sick, must be engaged daily on some duty connected with the camp, such as working in the garden or tending to the camp's cattle. This work was not onerous, and it was agreed that there would be no supervision by the Japanese.[81] Working parties were also drawn from the other ranks for maintenance and repair of the railway.

It was around this time that the Japanese announced that the camp canteen could no longer purchase meat, sugar and salt from the local Thai traders. The reason given was explained by Corporal 'Tom' Morris, with 22nd Infantry Brigade Headquarters, 'Under the Geneva Convention, you should get these things from us. If you have to buy them, it means we are not giving you enough. If we stop you from buying these things, therefore, it means you are getting enough.'[82]

Inevitably, the bridge was a prime target of the Allied bombers. The railway line curved round two sides of the POW camp which was only 150 yards from the bridge plus there was a Japanese anti-aircraft position within 300 yards of the camp. At first, the prisoners were allowed to disperse into the jungle when there was a raid, but this was stopped in September 1944. On

---
79. TNA, WO 325/157.
80. A.A. Apthorpe, *The British Sumatra Battalion* (Book Guild, Lewes, 1988), p .118.
81. Ramsay report, p.19.
82. Quoted in Gavan McCormack and Hank Nelson [eds.], *The Burma-Thailand Railway: Memory and History* (Allen & Unwin, Sydney, 1993), p.32.

29 November 1944, twenty-one aircraft attacked the anti-aircraft post and the bridge. Seventeen prisoners were killed in the raid and more than forty were wounded, though none of the bombs hit the bridge. Despite this, the then camp commandant, Lieutenant Noguchi, refused to allow the prisoners to dig slit trenches either during the working day or during rest hours for around a fortnight after the raid.

During this period there were two further air raids and at least one POW was killed. Finally, Noguchi permitted the prisoners to dig slit trenches, with alarms being what seemed like almost a daily occurrence, particularly at night. Further attacks were made on the bridge and with most raids at least some prisoners were hit from falling fragments of bombs or shells or machine-gun bullets. During one of these raids, Seargent Frederic Atherton led a stretcher party under heavy fire from the aircraft, to rescue two sick patients from an exposed position.

The damaged done to the bridge created very heavy work for the prisoners. Again, they were made to work day and night to repair the bridge quickly after each air raid which occurred with increasing frequency as the months progressed.

Casualty numbers continued to mount until the middle of December 1944, when the Japanese decided to move the whole hospital to Tamuang. It took around a month to transfer the approximately 1,500 patients.[83]

This move presented a problem for the prisoners. There was a hidden pile of 1.5-volt batteries which had been used to power the camp's secret radio. This was the same at Chungkai five kilometres up the line which was also being evacuated. Altogether there was around 300 batteries. The Chungkai batteries were concealed in a sack on top of which was placed fruit for the sick patients which was successfully smuggled into Tamarkan.

The batteries were then pushed down hollow bamboo poles, which were marked so that they could be identified. The following day, when the truck arrived to carry materials and equipment off to Kanburi, the officer-prisoner in charge of the operation placed the marked poles at the bottom. The truck was driven into Kanburi – passed the armed guard – and the batteries safely hidden away. The Tamarkan radio was eventually reconstructed and built into the structure of one of the clay ovens in the camp cookhouse.[84]

In January 1945, Toosey was sent with a detachment of 400 fit officers to form a new camp in Thailand unconnected with the maintenance of the railway at Nakon Nayok. It would be there that many of the POWs would see out the

---

83. Atherton later received the British Empire Medal, see *A Pharmacist on the Burma Thailand Railway*, POWs-of-japan.net.
84. Escritt Collection, *Beyond The Three Pagodas Pass*, p.39.

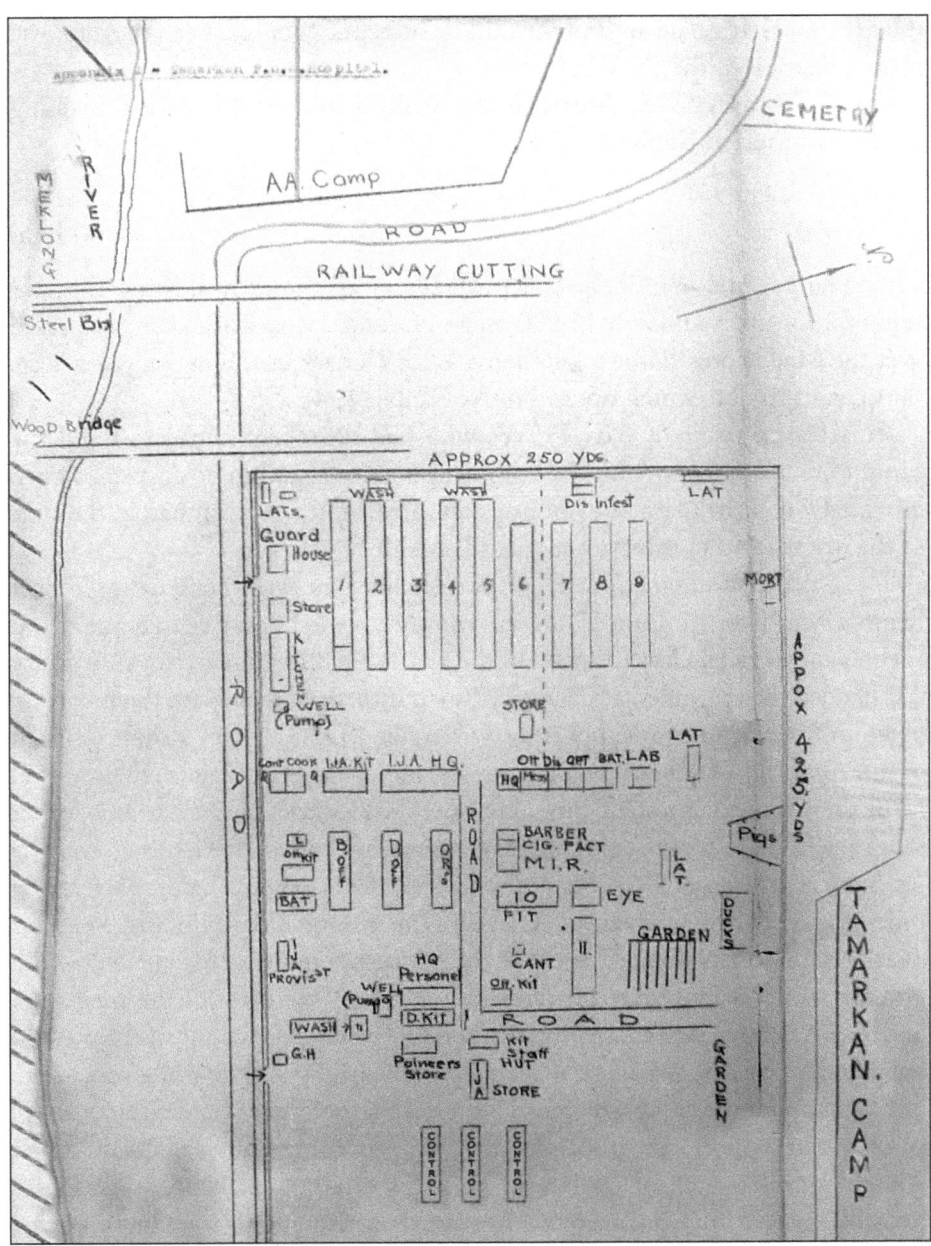

A partial sketch of Tamarkan camp.

final months of the war. There had been growing concerns that the prisoners would not be permitted to see the end of the war. It would seem they were only saved by the sudden surrender by Emperor Hirohito following the dropping of the atomic bombs on Hiroshima and Nagasaki. The prisoners were told after their release that a date around the middle of September had been fixed for the mass execution of the POWs.[85]

On 17 February 1945, Tamarkan was finally abandoned, and the remaining men transferred to Kanburi.

Chungkai   60 Kilo

Chungkai became one of the most notable of all the camps, being the HQ camp for the approximately 11,000 men of Group 2 who worked on the bridge over the Mae Klong. Some 6 kilometres from Tamarkan, Chungkai was a large camp of attap huts which opened in November 1942.

An advance party of sixty POWs who had been sent ahead to build the camp were taken to work on the railway upon arrival and so no cover had been provided when the main body of prisoners arrived. It was, fortunately, the start of the dry season, so this was no great hardship.

The British commander at Chungkai at this time was Lieutenant Colonel Sainter, who later (in June 1943) was moved up the line by the Japanese and Lieutenant Colonel Cary Owtram of the 137th Field Regiment, Royal Artillery, was handed the command at Chungkai. Owtram arrived there with the first main batch of 800 men from Kanburi in November 1942. Captain Ernest Gordon of the 93th Highlanders, was one of those men, who saw the area which would form the camp for the first time. He saw, 'loose stacks of cut bamboo, other loose stacks of atap grass, and a scraggly grass hut,' which he assumed was the Japanese guardhouse. They were told to clear an area about three-quarters of a mile long by half-a-mile wide.[86] Clearing the ground of bamboo thickets was a task the prisoners dreaded because the plants put out tendrils just below the ground, which were covered in 'needle-like' spikes. As most of the men were barefooted these spikes caused many injuries. A scratch from one of these could quickly develop into a tropical ulcer with the fearful possibility of amputation.

The plans for the camp which had been issued from the Japanese headquarters were for a vast open area, officers' houses, barracks for the other ranks, an office, a kitchen, toilets and a bath house. This was totally unrealistic, especially as Second Lieutenant Juji Tarumoto needed the prisoners to start work on the railway the day they arrived. As a compromise he split that first party of sixty in half, sending one half out to work while the other half built the camp as best as they could. As Tarumoto needed all the prisoners on the railway as soon as possible, he sent ten of his men to help with building the camp.

---

85. Owtram, pp.131-2.
86. Ernest Gordon, pp.65-6.

'We reached a clearing and saw three long huts complete, piles of bamboo poles on the ground and heaps of *attap* palm for roofing, recalled Colonel Owtram.'[87] The three huts could only accommodate 600 men, so the rest had to sleep on the open ground. As the camp was just a clearing in the jungle the Japanese knew there was no need to build a perimeter fence, however a 'flimsy' twelve-foot-high perimeter fence was erected with Japanese guards posted at several places around the perimeter and others patrolling the camp at regular intervals.[88] The fence was easily penetrated and four men tried to escape in December 1942 but, inevitably, they were caught. Later they were taken into the jungle, made to dig their own graves before being shot. About six weeks after this incident, Corporal Alfred Stoten of the Sherwood Foresters was permitted to go into the jungle to attend to the graves. 'There were four separate graves,' he later wrote, 'and at the end of each grave there was a bamboo pole which had been broken off about a foot from the ground. I concluded that these four men had been shot whilst tied to these poles and, after they had been killed, the poles had been broken and the men put into the graves.'[89]

The camp hospital was at first merely one end of one of the huts. That was until Owtram said to the Japanese that if they provided the materials, he and other officers would build a hospital. The Japanese were so surprised that the British officers were willing to do the work they agreed and Owtram and his fellow officers constructed two good huts in a clearing a little distance from the main camp. Unfortunately, at times during the wet season, the hospital had to be evacuated because of the inrush of water. It was also the case that the rain caused the latrines to overflow, and excreta was washed into the hospital area.

Corporal Stan Henderson with the Bedfordshire and Hertfordshire Regiment was placed in the camp hospital with bacillary dysentery where the only treatment available for the illness was boiled tapioca and as much boiled water as he could manage. This regime proved totally ineffective, and he was emptying his bowels up to fifty times a day and losing even more weight. He decided to leave the hospital to join the work parties where he could receive rice which, at least, kept him alive.[90]

When cholera struck in 1943, the Japanese ensured that all the prisoners were vaccinated twice, and only around twelve men died during the outbreak. The outbreak, as we have read, coincided with the monsoon period when, wrote Ernest Gordon, 'We worked and lived in a world of wetness. One day's labour

---

87. Owtram, p.33.
88. Gordon, pp.71-2.
89. TNA, WO 235/963.
90. Stan Henderson, *Comrades on the Kwai*, Socialist History Occasional Papers Series No.6 (Socialist History Society, 1997), p.40.

was washed away by the floods of the next. Torrents strewed rocks in our path. We understood then how unfortunate was the location of our camp at the junction of the Kwai and the Mae Klong. Both rivers overflowed and left us living on a raft of mud almost up to our sleeping platforms.'[91]

Corporal Joseph Curtiss of the 1st/5th Sherwood Forester claimed that 'Owing to the heat a lot of men used to go into the jungle to avoid work. When caught they were thrashed with bamboo sticks.'[92]

Private Ronald Sadler of the Royal Army Ordnance Corps was saved from severe injury or worse, by the courageous actions of Royal Army Service Corps Captain Mathew Dickson. Sadler had been ordered to rake loose rock with a chunkle, which is similar to a hoe but with a heavy head. Previously Sadler had been engaged on drilling and he had lost a lot of skin from his hands. He showed his hands to the Japanese engineer officer (possibly called Nazamoto) and tried to explain that he could not do the job. 'He struck me with a stick so I knocked him down,' explained Sadler. He jumped up and picking up the chunkle he tried to chop me in two with it, and it was only due to the prompt action of Captain Dickson that I was not killed. He, regardless of the consequences, grappled with Nazamoto and ordered me to get away.' Surprisingly, neither Dickson nor Sadler received any punishment over the incident, though the latter did suffer a broken rib.[93]

Bombardier Jack Chalker, whose drawings powerfully portray the human suffering in the camps, was able to find beauty in the jungle around the camp: 'Just before sundown each day white ibis would fly back up-river to their night roosts, their shapes reflected in the glassy, swift-flowing water, and hornbill might call. Sometimes at night flights of huge fruit bats would glide silently overhead, silhouetted against the velvet sky, and hang like black rags over a nearby mango tree. Gibbons gave an occasional whooping call or chattered intermittently as they settled for the night, and the large geckos would call from the bamboo supports of our huts. It was strange that these hauntingly beautiful moments could occur within a few yards of huts full of pitiful sights, stench, carnage and death.'[94]

The number of prisoners in the camp reached 6,000, but conditions there were much better than at most of the camps, food was comparatively plentiful. Sergeant George Priestman R.A.S.C., said that the prisoners had three meals a day of a pint pot of boiled rice with, at breakfast a half-pint of green stew

---

91. Ernest Gordon, p.68.
92. TNA, WO 235/857.
93. TNA, WO 235/857.
94. Quoted in Midge Gillies, *The Barbed-Wire University: The Real Lives of Prisoners of War in the Second World War* (Aurum, London, 2011), p.318.

made of a type of watercress, at lunch a teaspoon of sugar, and in the evening the same green stew with a little meat added.

Though, in theory, the prisoners were not supposed to interact with the natives, the guards generally turned a blind eye to these transactions and a number of Thai food stalls soon grew up just beyond the perimeter fence. The prisoners even constructed a soccer pitch, a church and a well-tended cemetery. Of the food available, there was coffee, lime juice, cakes, eggs, peanuts and bananas, all at reasonable prices. The prisoners also built a still from which they produced a 'tolerable' alcoholic concoction derived mainly from banana skins.

The previously lax attitude to prisoner-Thai interaction changed markedly after a confrontation on 20 December. The Japanese demanded that all officers not on administrative work in the camp had to work on the railway. By this time total numbers in the camp reached around 8,000 other ranks plus 900 officers of whom thirty were lieutenant colonels – all under the command of Lieutenant Colonel Yanagida.

The Japanese engineer, Second Lieutenant Juji Tarumuto, saw these officers, who were not doing anything to further the progress of the railway as an untapped source of labour, as Lieutenant James Bell later recalled: 'I was in Chungkai Camp when the Japanese Engineer officer called 2/Lieutenant Tarimoto [*sic*] ordered all British officers who were not needed to take charge of working parties to work on the construction of the Thailand-Burma Railway. We all refused to work when Tarimoto had us all on parade. He then told us he would use the most extreme measures to make us work. He then turned the guard out with fixed bayonets. The guards loaded their rifles.'[95] Yanagida also said that all food obtained from outside would be stopped if the officers did not work.

The Allied camp commander at the time, Lieutenant Colonel John Rowley Williamson, discussed the situation with his fellow officers and the decision was taken to comply, though Williamson asked Yanagida if the officers could be kept together rather than divided among the other working parties and that they should be supervised by an officer, not a Japanese NCO. This was agreed upon and an all-officers battalion was formed from officers below field rank which undertook bridge building work along the line. The Japanese took 'extreme delight' in beating the officers with tools in front of their men and giving them the dirtiest jobs, inflicting conditions on them equivalent to those of the *rōmusha*.[96]

Williamson's approach up to this point had been to suggest to his officers they 'should continue to appear willing, while doing as little as was absolutely

---

95. TNA, WO 235/857.
96. TNA, WO 235/857.

necessary' to keep the Japanese from imposing harsher treatment upon the prisoners.[97] After this, relations between the POWs and the Japanese became strained and all contact with the local Thais was strictly forbidden. A secret trade still went on but if a native was caught dealing with the prisoners he was tortured. The usual procedures was, as related by Cary Owtram, 'to tie the offender up to a post by the guard house and knock him about for hours on end with fists, feet or rifles. If the Thai fainted, they kicked him on the ground, and if that didn't bring him round, they would throw water over him and, when he recovered, they would start hitting him again.'[98]

Food became much tighter and when Company Sergeant Major Leslie Gilbert became Camp Regimental Quarter Master Seargent, he found that the bags of rice issued to the prisoners were not the stated weight, being as much as half the designated quantity. When he complained to the Japanese Quartermaster, Captain Goto, he was laughed at. Sometimes Gilbert would sweep the floor of the store to gather every last grain of rice he could. Even some of the small amount of rice left for the prisoners was taken by the Japanese. Leslie Gilbert saw the man in charge of the Japanese cookhouse, called Siragowa, 'on numerous occasions, beat up all the British cooks employed in the cookhouse and demand some of the British rations. They were forced to give them up.'[99]

Nevertheless, the prisoners were permitted a day off at Christmas, and while the Buddhist/Shintoist Japanese did not celebrate that day, they did celebrate the New Year, which meant the POWs had another day to themselves.

There were many complaints about Tarumoto, including that made by Corporal Roy Pearce of the Royal Army Service Corps who submitted an affidavit regarding the actions of Tarumoto during the building of an embankment about twenty kilometres from Ban Pong: 'As we each proceeded to our work Tarumoto kicked us in the back to start off ... When any of us started to tire Tarumoto would beat us with a bamboo stick, usually the first piece he could lay his hands on. He would always hit us where we had an injury or a sore, or on any part of the body, usually the head or the back. For another punishment if we lagged behind Tarumoto would make any offender hold a heavy piece of wood, which weighed 40 or 50 pounds, above his head for sometimes as long as an hour, in the blazing sun. Some of the men could not do this and were beaten with a bamboo stick by Tarumoto.'[100]

---

97. Richard William Noel Bishop, *Before the High King's Horses*, in private papers of Captain R.W.N. Bishop, p.46, IWM Catalogue No.3155.
98. Owtram, p.40.
99. TNA, WO 235/922.
100. TNA, WO 235/857.

Tarumoto was quite open about his feelings towards the prisoners: 'I loathe and detest all English people,' he once told a Staff Sergeant Leech of the Royal Army Ordnance Corps, 'and will make their bodies sleepers for my railway.'[101] Tarumoto was proud of his ability to speak English and if any of the prisoners failed to understand him, which happened quite often, he would hit them with his bamboo stick.[102]

The Japanese medical officer at Chungkai was Lieutenant Hisashi Nobusawa, who described his version of how sick parades were conducted at his subsequent trial for war crimes: 'The sick parades were held at a place about 200 metres from the Japanese medical office and about 50 metres off from the prisoners-of-war quarters and they were held under two big trees from about 3 o'clock in the afternoon. The Allied medical officer came with the patients together with the examination or the diagnosis sheets or papers, and they came to get re-examined, and while they were being examined the others sat under the tree. On the whole, the examination made by the Allied medical officers were the same as those made by the Japanese officer, but sometimes they differed.' Nobusawa claimed that those prisoners already in hospital did not have to take part in the sick parades or undertake any camp duties. Despite such claims, he was sentenced to death for his inhumane treatment of the prisoners.[103]

As in Tamakan, when Owtram took over as camp commandant at Chungkai in June 1943, contact was made with Boon Pong who offered to continue to supply money and medicines to the POWs. The deal was that Owtram would write a letter to the British Government to arrange repayment after the war. Owtram duly wrote the letter and the secret supply of money, initially in the form of 10,000 baht, was made. Boon Pong continued to help the prisoners at great personal risk to himself.

A radio set, referred to by the prisoners as the 'Canary', was concealed at Chungkai. It was operated and maintained by Captain Max Weber, his younger brother Donald, and a former BBC engineer. Aided by a select number of friends who served as lookouts to warn of approaching Japanese, they listened to the news broadcasts which they could pick up from New Delhi or San Francisco, keeping the prisoners informed of the progress of the war. A delay of a few days was instituted in passing on news down to the rank in case any of the Japanese (some of whom had picked up a little English over the months) should overhear the POWs discussing current topics. Batteries and spare parts for the wireless were obtained by the men who were allowed out of the camps

---

101. TNA, WO 235/857.
102. TNA, WO 235/857.
103. TNA, WO 234/957.

on anti-malarial duty to pour oil on the ponds and swamps where the insects could breed. They were able to make contact with friendly Thais who provided the required items. Batteries were also obtained quite openly with the doctors informing the Japanese that, as there was no electricity in the huts, they needed batteries for torches to examine patients.[104] Due to fears of discovery, the Canary was moved around and hidden in a variety of different locations.

Being such a large camp, the demand for wood was considerable, and Owtram established a wood-gathering group of fifty men and several officers who lived in a separate compound. They went out each day into the jungle to collect the wood to fuel the cookhouses and for the funeral pyres. The pyres were built by the river as far away from the accommodation huts as was possible. During the cholera outbreak an average of twenty bodies a day were cremated.

He also laid down a disciplinary code to ensure offences were dealt with in a uniform manner and so that everyone knew what punishment they would receive if they transgressed. This measure was put in place primarily to stop theft by prisoners of belongings of fellow prisoners. As was the case elsewhere, and even at a well-run camp such as Chungkai, it was 'common practice' for the men to steal from each other. Any objects of tradable value could not be left unguarded. Even during daylight some men would take advantage of another's carelessness. Ernest Gordon recounted the tale of one officer who had all his belongings (including his spectacles) in a bag which was stolen from under his head one night. The dead were even easier victims and men 'lurked about' those who appeared to be on their death beds, waiting for them to expire. Most of the prisoners 'left this world picked clean,' Gordon observed.[105]

Colonel Sainter had employed a former commando as the camps' Provost Marshal who used quite severe methods and when Owtram took over he replaced the commando with a former Inspector in the Malay Police in Kuala Lumpur who took a more considered approach but maintained the camp's tight disciplinary controls.

Such items, including blankets which were one of the few items which made sleeping on the hard bamboo platforms bearable, would be stolen to sell to the local Thais who were always keen to buy them. The camp covered fifty acres and despite the endeavours of Owtram's police force, it was impossible to prevent men sneaking out at night to conduct their illicit deals.

Another illicit trade which developed between the POWs and the local Thais was with cigarettes and tobacco. A number of enterprising prisoners, initially Dutch but soon copied by the British, went into business with the natives

---

104. Gill and Parkes, p.177.
105. Gordon, pp.76-7.

and some Chinese to scour the jungle for native-grown tobacco plants. They brought back to the camp large quantities of leaves which they converted into cigarettes. These were sold in the camp at a considerable profit, the turnover reaching hundreds of dollars a month.[106]

When Ernest Gordon was diagnosed with a condition related to diphtheria, in which he was unable to stand, he was confined to the hospital, or what he called the 'Death House', which had been built on one of the lowest points in the camp and, during the monsoon, the ground was always sodden. It was the smells from the hospital which Gordon recalled with horror: 'The smell of tropical ulcers eating into flesh and bone; the smell latrines overflowed; the smell of dirty men, untended men, sick men, of humanity rotting, humanity gone sour. Worst of all was the sweet, evil smell of bedbugs by the millions crawling over us to steal the little flesh that still clung to our bones.' Gordon appealed to his friends to help get him out of hospital but the MO refused to allow him to mix once again with men who were not sick. So, his friends built a little hut just for him. His wonderful friends saved his life.

Gordon also recounted in his memoirs a terrible tale concerning a fellow Argyll and Sutherland highlander. At the end of work one day, a count of the tools revealed one spade short. The Japanese guard angrily shouted that a prisoner had stolen it to sell to the Thais and he demanded the culprit stepped forward to receive his punishment. No one moved. This enraged the Japanese guard even further, shrieking 'All die! All die!'. To show he meant what he said, he raised his rifle, pulled back the bolt and aimed at the first prisoner in the line.

At this point a highlander did indeed step forward and, as he stood proudly to attention, declared that it was he who had taken the spade. 'The guard unleashed all his whipped-up hatred; he kicked the hapless prisoner and beat him with his fists. Still the Argyll stood stiffly to attention. The blood was streaming down his face, but he made no sound. His silence goaded the guard to an excess of rage. He seized his rifle by the barrel and lifted it high over his head. With a final howl he brought the butt down on the skull of the Argyll, who sank limply to the ground and did not move. Although it was perfectly evident that he was dead, the guard continued to beat him and stopped only when exhausted.' When the party returned to camp and the tools were recounted in the guardhouse, none were found to be missing.[107]

Though originally a work camp, Chungkai later became a base hospital camp (No. 3), along with two others, on the southern end of the railway. Being the most northerly of these three, Chungkai received many sick prisoners from the

---

106. Owtram, p.113.
107. Gordon, p.105.

farthest reaches of the railway. 'The condition of the people who came down to Chungkai hospital camp was very bad indeed,' reported Lieutenant Colonel Laming. 'Most of them had chronic dysentery or malaria – or in some cases both. In some cases, they were so far gone they died within 24 or 48 hours after being brought to the camp. Many had terrible ulcers, mostly on the lower leg, which in some cases were so bad that the leg had to be amputated.'[108]

The senior medical officer in the hospital, Lieutenant Colonel St. J. Barratt, noted that towards the end of October 1943, the hospital admitted its 10,000th patient in just over a year and on the last day of that month the 1,000th death had occurred.[109]

By March 1944 most of the prisoners had been moved from the jungle work camps to be placed in the main camps at Nacompaton, Non Pladuk, Tamuang, Kanchanaburi, Tamarkan and Chungkai. Those patients moved down river to the hospital camps were separated into two categories by the Japanese. Those termed 'walking' went on the railway, while the 'lying incurables' were transferred by barge.

The earlier orderliness of the camp seems to have dissipated, probably because it had been so overwhelmed with arrivals, as when Captain Reginald Newton, 2/19 Battalion A.I.F, passed through he saw 'it was in a disgraceful mess. Australians, nobody controlling them, looking after them, tending to them.'[110]

In a report submitted by 'Weary' Dunlop on conditions at Chungkai and Tarsao between October 1943 and May 1944, he wrote: 'This was the period of most terrible aftermath of railway construction. These areas being "cities of sickness". The morning ward rounds are becoming more and more difficult as patient after patient, with no drugs to help him gradually sinks into a final "total deficiency" state which often lasts for weeks before he eventually dies ... over 75% of the Hospital and Convalescent Depot patients have recently been covered in sores and septic skin conditions.'[111]

Gunner Fergus Anckorn found it impossible to sleep with the rain running off the roof of the accommodation hut onto the ground and splashing mud up onto the bamboo sleeping platforms. So he volunteered for one of the camp duties where he knew he could get some rest – preparing the bodies for burial. The bodies were stored in a small secure hut, just eight feet by six feet. Here he had to sew rice sacks together to cover each body. As Anckorn later wrote, he

---

108. TNA, WO 235/957.
109. Owtram, pp.79-80.
110. Interview with Captain Reg Newton (NX34734) Anzac Day 1992, secondtwentiethbattalionaif.wordpress.com/prisoner-of-war-POW.
111. AWM, 54 554/5/1 'D' Force (Thailand):] POW Camps, Thailand, Report on Kinsayok Camp and Hospital and Tarsau Base Hospital, 1943-1944.

had become so inured to death that it didn't bother him that he often laid on a pile of dead bodies as long as he had somewhere dry to sleep.[112]

Fergus Anckorn also acquired a natural defence against bedbugs and mosquitos – a chameleon which adopted Fergus as a friend. He placed himself on Fergus' chest during the night and snapped up any approaching insects. During the daytime he sat on the soldier's shoulder as he went about his duties.

Lieutenant Alfred 'Tommy' Atkins, R.A.S.C., also sought a means of dealing with another pest – rats – which swarmed through the huts at night. 'Damn things nibble anything eatable that isn't in a tin & run over us keeping us awake. To crown it all, they leave their droppings wherever they feel disposed – on blankets, plates, etc.' So, one of the men devoted much of his spare time in camp manufacturing 'snooses', which was a cross between a noose and a snare. Once caught, some of the prisoners skinned and boiled the rats.[113]

The cholera area at Chungkai was marked out and fenced off, where small huts were built to accommodate the victims. A pile of dry wood was placed under each hut. When those inside died, the wood pile was set on fire and the whole hut would go up in flames.

In the midst of all this misery and starvation, the Japanese camp adjutant, Osaka, decided to hold a dinner party and asked Owtram to select a suitable guest list of twenty. Osaka was as good as his word, and he produced a 'most excellent' dinner for twenty senior Allied officers. To Owtram, the whole episode was 'incomprehensible'.

Though there were numerous instances of prisoners stealing off each other in their efforts at personal survival, there were, on the other hand, many occasions when, without the sacrifices of others, men would not have survived. Such examples were the offer of blood to those undergoing medical procedures. At Chungkai it was known that men repeatedly donated blood. This even included direct transfusion from the donor to the patient.[114]

It was also the case that the Medical Officer at Chungkai, a Captain Hugh Edward de Wardener R.A.M.C., used the blood from surviving diphtheria patients to develop a serum which was used to treat other victims of the disease. This proved very successful and led to a rapid fall in the death rate from this illness.

When Robert Hardie returned to Chungkai in March 1944, he noted how much the camp had grown. Food was plentiful and included cakes and coffee-

---

112. Peter Fyans, *Conjuror on the Kwai: The Incredible Life of Fergus Anckorn* (Pen & Sword, Barnsley, 2011), p.133.
113. Gillies, p.336.
114. Stewart Mitchell, *Scattered Under The Sun: The Gordon Highlanders in the Far East 1941-1945* (Pen & Sword, Barnsley, 2012), p.131.

fudge. Earlier, in November 1943, Dunlop had issued a new level of rations, as follows:

Breakfast	Soft rice porridge with sugar
11.00 hours	Sweet white sauce
Lunch	Salted vegetable soup and tea with sugar
15.00 hours	Sweet white sauce
Evening	Salted soup and rice pudding pap with sugar plus tea with sugar
20.00 hours	Sweet tea

The prisoners were able to bathe in the river, and a bamboo and matting stage had been erected where shows and concerts were held. Being a large camp there were many talented individuals there, including Leo Britt, who was a professional actor having appeared in theatres in both London and New York (he continued his career after the war, featuring in a number of films). The Japanese accepted him as a producer and relieved him of other chores so that he could rehearse and produce the various musicals and plays which were put on. The Japanese watched the performances along with the prisoners, the former always taking up the best seats.

A sort of jungle university was formed with classes held whenever and wherever possible. There were seminars and courses held in history, philosophy, economics, mathematics, several of the sciences and in at least nine languages. A library was formed from a surprisingly large number of books that had been kept by the prisoners. Such a stock of literature was not always maintained for its intellectual or educational value, but because the pages were useful for rolling cigarettes or as toilet paper.

Artistic expression also found an outlet with wood carvings from the abundant trees and drawings with the artists crushing charcoal and pulverised rock as their mediums. They made brushes from hair plucked from their own beards. So many works of art were produced the prisoners held a exhibition in one of the huts where the efforts of thirty or forty prisoners were displayed.[115]

As well as establishing a Communist Party branch with meetings and educational talks on Marxism, there were corresponding meetings of the Conservative, Liberal and Labour parties. The prisoners even managed to put together a small orchestra, thanks in part to a shipment of six violins received from the International Y.M.C.A. Woodwind instruments were made from various sizes of bamboo and a surprisingly large brass section was formed from

---

115. Gordon, p.158.

several trumpets, trombones, and saxophones which prisoners had carried into captivity and kept throughout their internment.[116].

To Major Basil Peacock of the Royal Artillery, Chungkai was like 'paradise' compared to where he had been at Tarsao camp due to the abundance and variety of food available. There was a large and well run canteen supplied by official native traders who brought in peanuts, pig oil, duck eggs, vegetables, palm sugar and even toothbrushes and razor blades for those who could afford them.[117]

When Peacock's party first arrived there after the completion of the railway, they were employed in digging a large trench around the camp, repairing huts and in cutting wood. There was little direct supervision by the Japanese and, as long as the prisoners appeared to be doing something, they were largely left alone. Nevertheless, the completion of the railway did not mean the end of work, with parties required to repair and maintain the line. With so many POWs from the jungle camps still unfit having suffered so badly from the privations and ill-treatment of the speedo period, on 15 November 1944, Lieutenant Nabuswa took all the officers from Chungkai hospital and put them to work on camp duties, thus releasing the 'fit' men from those tasks to join the external work parties. Shortly afterwards the hospital at Chungkai was closed and the patients moved to Tamarkan. Following repeated Allied air attacks upon Tamarkan and the bridge over the Mae Klong in December saw that decision being reversed, the patients being sent back to Chungkai.

Around 1,000 prisoners were received from Tamarkan on 18 December and at the same time some forty casualties of the Allied raids, many of whom were stretcher cases, were also sent to Chungkai from Brankassi and Wang Yai camps and conditions at Chungkai deteriorated markedly. There were, Warrant Officer Tom Hampton recalled in January 1945, sick prisoners all over the camp with no proper accommodation for them.[118]

By the time Chungkai No. 3 Hospital Camp was closed in June 1945, 19,975 patients had been treated there with an average of 2,000 men in the hospital at any one time during its busiest period. The Commonwealth War Cemetery is very near the original site of the Chungkai Cemetery.[119]

---

116. Henderson, pp.43-4; Gordon, p.161.
117. Basil Peacock, *Prisoner on the Kwai* (Blackwood, London, 1966), p.220.
118. AWM, 54 1010/4/65.
119. Fyans, op. cit.

Wang Lan 69 Kilo
Also known as Wanran, Wun Lun or Lung

Wang Lan camp was situated on the west bank of the Khwae Noi. The workers here were responsible for constructing a stretch of track roughly five miles long linking up with parties from Chungkai in the south to Wang Yen, 75 kilo camp, in the north. At first the men worked continuously for ten days and had the eleventh day as a *yasume*, a rest day. This changed when the Japanese introduced the system where a given number of metres had to be completed each day. As the men found it difficult to achieve the specified distance rest days became less frequent.

J.R. Hill arrived there on 22 November 1942: 'The huts already erected looked reasonable and the location near the river favourable. During the day we were allocated the atap roofed huts and had our first good night's sleep for a week.

'At Wun Lun we were formed into a labour battalion of 790 officers and men. To begin with we were doing labour jobs about the camp. The camp was a flat plateau above the river, close to a small Thai village. There was insufficient accommodation so additional huts had to be built and we were the labour force. Large rafts of bamboo were floated down the river and it was our job to carry the bamboo from the river to the construction site.

'After carrying the bamboo to the building site came the task of cutting to size and erecting the framework of these huts. The frames were joined together with material obtained from local trees. The outer bark was removed and the pliable inner bark pulled off in strips. These strips made excellent binding material for tying the horizontal struts to the vertical posts.

'Bamboo was cut in approximately six-foot lengths and then split until we were left with pieces of bamboo six foot long by approximately one to one and a half inches wide. Long atap leaves approximately three feet long were doubled in two and positioned over the bamboo strips. By sewing along the atap leaves, where it was bent over the bamboo strips, we had sections six feet by one and a half feet wide, ready to tie on to the roof. Starting at the bamboo and overlapping each section we made our way to the apex. Beds were formed by constructing a frame about two feet from the ground. Bamboo was cut to size then split and flattened to the best of our ability. We washed in the river at night.'[120]

Breakfast consisted of a form of porridge made from rice that had been partially roasted on a steel plate and then placed in boiling water. To this was added a tiny amount of salt and pork fat. Accompanying h this was a mess tin of tea and the daily allowance of a teaspoon of sugar.

---

120. IWM, LBY 05/1096; J. R. Hill, *Unknown to the Emperor* (Zeebra, Manchester, 1998), pp.71-2.

Captain Barry Baker was involved in organising the siting and digging of the camp's latrines. The men had quickly learned that latrines should not be sited in 'some dark and secret corner ... but rather in the highest, openest [sic] and windiest part of the camp.'[121] Latrines, generally, were not built with seats, the men having developed the technique of squatting. Usually, just a bamboo rail was fitted on each side for the men to hold onto if necessary.

The work the prisoners were made to do included the building of a bridge, the first of many. The Japanese engineer in charge ordered some of the men to climb to the top of the pile-driving rig. The apparatus looked very unsafe, and the prisoners refused. After much abuse from the engineer said he would show them there was nothing for the men to be worried about. As he climbed up the rig it collapsed, to the delight of the prisoners, especially as the engineer broke his leg when he fell.[122]

Len 'Snowie' Baynes passed through Wang Lan which, he later wrote, 'had no perimeter fence as had the other camps we knew. One side was bounded by the river, one by the railway, one by jungle, and the last by a clearing which was being created by two very hard-working Chinese men, who were trying to make a small farm.'[123]

Jack Shuttle arrived at Wun Lun towards the end of the monsoon period of 1942 and 'gazed across at a muddy square of about an acre in size, which was a complete quagmire, at a few hastily assembled huts. Never had I seen such a morass.'[124] Conditions improved in the camp with the ending of the monsoon and the ground became baked hard. It was then that the Japanese insisted the Allied officers at Wun Lun must make up the numbers in the railway working parties. The officers, under Lieutenant Colonel Swinton, flatly refused. That was until a truck was driven up with a mounted machine gun on the rear which was trained on dissenting officers, who, of course, relented. Prior to this, there had been some resentment among the other ranks that the burden of suffering had not been shared fairly, with the officers receiving the same rates of pay as the Japanese Army equivalents even though they were not having to work.[125] The officers' pay, though, was considerably reduced because they were charged room and board by the Japanese.

At one point during the 'Speedo' period, the men were forced to work continuously for twenty-seven hours. Remarkably, this enforced labour did not break their morale and they marched back to camp defiantly singing *Colonel*

---

121. Hilary Green, p.84.
122. Newton and McGuinness, p.504.
123. Leslie Baynes, 'The Will To Live', BBC People's War, Article ID: A2147041.
124. Jack Shuttle, *Destination Kwai 'Reluctant Gypsy'* (Tucann, Heighington, 1994), 67.
125. Shuttle, pp.72-3.

Bogey. This infuriated the Japanese guards and the sergeant in charge, after failing to stop the singing, chose ten prisoners at random and made them stand outside the guardhouse for twenty-four hours where they were frequently hit on the head.[126]

As well as the punishing nature of the work, the prisoners had to endure attacks from insects. The men sweated profusely as they worked semi-naked. The blistering sun dried the sweat, leaving salt on their backs and stomachs which attracted large numbers of wasps. Trying to knock the wasps away often resulted in painful stings. Worse were the stings of centipedes and scorpions that were uncovered as the prisoners cleared the jungle, which could cause very serious swelling.

Rations, which were generally brought up by barge from Kanburi, consisted of sixteen ounces of rice plus two ounces of buffalo meat with a form of soybean called *kachang-ijau* and, at one point, a large number of black pigs. But, as elsewhere, as increasing numbers of men fell sick, those in hospital were reduced to half rations. To mitigate the effects of this all the food was 'lumped together' and shared equally among workers and patients. There was also a small local market where Thais had been allowed to set up stalls in a clearing between the camp and the river. The POWs were permitted to visit for one hour each day after returning from work.

Lieutenant Colonel Swinton regarded Wan Lung as a good camp: 'the attap accommodation was good of its kind. Food was satisfactory, and the cookhouse although about 400 yards from the huts was quite good, though ovens were not allowed.' A small hospital of fifty beds was built by officer labour which was always full to capacity. Altogether, throughout the course of three months, around 600 men were so debilitated by illness as to be of no practical use on the railway and were shipped out to base hospitals.

The number of POWs increased over time, eventually numbering between two and three thousand. Among there were about 300 spare officers not already employed with the battalions. Many were over forty-five years of age and there were eighteen lieutenant colonels amongst them. Swinton kept these officers busy with duties in the camp and in building the hospital. Soon, though, the Japanese wanted these men to work on the railway.

The day after being told of this Swinton paraded eighty-nine officers but he told the Japanese guards that he would not order his officers out to work unless the camp commandant himself came to say that. Eventually, as Swinton would not relent, the commandant made an appearance and repeated his order. Swinton reluctantly ordered his officers to join the work parties: 'Hardly had

---

126. Shuttle, pp.80-1.

they marched off when the engineers fired several rounds of ball ammunition apparently into the air, and the officers were brought back at the double and the parade ground picketed with armed sentries. All the sick and all officers were paraded and inspected by the Engineer officers and a large number of both were ordered onto work at once.' Swinton and his medical officers were struck hard several times in the face by two young engineer officers. 'From this date onwards,' Swinton later reported, 'the persecution of the sick gradually increased, until … it became inhumane cruelty.'[127]

Eventually, the Japanese also stopped the prisoners from trading with the natives, but this didn't deter many of the locals and POWs from engaging in clandestine dealings. Secret nighttime rendezvous resulted in many items, even medicines, changing hands, but always at prices commensurate with the enormous risk the natives undertook. Some of them made so much money they offered a banking service, loaning money on promissory notes to be redeemed after the war.

One of prisoners engaged in this illicit trade, a Corporal Bluestone, was caught by the Japanese and was subjected to two days of punishment beatings. Bizarrely, in between beatings, the Japanese gave the corporal coffee and biscuits. He suffered a badly broken jaw which the camp doctors were able to wire up, before sending him down to Chungkai hospital.[128]

While it was the case that at Konyu one of the prisoners had carried a gramophone and a collection of records into the camp, so it was at Wun Lun that one man had lugged his piano accordion all the way into Thailand. He played for the prisoners accompanied by another man on a cornet.

Wang Takhain 81 Kilo
Also known as Wun-tu-Kin, Wan Tow Kien

After Wang Lan, Len Baynes next stop was at what he called Wun-tu-Kin, which was run by a Japanese engineer called Yoshio Suzuki, who, it seems, did all he could to mitigate the ill-treatment the prisoners suffered at the hands of the Korean guards. Remarkably, Len found the opportunity numerous times to slip away from his workstation to wander round the local area and observe how the Thais lived in nearby villages.[129]

Dr Robert Hardie arrived at what he interpreted as Wan Tow Kien at the start of February 1943. He was also able to walk freely in the surrounding

---
127. TNA, WO 235/963.
128. Shuttle, pp.77-8.
129. Les Baynes, op. cit.

jungle, where he discovered an abandoned orchard of lime trees with ripe fruit. Food generally was good here, Hardie noting that cocoa, sugar and Japanese strawberry jam were available

Hardie found the hospital to be small but not overcrowded and there was no shortage of medicines, but that was soon to change. Large numbers of sick were transported to Wang Takhain and the hospital quickly became over-full. The fit men were sent to Ban Khao and only the unwell were retained at Wang Takhain which had become 'half-deserted and melancholy'.[130] This situation changed again and in March 1943 when the camp again became crowded. In April, the sick were evacuated to Chungkai and the fit men were moved upriver.

Ban Khao   88 Kilo
Also known as Bankao or Bankow

In January 1943, the first 700 British prisoners arrived at Ban Khao and were joined by 400 Dutch prisoners on 13 March 1943. The camp was close by a small Thai village consisting of around a dozen huts on stilts and a small temple. The huts of the Japanese were within a few yards of the river, almost touching the village. The senior Japanese in charge of Ban Khao was a 'peculiar' sergeant-major called Hibiju.[131] Not only was saluting of the Japanese mandatory, so was bowing on all occasions prisoners passed a guard, with failure to do so resulting in punishment.

Nevertheless, John Wyatt considered the camp to be in a 'beautiful location near a Thai village, with trees and shrubs which would provide us with much needed shade.' On arrival, the troops were greeted by local Thais who had eggs and other 'delicacies' to sell to the prisoners.[132]

Basil Peacock related a tricky situation in which one of the prisoners killed one of those local Thais. Two of Peacock's men had each carried a pair of boxing gloves all the way from Singapore. They enjoyed sparring with each other and on a *yasumi*, or rest day, had gone into the jungle to have a match. This had attracted the attention of some of the locals and one of them asked if he could have a go. The Thai donned a pair of the gloves and squared up to a Glaswegian called Mackay. According to the two Brits, the Thailander started hitting Mackay harder than was necessary. So Mackay responded and, after receiving a heavy body punch, the Thai collapsed and died. The other Thais pulled out knives

---

130. Robert Hardie, *The Burma-Siam Railway, The secret diary of Dr Robert Hardie 1943-45* (IWM, London, 1983), pp.65-75.
131. Peacock, p.114.
132. Wyatt & Lowry, p.79.

and Mackay and his friend Carlyle ran back to camp. A doctor was called who examined the dead man and found that he had an enlarged spleen, probably to recurrent malaria, and even the slightest punch to his body would have killed him. But the incident was reported to the Japanese and the two soldiers were arrested. The *Kempeitai* were also informed.

After an investigation, Peacock and his commanding officer, were told that the two soldiers had done nothing wrong and would not face any punishment, merely that a sum of money should be paid to the deceased's family. Yet the soldiers were badly bruised and bleeding. Peacock demanded to know why the soldiers had been beaten if there was no punishment. He was told that beating the truth out of people was how the *Kempeitai* gathered evidence. Mackay and Carlyle confirmed this, saying that all the Thai witnesses had also been beaten up![133]

In April 1943, there were – wonderfully – no deaths reported from the camp. This camp later became famous for the neolithic finds one of the Dutch prisoners, Hendrik Robert van Heekeren, who was an amateur archaeologist. He was assigned to the nail crew, which had to drive wire nails into the sleepers, which gave him the opportunity to dig into the ground. What is interesting is that he knew the route had been that taken by migrating tribes in the past, indicating that the railway was following a traditional path.[134] This was well-known by the Japanese. The railway was not a sudden idea forced on them by the exigencies of war, the route having been surveyed by the Japanese some years earlier.

Heekeren kept copious notes of his research and managed to keep a small collection of artifacts with him at the camp. The Japanese were quick to confiscate his collections and notes, and punish him, but van Heekeren continued to collect whenever possible. After the war, he returned to Thailand to continue his research. This included the discovery and excavation of one of the first, if not the first, Mesolithic human burials, likely dating to around 10,000 years ago.[135]

Len Baynes was transferred to Ban Khao on 21 February 1943 and the following day his party was taken by the guards into the jungle to gather materials for hut-building. 'I found out for the first time, wrote Len, 'where the "ties" came from that we used to tie the bamboo poles together. An oblong strip of bark was cut from a particular kind of tree, and from the inner side it was possible to peel off fifty to a hundred of the tough stringy tape-like pieces. They had to be soaked in water for a few days before becoming flexible enough to use.'[136] There was, though, a shortage of accommodation with some men, including the sick, having to sleep on the ground outside.

---

133. Peacock, pp.116-128.
134. www.tweedewereldwereld.nl
135. Taken from Cyler Conrad, 'An Archaeologist on the Railroad of Death', sapiens.org/archaeology.
136. Baynes, op. cit.

Lieutenant James Bell recorded a particularly unpleasant episode concerning Engineering officer Second Lieutenant Kuriyana, who 'harangued' two officers of the Gordon Highlanders, one of whom was Captain George Moir-Byres, for bringing in the work party too soon: 'When he had finished, he drew his sword, which he brandished above their heads. By pressing the edge of his sword onto their faces he forced them to kneel and then get up again. This procedure went on for some little time, and then he started beating them over their heads, shoulders and bodies with the flat if his sword. By the time Kuriyana had finished with these officers they were in a very sorry and distressed state.'

Lieutenant Colonel Johnson was told what was happening and he tried to intervene but was slapped on the face and made to stand to attention for a quarter of an hour before being allowed to go. The two Highlanders were made to stand outside the guard room all night.[137]

On another occasion, during a morning sick parade, Second Lieutenant Juji Tarumoto, who was responsible for the construction of the railway from Chungkai to Non Pladuc, took exception to one of the prisoners who was suffering from beriberi. 'Tarumoto ordered him to double about 20 or 30 yards and then double back again,' reported Private Thomas Claydon of the 1st Cambridgeshire Regiment. 'Owing to the fact that this man was suffering from beri-beri he fell after taking only two steps.' The man was carried back to the hospital where he remained for three days before being taken to Chungkai hospital where he died.[138]

R.E.M.E. Captain George Akester, the officer in charge of a Ban Khao sub-camp, was also a victim of Tarumoto's brutality. On 10 February 1943, Akester had eleven men who were too ill to work on the bridge that the team was building. Tarumoto decided that day to check on the progress of the work and investigate the camp. 'He saw that I had eleven men sick,' wrote Akester. 'He asked me if I knew I was only allowed to have five, which I admitted. He struck me across the face with his riding crop for disobeying his order, breaking the top plate of my teeth and smashing my glasses. He then ordered a Korean corporal to beat me. The Korean beat me on my bare back with the tooth edge of a hand saw ... I think I was struck six or eight times in all.'[139] Tarumoto made all but three of the eleven men work. One of the men later collapsed and was taken down to the main Ban Khao camp where he died. There were only three deaths in total at Ban Khao and by April 1943 work had moved on to Wang Pho.

---

137. TNA, WO 235/857.
138. TNA, WO 235/857.
139. TNA, WO 235/857.

Tha Kilen   98 Kilo
Also known as Takiren, Tarkilen, Tarki Len Tarkalin, or Ta Ki Len

It was to Tha Kilen camp that J.R. Hill arrived after marching up from Ban Khoa: 'When we reached Tarki Len in February 1943, the huts were already erected in military fashion, facing the huts was a Japanese guardroom, between these buildings was a clearing where we were allowed to sit when work for the day was finished.'[140]

Jack Shuttle was also moved to Tar Kilen in February 1943. He found the camp, which had been built close to the river, to be small and very cramped, but it's situation was 'very pleasant'[141] being located in a grass meadow not in the jungle. Private Alfred Arthur Allingham of 2/2 Pioneer Battalion, AIF, said that water was the 'main concern' at what he called Takelin. The prisoners had to roll 44-gallon drums down to the river, fill them up and roll them back.[142]

The camp was run by a Lieutenant Kokubo Nagataro who was feared and hated by prisoners and guards alike. One night, in a drunken rage and over no known specific incident, he demanded that everyone assembled outside. This included the senior British camp officer, a Lieutenant Colonel Milner. The colonel took his time to dress correctly before emerging from his hut. This delay infuriated Kokubo even further and he launched into a violent assault upon the colonel. He was repeatedly knocked to the ground, and every time he got back up again and stood rigidly to attention. The beating continued for at least fifteen minutes with Milner taking it all without uttering a word.[143]

A further batch of 300 Dutch prisoners arrived there on 9 March. Although officially there was supposed to be no contact between the natives and the prisoners, the local village was just forty feet away across a road and a brisk trade developed between the two with little Thai children running around as the go-betweens. There was also a small local market at Tha Kilen where locals sold eggs, vegetables and dried fish to the Japanese who sold the items on to the prisoners at, no doubt, a healthy profit.

Also in March 1943, four POWs escaped from Tha Kilen and a huge hunt was undertaken by heavily armed *Kempeitai* as well as Thais eager for the handsome reward on offer for the capture of the prisoners. Sergeants Francis Kelly and Edward Reay along with Fusilier Timothy Kenneally and Private Patrick Fitzgerald broke out of the camp with the aim of reaching the Burmese coast at Maungmagan, some sixty miles from Tha Kilen.

---
140. Hill, p.78.
141. TNA, WO 235/918.
142. AWM, 54 1010/4/3.
143. Shuttle, p.84.

Their absence was covered up by the other prisoners during *tenko* with men moving around as they made 'urgent' visits to the latrine. This deception was maintained for a couple of days before the commanding officer had to announce that four of his men were missing. They were caught just sixteen miles away near the Burmese border. Though it has been said that Fitzgerald was shot during capture and the other three were later executed, it would appear that all four were executed at Khao Pun on the 23 March 1943 they are now buried in Kanchanaburi War Cemetery Plot 8 Row K numbers 28/ 29/ 30 and 31

Lieutenant Christopher Raymond of the 3rd Indian Corps Signals saw the graves in the jungle two or three days after the execution. He saw the 'rough graves and bamboo frames in the shape of a cross. It looked as though some persons had been tied to them, they were marked, and there were some stains which looked blood stains … They were about three-quarters of a mile from the camp in a little clearing in the jungle. There were no names on them.' Major General Sasa, who ordered the executions, met a similar fate after being found guilty of war crimes in 1946.

It was also in March 1943 that Robert Hardie while being transferred to Takanun, the train he was on stopped at Tha Kilen. 'At this halt there were a hundred sick men waiting in what shade could find near the track … Some of them were very ill; two, in fact, were dead and more were dying.'[144] The sick prisoners had been sent from the camp to wait for a train to take them down to a base hospital camp. They had been told by the Japanese they could not take any dead bodies on the train, but the POWs had not been permitted spades to dig graves. So, the bodies just lay on the ground where they had died.

On 2 April, the prisoners were moved to Wampo, though some prisoners returned in April 1945 to conduct maintenance work on the railway.

Non Pradai   102 Kilo

A body of 300 selected men was taken by motor transport to what was described as a paddy field full of water, the prisoners being told they had to build their own huts. It took just two days for the men to construct two huts. The job the prisoners were given was the collection of gravel from the river for use as ballast on the railway.

---

144. Hardie, p,78.

Arrowhill 110 Kilo
Also known as Arruhiro or Arohuil

Robert Hardie spent a night at what the prisoners called Arrowhill. He noted that the officers had their own separate hut and mess. At the end of the hut were big bamboo seats around a large fire. The camp, which was on a stretch of level ground high above a 'shingly' stretch of the Khwae Noi, was well run with the commanding officer, Lieutenant Colonel Lilly, being given a relatively free hand by the Japanese commandant, Lieutenant Hatori.[145]

Reg Twigg initially painted a similarly favourable picture of what the, saying that it was the most beautiful place he had seen in South-East Asia: 'The Kawai ran, foaming and roaring, through a gorge carpeted with eild orchids, and thousands of monkeys chattered in the tree canopy.'[146] Before long, however, the ill treatment Reg endured and witnessed soon coloured his view of Arrowhill and that roaring river was where two POWs drowned.

Wampo 115 Kilo
Also known as Wang Po or Wang Pho

Near the village of Wampo the Khwae Noi takes an abrupt eastwards loop into a rocky gorge that cuts into the line of the railway and here it was necessary to build a viaduct about half a mile long to carry the track over the gorge by the river.[147]

As elsewhere, when the prisoners first arrived at Wampo there was no accommodation for the men. They had to roll up their blankets or whatever they had over their heads to protect them from the swarms of mosquitos, lying down wherever they could find some shelter from the weather.

There was an immediate requirement for a hospital to be established at Wampo as soon as the camp had been formed. After some persuasion the Japanese allowed two tents to be erected into which fifty of the worst cases were squeezed.

The men were told that they had to build a stretch of railway twelve miles long with a viaduct at one end and a bridge at the other. The camp for the men who would work on the Wampo Viaduct became known as Wampo South and the camp for the workers required to build a bridge was Wampo North.

---

145. Hardie, p.81.
146. Twigg, pp.236-7.
147. This description taken largely from wartimememoriesproject.com/ww2/POW/POWcamp.

A subsidiary camp was formed in early 1943. It may have been what Sergeant Leslie Burbridge, who was at Wampo North, identified as Pongysho. This was a small jungle camp close to the main camp. Motoyama – the Black Prince – was put in charge, which gave him free rein to abuse the prisoners. One of the more notable punishments he inflicted upon the POWs was to drive them into the fast-flowing river and make them stay there in water up to their navels for hours at a time.[148]

There was, additionally, a Wampo Central which was used to house sick prisoners. This camp was hemmed in by trees and mountain. The only open space was the parade ground. As the prisoners there did not work the men were on half-rations. There were no proper facilities and just a few orderlies to care for the patients. As elsewhere, there were complaints that a large number of perfectly fit young officers who could have helped dig latrines and improve the infrastructure of the camp instead stayed out of sight in their own hut, sitting 'around on their bums al day, playing bridge and reading and complaining about not being able to get decent pipe tobacco.'[149]

The viaduct and the bridge were quite complex structures, and their construction involved the communication of often complicated instructions from the Japanese engineers to the workers. Frequently, the prisoners failed to understand what was required of them, so they did what they thought was expected. Almost invariably it was not what the Japanese wanted, and such mistakes resulted in a beating. The POWs responsible were lined up and slapped hard. If a prisoner ducked the blow or fell after being hit, he received extra punishment. The only way to avoid further suffering was to stand to attention and take the bashing without flinching.[150]

The prisoners also received a bashing when one of the Japanese engineers fell to his death from the bridge. To a man, the prisoners cheered when they saw the engineer crash onto the rocks. The resultant beating from his comrades was one the POWs took without complaint.

The prisoners got a half-day holiday once a week. This, nonetheless, was used by the Japanese to their advantage. The Khwae Noi was 'teeming' with fish and the Japanese would gather a group of prisoners who were able to swim and line the up by the side of the river. The Japanese would then throw grenades into the river about 200 yards further upstream. This would stun scores of fish which would float down the river to be caught by the prisoners. The Japanese, of course, always took the best of the catch.

---

148. TNA, WO 235/918.
149. Ian Denys Peek, *One Fourteenth of an Elephant: A Memoir of Life and Death on the Burma-Thailand Railway* (Doubleday, London, 2004), p.126.
150. Hill, p.83.

Among the early arrivals at Wampo, often called Wang Yai, Wanyai or Wang Pho, was Alfred E. Nellis, a Regimental Quartermaster Sergeant with the 9th Coast Regiment Royal Artillery. At first, he considered conditions at Wampo not to be too unreasonable though, of course, the food was poor and the work hard. But, in February 1943, two subsidiary camps were opened three miles from the main camp, one to the north and one south, and the situation changed immeasurably.

'All good times ceased, the railway was being made too slowly, it must be speeded up, more men must go out to work, cook-house and administrative staff were reduced, sick were sorted out, the least sick were made to go out to work … Men commenced work at 7.00 am until their task was completed, often working until their tasks were completed at 2.00 am the next morning … Boots were becoming things of the past, P.O.W.s working barefooted or working with a piece of wood held by a piece of cloth around the toes on the feet. Clothing also became worn out or had been cut up for dressings, men had no shorts or shirts, but wore only a loin cloth or shorts made from rice sacks. Sickness increased, but men still had to work.'[151]

The weekly half-day rest was abolished, and the men had no chance to wash or air their clothes. Scabies, ringworm and other skin conditions became rife, and the huts became 'a living mass of bugs and lice' and the hospital became full.

The only 'medical' equipment available to Dr Stanley Pavillard was three pairs of artery forceps, one pair of rusty scissors, and some cat gut. As he didn't even have a knife, he used a cut-throat shaving razor.

It was around February 1943 that Pavillard took an immense gamble. He leaned that a supply of drugs had been sent to Wampo. These were on their way to Burma for use in Japanese hospitals. Pavillard asked for permission from Lieutenant Colonel Lilley to break into the Japanese store and steal some of the drugs the POWs desperately needed. Lilley agreed. Pavillard undertook a preliminary reconnaissance by himself that very same afternoon to ascertain what medicines had been received and where they were located. Had he been found he would have been severely punished, possibly even executed. 'It was imperative that the boxes be examined where we could not be surprised and the only course open was to bring them to our hospital 200 yards away,' Pavillard explained.

That night, along with four trusty men, he 'entered the store from a smithy shop, the idea being to lift the boxes some 8 ft. over a wall separating the rice stores from the smithy shop. We had to be careful dodging the guards. The first box came over though it was a slow job. Whilst I was examining the boxes in the Hospital the men went for the next one. I was surprised at the rate which

---

151. BBC People's War, Article ID: A2147041.

the boxes were arriving, but was too busy to enquire how they were bringing them so quickly. When the last box was examined I was told that they got tired of lifting the boxes over the 8 ft. wall. They thought it was quicker and easier to take them through the front door!' The front door was less than twenty feet from the Japanese Commandant's house. Taking just some medicines from each of the boxes, the Japanese were never aware that they had been looted by the prisoners, and Pavillard acquired a considerable stock of medicines and equipment which he shared equally between B, D and F Battalions. After the war, Pavillard named his four accomplices and asked that they receive due recognition for the enormous risk they took.[152]

In March, more prisoners arrived at the Wampo camps, and rations became even more stretched, and then at the end of April the hot, dry weather broke and the monsoon rains began. Conditions deteriorated further. To one of the Japanese, Yoshihiko Futamatsu, Wampo had a 'hot, stagnant, gloomy atmosphere. When rain fell, green jungle looked brilliant and lively, but … ending up by making clothes and matting damp. At night it was cold, and with the cold came mosquitoes which breed in the jungle, and they got inside our huts. Wherever you were you could hear the humming of insects.'[153]

Also, in April – the 29th – was Emperor Hirohito's birthday, to celebrate which the prisoners were given a full day's holiday. Sporting events were organised between the POWs and the Japanese and Koreans. These included long and short distance running and swimming races. The prisoners also joined the prisoners in collecting a 'big haul' of fish killed, or stunned, by throwing sticks of the engineers' dynamite into the Khwae Noi.

As in all the working camps, beatings by the Japanese were not uncommon – but it was not just prisoners who were subject to such punishment. Gunner Fergus Anckorn described one peculiar example of this when he was at Wampo. At one stage elephants were employed to move heavy timbers as the prisoners were becoming too weak to carry the larger logs for the bridge. Each elephant would drag the logs along with chains while one POW would follow behind. When the allotted place had been reached the prisoner would undo the chains. The elephant would then kneel down and roll the logs into place.

During the height of the rushed construction of the 'Speedo' period, some 200 elephants were employed along the line. One day, an additional load was added to one of the elephants above the usual two logs that the animals were expected to pull. The elephant refused to move. A guard deployed the normal

---

152. TNA, WO 235/963. The men were CQMS J.M. Metcalf, Private K.T. Wadsworth, Sergeant T.P. Cassidy, and Lance Corporal E.T. Miles.
153. Yoshihiko Futamatsu, *Across The Three Pagodas Pass: The Story of the Thai-Burma Railway* (Renaissance Books, Folkestone, 2013), p.101.

Japanese method for solving problems by hitting the elephant between the eyes with a heavy tool: 'The elephant roared and started on him. The guard turned and ran for his life. The elephant chased him, teak log and all in tow, as he crashed along at full pelt. Even with the load, the elephant gained on the guard, so he ran down the embankment towards the river. The elephant followed and down they both went – the elephant sliding down on his bottom like in a Walt Disney picture! They crashed into the river below and the elephant set about squirting water at him through his trunk. The terrified guard swam to the other side to get away.' A few days later when the guard was on duty, the elephant recognised him and charged after him again. Eventually the guard had to be transferred.[154]

Another strange instance of Japanese discipline was witnessed by Eric Roberts of the 1/5 Sherwood Foresters when something upset a visiting Japanese officer, 'who proceeded to beat up a Jap warrant officer standing nearby; he in turn beat up a Jap of lower rank who proceeded to beat up a Jap private soldier, who in his turn took it out of some prisoners who were nearby.'[155]

It is not impossible that the Japanese officer Eric Roberts referred to was Lieutenant Tarumoto as Herbert Jupp of the 5th Battalion Royal Norfolk Regiment specifically identified Tarumoto as he 'frequently walked around brandishing his sword and shouting, striking the men on their heads, shoulders and bodies with the sword in the scabbard for no reason at all. Some were knocked down, in fact they frequently could not stand after being struck. Tarra Motto [sic] would kick them and tell them to get up again.'[156]

Jupp also said that one of the jobs for the men at Wampo was that of quarrying stone for ballast. When working in the quarry, one of the guards, known only to him as 'Gold-rush' because of his 'hideous' set of gold teeth, would pick up pieces of rock and throw it at the workers for no particular reason other than pure malice: 'I have seen them knocked down,' Jupp reported, 'and then kicked because they could not get up'. The work usually lasted between fourteen and sixteen hours a day and, sometimes, the prisoners would then have to unload railway trucks for two or three hours.

Sergeant George Priestman of the Royal Army Service Corps was at Wampo in April 1943, when the food ration consisted of a pint pot of rice three times a day. With the morning meal they had half a pint of green stew made, he believed, from a form of watercress. For the midday meal they had a teaspoon

---

154. Fyans, pp.125-6.
155. Ian Roberts, *Survival & Separation on the River Kwai: The Ordeal of a Japanese Prisoner of War and His Family* (Pen & Sword, Barnsley, 2023), p.85.
156. TNA, WO 235/957.

of sugar on the rice, and with the evening meal they had the same green stew with their rice which had a little meat in it.[157]

Dr Pavillard saw that morale was of enormous importance among the patients in the hospital. Once a man lost the will to live, drugs or any other form of treatment became completely ineffective. The medical staff carried out any form of 'subterfuge' to cheer up the patients, even making up stories about the progress of the war to give them hope of soon being liberated. On occasion patients who had seemingly given up on life were 'ordered' to survive, telling them that they died they would be court martialled! So ingrained was military discipline in some of the men this trick sometimes really seems to have worked.[158]

Pavillard was allowed to journey to Kanchanaburi to buy food and medicines where he made contact with the remarkable Boon Pong, who agreed to help the prisoners at Wampo as he was doing at other camps. Pavillard also managed to add fifteen extra men, fifteen different men, to the number of sick each day. This was done on a rota basis so that he could give that number of men one day's rest from the tough work of clearing the jungle.

As well as a few species of edible plants the men discovered in the jungle, snakes provided valuable nutrients. While an acquired taste, boiled or grilled snake, especially Python, was regarded as being 'very acceptable'. The prisoners at Wampo also set traps to snare monkeys. The traps were simple affairs. A large bamboo with a narrow hole in the top would be pushed into the ground. Rice or fruit would be placed at the bottom of the hole. A monkey would come along, thrust his hand into the hole and grab the food. The clench fist would be too big for the monkey to pull back through the hole. Unwilling to let go of his prize, the monkey would still be trying to pull his hand free when the trap-setter returned. One day they killed and ate a six-foot iguana which they drove out of a tree it had climbed in a bid to escape the hungry horde of prisoners.

Even though a degree of cooperation existed between the prisoners and the Japanese because Doc Pavillard had helped one of the Japanese remove an enormous tapeworm from his intestines (the Japanese had no doctor or competent medical staff in the camp), beatings were still a feature of life at Wampo. In one instance, a guard on his rounds one night had looked in the POW mortuary. As he shone his torch on the mortuary table the body lying there suddenly shot upright. The guard rushed out of the hut screaming in terror. It transpired that the prisoner slept in the mortuary because there were fewer biting insects there than in the accommodation hut. The consequence

---

157. TNA, WO 235/957.
158. Pavillard, p.100.

was that the guard returned with three others and gave the prisoner a good beating for not being dead![159]

Pavillard was increasingly called upon to attend to medical problems among the Japanese which gave him the opportunity to inflict a little painful revenge upon the hated guards. This included, where possible, infecting them with dysentery. One way this was achieved was when polishing their teeth. The Japanese, seemingly, took great pride in their protruding 'horsey' teeth. If a guard had proven particularly vile, he would be targeted, being admired for his wonderful teeth and being told that there was a dentist in the camp who could repair teeth as well as polish them to make them sparklingly white. If the guard took the bait his tongue would be smeared unobtrusively with the prepared solution of bacillary and amoebic dysentery. This could result in the guard suffering the effects of severe dysentery and his transfer to the Japanese base hospital downriver and his absence from duties for up to six months.

The men that worked on the Wampo viaduct suffered terribly. They had to carve a ledge a quarter of a mile long out of a sheer face of rock sixty feet above the Khwae Noi. Many men collapsed, and some died, from heatstroke as they worked, being not just exposed to the direct effects of the sun but also to the reflection of the sun from the bare stone around them. The men worked 'blindly' Pavillard commented, 'in a jerky, mechanical fashion as if hypnotised or dazed, aware only of the harsh sunlight boring mercilessly through their eyeballs.'[160] This resulted in three men falling into the river and drowning.

To form the ledge for the railway the rock had to be blasted away in the same fashion as the Hellfire pass (see below) was excavated. The splinters from the explosions could fly considerable distances and, on one occasion, a piece of rock hit one of the POW cooks in the camp across the river. It entered his skull, exposing his brain. He survived with no lasting effects, but another prisoner working of the viaduct was not so lucky. A large piece of rock struck him in the face which resulted in permanent disfigurement and partial facial paralysis.

Yoshihiko Futamatsu considered the POWs on the job to be 'rather negligent'! He continued: 'The Japanese engineers could not permit negligence and constantly scolded them, shouting "Supeedo" and "Hurry uppu" to them. The prisoners-of-war thought this was callous cruelty.'[161]

As at Chungkai, and as at some other camps, a library was formed at Wampo. To join the library prisoners had to contribute at least one book. The prisoners were also allowed to perform a concert once every three weeks.

---

159. Pavillard, pp.101-2.
160. Pavillard, p.112.
161. Futamatsu, p.104.

On 10 May 1943, the railway reached Wampo and the prisoners that were fit to walk were marched to Tonchan South, while the 150 sick men were taken by barge down to Chungkai Base Hospital Camp. Though the work they had been engaged on was for the benefit of the Japanese war effort, the men, quite justifiably, felt a degree of pride with what they had accomplished as they gazed at the viaduct which still stands today.

Pukai   119 Kilo
Also known as Monkey Bend Camp

Major Basil Peacock was part of a group of men under Lieutenant Colonel Johnson of the 4th Suffolks which worked at Pukai, known by the troops as Monkey Bend camp, during March and April 1943. This was during the speedo period and the Japanese lieutenant in charge of the camp only permitted one officer and seven men per battalion for camp duties. This meant that all the sick had to contribute to cutting wood, digging latrines, and carrying water. To ensure there was always enough boiled water, the cooks, as was the case throughout the camps, kept their fire going, even through the night, so that the men could fill their water bottles in the morning. Many of those sent out to work were so ill that all they could do was sit and break pebbles to a suitable size for use as ballast between the railway sleepers.

One day, Peacock was summoned by one of the particularly brutal Korean guards to join him on a monkey hunt. The guard was frequently using a stick to beat the prisoners and, it seemed, he was eager to use his rifle. To save the guard finding some excuse to shoot one of the POWs the killing of a monkey or two seemed worth the sacrifice. Fortunately for the primates in the area, the guard proved to be a terrible shot and after a futile hour the pair returned to camp.[162]

During the 'speedo' period, the work slipped behind schedule because there were so few men available and because of contradictory instructions and the Japanese engineers 'hustling' the men from job to job with no discernible plan. This meant the prisoners were worked increasingly longer hours, bring driven off to work in the dark and returning to camp in the dark. In the end, the prisoners decided the best way to ease the pressure being put upon them was for Peacock –being regarded by the Japanese as the 'Number One' prisoner – to suggest to the Japanese that they should let the men get on with the job without interference from the Japanese engineers.

---

162. Peacock, p.101.

This was accepted and the work completed so that the prisoners were able to have a half-day rest. The Japanese were so pleased that the work had been completed they told the prisoners – in fact insisted – they could arrange a concert. Two days later the camp was broken up and the prisoners were rewarded for their conduct with a large sack of peanuts.

Wang Yai   125 Kilo

Basil Peacock's party was moved to Wang Yai in April 1943. He had become accustomed to ramshackle huts but the ones here were the worst he had so far seen. They were only roughly ten or twelve feet high with no walls, the roofs simply sloping down from the ridge poles to within eighteen inches of the ground. Even some of the ridge poles had sagged down and the prisoners had to bend over to walk from one end of the hut to the other.[163]

Cholera first raised its head in this regio at the *rŏmusha* camps resulting in the natives running away in large numbers. News of the outbreak was passed onto new arrivals who also took to their heels. There was a great danger that infected natives would spread the disease. Efforts were undertaken to try and round up the escaped *rŏŏmusha* and the *Kempeitai* set up a holding cage at Wang Yai for those they captured. It was, though, too late as cholera as too deeply rooted in the native workforce.[164]

Tarsao   130 Kilo
Also known as Tarsau, Tahsao or Tha Sao

Tarsao was a very large HQ camp situated by the road leading up alongside the railway towards Burma and close to the Khwae Noi. Originally constructed by 400 men of the 4th Battalion, Royal Norfolk Regiment under Lieutenant Colonel Alfred Ernest Knights, the camp had a hospital and a cemetery, as well as a charcoal pit operated by the prisoners. Unlike many of the camps, it was surrounded by a ten-foot-high bamboo fence. It became the headquarters of No.4 Group, and it was from here that the payments of money from the Japanese for those classed as working was received for distribution to the other camps in the group. There was on occasions some difficulty getting money to the camps further up the line due to the difficulty of moving around during the monsoon. The camp had a population of between 1,700 and 2,500.

---

163. Peacock, pp.131-2.
164. TNA, WO 203/6325.

The camp commander was at first Major Cheda and later Lieutenant Colonel Ishii, with approximately 200 men under them. The guards were mostly Korean. The camp adjutant was Lieutenant Tanaka who had a little compound of his own. The Japanese camp doctor was Lieutenant Maruoka, who was 'weak, drunken and useless and left everything in the hands of Tanaka', according to Major John Parsons of 2nd Battalion, 18th Royal Garhwal Rifles, who was Colonel Knights' Assistant Camp Commandant. The interpreter was a civilian called Oseiki who also had considerable influence on how the camp was run.

The Malayan Prisoner of War Administration also had a separate fenced off area (described as a like a quadrangle or yard), in which there were a number of bamboo and attap storehouses. In this area were fifty prisoners (two Australians, eighteen British and thirty Dutch) under the command of the Dutch Captain D. Gerritsen, later replaced (on Japanese orders) by Captain J. Swartjes. The purpose of this group was that of drawing rations etc., from where they had been taken off the arriving trains and carrying them to the Camp Administration's place of storage. From there the goods were put onto trucks for distribution to the camps along the line until the monsoon washed away the road, and then the supplies were sent by river barge. Compared with the jungle camps, food supply was reasonable, with the rice ration being supplemented by vegetables and, occasionally, meat. A canteen was run from a warehouse, where it was possible to buy eggs, biscuits fruit and tinned fish.[165]

This group of prisoners, which had been assembled from the groups that had passed through Tarsao, was also supposed to look after the baggage of the POWs but, because the Japanese were continually using the men on other tasks, this did not happen. Inevitably, this meant that items were stolen from the baggage, including some medical supplies. Though the thefts were investigated, the culprits were never identified.

The camp, in its original form, had just one hospital hut, set up in October 1942 under Lieutenant Colonel W. Harvey,[166] which could house twenty men in very cramped conditions. Later this was increased with a second hut making a total of 250 beds. Unfortunately, the number of sick was never less than 400.[167] Colonel Knights wrote of conditions at Tarsao: 'Already, my daily visits to the hospital were becoming something of a nightmare, the suffering was indescribable, the atmosphere of frustration amongst the medical officers at the inability adequately to attend to the need of their charges through lack

---

165. English, p.105.
166. AWM, 54 554/5/1.
167. TNA, WO 235/963.

of medical supplies, and their feeling that they were fighting a losing battle in spite of all their superhuman efforts, was pathetic.'

One of the few brighter moments was when Knights was introduced to the 'V' Organisation. A note was handed to Knights by one of the prisoners who said it had been given to him by a Thai native on one of the barges which sailed up and down the river. The note said that if Knights needed drugs, medical supplies or money he was to contact a native on a barge at the riverbank adjacent to a disused mill at a specified day and time. The note was dimply signed 'V'. Knights, of course, did make contact and, after the war, he stated that Boon Pong's organisation supplied him with 35,408 ticals throughout the period Tarsao was open, which Knights calculated was the equivalent of £2,400 (around £130,000 today).[168]

Major Bruce Hunt AAMC reported an incident which led to a savage beating of him and the camp's Australian interpreter, Major Wild. Hunt was told that all those unfit for work had to be subjected to an inspection to determine their state of health. This was done and the Japanese medical officer, Lieutenant Maruoka, agreed that the thirty-seven men presented were too ill to be sent out to work. However, Maruoka was 'weak, drunken and useless' and the Japanese corporal in charge of the guards over-ruled him and said that only ten were permitted to remain in camp.

Hunt and Wild were determined to stand their ground – quite literally – placing themselves in front of the thirty-seven men which were separated from the main group preparing to leave for the day's work on the railway. Bruce Hunt takes up the story: 'The corporal approached with a large bamboo in his hand and spoke menacingly to Major Wild who answered in a placatory fashion. The corporal's only reply was to hit Major Wild in the face. Another guard followed suit and as Major Wild staggered back the corporal thrust at the Major's genitals with his bamboo. I was left standing in front of the patients and was immediately set upon by the Corporal and two other guards – one tripped me while the two others pushed me to the ground. The three then set about me with bamboos, causing extensive bruising of scull, back, hands and arms, and a fractured left 5th metacarpal bone. This episode took place in front of the whole parade of troops. After I was disposed of the corporal then made the majority of the sick men march with the rest of the troops.'[169]

There was also the shocking episode concerning Private Eric Bertrand Hilton of the 5th Bedfordshire and Hertfordshire Regiment. In late October or early November 1943, Hilton had been struck by one of the Koreans at the work

---

168. IWM, Escritt Collection.
169. Grehan, p.46.

site for going to urinate in the jungle without permission and Hilton had hit back at the guard. A Court of Inquiry had been conducted but the verdict had already been decided. On day two of the inquiry, Hilton, having loosened his bindings, made a bid to escape. He only got about twenty-five yards before he was caught. Private G.V. Hunt (4th Battalion Royal Norfolks) saw Hilton 'unmercifully beaten up' by Korean guards after his recapture. He was 'kicked and stoned, with his hands tied behind him, and finally bayonetted, causing him to bleed badly, leaving him in a very distressed condition in a small cell'. Hilton was later taken away by a Japanese officer. It was presumed that Hilton had been shot, as he was not seen again.[170]

Though Lieutenant Colonel Knights was unable to find out officially what had happened to Hilton, it is said that the Japanese let it be known that Hilton had been executed, the message being that any POW who retaliated when being disciplined would meet the same fate as Hilton.[171]

Signalman Reg Bulled wrote of the shambolic nature of the morning count at Tarsau. The men were paraded in three ranks and numbered off in Japanese. This process was repeated to confirm the count. Then the guards conducted their own count. When all the totals tallied, the men in hospital would be counted. The whole episode could last thirty or forty-five minutes, which was an agonisingly long time for the dysentery sufferers to stand.[172]

The latrines were particularly dreadful at Tarsao with only six partially sick men allowed to undertake hygiene duties, meaning that the digging of new latrine trenches was 'impossible'. The latrines were home to thousands of flies and maggots.

When Arch Flannagan arrived at Tarsau it was thought he had cholera and he was placed in what was called, as in many of the camps, 'Cholera Gulch', which he described as 'just a collection of tents, down in a hollow'. As it transpired, he did not have cholera and, despite so many dying around him, he survived. In fact, he believed that it saved his life as it meant he did have to work on the railway during the intense 'speedo' period.[173]

Pilfering from the Japanese engineers' store was not uncommon at Tarsao and considerable quantities of food were, according to one account, stolen at night through the attap of the store hut. The items mentioned were tins of salt pork and bags of sugar.[174]

---

170. TNA, WO 235/918; War Crimes Courts, 6 March 1947, legal-tools.org/doc.
171. TNA, WO 235/963.
172. www.far-eastern-heroes.org.uk/Memoirs_of_Reg_Bulled.
173. Wright, p.44.
174. Brune, pp.628-9.

Over the months the camp grew considerably, eventually numbering eighty-four attap huts and, along with Kanchanaburi and Chungkai, became a base hospital in April 1943 with a small working camp nearby for fit prisoners maintaining the road. Thousands of sick prisoners were transported to Tarsao, including those from the awful Tonchan South Camp.

Badly situated close to the Khwae Noi, conditions at Tarsao hospital camp – which then consisted of twenty-four 'tumbling' huts – were dreadful, which Dick Ridgwell described to Cheryl Mellor in 2017: 'It was terrible. Overcrowded with sick men everywhere and very few medical orderlies to care for them. There was always a terrible odour accompanying the men with ulcers. I gathered up blankets and tore them up for the ulcer ward.

'I assisted around the hospital as much as I was able and helped hold down those men while orderlies scraped away the maggoty pus from POWs' limbs using a silver spoon. The pain was terrible for these men. Following this appalling procedure doctors would take the torn blankets which had been sterilised in boiling water in nearby 44-gallon drums placed over fires. These would be placed over the cleaned wound. This was the only procedure available for ulcer patients. There was nothing else.'[175]

Hugh de Wardener, was transferred to Tarsao hospital camp: 'It was a terrible place to start with and the Nips would not allow enough people to dig latrines and there weren't sufficient huts. And a few days after we arrived the monsoon started. So we had faeces all over the place … we also got into the camp all the people that would die in the smaller camps above us … and these dying people would be sent to us and all we had to do was give them the last rites.'[176]

The dreadful conditions at Tarsao when it had become a base hospital were the subject of investigation during the war crimes trials after the war: 'The whole area gave out a stench of foulness, staleness and death … Sick men were regarded as a waste of time, and better dead … Lack of supervision allowed greater responsibility to be taken by most junior guards who exercised their native flair for brutality. These guards in a number of cases had the mentality of apes and the experience of imbeciles.'[177]

'Weary' Dunlop visited Tarsao in October 1943: 'Conditions fulfilled my worst fears,' he reported, 'owing to the flooding of the sick of the wretched ill-equipped hovels many had deteriorated grossly instead of improving.' He cited the example of a Warrant Officer of 2 A.I.F. who had left Hintok a few weeks before with an almost completely healed small tropical ulcer 'now presented

---

175. 2/4th Machine Gun Battalion, 2nd4thmgb.com.au.
176. Gill and Parkes, p 180.
177. TNA, WO 235/957.

with 2/3 with the tibia exposed a radical spreading foul gangrene and was nigh unto death with the exhaustion and toxaemia'. Dunlop carried out a thigh amputation on the patient, who suffered a cardiac arrest during the operation but was resuscitated. The man died twenty-four hours later.[178]

The old, decrepit huts were in such a state that at times they collapsed on the patients. Yet Dunlop was full of praise about the camp's operating hut which 'surpassed any previous experience'. He wrote that it had a 'built up bamboo floor, a built-in operating table to take a stretcher, and even some rather ineffectual attempts at fly-proof wiring'. The hut had a microscope and a rudimentary laboratory.

Despite its obvious failings, some men who moved from the jungle working camps after the completion of the railway to Tarsao described it as like 'entering the gates of paradise'. The huts were waterproof, the camp was clean and the food 'more plentiful than the prisoners had known for weeks'.[179] Lieutenant John Durnford wrote of Tarsao that it 'lay in trees at the top of the steep hill leading down towards Tarsao. Through it ran a pleasant, slow-moving stream, to fall in a mare's-tail waterfall over the cliff's edge into the cutting below.'[180]

Because, as a hospital camp there was no external work, rations were severely restricted by the Japanese. The only way the patients were able to survive was through contributions from battalions working in other camps according to the number of their sick sent to Tarsao. Sometimes, though, this did not happen.

A report on conditions at Tarsao between 17 March 1943 and 15 June 1944 states that there were more than 5,000 prisoners accommodated there: 'Hospital poorly situated – layout bad – ground foul, atap huts in poor condition, overcrowded – less than 1 metre per man making task of MOs difficult in attending individual patient. Practically no effective isolation of dysentery cases possible ... The effect on morale on patients when evacuated from this area [at the] latter end of April 44 was remarkable.'[181]

One of the tasks forced upon the POWs at Tarsao was the burial of dead native workers. The prisoners had to dig several holes in the ground, into which the bodies were thrown. Sergeant Johnny Sherwood described this as a 'sickening' job: 'These bodies had lain festering for several days and it made me retch at the stench of blackened, putrefying corpses and the swarms of flies.'[182]

---

178. AWM, 54 55/5/1.
179. Alan S. Walker, *Australia in the War of 1939–1945*, Series Five, Medical, Volume II, Middle Est and Far East, (Australian War Memorial, Canberra, 1962), p.571.
180. Durnford, p.76.
181. TNA, WO 235/963.
182. Johnny Sherwood and Michael Doe, *Lucky Johnny: The Footballer who Survived the River Kwai Death Camps* (Hodder & Stoughton, London, 2014), p.55.

Another task Johnny Sherwood hated was the carrying up of supplies from the river, where barges were tied at the bottom of steep banks that had been turned into mudslides: 'We slid down this slimy skid-pan so fast that we often collided with the barges, or fell into the river. But coming up was a nightmare, trying to carry heavy barrels or chests, while at the same time trying to get a grip with our bare feet on the mud.' Sherwood lost count of how many times he dropped his load and slithered down the bank, to start the whole laborious climb again. 'It was a bruising and exhausting task for a fit man, and none of us were up to it. But the guards didn't care, laying into us every time we fell. The only thing that kept us going was the knowledge this was food and medicine, and we somehow wrestled everything up the bank in the end.'[183]

One particularly distressing scene at Tarsao affected Captain John Barnard of the 2nd East Surreys. One night, as he was walking across the camp, he saw a dark object by the side of the path: 'I bent down and found that it was a youngster who had been ill for some time, lying face downwards in the mud. He was only just over five feet high, and even in pre-war days was very slight, but now after weeks of sickness he was more like a little boy.

'I picked him up and carried him to the tents and sent for Doc., but there was little we could do. Repeated attacks of dysentery and innumerable bouts of malaria had now been followed by black water fever.' The young man died the following day.[184]

Another who died at the hands of the Japanese was a man Bill Reed, of 85th Anti-tank Regiment Royal Artillery, knew only to be a soldier from the Sherwood Foresters. The very ill and weak man had been accused of attempting to escape. The prisoners were lined up to observe what happened to escapees who were caught. The unfortunate Forester was tied to the front of a locomotive on the orders of the camp commandant, Lieutenant Sugano: 'at Sugano's signal to the engine driver, exhaust steam gushed from the locomotive's cylinders and it moved slowly forward with its living human buffers, and commenced shunting work in the sidings.'[185]

One event caused a smile on the POWs faces came when they were ordered to build a 'biggish' bungalow for, it was said, a Japanese general. The prisoners collected as many live bugs and lice as they could, placed them in matchboxes and released them in the bungalow.

John Durnford was told that Boon Pong of the 'V' Organisation was planning an escape route out of Tarsao to China for POWs. The plans were put on hold

---

183. Sherwood and Doe, pp.57-8.
184. Lowry, *Last Post*, pp.110-111.
185. Reed and Peeke, pp.76-7.

due to the imposition of harsher measures following the discovery of a diary in which, it was said, were details of a scheme to the capture of one of the guard huts. Suspecting an armed insurrection, several officers were imprisoned in bamboo cages and interrogated. The escape plan, if it did really exist, was never revived.[186]

Morale was maintained, as far as was possible in such conditions, with the news from four 2-valve wireless sets which had been constructed by men who were formerly electricians of the British Malaya Broadcasting Corporation. They were concealed inside large Dutch water bottles and the information passed along to other camps.[187]

One party, including men of 2/19 Battalion A.I.F, were moved to what was referred to as 'North' Tarsao, though was probably Tonchan South, where they were made responsible for some 2,000 rŏmusha, composed of Malays, Chinese, Tamils, Thais, Khmers, Cambodians, Laotians, Vietnamese, Indonesians, Sumatrans and 'Ambonians'.[188]

Colonel Humphries of 'H' Force passed through Tarsao on his way north in May 1943. He found there was a 'severe lack or total absence of tentage, or water, primitive and totally inadequate sanitary arrangements, mud, rain with general squalor and misery.' This was echoed by Dental Officer, Captain M.K. Winchester A.A.M.C: 'The outstanding impression here were the filth, the exhausted look of the men, the hardships due to the lack of drinking water, mud and incessant rain.'[189]

Basil Peacock, from No.2 Group, had a similar opinion of Tarsao. He later wrote that he was used to terrible accommodation at other camps but the huts sat Tarsao were the worst he had seen: 'They were only about ten or twelve feet high, with no walls, and the roofs simply sloped from the ridge poles to within eighteen inches of the ground.' The ridge poles of some of the huts had sagged to such an extent that the prisoners had to bend down to walk from one end to the other.[190]

The party from No.2 Group were given accommodation a short distance away from the main part of the camp. Their duties were to load sampans travelling up-river and to receive sick and dying prisoners that came down river.

Dunlop wrote that, when he was first associated with Tarsao hospital, the camp was 'close to the Kwai Noi River handy to a barge point and consisted of 24 of those tumbling bamboo and attap structures provided with the usual

---

186. Durnford, p.79.
187. TNA, 203/6325.
188. Newton and McGuinness, p.585.
189. TNA, WO 325/17.
190. Peacock, pp.131-2.

rough continuous platforms of bamboo on either side of the building. The patients usually lay with their feet directed to the central pathway so that, with the overcrowding, access to the sick patients was most difficult.' He was later to further report on the 'alarming death toll' following the mass evacuation [from the jungle camps] of the sick by 'barbarous' methods. 'Conditions then fulfilled my worse fears since, owing to the flooding [of the hospital] with sick of the wretched ill-equipped hovels.'[191]

Dunlop's report continued: 'The hospital at this time ... presented an appalling spectacle. The huts were practically all old, decrepit, and leaking badly, and at times collapsed on the patients. With the overcrowding of huts there was no room for site latrines at reasonable distances and these were of the open trench type, swarming with maggots and horribly offensive.' Not only were the latrines too close to the accommodation huts, some were also crumbling and falling in. The run-off for all the waste water, from the camp, including the soiled remnants of dressings from the hospital, was down to the river, but the current at that spot was very weak and often, as barges passed by, the refuge was washed back to the prisoners' ablutions area. The open cholera tents were also situated close to the hospital – only about twenty yards away.

Due to the absence of medicines, some of the dysentery patients were 'merely skin stretched over a skeleton' and others were 'horribly bloated and swollen'. But what Dunlop regarded as presenting the most distressing picture of all was seen in the tropical ulcer wards. These 'resembled horrible "butchers" shops filled with the stench of gangrene and buzzing with flies which hovered tenaciously above the crude rags of clothing etc., which were boiled and reboiled for dressings.' These wards were 'pools of infection' with the courageous volunteer orderlies who tried to look after the patients just ordinary combat soldiers with little or no previous experience of medical work.

Proper nursing care became simply impossible as the number of severely sick patients grew. The condition of the patients having deteriorated with 'shocking rapidity', observed Dunlop, owing to 'wracking' pain and toxaemia. 'The general appearance was striking, notably the pale, lined, harassed face and haunted eyes, telling of pain and loss of sleep.'[192]

Dunlop was so moved by what he witnessed at Tarsao he sought permission to be stationed there for as long as necessary. This was approved, and on 25 October Dunlop was appointed Officer Commanding Tarsao Hospital.

His first task was to have the boundary fence extended so that the hospital grounds could be extended to allow greater space between the main wards and

---

191. AWM, 54 554/2/1C.
192. AWM, 54 554/5/1.

the cholera ward as well as giving more room for proper latrines to be dug. Despite the weak state of the patients, the latrines were dug to a depth of at least fifteen feet. A large petrol drum was also stolen from the Japanese and disguised with mud for use as a steam disinfector and a scabies disinfectant centre was established. Interestingly, permission was granted for the construction of a ward, surrounded by a fence, for men with mental health issues. The hospital huts were rebuilt but in stages to avoid having to move large numbers of very sick patients around.

Despite having no nails, wire or solder the little prisoners' workshop produced some ward and hygiene equipment, including charcoal sterilisers made from biscuit tins and mud, irrigators, splints and bedpans. Over the weeks these men became increasingly skilful and were soon making bowls, buckets, trays, ladles, mugs, pillows and mattresses (of rice sacks and straw), brooms, pneumonia jackets, lamps, urine bottles, latrine lids, vegetable scrapers and even bamboo needles and scalpels. Charcoal was also used by the prisoners as toothpaste, with a bamboo stick the usual toothbrush. Men washed themselves with gravel or wood ash from the cookhouse fires and dried themselves with jungle leaves.

On 5 November Dunlop was arrested by the Japanese who were convinced he had a secret wireless (there was, of course, one in operation in the camp). He was told by the *Kempeitai* he would be executed. He was tied with his hands behind his back round a tree, Four Japanese soldiers, bayonets levelled, stood in front of him as the seconds were counted down. At the last moment, he was reprieved. He was beaten and placed in a cell, face to the wall, awaiting his fate. Again, he was taken to the tree where the same ritual was re-enacted. Eventually, after four days and finding no wireless, he was released.

Also, the previous month, October 1943, Captain Vinton of the 4th Suffolks was beaten up by one of the Japanese and as a result, developed a mastoid. Captain McConachie operated on him with the only equipment available to him – a carpenter's hammer and chisel.[193]

In November 1943, the weather started to turn, and the nights became increasingly cold. Most patients had no blankets, in some cases due to them having been sold by the men for food during the warmer weather. Large numbers had no covering other than just a loin cloth and an old rice sack. The Japanese did try to help, providing bamboo matting for the men to lie on. The mats also acted as wind breaks, making the huts a little warmer. Dunlop also put in place measures to make use of every scrap of food. If an animal was killed all the beast's blood was captured and added to the daily stew. Every organ was taken and used in some form or other and animal fat was used as ointment.

---

193. TNA, WO 325/157.

Incredibly, the rehabilitation of patients with long-term or life-changing conditions was instigated. In the midst of conditions more dreadful than any of the medical staff could ever have imagined working, arts and crafts schemes for such as amputees were introduced, encouraging these men to produce useful items for the hospital in exchanged for small amounts of money. In addition, there were lectures, classes and readings (books being very scarce), quizzes and debates.

The food situation had become so bad the prisoners took to stealing from the Japanese food store. Two prisoners – drivers Leggett and Newham – were caught in the act. As punishment, they were made to stand at attention outside the guard hut for seven days continuously except during the hours of darkness when they were allowed to lie on the ground. At the end of the week they were in great distress, with their legs swollen to three times their normal size, and they were immediately taken to hospital. It took them some weeks to recover.[194]

John Durnford saw Tarsao in a different light, calling it a sort of Aldershot of the jungle: 'There was saluting, the blowing of reveille and retreat, officers' compounds officers' huts, officers' messes, dinners, bathing – and, final absurdity, officers' latrines.' Durnford also mocked that the officers' faces, which he wrote bore an unhealthy pallor because they never saw the sun, 'sheltered behind enclosures with palm-thatched walls at their entrances. Within these, officers took the evening air rather as they might on the veranda of a permanent of a permanent station mess.'[195]

In November 1943 rations became so poor that a considerable amount of thieving of Japanese stores took place until two prisoners – Driver Legget and Driver Newham – were caught in the act. The punishment which followed resulted in the two men being made to stand to attention outside the guard house during daylight hours for seven days, being permitted to lie on the ground at night. If either man failed to hold himself at attention one of the Japanese would come out of the guardhouse and beat him.[196]

Towards the end of November, after repeated urgings by the senior officers at Tarsao, the IJA sent a representative to Bangkok to obtain medicines. He returned with a number of important items. However, there were never enough medicines to treat the more than 2,000 patients. Almost every POW suffered from malaria and quinine was in very short supply. When they did receive some from Japan, disturbing side-effects were noticed including irregular heart rhythms and, in some cases unconsciousness and even dementia.

---

194. TNA, WO 235/963.
195. Durnford, p.38.
196. AWM, 54 1010/4/68 Part1.

Patients suffering from acute pellagra often soiled themselves merely by the act of turning over on the bed. In the final stages of the illness, Dunlop noted, some of these patients 'developed a strange mental apathy with indifference to death'.

In December, Dunlop wrote: 'The misery of cold at night was at this stage most pathetic and very few patients were able to sleep. Men who were ambulatory moved about the area huddling before the kitchen fires and other warmer places. The majority crawled out and slept in the open on the ground because it was much warmer than on the bamboo beds and the whole bedding could be used above the body.'

It was on 18 December that Allied aircraft were heard above Tarsao, following which the Japanese became very strict about fires at night. The prisoners were not permitted to leave their huts when aircraft were heard, being told if they wanted to shelter from any bombs that might be dropped, they should hide under their bamboo beds!

As in other camps, the cooks prepared special meals on Christmas Day from items they had been accumulating over the previous weeks. Men from the main camp took small gifts to those in the hospital, and a stage was built for a performance of *Cinderella*. There was even a lottery overseen by Father Christmas.

Altogether, 15,029 patients were admitted to Tarsao during its period of operation, which ended in April 1944, when the survivors were transported to Kanchanaburi. In anticipation of the move, a major operation was put in hand. A production line was set up to produce 3,000 wooden clogs from felled trees; 300 stretchers were made from bamboo and rice sacks; wooden food containers were made for those men without mess tins; and bamboo water bottles were manufactured.

Tarsao eventually had three cemeteries, where 806 men were buried.

Tonchan South   131 Kilo

There were three camps at Tonchan. The southern one, which was under the command of Lieutenant Colonel T. Newey, was nine kilometres from the central Touchan camp. 'H' Force commenced work here, at what became the force's No. 5 Camp, on arrival from Singapore in May 1943. It was the most southerly of the 'H' Force camps, incorporating groups 5 and 6 which were administered individually.

It was composed of two lean-to shelters plus nine tents of varying sizes, all of which, Colonel Humphries wrote, 'were uniform in one respect – that they did not keep out the rain'. These tents could not house all the prisoners and, until attap huts could be built, many men had to sleep on the open ground. Two more tents were later added which had been found on the road. The camp held a total of around 800 men at that stage.

Water came from a stream which, rising from a hillside, ran adjacent to the camp and finally tumbled as a waterfall down into a valley 100 feet below. At first the men used buckets to scoop out the water from the stream but later pumps with an inbuilt filtration unit were issued.

Captain Reginald Burton of the Royal Norfolk Regiment wrote that the quarters of the Japanese engineers at Tonchan were comparatively luxurious: 'They had well-built huts, good quality tents and all the amenities, including beds and raffia matting.'[197]

The men were mainly employed in clearing jungle, excavating cuttings, moving earth and stones, felling trees and bridge building, which included the laborious task of piledriving. For this, the prisoners would cut down a thick tree trunk and 'wedge' four handles into it. The men would then lift up the trunk and then drop it into the riverbed. They would have to repeat this process until the trunk was securely embedded into the ground.[198] Officers were also made to work and as these men had largely been used for administrative duties, they were unfit for heavy manual labour. They were, in many cases, less efficient than the other ranks and beatings by the Japanese with pick handles or even iron bars was a daily occurrence.

As with other camps, the prisoners had to work until as late as 20.30 hours each day. Often, even after they had been out all day, officers would be called on to perform essential work around the camp, such as laying paths, fetching water for the cookhouse and other chores to make the camp 'habitable'.

During 'speedo' a night shift was introduced which saw the men start work in the afternoon, finishing at around 04.00 hours. They would then have to wake up at 07.00 hours but were given the morning off.

Not only was the work hard, but the language difficulties often led to misunderstanding instructions given by the Japanese engineers. The Japanese way to deal with this was, as usual, to beat the officers, again with bamboo sticks or iron bars.

At one point, elephants were brought in to help with the dragging of heavy logs from the forest. But the elephants were considered to be too slow, and they were sent away. The prisoners were told that ten men must do the work of one elephant.[199] It was not long before footwear and clothes began to wear out and there was nothing to replace them with.

---

197. Reginald Burton, *Railway of Hell, War: Captivity and Forced Labour at the Hands of the Japanese* (Pen & Sword, Barnsley, 2002), p.87.
198. 2/4th Machine Gun Battalion, 2nd4thmgb.com.au.
199. TNA, WO 325/157.

Sanitation was always a matter of great concern and at Tonchan South, and one of the first tasks to be undertaken was that of digging the latrines. The first attempt at digging the pits came to a halt when the men struck solid rock just a few inches below ground level. It took just a day or so of exploration to find suitable soft ground, though the intended depth of forty feet proved impossible to achieve. Though bamboo walls and an attap roof was fitted to the latrine, these only held back the 'loathsome bloated' flies for twenty-four hours.

At first rations were received by truck from Tarsao until the monsoon made that impossible when rations had to be manhandled from the river. On some occasions, parties had to be sent to Tarsao to carry supplies back to the camp on foot.

There were instances at Tonchan South of Allied officers being forced to act as servants to IJA personnel. The presumption must be that this was to humiliate the captured officers.

Almost as soon as Tonchan South had been established, native work camps quickly sprung up around the POW camp. By June 1943, the prisoners were surrounded by Tamil, Chinese, Malay and Indian camps. Altogether there were some 3,000 POWs and 2,000 Asiatic workers in an area of less than half a square mile. The native areas were so severely congested that not even the most basic hygiene measures could be undertaken. The Tamil camp was upstream of the POW camp and when cholera struck the native camp, the disease was carried downstream. Tonchan South became known as the 'cholera camp'. This was in spite of strict measures ordered by Stanley Pavillard, who had moved with D Battalion from Wampo. As soon as the very first case was diagnosed on 10 June, Pavillard set up an isolation area with the only tent that was available, old and leaky that it was.

Outside work was halted for two days and when it was resumed some of the sick were allowed to stay in camp to carry out cremations and for grave digging. Unsurprisingly, few wanted to report themselves as sick. But these jobs had to be performed by someone, so this duty was allocated to fit and light sick alike on a rota basis – everyone had to take a turn.

Pavillard immediately insisted that only boiled water should be used for drinking and brushing teeth and that all eating and cooking utensils should be dipped in boiling water before use. Bathing in the river was prohibited and any food touched by flies or ants had to be thrown away – a measure which must have caused anguish among the hungry prisoners and was impossible to enforce. The men were also warned not to lick paper when they rolled up their cigarettes. Despite these measures, by the first night ten men had been diagnosed with cholera, some of whom had already died. The cholera compound quickly became 'hellish in every way', Stanley Pavillard recalled. 'and from the compound there rose continually … a faint desperate moaning which was terrible to hear punctuated at intervals by appalling shrieks.'[200]

Pavillard asked the Japanese camp commander for more tents, plus larger parties being permitted for clearing the jungle for graves and for the actual grave digging. All his requests were refused, the camp commander merely saying that nothing could be done, and the men must be allowed to die. Pavillard had to take tents from the working POWs leaving them to sleep out in the open, and the grave digging parties had to be composed of officers and other sick patients. The men were soon dying in such large numbers, the burial pits were dug just thirty feet from the tents as there simply was not enough men to clear the jungle.

As a consequence, the disease struck with frightening severity in the summer of 1943. Not only were the native work camps situated 'cheek by jowl' with those of the 'H' Force, the prisoners also worked side by side and on the same jobs as the Asiatics. They even had to walk through their camps along 'faeces-splattered' paths, and the ground, the vegetation and the tools they had to share with the *rŏmusha* were all covered and contaminated with excrement. The Tamils also used the stream which supplied the POW camp as a latrine. This was reported to Sergeant-Major Hiromatz, the senior Japanese at Tonchan South, but he did nothing to stop this practice. Indeed, Hiromatz showed no sympathy for the sick and at one point he went into a hospital latrine and brutally assaulted the dysentery and cholera patients he found there.[201]

Many of the *rŏmusha* fled into the jungle, but they could not escape the disease and the POW working parties were constantly finding and burying the bodies on their journeys to and from their workstations. To make matters even worse the Japanese moved the *rŏmusha* cholera tent next to that of the POWs. 'They had no doctors or orderlies and were allowed neither food nor water,' wrote Pavillard, 'Their cries for water were pitiful to hear.' Nevertheless, Pavillard's orderlies managed to pass some food and water to them.

The Japanese were so terrified of the disease, they would not go anywhere near the *rŏmusha* cholera area and suspected cases from the *rŏmusha* camps were just dropped in the prisoner of war cholera camp where they were left on the ground to die. In some cases, where the Tamils were not quite dead, they were killed by the Japanese or were ordered to be buried alive.

The disease took a grip on its victims with shocking rapidity. The cholera cases who were stricken while at work were merely placed to one side and carried back to camp at the end of the day over undulating, slippery, muddy paths through the jungle, often for distances of up to two miles, by their exhausted comrades.

---

200. Pavillard, p.136.
201. TNA, WO 235/936.

Appeals to prevent the spread of the disease by stopping the movement of men from the camps to the work sites during the epidemic, where they would be handling the same tools used by the natives, were ignored. By 25 June, only 50 per cent of the prisoners were capable of heavy work.

At first the prisoners burned the bodies of those that had died but such was the death rate the bodies began to pile up and so they had to be buried in a mass grave. For this a huge pit was dug which was 18 feet long, 8 feet wide and 20 feet deep. During the period when cholera was at its height the Tamil and Chinese workers at the camp were dying at a rate of around forty to fifty a week.

Eventually, parties of officers were forced to clear the surrounding native encampments of dead and dying *rŏmusha*. They burnt and buried the dead natives and built new camps for the survivors. Officers were also employed in bringing supplies to the camp when the monsoon put a stop to road transport. They walked to Tarsao from where they carried back bags of rice and vegetables.

Lance Corporal Ian Denys Peek, a member of the Singapore Volunteers, saw British Other Ranks at Tonchan South in June 1943 during the height of the monsoon, with 'sunken eyes, tight skin over shrunken bodies and stringy muscles ... some have the muck of dysentery and raddled bowels trickling down their legs, washed away by the pouring rain. They don't pay any heed to it. It has been their condition for so long, they are past caring and can't stop it anyway. And they have nothing to wipe the mess away – not a bit of rag or anything else.'[202]

As well as stealing a portion of the food allocated to the prisoners (particularly peanuts and sugar) at one point, not only were the sick driven out to work, but the Korean guards also made the cooks leave the camp to make up the numbers required for the work parties. After what Private C.F. Taylor described as 'a great deal of trouble' the Koreans were 'made to see a little sense and eventually returned [the] P.W. cooks to cookhouse'.[203]

The Thai trader, Boon Pong, also helped the prisoners at Tonchan South, particularly with regards to the supply of drugs. He also took reports on the conditions being experienced by the POWs written by Pavillard to the Swiss consul in Bangkok via a Mr Tannar, a Swiss gentleman who worked in Bangkok. As a result, Pavillard received drugs through the Tannar-Boon Pong link, helping to save the lives of many at Tonchan South.

As in some other camps, the first Tuesday in November meant Melbourne Cup day. For this, it was those who had lost a limb who lined up at the start. Every runner had three legs – two of bamboo crutches and one of their own. Betting was heavy, but the runners collapsed together in a heap over the finish

---

202. Peek, p.147.
203. TNA, WO 235/918.

line and no clear winner could be declared, which, happily, meant there were no losers.[204]

Conditions at Tonchan South only began to improve after Colonel Humphries managed to persuade Lieutenant Sanjionchi, the IJA Guard Commander, to inspect the camp. Sanjionchi was clearly concerned with what he saw as improvements were put in hand almost immediately.

When work finished at Tonchan South this terrible camp was not merely abandoned, it was actually dismantled.

Tonchan Central   139 Kilo

Stuart Young was one of the early arrivals at Tonchan, as part of C Work Battalion. 'The camp was situated at the top of a slope.' He later wrote, 'at the bottom of which flowed the northwest tributary of the Mekong. The slope was very steep and approximately 200 feet high from the river. Cookhouses were built on the banks of the river to be near our only source of water.' When they arrived, the men of C Battalion had to clamber down a rocky precipice to a small clearing perched on a ledge above the river. There was just one hut to accommodate the 600 men of the battalion. The camp was, without exaggeration, knee-deep in mud and the latrine was a bamboo platform built over the cliff directly above the cookhouse. That cookhouse was, as Young wrote, in a clearing on the river's edge, and there, in holes scraped in the bank, were installed four 12-gallon cast metal boilers. The rain was torrential at that time and the task of preparing the food was 'overwhelming'.[205]

After they had completed building the huts for themselves, the prisoners were set to work to build six kilometres of road to the north and the south of the camp. After they had done this, they were ordered to clear a path 50 metres wide through the jungle for the railway.

Meals were carried up the steep slope from the cookhouse by relays of men cursing under the weight of six-gallon 'dixies', as they slithered on mud and stumbled over tree roots. The food was always cold on arrival at the camp.[206]

As well as building huts for the other work battalions – H and K – which were to follow, Stuart and his fellow prisoners had to build accommodation for the Japanese who were still living in tents: 'This hut, overlooking the entire camp area from an eminence nearby, turned out to be a magnificent structure of several rooms, the whole supported on stilts and having an imposing flight of steps leading up to the main doorway. A separate cookhouse was added and,

---
204. Peek, p.334.
205. AWM, 54 554/2/1C.
206. Dunford, p.46.

some weeks later, a stream was diverted through the Japanese lines, by means of improvised bamboo pipes, to provide showers and baths.'[207]

Sergeant H. Jones was in No. 12 Battalion, which arrived at Tonchan on 12 November 1942. As the Japanese had not permitted the prisoners to build accommodation for all the new arrivals, there were still only two huts for the prisoners which were, of course, already occupied and the new arrivals had to sleep on the ground. The Japanese never allowed prisoners enough time to build enough huts to accommodate the men and the camp remained an overcrowded swamp.

With the camp's original strength of 1,647 rising to 2,700 all crammed into such a small area, with its collapsing huts, ragged tents and flimsy bivouacs, the place soon became virtually uninhabitable. Inevitably, beriberi, malaria, cholera and dysentery spread throughout the congested camp, resulting in a death rate of around 25 per cent. A 'decent' cemetery was created for the prisoners who died, which had a 15-foot-high cross at its entrance.

On 24 November No.11 Battalion arrived at Tonchan, the entire camp being placed under the command of Lieutenant Colonel Clark, with Staff Sergeant 'Tiger' Hiramatsu (he acquired his nickname partly through his fearsome appearance and partly due to 'the bestial roaring noises' he made when enforcing his will) as the Japanese camp commandant with twenty-three Korean guards. Hiramatsu told the POWs they had to salute him and the Koreans and, any man that didn't, would be beaten up – and many were.

In January 1943, pay was increased to the following: privates 25 cents per day, corporals and sergeants 30 cents per day and warrant officer 35 cents per day, with each man in the camp contributing 10 per cent of his pay to buy food for the hospital.

It was in the last week of this month all work on the railway ceased owing to the Japanese surveyors having made miscalculations which would cause the ends of the railway working towards each other to miss by about 1 kilometre. This meant a cutting had to be made through solid rock to make the two ends of the track line up and the consequence of this was more punishing work for the prisoners and more deaths. It would become known as Hellfire Pass.

The prisoners also took whatever opportunities presented themselves for delaying or sabotaging the construction of the railway. This included, when unobserved, prisoners putting huge tree logs under the earth where the track was to be laid. These, it was hoped, would quickly be eaten away by the jungle's insects and the track would sink.[208]

---

207. Young, p.55.
208. TNA, WO 203/5823.

As regards food, breakfast consisted of one pint of rice with the luxury of a spoonful of sugar every third day. Other meals included pumpkin stew and in February 1943 the men received their first issue of meat. According to John Durnford, the meat arrived in the form of black pigs brought upriver on Thai barges in wicker crates. The meat was made into a 'greasy pink broth in which small chunks of meat appeared almost fortuitously'. The Japanese took the body of any animal they wanted for themselves and gave the prisoners the head. The animals were slaughtered and dressed by the POW butchers who removed the head as far down the neck as they could. It was said that it was not unknown for the 'head' to have kidneys attached – such evidence quickly disappearing.[209]

The other source of nutrition came from throwing hand grenades into the river to kill fish. On one occasion this resulted in the capture of an approximately ten-foot-long dogfish. In another incident, an enormous snake, twice the length of the dogfish, was spotted swimming across the river and was despatched with a felling axe when it reached the bank.[210]

There was some resentment against the easy life of the officers in the camp. There was around thirty of them who spent their days leisurely playing cards and other indoor games. 'Tiger' Hiramatsu hated seeing this and eventually most officers were forced to work. As noted at Chungkai, they were given the worst and dirtiest jobs, and the Korean guards would beat the officers in front of their men on the slightest pretext.

The pressure of the 'speedo' period proved too much for the 'Tiger' who had a 'nervous collapse'. He was replaced at first by a Lieutenant Hattori and then by Lieutenant Tanaka who arrived at Tonchan in March 1943. Tanaka's first act was to order all the prisoners onto parade. He informed the POWs that they must let the sick die so that their rations could be given to the fit men. When the monsoon broke in June 1943, no man was permitted to remain in hospital unless they were 'completely finished' the other sick men were carried to work by their comrades. If men collapsed from malaria and dysentery while at work, they were beaten to make them get up. Of course, this rarely succeeded and the men were just left on the ground where they fell until work finished for the day when they could be carried back to camp. That same month, generators were brought in by the Japanese to provide electric lighting so that the prisoners could work all night.

Theft from those that died in the hospital was a feature at Tonchan, as in other camps. One of the worse culprits turned out to be a hospital orderly.

---

209. Newton and McGuinness, p.610.
210. Durnford, p.47.

When he died, the jewellery and watches he had stolen from the very men he had looked after were found in his pack.

Jack Holland, Doug Newton and Charlie Hewitt were at Tonchan camp, as one of them recalled: 'My friend and I whilst working near the river, had noticed that the Japanese in their cookhouse, which overlooked the river, would throw waste food down into the water, which would then be carried away by the current. This seemed to offer some way of obtaining an addition to our diet. Charlie suggested that if we left the camp during the hours of darkness, made our way to the river below the Jap cookhouse, we could collect most of the rubbish being discarded.

'The thought of being caught out of the camp at night was a sobering deterrent. The brutality of the Japanese and, in particular, the Korean guards towards European prisoners, was well known to us, but we were slowly dying of starvation, and the risk seemed worthwhile. The first attempt was very successful. We made our way down to the river under the cover of darkness and settled down in the water up to our necks. We could hear the Nip cooks laughing and joking, as they threw their rubbish into the river. Our collection was increasing, cabbage leaves, bits of pork fat and skin, chicken heads and feet, fish heads and tails, to us a veritable banquet was spread before us. We carried as much of our spoils as we could back to the camp, quite a hard task, as the bank was very steep, and we were in poor physical condition. The next problem was how to cook our capture? After some hard bargaining with a POW who owned a petrol tin, (the ultimate POW luxury), we made a very acceptable stew.'[211]

A group of half-a-dozen officers at Tonchan formed an 'escape committee'. With what information the officers had, they concluded that the only way for them to escape would be to trek through the jungle to the ports on the Andaman Sea where they hoped to bribe a local Thai to take them to safety. One day John Durnford undertook a solo reconnaissance to gauge the practicality of their plan. He sneaked out of camp and climbed 1,000 feet to the top of a hill behind the railway clearing. He saw in every direction endless jungle-clad, rock-tipped, mountains. He knew then that the terrain held the prisoners captive more effectively than any barbed-wire fence or machine-gun post ever could.

A post-war report on the treatment of the prisoners noted the following: 'In about June 43, when many P.O.W. were dead and few available for work, thousands of Malay, Tamil, Chinese and Siamese coolies were brought into the area and lived and worked side by side with P.O.W. The proximity of these men

---

211. *Tonchan POW Camp, Thailand* by Lancshomeguard on BBC People's War, Article ID: A4091230.

facilitated the spread of disease and plague and cholera, and epidemics killed hundreds of P.O.W. and natives in thousands.'[212]

The Japanese were terribly afraid of cholera. Work on the railway stopped for a week when the disease first struck and the Japanese built a small stockade around their own quarters into which nobody was allowed unless he was first 'covered' with disinfectant. When work resumed it was carried on at the usual pace, with the men working up to fourteen hours a day.

After a period at Tonchan South Sergeant Jones returned to Tonchan central in July 1943 and found it in a 'hopeless' condition: 'The bamboo sleeping platforms were alive with bugs and lice, and men were now going down with typhus fever.' Conditions were so bad, at the end of July, the Japanese allowed the huts to be rebuilt.

One day, a POW was struck by a guard. The prisoner hit back and ran towards the river, where he was caught and held by five Koreans while a fifth bayonetted him in the stomach. He was dragged back to the guard room where, still alive, his hands were tied to his feet. He was kept outside the guard room for five days without food or water then he was taken away by lorry and never seen again.[213]

After the completion of the line in October 1943, the prisoners continued to undertake maintenance of the track and the road. One day, as the men were cutting back foliage to keep the road clear, two Japanese engineers sawed down a large tree which fell among the working prisoners, hitting one man, Tommy Warfield of 2/20 Battalion A.I.F. on his head. His skull was fractured, and he died two days later. Remarkably, the Japanese commander decreed that Warfield had died while serving with the Imperial Japanese Army and not as a POW. As a result, he received a full IJA funeral with a coffin and pall bearers and even a military salute from ten Japanese soldiers firing two volleys over the grave.[214]

Tonchan Spring   140 Kilo

The men of 'H' Force arrived at Tonchan Spring (No.4 Camp) on 18 May 1943, with more arriving the following day. As was the case in many camps. The prisoners were given just one day to build their bivouacs before being ordered out to work on the railway.

Tonchan Spring camp was some 500 yards off the main jungle track and had acquired its name because of its proximity to a spring which provided the water supply for the camp. Large land crabs were to be found there. The camp consisted of thirty tents of varying sizes. In addition to the 468 Dutch prisoners here,

---

212. AWM, 54 554/2/1C.
213. TNA, WO 325/157.
214. Newton and McGuinness, p.611.

an attached party of British, commanded by Captain T. Bouch of the Suffolk Regiment was also present, bringing the total up to 567. The accommodation was totally inadequate for these numbers, and the prisoners had to erect shelters with leaves as roofing. There was also a problem with the latrines. The ground was very rocky, and the latrines could not be dug to the usual depth.

The camp was run for the Japanese by a senior Korean guard whose conduct in hitting prisoners prompted Commander J.C. Cornelis of the Royal Netherlands Navy to approach Lieutenant Shingyochi, who managed to put a stop to this.

The prisoners were employed on bridge building, creating cuttings and embankments and, later, metalling of the railway. Though the workstations were initially close to the camp, eventually, this work took the men three to four miles away from the camp, which distance they had to walk each day before beginning their labours. The men worked every day without a break until the middle of July 1943, when they were granted their first half-day rest.

The health of the prisoners deteriorated very rapidly, the men being struck down with dysentery. After just one month there were already 300 cases but the men were still made to work. Malaria was also a problem, but the prisoners were very fortunate in that cholera missed Tonchan Spring altogether. This was despite the frequent sight of dead Tamil workers from the corresponding *rŏmusha* camp which succumbed to the disease and, as at other places, were just left to die where they fell.

Supplies to the camp were initially received by truck until road conditions made this impossible when the monsoon struck. Rations then had to be carried from the river by fatigue parties and this continued until the end of the work at Tonchan. The local knowledge of the Dutch Eurasians in seeking out edible plants in the jungle, as in other camps, proved immensely valuable. Two particular high points were remarked on in the official report on Tonchan Spring. The first of these was the purchase of eggs with camp funds (which the men contributed towards) for the first time on 21 May and, almost a month later on 22 June the prisoners were able to buy a water buffalo.

Another event of note was the escape by one of the Dutch prisoners in the second half of August. He was never heard of again.

At the end of August Camp No.5 joined Camp No.4 and then on 8 September a party of twenty Dutch prisoners were despatched to Kanburi to help with the building of the base hospital there. The remainder of the men followed on 23 September.

Tampi South   143 Kilo

This camp was situated in the heart of the jungle, with a total of 397 prisoners. It was a tented camp of thirteen very poor tents. Ankle-deep mud, of a 'custardy' nature was a feature of Tampi South from the outset and the creation of any form of drainage proved virtually impossible. The men here had to walk 1.5 miles to their work place each day, where they had to cut their way through hard and rocky terrain, and a good deal of the labour was the 'sledge and wedge' kind.[215]

Captain Jeffery English with H4 party of 'H' Force arrived there in May 1943 and saw it for the first time: 'Set in a minute clearing, with a tall bamboo stockade which rather pointlessly only ran around two sides, it was no more than about 50 yards across and maybe 100 yards deep. A swampy little "square" of churned-up mud occupied the foreground, a number of tents and two extremely home-made attap huts lined the periphery, while just by the gate, on the left of the square, an open-sided, smoke-wreathed cookhouse crouched in dismal squalor beneath a rough matting shelter.'[216]

As for English and his party there was no room in the existing camp and they had to create their own camp. They were shown a rough area of virgin jungle where the space allocated to them was marked on a tree with a chalk cross. From that point they were to clear the ground on the same rectangular basis as the existing camp – 50 yards by 100 yards. This was where they erected their old Indian Army tents. By using flysheets as well as the tents – which were meant to accommodate eight men – there was enough for one to every forty men. To fit all these men into each would have meant just seven inches of space. So a rota system was introduced. Half of the forty allocated to each tent or flysheet slept under cover, while the other twenty slept outside. The following night they exchanged places. The prisoners fitted out the tents with bamboo floorboards. Two of the better tents were given over to the medical staff as the hospital. Three 'sumps' were dug next to the small steam which supplied the camp with water. One was for the cookhouse, one for clothes washing, and the third was used as a communal bath. After just two days it was considered that the prisoners had been given sufficient time to build their camp and the first parties set out to their work stations.[217]

The Japanese allowed the POWs twenty men to run the camp. This included the doctors, medical orderlies, the cooks and two men to collect wood for the cookhouse fire.

---

215. TNA, WO 325/17.
216. English, pp.110-1.
217. English. p.117.

The work was on the Kanu cutting – Hellfire Pass – where the prisoners were supervised by particularly aggressive and vindictive Japanese corporal and seven privates. If they considered any prisoner was slacking, even to pause momentarily to wipe sweat from his eyes, they would beat the man around the head or his body or his legs with a bamboo stick.

If they though a POW was deliberately disobeying instruction – though, of course, it was usually the case of mis-interpreting the Japanese orders – a more severe beating followed, often by more than one guard, the punishment only ending when the attackers became exhausted. One of the corporal's frequent punishments was to make the unfortunate victim stand on the edge of the ravine and hold two 12-pounder hammers out at arms' length. While he was stood precariously on the brink the Japanese would kick him on the legs or in the groin. One day, a prisoner suffering such treatment, realising he was about to topple over the edge, grabbed the shirt of one of the Japanese and together they fell to their deaths. Not only did the Japanese lose a worker and one of their own, more importantly, they also lost two precious sledgehammers. This put an end to the practice.[218]

The 'speedo' period saw the prisoners working until 21.30 hours or later, the men trailing the two miles back to camp in the dark, arriving as late as midnight. It was easy for the prisoners to get lost on the jungle path in the dark, the men only reaching camp the following morning. If such individuals were lucky they would be in time for breakfast, if not they had to rejoin the working parties marching back to their work stations for the day.

The incidence of sickness was high from the beginning and by June 1943 sickness, injuries inflicted upon the men by the Japanese and exhaustion had reduced the strength of working shifts at Tampi South from 200 to 150 men, and on the 16th of that month the first cholera disease was reported. That same day, 266 British prisoners arrived. Within nine days seventy-two men had died from cholera, and by the end of June only 120 men were capable of work. This meant there were not enough men fit to maintain the camp which had become overrun by lice and rats.

Nobody escaped illness. The area was infested with malarial mosquitos and everyone, at one time or another, suffered from malaria in one or more of its forms, sometimes men being doubly infected. Diarrhoea and dysentery abounded.

After a visit to Tampi among other 'H' Force camps, in the middle of July 1943, Colonel Humphries wrote: 'I thus gained first hand knowledge of the terrible condition under which the personnel of my party were working. It was indeed tragic to see the state to which, what had been a fairly healthy body

---

218. English, pp.121-2.

of men, had been reduced.' He did, nevertheless, see 'a dogged determination to win through … even though their faces were emaciated and drawn'. By 22 August 1943, Tampi South, had been the scene of 217 deaths, and 100 'fit' men were moved north to Konkoita for further railway work.[219]

Tampi 148 Kilo
Also known as Tampii or Tampie

Tampi was the Headquarters IJA Malay Prisoner of War Administration led by Captain Hachisuka. There were two camps in the Tampi area, some seven kilometres apart. Of these, Tampi was occupied by 'H' Force and it became its headquarters camp, and Tampi South occupied by 'D' Force. 'H' Force consisted of 3270 British, Dutch, American and Australian prisoners under the command of Lieutenant Colonel Humphries with Lieutenant Colonel Oakes as second in command.

Initially at Tampi, in addition to the semi-permanent buildings which comprised the IJA Headquarters office, sleeping and eating accommodation, there were four tents, one of which was divided into two with one half being for Force headquarters and the other half for sleeping and eating. One tent was used as a sick bay for the POWs. the other two were for sleeping and living accommodation for officers of the staff and the other ranks who made up the establishment. There was also a small attap structure which was used as a medical inspection room for the camp and as a distribution centre from which drugs etc., could be collected (when available) by representatives from the Tampi and Tampi South work camps.

The water supply at Tampi was from a stream which 'gushed' out from a hole about six feet high in the rocky hillside. It was plentiful and pure, but to be on the safe side all drinking water was boiled. It was the water supply which Captain Reg Newton said made Tampi the best camp he stayed in. He found it 'wonderful' to shower in the clean, fresh water that poured out of the rock. The water was also transported along a split bamboo channel straight into the cooks' kwalis.[220] Because of the fine water supply, Tampi was the base for a troop of Japanese cavalry.

Two slit-trench latrines were dug and, later, surface drainage channels were dug which improved ground conditions. Rations had to be carried from the river by the prisoners. This was a distance of some two miles, involving an exhausting climb out of the river valley up jungle paths.

---

219. routeyou.com/en-th/location/view/47448723/tampi-POW-camps.
220. Wright, p.63.

As might be expected being an IJA headquarters, discipline was very strictly enforced by the Japanese, with morning and evening roll calls, plus the prisoner cooking staff had to cook for the Japanese as well as the POWs.

Tampi gradually took on a semi-permanent status and part of the village of Tampi began 'springing up' on sites adjacent to the camp. On several occasions, Tampi had to host large parties of prisoners on their way to other camps. Though the POWs were not permitted to go out of the camp individually, they could go out without any restrictions if escorted by a Japanese soldier.

The food ration provided for 'H' Force was as bad as any on the railway. A small amount of rice with 'seaweed like' vegetable and water, was all that was on offer. With the heavy work and long hours, the prisoners had to endure, it was not long before the men in all 'H' Force camps, covering approximately twenty miles of jungle, were, according to one officer 'emaciated, glassy-eyed, bootless, practically clotheless [sic], fever and dysentery ridden, but still working! working! working!'[221]

As with Tampi South, one of the biggest problems was with malarial mosquitos, and while everyone was infected with malaria, cholera passed the camp by. Only five deaths were reported here – two Australian and three British.

A party was being transported to Tampi on 8 December 1944, when the train they were on was attacked by Allied bombers. 'We dismounted from the train,' explained Driver Thomas Litherland, 'and took certain sick patients off the train and removed them down the line away from the station for safety. The Japanese guards under a Korean attached to the Japanese engineers … forced us back to the train at the point of their rifles and we were kept there whilst the bombs were falling. The first bomb hit the engine and other bombs hit the train with the result that forty-three Prisoners of War were killed and about twelve were wounded.' Four of the guards were also killed.[222]

Konyu Camps 151 Kilo
Also known as Kannyu, Kanyu, or Kanu

There was a collection of camps in the area around Konyu and the job of the prisoners the camps held would be to excavate the notorious Hellfire Pass. The main camp was situated on a bamboo-covered plateau about three miles above the river. Konyu River camp, which was also known as Lower Konyu or Konyu III, was on the Khwae Noi below the escarpment on which Hellfire Pass was cut. There was also an Upper Konyu camp on the road just above Hellfire Pass. In

---

221. TNA, WO 325/17.
222. TNA, WO 235/918.

the other direction from Hellfire Pass, towards Tampi and Kanchanaburi, were yet more road camps, probably called Konyu I, Konyu Road or, again, Konyu II.[223]

When Kanu II and III were formed, Kanu I became principally a post where supplies were unloaded for work on the Hellfire Pass, and for the evacuation of the sick to hospitals down river. It was completely swamped as the river swelled during the monsoon.

Some of those new arrivals came by barge from Kanburi, with fifty-five prisoners per barge, plus crew and guard. The prisoners were crammed into a space measuring twelve feet by six. They were not allowed to leave the barges even though they stopped at night until they got to Tarsao where they were given a drink. The following day they were given a rice breakfast and put back on the barges. That was the only food they received in five days apart from two bananas a day. No drink was provided when they were on the barges, the prisoners having to drink from the river as they went along.[224]

The Australians of Dunlop Force (which consisted of two battalions, 'O' and 'P' each 450-strong and commanded respectively by Major H. G. Grenier and Major F. A. Woods) arrived at Konyu 3 on 25 January 1943 to find there was no shelter and precious little food. The men were exhausted from their terrible march and were scarcely capable of any meaningful work. The Japanese saw this and ordered them to rest until the next day. The following morning the prisoners were split into two groups. While one group continued clearing the jungle, killing venomous snakes and lizards in the process which they later roasted and ate, the second group began building the huts. The great bamboo which they cut down to make the huts, stretched as far as sixty feet into the air and were entwined with thick vines. Even after the base of the bamboo had been cut through, they remained upright, held in the grip of the vines until the prisoners shinned up the stem and hacked the vines clear.

The prisoners quickly formed temporary latrines, and cooking trenches were dug, while bamboo fences were erected upon which mosquito nets were spread. Due to the rocky nature of the ground, the latrines could only be dug to a depth of around six feet.

The prisoners were required to build five huts in total. After three days they were informed that the next day they would be required to start work on the railway and that they should finish the huts 'in their own time.'

Agreement was reached with the Japanese camp commander, Lieutenant Usuki (or Osuki) on the layout of the camp and the next day the building work began. The camp was to have nine large barracks for the men with a smaller one

---

223. Camps near Hellfire Pass, Anzac Portal.
224. TNA, WO 235/918.

for the officers. There was also to be a cookhouse, hospital and rations' store. Lieutenant Colonel 'Weary' Dunlop went with Usuki to the nearby British camp to see how their buildings had been constructed from local materials. When he got there, he was impressed with the latrines but was appalled at the condition of the men and the state of the camp. It was a glimpse into the future.

It was agreed that Dunlop's men would build nine barracks 50 metres by 6.5 metres that would be 3 metres high to the ridge pole. Each would accommodate 100 men. There was also to be an officers' hut of 13 metres by 6.5 metres, including 3 metres for an office. Beds were to be made of bamboo platforms 2.5 metres wide that ran the length of the barracks. There was also to be a hospital hut, 50 metres long, 8 metres wide and 4 metres high. Following the English camp's pattern, the kitchen was to be dug out of one block of solid earth, with rice bowls, or *kwalis* resting over them. The allowance was for twenty-two ovens per 1,000 men. Dunlop was told that 100 men could make two buildings a day.[225] It was also made clear by Usuki that: 'much work, much food, much pay; little work, little food, little pay', which meant that as sick numbers increased, food and pay – essential for buying more food – diminished. As mentioned earlier, it was standard practice in the camps for a proportion of each soldier's pay to be handed over for camp funds, in the case of Dunlop Force this amount was one third from both officers and other ranks, though this was later reduced to one-fifth following the increase in pay also previously mentioned. Canteen items were sold to the men at 10 per cent profit, with that money also going into camp funds.

Food was always going to be an issue with the influx into the region of thousands of workers and prisoners. Nevertheless. Japanese and Chinese civilian contractors were found who took goods up river to the Konyu area for sale to the camps' canteens. Such was the case, that in February 1943, eggs were made available in 'embarrassing' quantities, plus tea, coffee, sugar, small calves, peanut toffee, limes, pig fat and coconut oil were sometimes available.'[226]

When a concert was held on 20 February 1943, the senior officers enjoyed a dinner of asparagus, eggs, soup, meat stew and rice. This was followed by peanut toffee and cigars.[227] What was in short supply, though, were medicines, with the Japanese showing scant regard for the health of the prisoners. Dunlop described this as 'an everlasting appalling disgrace'.

With almost no resources, the prisoners had to be inventive. Fishhooks were made out of safety pins and sharpened bone and bamboo was used to

---

225. Dunlop, p.177.
226. Dunlop, p.194.
227. Dunlop, p.199.

make baskets and containers for food and water. On a rest day, or *yasumi*, the prisoners were able to make good use of their improvised gear to go fishing in the river and even to dive for giant clams. There was even an area where there were hot springs and the POWs cut a large square out of the river bank to create a warm baths.

During the monsoon the men had to walk the two miles to the Konyu cutting each day through deep, sticky mud. Those that still had boots tied string around them to prevent the soles being sucked off into the mud.

It was noticed that fights sometimes broke out among the guards, often over cigarettes. Fights also occurred among the prisoners, though discipline was usually well maintained with punishments being for the common good, such as extra tasks like chopping wood or carrying water. Even so, a 'lock-up' was built for those who committed more serious offences.

Ron Lun, who had claimed to be a Chinese cook on a rubber plantation to avoid being interned in a POW camp, did not get away with it. He was tortured in Konyu jail, eventually admitting that he was Australian soldier. He suffered five weeks solitary confinement and a whole series of shocking assaults. At night, his hands were chained behind his back as he laid on a stone floor with no bedding. He was slapped and kicked and hit with knotted ropes and sticks and was tied with his hands above his head and left hanging for half a day. He was also water-boarded.[228]

Though the dense jungle and the forbidding distant mountains made escape an impossible ambition, Dunlop never forgot he was a soldier and, before the monsoon began, he tried to start a bushfire in a bid to cause as much disruption to the building of the railway as he could. The trees which were dry and leafless but the undergrowth was still wet and green and his efforts were to no avail.

It was only a few weeks after Dunlop Force moved in that cases of primary malaria revealed themselves. The cause was found not far away from Konyu 3 where 'an abundance' of stagnant pools and water lying in the cut stumps of bamboo. There was found a small striped malarial mosquito *Anopheles minimus*. Other dangers were venomous snakes (cobras and kraits), pythons, scorpions, tarantulas, centipedes and even tigers.[229]

Despite inoculations against dysentery, cholera, plague and typhus, sickness rates rose, and the tents of the camp hospital were soon full. New, temporary structures 'jerry-built with no roof' were erected on uneven ground by the river.[230] Due to the appearance of cholera, in early March washing and bathing in the

---

228. Dunlop, pp.229-30.
229. Sue Ebury, *Weary, The Life of Sir Edward Dunlop of the Burma-Thailand Railway* (Viking, Harmondsworth, 1994), p.389.
230. Sue Ebury, p.393.

river was no longer permitted. New rules were brought in at the same time in which the Allied sections were to be numbered in Japanese as were bugle calls. On 12 March Dunlop Force began its enforced move to Hintok Mountain camp, the move being completed by the 17th.

One notable incident occurred at the beginning of April 1943. A sailor, somehow, had managed to keep his gramophone and forty-seven records. These he sold to a Thai man in the camp canteen. The Japanese frequently borrowed the gramophone and that same evening they asked if they could use it. When they were told it had been sold, the Japanese were furious. Both the sailor and the Thai were beaten up and the gramophone was confiscated by the Japanese.

Hugh Clarke was one of a batch of 600 men of 'F' Force which arrived at Konyu 3 on 25 April 1943. They 'halted in a small clearing in the jungle-covered plateau and were informed that this was our new camp – when we built it ... The job site was at the end of a 500 metre track under a canopy of towering bamboo and was to be a cutting through a great rocky spur. Far below, beyond a sea of bamboo, the river wound north like a silver ribbon.'[231]

With the addition of this new group, work on the cutting was extended around the clock, with the new arrivals forming the night shift. At night the cutting was illuminated by bamboo fires, some carbide lights and bamboo containers filled with diesel oil with hessian sacks. Two British prisoners were made responsible for keeping the containers filled with oil. They were beaten 'incessantly' by the Japanese. They were beaten for not refilling the containers quickly enough; they were beaten for moving a container to fill it; they were beaten for letting one burn down too low; they were beaten for falling down, being too slow; or just for being there.[232]

It was a similar story for the men moving the spoil. The excavated rock was piled onto wheeled skips, referred to as ore trucks, which the prisoners had to push along a narrow track that had been laid. These rails were out of alignment at certain points and with the prisoners being beaten to move as fast as they could, the skips would jump the tracks. This happened on every trip to the increasing anger of the Japanese who would beat the prisoners to go faster and them beat them for allowing the skip to fall of the line. Even though the prisoners argued that if work was halted for a short time to realign the track properly it would ultimately save a lot of time, they were told the work must not stop for any reason. The insane merry-go-round continued.

---

231. Hugh V. Clarke, *A Life For Every Sleeper: A Pictorial Record of the Burma-Thailand Railway* (Allan & Unwin, Sydney, 1986), p.22.
232. Newton and McGuinness, pp.602-3.

The Australians of T Battalion arrived at Konyu in April 1943. Almost as soon as they arrived, and while the prisoners were still trying to build their huts, half of their number were sent to work on Hellfire Pass. This was in two sections, one about 500 yards long by about twenty-five feet high, and the other about eighty yards long by eighty feet high. The cuttings were excavated by the 'hammer and tap' method. One man would hold a spike sharpened at one end against the rock face while his partner would hit the spike with an eight-pound sledgehammer. They had to repeat this process with increasingly longer drills until the hole was 60cm deep. Into the holes the Japanese engineers placed an explosive charge, as explained by Australian Hugh Clarke. 'The engineers would get six or seven of us out and give us a cigarette. We would light a cigarette each. With these we would have to light four or five fuses and then go for our lives up into the bush before the charges blew.'[233]

Often the weaken and exhausted men would miss the spike and hit the poor partner holding it causing severe injuries as did the flying splinters of rock. Crude hand drills were also used which spat out rock dust which covered the sweating workers, with larger splinters flying everywhere causing many injuries.

When the dynamite had blasted away the rock, the prisoners had to clear away the resultant spoil with shovels and bare hands, after breaking the rocks down to a manageable size with sledgehammers. Some of the larger pieces of rock were dumped in the riverbed to strengthen the base of the pylons of bridges, while the smaller pieces were used to form the base for the railway sleepers.

Apart from the few ore trucks, the stones had to be moved, as elsewhere, by rice sacks slung between bamboo poles, while others worked continually cutting down trees with two-handed saws and then cutting them into the required lengths. At first it would only take between eight and twelve men to haul the huge teal logs which were used as railway sleepers but, as the prisoners became weaker, twenty or thirty men were needed. Many of the weaker men simply could not bear the weight and their knees buckled under the strain.[234] After the track had been laid, further small pieces of rock were spread between the sleepers.

Elephants were introduced to carry containers of water for the hammer and tap teams but the Burmese drivers soon contracted cholera and died. The Japanese tried to take command of the elephants but the great beasts refused to cooperate. When one Japanese tried beating an elephant to make it obey, it picked the man up with his trunk and hit him against a tree.[235]

---

233. 'Of elephants and men' in McCormack and Nelson, p.40.
234. Lionel de Rosario, *Nippon Slaves* (Janus Publishing, 1995), pp.120-1.
235. McCormack and Nelson, p.40.

The men that Stanley Pavillard saw at Konyu No.3 camp, which he called resembled a big cattle pen when he was transferred there in June 1943, were virtually naked skeletons that were so weak they were almost incapable of any movement. They had been transferred from Konyu 1 and 2 camps and were due to be transported to a base hospital – though it is claimed their departure had been intentionally delayed and they had been half-starved by the Japanese in the hope that more might die.[236]

There was just one stream to provide the water needs of the men at Kanyu No.3 camp. The camp's cholera isolation compound was on the opposite side of the stream from the main part of the camp. The Japanese had not allowed a bridge to be built which meant that all those going to the compound tramped their muddy feet through the stream. The stream then continued into the camp. To make matters worse, the stream was used by elephants as a watering spot where they also defecated. 'Conditions in the Kayu [sic] area were truly appalling,' wrote Pavillard. 'At the river camp there were some 500 living skeletons barely capable of movement'. Deaths were at the rate of 100 per month.[237]

As in other camps there were those that feigned illness to avoid being forced to work on the railway. The problem with this was that if there were insufficient numbers available for work there was always the danger that the Japanese would drag men out of the hospital indiscriminately. It was essential for the doctors to identify the malingerers for the benefit of those who were really sick. Stanley Pavillard did this by insisting that those reporting with dysentery should bring a sample of their stools carried on, for example, a leaf. It was not long before the doctor became suspicious – the stools were beginning to look familiar. He discovered that there was indeed 'a brisk trade' in genuine dysentery stools!

Ian Denys Peek also arrived at Konyu in July 1943: 'The camp layout in front of us is the usual one: bamboo and attap huts on three sides of a parade area, with a Nip guardhouse on the side nearest to us, close to the lorry track. All of the huts have collapsed and small shrubs grow in the open spaces, so clearly it has been unoccupied for some time. And there is something we have not seen in any camp so far: a formal entrance to the parade ground, made of tree trunks put together somewhat in the style of a traditional Japanese gateway, by the guardhouse.'[238] Part of the camp was already occupied by fifty or sixty prisoners too ill to maintain the place which was in a dreadful condition.

The camp was by the river (considered essential for the supply of fresh water) and every morning when going to work on the railway the men had to climb

---

236. Pavillard, p.146.
237. TNA, WO 235/963.
238. Peek, p.195.

a steep cliff and then back again to the camp for lunch. This was repeated in the afternoon, the men having to return to the camp down the 'rain-slippery' slope in the dark. Such was the loss of working time with this arrangement, the Japanese eventually moved the camp to the top of the cliff where, inevitably, water was scarce. The Japanese also demanded more men for the working parties, with only the weakest left in the camp – there were not even any men left in the camp to bury the dead. The only result was more deaths among the prisoners. Then cholera struck and the death toll grew to such alarming proportions the upper camp had to be abandoned.[239]

As was the case in some of the other camps, there was resentment that many of the officers did very little, often leaving NCOs to lead the work parties. 'They were supposed to be a go-between for us with the Japs,' complained Jim Kerr of the 4th Anti-Tank Regiment, 'in order to get the men a rest or simply to look after us when they could.' Not many did.[240]

Most of the soldiers smoked and, as paper was scarce throughout the camps, an alternative was found in the form of banana leaves. Green banana leaves, when not used as toilet paper, would be laid out under the prisoners' beds or in rice sacks to dry out. They could then be cut and rolled with native tobacco the form cigarettes. That local tobacco was washed in the river, dried and then sweetened with brown sugar before being rolled into cigarettes.

The poor diet of the prisoners meant serious vitamin deficiency which led in some instances to temporary blindness. This condition was suffered by Private George McNab of the Gordon Highlanders. He knew that if he didn't work his rations would be reduced but he was able to avoid this thanks to a fellow highlander. Sergeant James Burnett worked with McNab on the hammer and tap excavation in the Pass. McNab held the spike in place while Burnett wielded the hammer. This continued until one day McNab's sight was suddenly restored.[241]

Charles Steel was at Kanu in May 1943 and remarked on how the Australians had built a system which carried water from a stream through bamboo pipes to all parts of the camp.

By June, as the Japanese strove to finish the line, the men were worked for eighteen hours a day. This continued for around six weeks. Sickness levels were alarming during this period. At Konyu Road, only sixty men were working out of the camp's 600 British prisoners. The officers, in particular, suffered greatly. This was because their hut was adjacent to an open latrine used by hospital

---

239. ibid, 198-9.
240. Wright, p.80.
241. Mitchell, p.124.

dysentery cases. Thirty-two died within the course of eleven days and six men were employed continually digging graves.[242]

E.S. Benford was with 'W' Battalion which was transported to Kanu on barges pulled by motorboats which struggled against the swiftly flowing currents of the Khwae Noi. At bends in the river where the water ran more rapidly, a rope would be tied to a tree and the prisoners would haul the barge against the rushing waters, being bashed into greater efforts by the Japanese as the men tugged and pulled. They arrived at Kanu covered in bruises and contusions.[243]

A hospital of three huts was formed at Kanu a short distance away from the main accommodation which were reached by crossing a log bridge over a fifteen-foot ravine. Lance Bombardier Benford volunteered to act as a medical orderly. He described his first night duty, with 'the flickering light from our log fire barely penetrating the dark interior of the long huts and the animal like noises that men in their death throes involuntary make.'[244]

Gordon Highlander, Alistair Urquhart at Kanu, wrote about the mental health issues with which many of the prisoners struggled. On occasion this manifested itself in uncontrollable violent behaviour. To protect fellow prisoners a 'lunatic asylum' bamboo cage was built with the agreement of the Japanese. It was six feet square with a bench for the patients to sit down on. They were given food and water but then largely ignored.[245]

With no rations being provided by the Japanese for those who did not work, the food supplied for the workers had to be spread every more thinly as the number in hospital grew. The total amount of food was calculated by the Japanese and handed to the prisoners' commanding officer who organised its distribution on, what it was hoped, a fair basis.

The latrines at Kanu were, at first 'revolting, vast open pits'. Later they were fitted with covers after weakened prisoners collapsed into them and drowned.[246]

There were only a few reported assaults here by guards, none of which were of a serious nature. One of these was when an officer was struck in the face with a stick by the guard called Harimoto. The reason for this was that he failed to salute the guard. The officer had very poor eyesight (his spectacles were knocked off and broken when he was hit) and he simply did not see the guard at a distance. His eyesight was so poor that Colonel Humphries demanded Harimoto should pay for the repair of the spectacles. Another instance of an

---

242. Edbury, p.421.
243. E.S. Benford, op cit.
244. ibid.
245. Urquhart, pp.157-8.
246. Urquhart, p.165.

officer being struck was when the camp commander, Major Spencer, failed to produce the number of men demanded for work.

The camp was abandoned after two months, though supplies for Kanu II and III camps continued to be unloaded there.

Kanu II ? Kilo

The 'D' Force Group 4 area was said to be the busiest and most congested along the entire length of the rail link. No.4 Group was under the command of Lieutenant Colonel Iichi. The terrain was mountainous and rugged, making excavation of cuttings through rock face and bridge building, extremely difficult. Kanu II was situated on top of a plateau above Kanu I and it was at the former where the men who would excavate the Hellfire Pass were held. Apart from the hospital, the Japanese headquarters and the guards' and store huts, the rest of the camp was under canvas. Another tented area was set up some 350 yards deeper into the jungle as a cholera isolation hospital.

Ronald Searle was with 'H' Force and his party had to wade through mud, often waist-deep, in the latter stages of its march from Ban Pong to Kanu: 'On immediate arrival, despite our condition, we were made to clear a jungle area and construct a camp. This was completed the following day and at once work commenced on the cutting [Hellfire Pass]. Blasting and clearing, blasting and clearing, in frantic forced shifts, from that moment until the railway completed, we were given no rest or quarter.

'Thrashings began immediately, and the deathroll set off … Cholera swept through the camp, hour after hour, day after day, thrashings and beating continued unmercifully, 12 – 16 hour shifts became the rule, a little food could be hurriedly eaten only when blasting began … Throughout the months in scorching sun and, more often, in stabbing monsoon rain, we dug away blast spoil and dragged great rocks to the cliff edge, tearing our flesh, straining our bellies, huddling under our remaining rags to get what protection we could against the bitter night of the mountains…

'Beatings continued with monotonous regularity. Scalps were split with blows from a shovel blade, heavy bamboo rods were a favourite weapon, as was the pick helve. Heads and shoulders were battered black and blue …

'Men with cholera falling, doubled up in agony, vomiting the dreaded green bile, were unmercifully clubbed with iron bolts in an effort to get them to rise. Any sign of exhaustion or weakness would bring a "beating up". If a club wasn't handy then sharp flints would be used to gouge the prisoner's arms. Legs swollen with beri-beri or eaten away with maggot infested ulcers would be kicked or struck. Japs would gather and laugh at this; it was their daily entertainment.'[247]

At the height of the cholera epidemic the cremation fires flared continuously at every camp along the line: 'They lighted the way out to work in the dark before dawn,' E.S. Benford; 'they guided us back through the dark wetness of the jungle long after dusk. And always, lying round them in stick-like bundles were the bodies that awaited cremation.'[248] The prisoners were not permitted to wash their faces or brush their teeth during the epidemic, receiving just one pint of boiled water a day for drinking.

During the 'speedo', a party of around sixty officers from Kanu II were sent to work on the pass. The senior officer was Captain Berniscondi whose first task each day was to collect a pile of rock splinters for the Japanese guards. These would be thrown at any of the officers not seen to be working hard enough. If that was not regarded as sufficient inducement to greater efforts, they would give Berniscondi a beating. These varied from four 'rattling' punches to the face to being hit with a bamboo stick or kicked. Berniscondi would receive up to fifteen beatings a day.[249]

One morning a group of twenty-four POWs was marched out to the nearby Tamil camp which was littered with the bodies of those who had died of cholera. The officers were ordered to dig pits into which they dropped the bodies while the fearful Japanese kept well away. Lance Bombardier Benford was one of that group who tried not to breathe in the 'sickening … ghastly stench from hundreds of … black wasted bodies, with their skeleton like limbs spread grotesquely at every angle … lying in a pool of grey liquid vomit and excreta'. After disposing of the bodies, the whole Tamil camp was burned down by the POWs.[250]

Gunner J. Blyth, 4th Australian Anti-Tank Regiment, and Gunner Horgan, stopped to talk to fellow prisoners on a convoy passing by the camp and were accused of trying to escape by a Korean guard. As punishment, the two men were forced to stand three feet in front of a roaring bamboo fire for approximately twenty minutes at bayonet point. Both men were badly burned, particularly Horgan, who was not wearing a shirt. Though evacuated Tarsao hospital, Horgan died approximately two weeks later.[251]

Alistair Urquhart described working on the pass: 'under the scorching Thai sun and without a shirt or hat for protection, or shade from the nearby jungle canopy, the work soon became exhausting. Minute after minute, hour after

---

247. TNA, WO 325/18.
248. Benford, op. cit.
249. Benford, op. cit.
250. ibid.
251. TNA, WO235/918.

hour, I wondered when the sun would drop and we could go back to camp … We were all in various stages of beriberi, pellagra, malaria, dengue fever and dysentery. A new illness had also started to ravage some unfortunate prisoners. Called tinea, it was nick- named 'rice balls' because the hideous swelling had the tormenting tendency to attack, crack and inflame the scrotum.'[252] Life was no easier for those who worked in the camp cookhouse. As cookhouse staff was always kept to minimum levels those men had to cut their own bamboo, carry their own water and carry all the rations from the railhead or the riverside, casualties among them were high throughout the camps, and at Kanu this reached 50 per cent. The food at Kanu II, Major George Schneid wrote, was 'frightful'.

Among the terrible stories of maltreatment of the prisoners is one that occurred at Kanu, as related by Lieutenant G. Mansfield of the Australian 8th Division Signals. One day, the party which he was responsible for arrived at the work site one man short. Mansfield was ordered to go back and find the missing man. He found a British soldier lying on the roadside suffering from dysentery and diarrhoea unable to walk any further. But Mansfield was able to raise him to his feet and helped him to reach the valley where his comrades were working, where the soldier collapsed and fell unconscious: 'whereupon, the I.J.A. guard rushed up and commenced to beat the inert body with a large bamboo rod. He also brutally pushed the rod into the mouth of the unconscious man, and prodded him about the private parts of the body …

'An hour later, the same I.J.A. guard dragged the still unconscious body down to the end of the trolley line and indicated to me that I was to place the man under the railway line and empty the next load over him.' Mansfield, of course, refused and he was beaten about the face: 'I was again ordered to dispose of the body and again refused, 'and this time I was struck on the head with a 4lb sledgehammer and a crowbar.'

The next trolly of spoil arrived and the Korean threw the unconscious body under the end of the track and tried to dump the contents onto the man, but he could not do it by himself. So, once again, he ordered Mansfield to help him. Again Mansfield refused, and again he was hit repeatedly by the guard for disobeying an order. 'The wretched man now regained partial consciousness,' continued Mansfield, 'and grasped the projecting rails, and attempted to raise himself. Immediately the guard saw this, he seized a shovel and struck the unfortunate man on the head with all the force he could muster. This completely knocked the man out again with the result he slid and rolled down the side, amongst the loose rubble and rock, a distance of about 150 feet into the valley

---

252. WW2today.com via pacificparatrooper.wordpress.com.

below.' Remarkably, the poor soldier did not die and was later taken to the camp hospital.[253]

Major George Graydon arrived at Kanu II camp on 27 April with a mixed force of 225 men. Initially, they were housed twenty-three at a time in eight-man tents. The entire area of the camp at this time was covered in ankle-deep mud.

On 30 June 1943, Colonel Humphries wrote from Kanu to the Commanding Officer of the Malay POW Administration: 'Every medical officer in the force has now sent a despairing note, and everyone has given the same independent report, namely that the men are starving to death, are mentally and physically worn out and 20 per cent of the force is suffering from beri-beri of advanced type indicating widespread inanition. A general collapse is inevitable unless the food improves at once and the sick are afforded proper medical care and attention.' The following day, Humphries then wrote to complain about the 'brutal assaults' on the prisoners working on the railway. No reply is to be found in the 'H' Force papers.

On one occasion at Kanu in September 1943, two Australians were caught stealing Japanese construction tools to exchange for food with local Thais. The Japanese shot the Thais dead and then tortured the Australians for several days, forcing them to stand naked in the sun. When the two prisoners could no longer stand, they were taken into the jungle where they were made to dig their own graves before they too were killed.[254]

Despite all this, the officers tried to maintain morale by organising camp concerts about twice a week. Men would sing songs, or recite poetry they remembered from school days, and others would tell jokes. 'Lucky' Johnny Sherwood regarded these events as 'life-savers', lifting the spirits of the prisoners, if only fleetingly.

When the completed line passed Kanu, the prisoners were made to cut trees into logs for the wood-burning engines. Once what was deemed a suitable pile of logs had been cut, the prisoners were transported to Tamuang.

Captain Richard Parker was the medical officer responsible for approximately 400 Australians and 270 British at Kanu III camp, from 23 April until the end of July 1943. The camp was situated on a flat area of ground which was turned into mud during the monsoon. The men were housed in leaking tents. Latrines could only be dug to a depth of around six feet due to solid rock being encountered at that depth. When cholera broke out, the Japanese did give Parker some vaccine.[255]

---

253. TNA, WO 325/17.
254. Sherwood and Doe, p.109.
255. TNA, WO 235/963.

Malay Hamlet 153 Kilo

Situated approximately 450 yards east of Hellfire Pass, Malay Hamlet was established by 'H' Force on 21 May 1943, with the arrival of 347 Australians and 114 British. The site was unprepared, and a small area was cleared during the afternoon and twenty tents erected. During the next two days the camp was enlarged, the tents floored with bamboo, latrines dug, and a cookhouse prepared. The men, though, were worn out by the long march to the camp and it was with difficulty that the officers persuaded them to help build the camp – even to the point of insubordination.

On the 24th a working party of 200 was demanded for the day shift and a further 200 for the night shift to work on Hellfire Pass. These were broken up into parties of fifty with an officer in charge of each. The Japanese allowed fifteen officers to administer the camp. Further arrivals saw camp numbers rise to some 500 Australians, 200 British and a few Americans.[256] It straddled the road to northern Thailand (now Highway 323) the ground sloping gently from right to left, the former being where the Japanese had their tent. On the left side were most of the POW tents and the cookhouse. It was only a few hundred metres from Konyu 3, where Australians from 'D' Force were based.

Alongside the road was a small stream, seepage from which made the left i.e., the POW side, damper and muddier. Altogether it consisted of about twenty 'half rotten, leaking tents, set up in a small clearing', with bamboo pathways connecting parts of the camp, but it was approximately four kilometres from the river, with the men having to carry the supplies from there on their backs.

Lieutenant Colonel Roland 'Roly' Oates was the camp's senior Allied commander: 'We had a heart breaking job building that camp,' Oakes recalled, 'but it was done at last and we found ourselves at the end of two days with 24 half rotten, leaking tents, set up in a small clearing amongst giant bamboos in the wilds of Siam ... Almost immediately the monsoon rains began, pouring down day after day, until the country became like a wet sponge. In our confined area, and on the track outside which carried the traffic, mud was often knee deep – filthy, oozing mud which stuck to everything like glue ... I doubt if any of us or our belongings were dry during the first month in that camp.'[257]

The latrine was some yards away at the end of a narrow, winding, muddy track through the jungle. It was an unrealistic distance for dysentery patients to reach in time during daylight hours and difficult for any of the prisoners to navigate at night. Many dysentery patients would not even attempt to reach the latrine during the dark, squatting on the ground near their tents.

---

256. 2nd4thmgb.com.au/camp/malay-hamlet.
257. R.F. Oakes, 'Work and be happy', AWM, MSS 1037, quoted on anzacportal.dva.gov.au.

The Japanese allowed fifteen men to remain in the camp, including officers responsible for pay and records, for the maintenance and issuing of tools, camp hygiene, the chaplain, a quartermaster, the dentist, Captain Winchester, and the interpreter, Lieutenant Austin. In addition, there were around forty cooks, sanitation and medical personnel.

Within a week of the establishment of the camp, the number of sick had risen to more than 200, and the decision was taken to build a hospital. Work began on a thirty-bed facility on 31 May, the place being built by the Colonel Oakes who, almost practically unaided, designed and collected the materials for the bamboo and attap huts.

According to Stuart Lloyd, the site of the camp 'was on a beautiful sloping hill with a stream running and gurgling some 20 yards away. It was surrounded by dense bamboo thickets while behind it towered sheer and majestic huge rugged, jungle covered limestone cliffs. A sight that even when things were at their worst always pleased me … the air when arrived was thick with the nauseating smell of burning bodies the day's batch of burning cholera victims.'[258] The first cholera case had been diagnosed on 16 June, but the facilities at the camp hospital, 'were meagre', the official 'H' Force report stated, 'the hospital itself simply consisted of those tents which housed the sick'. All ranks were inoculated, and an isolation ward was formed about 100 yards from the camp, but the disease continued to spread.

Lawrence Field of 242 Squadron RAF was at Malay Hamlet from May 1943: 'We had to get up at about 6 o'clock, collect breakfast from our own cookhouse and be ready for work at 7.30 a.m. There was no bedding provided and no washing facilities, except for a small stream which everyone had to use. This in time became infected and when eventually cholera broke out our medical officer forbade us to use the stream. It was a very bad wet season all the time we were there, and what little clothing we had was soon unserviceable. It was very cold at night and, as a result of this and shortage of food, all the men were ill, many suffered with beri-beri …

'At one period as many as sixteen men died in one day, as we hadn't got the labour, we had to cremate the bodies. When the Japanese stopped this because of the smell, we used to bury the dead men in one grave.'[259] These mass graves held as many as ten men each. Even though the blankets of the men who died of cholera were heavily fouled with excreta such was the shortage of blankets these were retained and reused, the corpses being carried naked to the cemetery. That cemetery was around 200 metres away from the camp.

---

258. Stuart Lloyd, *The Missing Years: A POW's Story from Changi to Hellfire Pass 1942–45* (Rosenberg Publishing, Dural, NSW, 2009), p.162.
259. TNA, WO 325/18.

One of the wagons presumed to have been used to carry the prisoners from Singapore to Bam Pong. This is now on display at Hellfire Pass.

The point at which the railway crossed the Thailand-Burma border, the Three Pagodas Pass.

The route of the railway can still be seen leading up to the border by the Three Pagods Pass.

A photo looking towards the Kwai Noi near Hellfire Pass which gives some indication of the nature of jungle in this area that had to be cleared by the PoWs before they could build their camps.

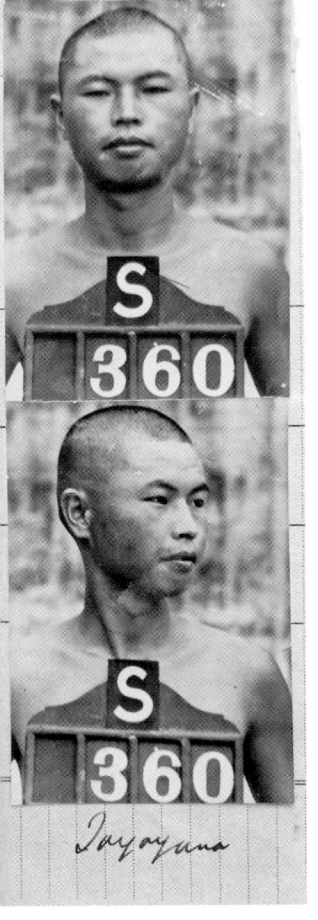

The Korean guard, Toyoyama Kise, who became notorious for beating prisoners with a golf club, photographed for the war crimes trials at which he was sentenced to death, though this was commuted to life imprisonment.

First Lieutenant Tsuneo Fukuda, the camp commander at Shimo Songkurai.

Hellfire Pass has been preserved as a memorial to those who worked and died on the cutting. As you can see some of the original rails are still in place.

Thakilen station on the part of the line still in use.

A portion of the old track can still be seen at Takunun.

Looking across at the ground where Shimo, or Lower, Sonkurai once stood.

Chungkai cutting was cut through solid rock in the same manner as Hellfire Pass. Nearby is Chungkai cemetery which holds the graves of 1,426 British and 313 Dutch servicemen.

The famous Wampo viaduct perched above the Kwai Noi is still in use, carrying both local passengers and tourists.

Base camp at Tamuang. (Australian War Memorial; PO1932.003)

Inside a hospital hut at Wampo. (Australian War Memorial; 157878)

Near the busy town of Kanchanaburi lies the most photographed bridge built along the railway. Often believed, though possibly erroneously, to be the one featured in Pierre Boulle's *The Bridge On The River Kwai*, it is not on the Kwai Noi at all but spans what was formally called the Mae Klong River, though is now known as the Khwae Yai. Also, unlike the film of the book, the bridge was not a wooden affair. It is a concrete and steel structure which is still in use today.

It is understood that it was across this section of the Songkalia River near Songkurai where the bridge was built which inspired the Pierre Boulle novel, not the more famous one near Kanchanaburi. The Songkalia is shown here in flood during the monsoon.

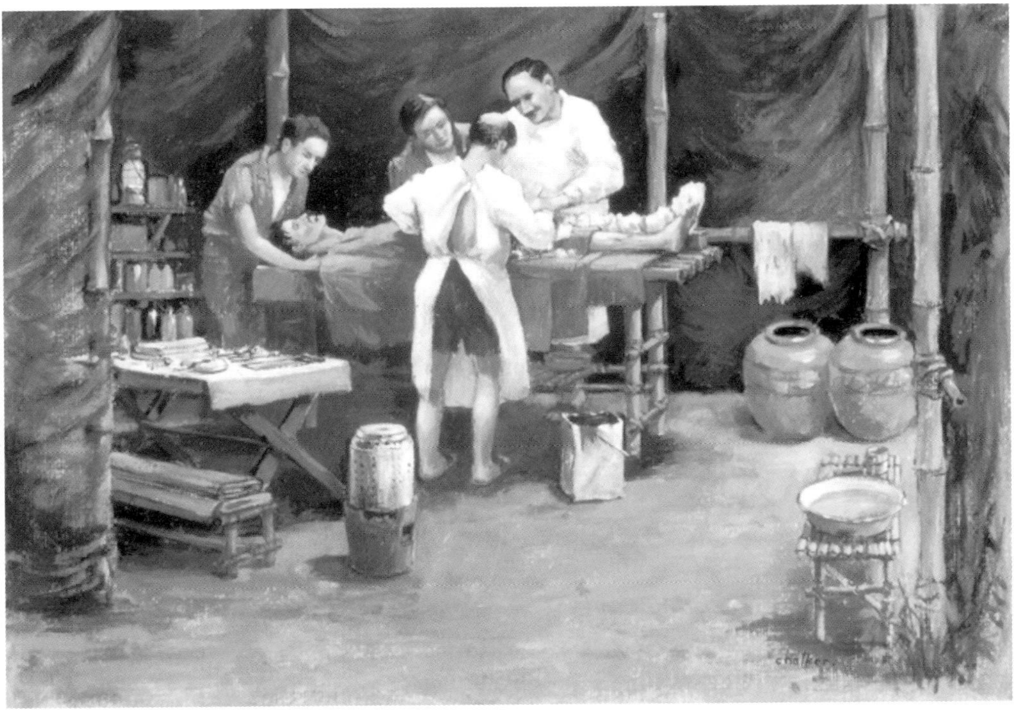

Colonel Edward 'Weary' Dunlop and Captain Jacob Markowitz working on a thigh operation, at Chungkai. (Australian War Memorial; ART91848)

The often-reproduced photograph of three 'fit' workers at Shimo Sonkurai No 1 Camp, standing outside the camp hospital. Left to right, it is believed these men are Bruce Pearce, Oscar Jackson, and Reuben Niles Pearce, all of the 2/30th Battalion A.I.F. Reuben Pearce is unable to fasten his shorts because his stomach is swollen with beri-beri. (AWM P02569.192)

At Kanchanaburi engines used on the railway have been preserved. This is one of the powerful coal-burning engines which used to pull the train up the mountainous stretch of the railway beyond Wang Po.

Australian and Dutch prisoners of war, suffering from beriberi, at Tarsau in 1943.

Most of the camps have disappeared, with little or nothing of them to be seen other than a patch on the ground. So it is with Brankassi/Prang Kasi.

A large area of where the 'F' Force camps were situated.

Wan Lan station is one of those still in use.

Old railway sleepers lay rotting at Wang Yen station at the 75 kilometre mark from Nong Pluduc.

Aerial view of Tamarkan PoW camp taken by 684 Squadron, Royal Air Force, on 2 January 1945. The layout of the camp can be seen adjacent to the bridge which still stands today. The bridge was repeatedly attacked by Allied bombers, the worst, as far as the prisoners were concerned, was on 29 November 1944. During this attack on an anti-aircraft battery, three bombs over-carried and demolished the top ends of PoW huts 1 and 2, burying a number of the occupants. (HMP)

One of the spikes used to cut through the rock at Hellfire Pass by the 'hammer and tap' method is still embedded in the stone.

'Cholera Hill', an isolation hospital for members of "F" Force suffering from the disease at Shimo Sonkurai No 1 Camp. To the right of the hospital tents is a make-shift operating table where amputations, treatment for tropical ulcers and autopsies were done. (Australian War Memorial; P02569.189)

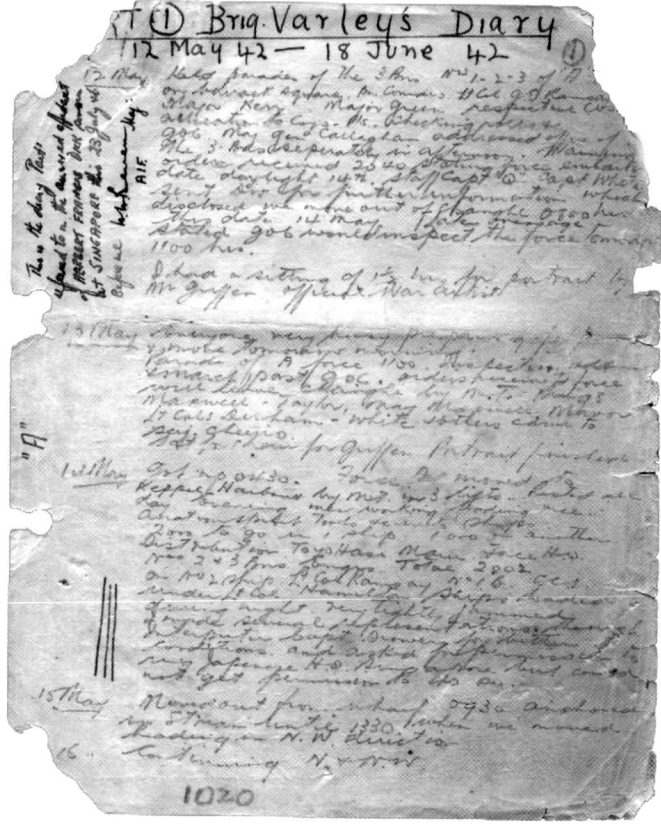

Brigadier Arthur Varley's diary which he managed to keep hidden from the Japanese and which has survived until the present day. (AWM 2019.22.89)

In June H4 party was moved to Malay Hamlet where the available workforce had been severely reduced by the cholera outbreak. The camp had been reorganised from its original layout to create distinct areas of medica concern. To the left of the 'fit' camp were the tents for the malaria and beriberi cases. Further left were the dysentery tents and then the most recently arranged area, the cholera tents. Access to the cholera area was across a trench filled with lime.

One day, Dick Austin, of 2/19 Battalion A.I.F., acting as a translator in the camp, told Colonel Oates that one of the POWs had sold his shirt to a native. With clothing being so scare, this was not permitted and the Japanese insisted that Oates would pick out the culprit and beat him up in front of the paraded prisoners. 'We got out of it after some sticky argument by assuring the Japas that the bad man was very wicked, but that he would not own up for fear of what they would do to him. If they left it to Col. Rowley he would soon confess and he would be fined 10/-'.[260]

The men worked on the Hellfire Pass in twelve-hour shifts from 08.00 to 20.00 hours when the night shift took over. The pass was around a mile away which meant that the working parties were paraded in camp at 07.00 hours each morning for the march along the muddy track to the cutting. The off-going shift arrived back in camp around 08.30. But this did not mean theses unfortunate night shift workers had the rest of the day to themselves. Five days a week the night shift workers were roused early to collect rations from the river, including the rations for the Japanese. This task lasted from around 13.30 hours until 17.00 or 18.00 hours. As the number of sick increased, so too did the burden placed on those fit enough to work and gather rations. This only led to more men falling ill in a truly vicious cycle which could only end when there were no longer any fit men left to work on the railway. This logic was, seemingly, lost on the Japanese, who drove the remaining workers on beyond their strength with beatings and punishments.

The workers on the night shift suffered the worst treatment, being lashed with knotted ropes or by split-ended bamboo sticks which snared the skin of the prisoners when it struck bare flesh. While it was standard practice of the Japanese to kick prisoners who had collapsed onto the ground to make sure they were not feigning, they would use their boots to grind the unconscious prisoner's face into the gravel just to be certain. One of the night shift guards, whose treatment of the prisoners was so appalling, the POWs made a point of finding out his name – it was Superior Private Kanaga. He was hanged for his crimes after the war.[261]

---

260. Newton and McGuinness, p.656.
261. English, pp.138-41.

Eventually, the officers at Malay Hamlet came to a chilling decision. As they were compelled to send even sick men to work to make up the required numbers, they naturally tried to keep the most severely ill men in hospital. But these were the ones most likely to die anyway. It made little sense to send out sick men who, as a result, were only going to become even more unwell. So, the officers reversed the policy. Those that stood the best chance of recovery were kept in hospital and the ones least likely to survive were sent to work, even though this was an almost certain death sentence.[262]

'Men taken from hospital were lined up with the others,' wrote Major A.E. Saggers, the second in command at Malay Hamlet. 'Many would break down and cry, others would vomit, while others would defecate from nervousness and/or illness. Others sat in the mud in the ranks, awaiting the order to move, pitifully conserving their strength. The faces of all appeared haggard and drawn and it was perfectly apparent that all were suffering from extreme exhaustion, lack of sleep and undernourishment.'[263]

By the first week of July 1943, more than 400 patients were in the hospital, 200 of whom were suffering from cholera. The maximum number of 'fit' men available for work was down to just 120 men per twenty-four hours (eighty during the day and forty at night). Just a week or so later total deaths had reached 134, of whom 118 were victims of cholera. A total of 111 Australians and 106 British POWs died at Malayan Hamlet.

Colonel Oakes also, again single-handed, felled and dressed two trees and from them constructed a 'beautiful and massive' cross as a memorial to those who had died at the camp which was erected at the cemetery. Colonel Humphries unveiled the memorial on 22 August 1943, the ceremony being attended by the IJA Adjutant from Administrative Headquarters of the IJA Malaya Prisoners of War Administration, Lieutenant Matsumoto. Carved into the crossbar were the words 'To our Australian and English comrades laid here to rest – amatos, eurum deus, aspicat'.[264] Work on the railway practically seized on that day, apart from maintenance of the camp.

Earlier, on 27 June 1943, Captain Pilkington returned to camp after having worked all night, to report to his commanding officer what had happened the previous evening: 'The Nippon guards started beating them up before they had even begun to work,' Pilkington said. 'and he had been beaten up for what reason he did not know with bamboo, a crowbar on the head, and his ears had been struck so hard that he feared both his ear drums had been broken.'[265]

---

262. English, pp.143-4.
263. Quoted in Rod Beattie, *The Death Railway, A Brief History of the Thailand-Burma Railway* (T.B.R.C, Kanchanaburi, 2015), p.114.
264. TNA, WO 325/17.
265. TNA, WO 325/17.

So many men had died and so many were incapable of any meaningful labour, the Japanese eased the burden on those still able to work by ending the two twelve-hour shifts, introducing instead three eight-hour shifts. Though this was an improvement, it came too late to make much difference as too many men had already died or been reduced by illness, semi-starvation and overwork into physical and mental wrecks.

One surprising boost at this time was the issuing of cooking tins to each man. This meant each prisoner could cook for themselves which was a 'tremendous' help, both 'morally and physically'. August also saw a marked improvement in the rations issued to the prisoners, with supplies being received by train. A large number of eggs were available, and Captain Smith set up a 'snack bar' where hundreds of eggs were beaten and cooked daily for the sick.

With the completion of the Hellfire Pass, the first evacuation of the sick to Kanburi took place on 8 September 1943. Eventually, just 100 fit men remained at Malay Hamlet. They stayed at Malay Hamlet until 10 December before being sent south, during which time conditions were 'very pleasant, good food, plenty of canteen supplies and good treatment by Nippon'. The Japanese also issued a large quantity of rubber boots, shorts and jackets to the prisoners.

Hintok Valley Camp 154 Kilo

Hintok Valley Camp – 'H' Force No.1 Camp – was situated on low-lying ground between Hintok Road Camp (Hin Tok or Hintoku) and the base of a limestone cliff. Major George Gaskell's party arrived here at 09.00 hours on 19 May 1943 after marching through the night and were told they had the rest of the day to prepare the camp. Part of the jungle had been cleared by a party of twenty-six men under Major H. Harrison who had arrived thirty-six hours earlier. Together, the two parties set to work clearing the rest of the ground, the digging of latrines, and the pitching of a few rotten 'tent flies' sufficient to cover less than half the number herded into them and pitched on sodden ground as the monsoon broke that very day.

The work required of the prisoners was extremely strenuous, being the building a high and long viaduct and the blasting and excavation of the deep cutting of the Hellfire Pass. At first the only food available was a very small quantity of watery rice and some boiled water.

Added to this was the fact that the camp was some three miles from the railway, which meant a long trek through difficult terrain for the working parties, with all the intendant risks of injury to the bare feet of the workers. Some were so exhausted after a day's forced labour that they were unable to make it back to the camp, and they simply slept, or died, in the jungle.

All the food for the camp had to be carried four miles from the river camp, the last half-a-mile being a climb over limestone rocks. In an effort to make the journey a little easier the POWs built a thirty-rung bamboo and rope ladder over the rock face of an escarpment to the south of the camp site, as Major Gaskell later recorded: 'The conditions of this camp were appalling. Men were sent to work before daylight and returned after dark without a single day's rest and were allowed no opportunity to dry, wash or mend their clothing, with the result that in a very short time many had only a piece of rag around their loins and went to work unshod. The journey to work was over a track deep with mud and necessitated climbing over a hill so precipitous that in one part ladders had to be scaled over the cliff face. The exhausted men had to use this track in the dark, often carrying their sick comrades on their back which, in the case of cholera, meant that those assisting were covered in the vomit and faeces of the sick.'[266] The sick who were ordered to make up the numbers of the working parties often had to be bound to bamboo stretchers and lowered by rope down the cliff face. At night this frightful operation was conducted by the light of a bamboo fire at the foot of the cliff.[267]

Hintok Valley camp was also a long way from the supply route of the Khwae Noi. During the monsoon, the road from Ban Pong became virtually impassable leaving only the river as a reliable supply route. The Japanese refused to provide trucks or release men from railway work, so supplies had to be carried from the river – often by officers as no other men were available – up the steep and rugged slopes.

The Japanese commandant, Lieutenant Hiroda, (sometimes referred to as Hirota) had insisted that the latrines should be placed about 200 yards from the camp but, as many of the men were suffering from dysentery and were bedridden, they could not reach the latrines. As a result, conditions soon became 'indescribable'. It became a daily feature of camp life for one or two officers to volunteer to clean up the faeces that were spread over the camp area. None of the patients themselves could help in this cleaning up process because if they were seen walking, they were immediately considered to be fit enough to be sent out to work.

Parties of prisoners were detailed to assist in the Japanese engineers' cookhouse, and these men returned daily with bruised faces and bodies from being hit with bamboo sticks or fists. In one instance, a Private Bird returned to camp with his jaw broken from being struck with a wooden sandal.[268]

---

266. TNA, WO 325/17.
267. Walker, *Australia in the War of 1939–1945*, p.618.
268. ibid.

On 8 June 1943, Hirota demanded an additional 100 men for the working party. Despite protests from Gaskell (who was beaten by two Japanese privates for daring to interfere) 100 seriously ill prisoners were forced to go to the railway cutting. 'All these men were driven by Japanese Engineer personnel armed with bamboos,' Gaskell later wrote, 'just as cattle are driven, towards the site of the work, 2½ miles distant.'

Many collapsed on the way but were beaten to their feet by the guards. Some, though, could not rise from the ground and they were left where they had fallen. They were collected and taken back to the camp only after work had finished that night. One of these men died that evening as did many others over the course of the following days.

Gaskell also saw many instances of prisoners forced by illness, exhaustion, fatigue, or collapse, to return from the working site, being seized upon by the guards immediately they crawled or staggered into camp. They were made to perform the 'most strenuous' tasks which could be found as punishment, such as chopping wood. They were not allowed to see a doctor and should any officer protest at this treatment, they too would be forced onto similar work.[269]

There were a number of recorded incidents at this camp, one of which was reported by J. Lucas of the 2nd Gurkhas who was attacked on the night of 16/17 July 1943, while working on a bridge. For no specified reason, he was assaulted by two Japanese engineers: 'Whilst one belaboured me with a bamboo causing numerous lacerations to my back, legs and chest, the other, who was on the bridge, kicked and stamped with his boots on my head.' Lucas stated that one of the Japanese then tried to shove a bamboo stick down his throat. Even though he was badly cut and bruised, he was made to continue working.

Cholera broke out at Hintok Valley camp on 19 June 1943, brought by new arrivals from Kinsaiyok. So virulent was the disease, one man in Charles Steel's battery was well at 21.00 hours and dead at 03.00, just six hours later.[270]

The sick patients were forcibly quarantined at 'Cholera Gulch' a 'dismal flooded area' a short distance away from the camp. Jeffery English saw the cholera tents which were 'frightful beyond description'. 'The blotched, stinking emaciated victims lay packed like sardines twenty or thirty to a tent, occasionally groaning or twitching into activity and crying feebly for orderlies with bedpans, but most of them lying quite still'.[271]

---

269. TNA, WO 325/17.
270. Best, p.83.
271. English, p.148.

During the height of the epidemic, Hiroda ordered that any man who collapsed with suspected cholera had to be left where he had fallen. No one was permitted to assist him in any way, nor was he to be taken to hospital.[272]

The outbreak was actually a relief for many as the Japanese were so fearful of the disease, they kept well away from the POW camp. Eventually, as with other camps, sickness and death from the many tropical illnesses the men contracted, compelled the Japanese to allow some of the sick to be evacuated by barge from the river camps to hospitals further downstream. Hintok Valley camp became known as 'Death Valley' and of the men 489 who started work there 144 died at the camp or after the evacuation to the base hospital in late July. Among those who died were the walking sick who were forced to make the four-mile journey to the river camp. Seventeen out of those 110 walking sick died within forty-eight hours of the move, and twenty-six other seriously ill men, who had to be carried in pouring rain, all died later.[273]

Hintok Mountain Camp   154 Kilo
Also known as Hintok Road Camp, Hintok Jungle Camp, and later named Hintok Camp No.5

Hintok Mountain Camp, also often referred to as Hintok Road Camp, Hintok Jungle Camp, and later named Hintok Camp No.5, was the northernmost camp in the vicinity of Hellfire Pass. It also served as a staging post for other groups of prisoners moving to camps further north.

Captain John Lawrence Hands arrived at Hintok with 'A' battalion (337 men) and approximately 600 Dutch troops. First of all, the prisoners had to burn an area of jungle to create space to erect the six small tents with which they had been provided. Each could only hold a maximum of fifteen men, the rest of the prisoners had to sleep outside on the ground with no shelter whatsoever. Only later were a further nine old and unserviceable tents provided. After only about a week, 200 of the Dutch prisoners had been struck with dysentery though there were no cases among the Australians.[274]

'Weary' Dunlop inspected the mountain camp on 12 February 1943. He found Dutch sanitation to be 'pretty grim'. He noticed that instead of the bottles with water which the men usually took with them into the latrines to wash themselves, the Dutch prisoners used their mess tins which they used for eating.

---

272. TNA, WO 325/17.
273. Walker, *Australia in the War of 1939–1945*, p.618.
274. TNA, WO 235/963; AWM 54 1010/4/65.

It was, Dunlop wrote when he arrived a month later with O Battalion (and later P Battalion), a 'waterless bog', where there were just two broken-down barracks and eight other incomplete structures. These had previously held Indonesian labourers and were in such a filthy condition they had to be burned down. Most of Dunlop's men had to sleep in the tattered, leaking tents mentioned above left by Captain Jack Hand's party of Australians and Dutch prisoners of A and R battalions who had moved on to Kinsayok.

As this camp was on an embankment between about five to seven five kilometres from the river, water was drawn from a 'miserable' little spring stream, which passed through a Japanese pressure filter pump and taken out to the workers by elephant. There was no possibility of boiling (i.e., sterilising) the water.[275] All stores and rations had to be carried by the POWs from a staging post on the river all the way back to the camp along a poor track over rough hills.

Dunlop had managed to convince the Japanese camp commander, an IJA private called Ikimoto, that fresh and deeper latrines needed to be dug, a new water supply scheme created and anti-malarial measures undertaken. But the Japanese officer, Hiroda, demanded every man, other than those who were bedridden, for work on the railway even if they had no boots. Those without boots soon had cuts which developed into the deadly tropical ulcers. With the onset of the monsoon and a shortage of tents, the men had nowhere dry to sleep. 'Things can't go on long like this,' Dunlop wrote, calling this 'the next thing to murder' and was a 'cold-blooded, merciless crime against mankind'. Quinine was supplied by the Japanese to help fight malaria. However, the medication was thought to be impure as there were numerous cases of unusual side-effects, including wild 'maniacal' fits and even sudden, otherwise inexplicable, deaths.

Dunlop Force was given a stretch of ground of more than four kilometres where they had to clear the jungle and build cuttings, embankments and trestle bridges. Each man had to excavate a cubic metre of ground per day with just picks and shovels. The spoil was taken to where a seven-metre-high embankment was to be made, the spoil being compacted by the stamping feet of the prisoners. The men had to work from dawn until it was dark, walking around three to four miles to get to their workstations. Because most had no boots and their feet were in terrible condition, they did not limp back in camp until after midnight.[276]

Dunlop fought a daily battle with Hiroda, who demanded that all the prisoners, regardless of the health or condition, were sent to work. In response Dunlop said that all his men would go on strike. When Hiroda threatened to

---

275. Dunlop, pp.217-8.
276. TNA, WO 235/963.

shoot Dunlop, the Australian replied 'you will have to shoot them all. Then you will have no workmen'. Nevertheless, no light duty prisoners were left in the camp for maintenance, and it was left to Colonel Dunlop himself to dig new latrines. The actual numbers permitted to remain in the camp of around 1,000 prisoners, were twenty-nine cooks (who had to also collect their own firewood), fifteen medical personnel (including two doctors, Majors A.A. Moon and E.L. Corlette), eleven clerks, six men for anti-malarial work and hygiene, five for water-carrying duties, one bugler, and three batmen for the Japanese.[277]

On or around 22 June 1943, Private Joseph Moate and sixteen others decided they were not fit to work. They left the camp but did not report for duty at the railway. That evening when all the prisoners had returned to camp, those that had failed to report for duty were summoned to the Japanese guard house. Just seven men did do, including Moate and Sergeant M. Hallam. They were taken by the guards to the parade ground where all the other prisoners were assembled to watch the punishment take place and lined up.

'Starting from one end of the line of the seven prisoners,' wrote Moate, 'the Japanese soldiers took one man after another and thrashed him. First they hit the man with their fists until he fell, then they set to and kicked him with their boots. In each case, three Japanese soldiers did the main punching and kicking of the prisoner and the other Japanese soldiers [there were around fifteen in total in the camp] stood near and struck the prisoner with bamboo sticks and wooden slippers.' The beatings began at 19.50 hours and continued until 23.15. Two of the prisoners were so badly beaten they developed tropical ulcers in their wounds and had limbs amputated and Sergeant Hallam died forty hours after the punishment.[278]

Along with two older other ranks, who Dunlop was able to keep behind, and the camp's carpenter, Jock Clarke, he constructed a system whereby a nearby stream was dammed with felled bamboo trees and the water was channelled 200 metres to the camp. John Coast, who passed through Hintok Road camp, was impressed with the ingenuity of the water supply: 'The latrines were made of wood, were clean and sixteen feet deep; they had made a complete water system out of hollow bamboo pipes and had rigged up showers in a bath place entirely carpentered from bamboo.'[279] This channelled water was also used to cool condensers in a water distillery plant. Water stills to help hydrate the cholera victims were made from stolen petrol piping and bamboo. At the height of the cholera epidemic the camp had three stills working non-stop, being serviced

---

277. Walker, *Australia in the War of 1939–1945*, p.564.
278. AWM, 54 1010//4/92.
279. John Coast, *Railroad of Death* (Hyperon, London, 1946), p.104.

by officers operating in shifts. These stills maintained an output of 100 pints of distilled water a day.

Large numbers of troops from other forces passed through Hintok Road camp, including an estimated 9,000 in April 1943. Each party in this force was to halt at the camp for a day and a night and all had to be fed. Most of these, some 7,000, were the men of 'F' Force. But their stay was only for two hours before they were driven on again. Some did not even stop.

In April, medical non-commissioned officer, Sergeant Seiichi Okada, often called 'Doctor Death' by the prisoners, set standards for the men with dysentery. If they had 'ten' motions a day, they were fit for duties in the camp. At twenty motions, they 'perhaps' could do some light work, but he accepted that at thirty motions or more a day they were genuinely unfit for work of any description.

The Japanese also hit on a plan to get more out of the workers with an incentive scheme. They confiscated goods from the canteen and then a list was compiled of those men who had worked well each day who were called out at *tenko* in the evening and handed a 'presento'.[280] This worked and the prisoners competed with each other. This angered Dunlop as it meant there was no longer a fair and even distribution of goods. What was also noticeable at this time was an increase theft of items by parties transiting through the camp. Indeed, petty theft was common across most of the camps. These were examples of self-preservation in desperate situations where life hung by a thread. This also manifested itself in other ways. For example, Dunlop cites an instance where a party passing along the line were given a quantity of medicines to take to Hintok Mountain. None arrived. The prisoners 'flogged the lot'. It was also found that men sent to work at Hintok River Camp were purchasing items from its canteen and then selling them to fellow prisoners for a profit when they returned to Hintok Mountain Camp. Men were also taking cattle from the compound, killing them in the scrub and selling the meat. There was also the case of a young soldier having his boots stolen by another POW while he was undergoing a minor operation. Such behaviour 'sickened' Dunlop's soul.

The speedo period not only resulted in longer working hours on the railway but also in more work being demanded from each individual every day, and the number of men in each crew being reduced to make more crews. To make up the required quota of workers for the day, the Japanese took many of those men considered too ill to go out to work and put them on light duties. Those that still had boots were chosen first by the Japanese. Of those left, any who had few

---

280. Later 'presento' items were pooled and distributed evenly, as was the additional 'danger' money earned by the workers.

or no bandages (i.e. no immediately visible signs of illness) were the next to be selected. The tasks these men had to perform were tree felling and hauling.[281]

Being allowed to stay in camp on light duties did not necessarily mean having an easier time. The camp guards made such men 'work like hell' all day to the extent that many asked to join the railway working parties where the Japanese engineers 'at least have some sense'.

There was, nevertheless, some recognition of the work some of the men were doing in the form of 'Danger Money'. Those using hammer drills, pneumatic drills, compressor units and drivers of motor vehicles, were granted an increase in their pay of 5 cents per day (though this was later amended).

When the monsoon broke, the workers were simply not able to achieve as much as during the dry period – the earth was heavier to shift, and the men slipped and slithered in the mud. To compensate for the loss of productivity, the Japanese engineers made the prisoners work even longer hours. For the men of Hintok Mountain even getting to their workstations was a 'slippery struggle', many with little or no footwear. One man who was considered not to be moving quickly enough was assaulted by the Japanese guards and was badly beaten. He died the following day. Even when they had reached their place of work, beatings were frequent and Hiroda was known to throw stones at men to make them work faster. As the days passed many of the workers could barely crawl back at the end of their shift in the pitch dark. One exhausted individual took five hours to return to camp.[282]

Dunlop's battles with Hiroda became more intense and prolonged. The catalogue of crimes committed during this period is too long to list here, but some are worthy of mention. A number of men who were very ill with malaria were dragged out of the hospital and beaten by an engineer sergeant. This beating included being 'hammered' on the face and head with wooden clogs, then being repeatedly thrown 'over the shoulder heavily onto the ground with a sort of fireman's lift action'. The prisoners were then kicked in the stomach, scrotum and ribs, as well as being 'thrashed' with bamboo sticks. This was far from being a unique case. On 22 June 1943, a Sergeant 'Micky' Hallum was so ill with malaria and enteritis he collapsed on the way to his work station. Unable to carry on, he returned to camp. On his own volition he lined up with others who had failed to reach the railway. As punishment for failing to attend work he was beaten – and beaten so badly that he died in hospital four days later.[283]

The clothes of many of the prisoners had perished and an ingenious scheme was devised to provide shorts for all that needed them. The bottoms of all the

---

281. Dunlop, p.287.
282. Dunlop, pp.272-6.
283. Dunlop, pp.285-6 & 288.

tents were cut off and the camp's one tailor converted the material into quite satisfactory shorts. To prevent the Japanese accusing the prisoners of destroying Japanese property, the shorts were disguised by being dyed a purplish colour with weed tobacco.

Periodically, cards were issued for the prisoners to write home. Except under special circumstances these had to be addressed to a relative with the same last name as the sender. The cards were pre-written, and all the prisoners were permitted to do was cross out the sentences which did not apply:

> I am interned in Thailand
> My health is excellent
> I am ill in hospital
> I am working for pay
> I am not working
> Please see that .... is taken care of
> My love to you.
> [Signature][284]

Letters from home were also received, though as late as eighteen months old.

Large numbers of native labourers, Tamils, Malays, Chinese and Thais, moved into the area, who quickly made the ground around their encampment a filthy mess and the area was soon swarming with vermin. Worse still, they fouled the stream above the point where Dunlop Force drew its water – and already there were rumours of cholera among the natives.

Sick rates rose with the onset of the monsoon, but still the same number of men were required for work on the railway. Dunlop wrote of this in his diary: 'Work parades ultimately became a deplorable spectacle with men tottering with the support of sticks and carried piggyback on to a parade ground, unable to work, in order that fixed figures could be met. Lying cases were frequently carried to the engineers' lines and ordered to work with hammer, axe etc., in a sitting position. The sick were frequently treated with special savagery in order to discourage illness.'[285] Dunlop was frequently beaten by the guards for trying to keep desperately ill patients from being forced onto the work parties. Dunlop towered over the short Japanese soldiers and had to kneel down so that the guards could hit him in the face.

Lieutenant Usuki, of Kouyu, who had jurisdiction over Hintok, arranged with the aid of Dunlop's camp funds and a collection from the officers, to buy

---

284. Owtram, p.41.
285. Walker, *Australia in the War of 1939–1945*, p.569.

fifty-four bullocks which were being driven on the road past the camp by locals, bringing much-appreciated meat to the men. He insisted, however, that all POW officers not employed on camp duties were to be sent out with the work parties. This amounted to very few officers as the light duties numbers had become so depleted most officers were already performing manual tasks around the camp.

In January 1943 a pig which had been supplied as rations escaped, swam across the river and disappeared into the jungle. The prisoners and the guards went off on a 'great hunt' to track down the enterprising animal, but it was never seen again.

Though Dunlop had assumed command of the force, there was, in fact, a more senior officer at Hintok Camp No. 5. This was Lieutenant Colonel, later Brigadier, C.A. McEachern, who was a combat soldier. With almost all Dunlop's time being taken in looking after the sick, he handed over responsibility for the administration of the camp to McEachern on 10 May 1943.

The constant battles with Dunlop over the number of men who were fit enough to go to work resulted in an incident which McEachern later recorded. He was informed that a senior officer was due to visit the camp and the then camp commander, Sergeant Okada, told McEachern that he did not want the officer to see so many sick in the camp. He selected fifty men from the sick parade and marched them into the jungle, ostensibly to hide from the senior officer. McEachern found out that the men had actually been driven to work.[286]

The Thai trader, Boon Pong, who helped the prisoners in Chungkai and Tamarkan also helped smuggle small quantities of precious drugs into Hintok concealed in foodstuffs (eggs, whitebait, salt, peanuts, oil sugar, and the much sought-after tobacco), delivered by barge from Kanchanaburi. As mentioned previously, Boon Pong took considerable risks in helping the prisoners and he was awarded the King's Medal for Courage in the Cause of Freedom after the war and was also made an Officer of the Order of Orange-Nassau by the Dutch.[287]

The rumours of the appearance of cholera proved to be unfortunately true. It took just two days from first diagnosis for allegedly 240 *rōmusha* to die of the disease. It struck at Hintok No.5 on 19 July 1943.

The Japanese were so terrified of cholera that they took extraordinary steps to stay away from anyone who had contracted the disease. On one occasion they tried to bury alive one cholera sufferer where he had fallen to avoid touching him. Another time, the Japanese wished to execute a prisoner who was lying in a tent, to avoid the spread of the disease. The Japanese were too frightened to go into the tent and were going to shoot wildly into the tent in the hope that

---

286. TNA, WO 235/867.
287. Though it is widely believed he received the George Medal, there is no record of this.

some of their bullets might hit the poor victim, until an Allied officer stepped forward and shot his companion.[288]

Saline solution was the most widely used treatment for cholera and Dunlop devised eight intravenous drips made from beer or saki bottles, fragments of rubber tubing, bamboo pipes and other 'odds and ends' fitted onto bamboo frames.'[289] The cholera camp became a 'dreadful quagmire', with the patients lying on flattened bamboo just a few inches above the mud. At night the only light came from condensed milk tins of oil with fibrous material wicks. The patients vomited into bamboo containers and excreted into cut-down tins. 'Blue' Butterworth, of 2/2nd Casualty Clearing Station, who served in 'Cholera Gulch' believed that working there was worse than being on the railway: 'It was a horrid, dark little place with people dying in their own muck.' As cholera could be transmitted orally, those working in the isolation area were advised to give up smoking.[290]

Despite the frequency of deaths, as much dignity as was possible was shown to each prisoner who died. The body was sewn into a grey Army blanket and carried to the cemetery on a rice sack suspended between bamboo poles. A bugle played The Last Post and Reveille, the sound reaching as far as the camp where those present would stand to attention.

On 19 July 1943, the railway having been completed up to Konyu, the fit men of were despatched to Hintok River Camp, only the hospitalised patients and those tending to them remained at the mountain camp, i.e., 342 sick, nine cooks, a duty section of eleven and eight orderlies, all under Dunlop's command. Then, starting on 20 August, all the sick, including cholera cases, were moved to Tarsao. This was no easy task as the patients had to be taken over a cliff. This necessitated some men being lifted or hoisted up and others being tied onto stretchers to prevent them sliding off.

Hintok River Camp   155 Kilo

On 29 June 1943, parties of groups 5 and 6 (Officers) began to arrive at Hintok and an overflow camp, nearer to the work area and situated close to the river about two and a half miles from the existing camp, was formed. This camp, which became known as Hintok River Camp, was actually composed of several camps. A British camp, under the command of Lieutenant Colonel T.H. Nevey of the Straits Settlements Volunteer Force, sat perched on cliffs high above a bend in the Khwae Noi on ground now taken over as a tourist resort; an Australian

---
288. Edbury, p.423.
289. ibid, 427.
290. Wright, pp.86-7.

camp under Colonel McEachern, was situated near the river bend; and a Tamil camp was located further upstream. The supply of clean water was often an issue in the camps, but at the Hintok River camp there was a natural spring emerging through the cliff face – although access to this became precarious as the river levels rose with the monsoon. In contrast to Hintok Valley camp, supplies could be brought in by river, though hauling the supplies and water up the cliffs was no simple task and tested the engineering skills of the prisoners.

Hintok Valley camp later assumed the form of a sick camp and was eventually closed down. It was here that that most of the Chaplaincy of 'F' and 'H' forces work was carried out.[291]

The men at Hintok River worked on the excavation of Compressor Cutting on the railway high above the camp. To reach their workstation, the prisoners had to clamber up a steep hill which, like so many places, became treacherously slippery with mud during the monsoon. Even though their workstation was only a short distance away – it was within blasting distance of the camp and chunks of rock would often land in the camp, on two occasions almost demolishing the kitchen – it took the prisoners an hour to slowly struggle there.

Working next to the Australians were a force of Tamil labourers who worked with the prisoners in building a bridge, 400 yards long by eighty feet high. This collapsed so many times, the POWs nicknamed it the 'Pack of Cards' bridge. The story of the collapsing bridge was told by then Captain Reg Newton: 'The Japanese survey people, the railway survey, they made a hell of an error of judgement when they hit this particular place Hell Fire Pass at Hintok. Instead of going around the ravine and out again like that, they came straight up against the brick wall, Hell Fire Pass, and nowhere to go. They'd just all of a sudden, drive this Hell Fire Pass through solid rock. We lost a lot of blokes there. And then when they came to the other end of it, there's a sixty–seventy-foot drop and there's the ravine. And there's the other side over there, the same. So they had to put this bridge across,'[292] Thirty-one men were killed in falls from the bridge to rocks below, and twenty-nine were beaten to death by the guards.[293] Eventually, the bridge was abandoned, being replaced instead with an embankment leading up to Compressor Cutting.

At one point in time, the officers of No.6 Group were compelled to carry and bury the bodies of dead Tamils. When Major A.M.S. Babbington MC protested at this he was severely beaten. This practice then continued until the completion of the work at Hintok.

---

291. TNA, WO 325/17.
292. Interview with Capt. Reg Newton (NX34734) Anzac Day 1992, secondtwentieth battalionaif.wordpress.com/prisoner-of-war-POW.
293. Walker, *Australia in the War of 1939–1945*, p.569.

This, though, was overshadowed by the treatment suffered by Lieutenant Duncan Barbour of the Royal Artillery, who was acting as the officer in charge of the kitchen. He had been ordered by the Japanese to build a bamboo extension over the fireplaces. As only very sick men were available to cut and split the bamboo, progress was slow. The Korean Medical Orderly, Harimoto, incensed at how long the work was taking, ordered Barbour to stand to attention and began to hit Barbour in the face and head, the British officer finally being knocked to the ground. Barbour was then told he had to carry all the water required for the kitchen and find all the wood necessary for the fire which would sterilise the water by himself. He started on this task at 04.00 hours. Just before breakfast, Harimoto went to the cookhouse. A 4-gallon container was on the fire at that time and was just reaching boiling point.

Harimoto, once again, ordered Barbour to stand to attention: 'I was clad in sarong and cotton singlet. The Korean was in a state of frenzied anger, and struck me on both sides of the face with all his strength so that I was completely dazed. I was still forced to stand to attention and to my horror picked up the still bubbling can of boiling water and flung the entire contents into my face ... as he swung the can I instinctively jumped and turned my back, but could not avoid the boiling stream, and the whole four gallons poured over my head, shoulders and buttocks.' Barbour ran away but was stopped by another guard as the boiling water seared into his flesh and seeped between his legs and arms. Eventually, he was allowed to be treated. The whole of his back area turned into one huge blister and he was incapacitated for a month. Barbour still carried scars from the incident when the war finished.[294]

One of the Korean guards (Army Civilian Employee Lee Han-ne) described the disciplinary methods which the Koreans as well as the Japanese soldiers were subjected to and which explains, to some degree, the behaviour of the Japanese and Korean guards: 'The training included marching, rifle shooting and fighting with bayonets, and the most remarkable thing was for us was that we were slapped on the cheek very often for even a minor error or misconduct. Sometimes everybody in the group was slapped for a mistake made by one person, or we had to stand in two lines facing each other and slap the comrade in front of us.'[295] With just a handful of teenage guards controlling hundreds of prisoners, the guards felt they had to be firm with the POWs or they would lose control, which explains why they slapped the prisoners at the first sign of perceived dissension.

The prisoners found their own way to fight back by taking every opportunity to sabotage the railway line. Spikes and bolts were put in the wrong place or

---

294. TNA, WO 325/17.
295. Tamayama, p.77.

left loose so that bridges or raised carriageways collapsed when the Japanese tried to run their heavy goods trains along them.[296]

While the behaviour of the Japanese towards the prisoners was less brutal than at some of the other camps, the unending heavy work and the incessant monsoon rains severely affected the health of the workers. 'The strain and malnutrition of the past months now began to affect the health of even the fittest,' the 'H' Force report read. 'In a very short time personnel who until now had escaped disease fell victim to the old complaints of malaria, dysentery, and septic ulcers. Eventually, even the cholera caught up with them.' The 'wretched' British camp was particularly badly hit with 220 men reportedly to have died in thirteen weeks. By August 1943, only seventy men remained there with nothing to eat but rice. As with Hintok Mountain camp, some of the more seriously ill men were sent to hospitals down the Khwae Noi.

Kinsaiyok Camps   171 Kilo
Also known as Kinsayok, Kinsick and Kinsayoke

Located a short distance beyond Hellfire Pass, Kinsaiyok consisted of a cluster of camps where Australians of 'D' Force, Dunlop Force, and 'K' and 'L' Forces were accommodated. These camps were Kinsaiyok Jungle Camp 1, Kinsaiyok Jungle Camp 2, a rock quarry for rail ballast and Kinsaiyok Jungle Camp 3.

The camps were situated beneath a major rail terminus and marshalling yard. As the camps were situated on flat ground near the Khwae Noi, which was swollen with the monsoon rains, the camps were for the most part, as 'Weary' Dunlop the Senior Medical Officer, Hospital area, reported, a 'quagmire', and the kitchens liable to frequent flooding.[297] The camps were of the usual long attap huts, most in a state of virtual collapse, with the monsoon rains pouring through the utterly inadequate roofs.

Dunlop wrote of his first impression of the camps: 'Things at Kinsaiyok are very much at sixes and sevens … Each group looks after its own sick, the hospital being run by a "Soviet of captains", but no common policy, no common stores, no arrangements for diets or special segregation of disease…. Sanitation poor, with only one big latrine for all … More latrines are being put down, of the open type unfortunately, though otherwise well made. Flies as usual and an offensive smell. For ablution a little stream pouring down to the river with a walk of 440 yards. This is also, alas, used by numerous [unsanitary] Tamils.'[298]

---

296. Pavillard, p.126.
297. AWM, 54 554/5/1.
298. Dunlop, pp.283-4.

Among the tasks the prisoners had to undertake at Kinsaiyok, was cutting a path through the jungle ahead of the rail-laying gangs and to excavate a long cutting, as well the construction and maintenance of a number of bridges in the area for the railway.[299] By the end of March 1943, all officers were engaged in heavy camp duties.

At the most northerly of the Kinsaiyok camps the Japanese were very worried about the great hordes of rats which infested the camp getting at their foods and even eating any leather shoes prisoners still had, so they had a deep ditch dug around their store. They also offered the prisoners 5 cents for every rat's tail they brought to them. In their efforts to get to the food store the rats dropped into the ditch where they were chased and killed. In the course of little more than three days, the Japanese were presented with around 2,500 rats' tails.[300] Such was the success of this measure, the whole camp was turned out to kill rats and by the end of six week some 10,000 had been killed.

Charles Steel was one of those transferred from Tamarkan to Kinsaiyok in May 1943. He found that 'all the huts are rotten and have collapsed, so that the eaves rest on the ground. Have to stoop to get in. Next hut (used as a transit hut) in deplorable state. Loads of mice, excreta, old worn-out boots all over the place.

'No POW administration in this Camp. IJA take all men out on work. Chased out with bamboos quite often. No hospital recognised. MO made to carry rice only yesterday. Capt. Keane beaten up for protesting.'[301]

Captain John Hands was transferred from Hintok to Kinsaiyok (which Hands called Kinsick) in March 1943 with his force of Australian and Dutch troops. Later these were joined by around 1,000 British prisoners. Of the Australians, Hands was only permitted to leave twelve sick in camp, all the rest had to work regardless of their condition. Those that were sent out to the railway worked for sixty-three days without a break.[302]

At one point, Hands decided that had had had enough of selecting the worst twelve cases and he kept back forty patients. The camp commander, Lieutenant Tanaka, tried to hit Hands with his bamboo stick, but Hands wrenched the stick from Tanaka hands and threw it away. Tanaka went back to get the other guards and they took all the sick men, some of whom were already dying and did indeed die shortly afterwards.

Two British soldiers tried to escape but were caught at another camp about twenty kilometres away. They were taken back to Kinsaiyok. They were beaten

---

299. anzacportal.dva.gov.au/ kinsaiyok-camps.
300. Roberts, pp.107-8.
301. Brian Best, p.78.
302. AWM, 54 1010/4/65.

every day for two weeks by the Japanese using bamboo, rifles, shovels and fists. Finally they were taken into the jungle where they were shot.[303]

Lieutenant Geoffrey Pharaoh Adams, also transferred to Kinsaiyok in April 1943: 'The first, last and indelible impression of the camp was the stench, a miasma of dysentery, excrement, decay and death.' This was also just as the 'Speedo' period was to begin: 'Beatings, from both camp guards and engineers, became such a part of everyday life that no one bothers to report them. Impossible tasks were set, and the work would go on for forty-eight hours continuously, or even longer. When darkness fell, we slaved on by the light of petrol lanterns, and time lost its meaning.'[304]

There was a series of incidents witnessed by a number of prisoners concerning the Korean guard known to the men as the 'Mad Mongrel' and a Corporal Martin. The Korean kept offering Martin trivial amounts for his groundsheet, but Martin refused to sell. 'You no sell. I fix,' the Korean said, and from that moment onwards he conducted a campaign of harassment to make Martin surrender the item. For any reason he could find, the Korean punished Martin with repeated beatings, but the doughty corporal would not release his precious groundsheet.[305]

John Wyatt was at Kinsaiyok: 'The camp was also a sea of mud and just to get to the latrines we had to wade ankle deep in this cloying, clinging, maggot-infested brown sludge … The latrines were simply long trenches about four feet deep with flattened bamboo slats stretched across. A gap of only two feet separated each "toilet" seat on which you squatted side by side, back to back, officers and men together. It was a most degrading and horrifying experience to endure. The pits were just a writhing, heaving mass of insects and the stench was so bad that it made your eyes water. The men with dysentery had to sit on these evil "thrones" sometimes up to twenty times a day.'[306]

Most of the prisoners smoked which meant those who did not smoke could barter their small allowance with the smokers for extra food. It was remarked on by non-smoker John Wyatt, that even those dysentery suffers in very poor condition who needed food for their very survival, if they were heavily addicted would still be keen to exchange rations for cigarettes.[307]

Charles Steel wrote that the cholera hospital was really just 'a dying hut', as there was no effective treatment available. There, Thai, British, Dutch and Tamils (males and females) were lying next to each other.[308] It was said that

---

303. AWM, 54 1010/4/65.
304. G.P. Adams, *No Time For Geishas* (Lee Cooper, London, 1973), pp.78 & 80.
305. TNA, WO 235/918.
306. Wyatt & Lowry, pp.81-2.
307. Wyatt & Lowry, p.82.
308. Best, p.85.

when the first cholera case was diagnosed at Kinsayok the Japanese were so alarmed they ordered the prisoner – a British solder – to be immediately shot and buried, which was carried out by Korean guards.

Geoffrey Adams described similar conditions in May 1943 as cholera struck in the midst of the monsoon: 'With the rain the ground around the camp never dried. One could not rest for a moment. Ditches overflowed and the stench of the filth assailed our nostrils to a degree hard to bear. We were worried about the swarms of flies scattering germs. Medical officers trying to stem the disease were themselves infected by it and some died.'

The Asiatics in the adjacent camp suffered the worst and special parties of British prisoners were sent to bury their dead, amounting to about twenty natives a day – sometimes even before they were dead. The British were forced to do this at loaded gun point, but they adamantly refused to do more than just dig the graves. It was also claimed that such was the Japanese fear of cholera, men were sometimes compelled to 'brain cholera cases with a hammer'.[309]

During the outbreak, 'the whole place, short-staffed and more like a fever hospital in the Crimea than a labour camp in the twentieth century, swarmed with flies and stank like a cesspool,' wrote Geoffrey Adams. 'The heat and humidity were overpowering.'[310]

John Coast had a similar view of Kinsaiyok when he was there in October 1943 'The greater number of bamboo and attap huts were collapsing hovels with gross deficiencies in the roofs. The hospital was accommodated in the worst of these huts and had been expanded into tents.

'The kitchens were for the most part on the river bank and experienced difficulties owing to flooding. The Camp hygiene arrangements reflected the previous struggle to obtain any tools or labour, and the latrines were foul and of the open trench type; anti-malarial measures as usual utterly inadequate.

'Ablutions were carried out in small running streams which were unfortunately frequented by many natives from surrounding labour camps. Cholera was still occurring amongst the natives.

'At this time the I.J.A. agreed to an extensive rebuilding program and the new bamboo and attap huts were more satisfactory. The new latrines laid down were of the deep trench type and were covered and made as fly proof as possible, and it was permitted to build suitable shelters over them.

'The 1.J.A. were induced to build a new hospital of much more satisfactory bamboo and attap construction. They consented to allow longitudinal bamboo platforms for the "beds" with passages between to allow some nursing access to

---
309. Hardie, pp.106-7, 109.
310. G.P. Adams, p.83.

patients. The beds of course still consisted of rough baboo without any sort of mattress or matting. This construction was somewhat marred by the independent notions of Koreans in charge who largely ignored plans and specifications. The buildings included a small administrative hut and operating room with earthen floor. A central hut was converted into a common M.I. Room where various M.O.s could see cases.[311] All the medical officers were to live together in a 'medical house'. Unfortunately, the four large tropical ulcer wards were a 'butcher's shop', with the nauseating stench of gangrene filling the air. The ulcers extended beyond their lower limbs, up to the thighs and buttocks. A number even had ulcers on their arms.

Nevertheless, the improvements to the camp were appreciated by Johnny Sherwood when he was transferred to Kinsaiyok in January 1944. He found the camp to be clean and tidy and was particularly impressed with the camp's cemetery: 'It was immaculately kept, with not a weed out of place, and dozens of little graves with home-made bamboo crosses stuck neatly into the ground.'[312]

Also, an area was cleared for a football pitch and recreation was encouraged. Often the guards would play a football match against the prisoners. The prisoners tried hard not to win every time! The spirits of the men were also lifted by the introduction, in the autumn of 1943, with a singsong each day before the men went off to work and upon their return at night. Among the songs was *Rule Britannia*, in which the words 'Britons never, never shall be slaves' must have stuck in the throats of many of the prisoners.

The Japanese also made all the prisoners parade after roll-call to learn Japanese patriotic songs during November and December 1943. This occupied all the otherwise free time during daylight hours the POWs had after work.

The POWs clubbed together to buy a few water buffalos. These animals were slaughtered by the Japanese as the prisoners were not permitted any weapons. The method adopted for this was for the prisoners to tie the head of the buffalo to a tree and a guard would shoot into the front of the skull – but this was not always immediately successful for the unfortunate animal.

There was another uplifting source for the prisoners in the form of news from a concealed wireless. From November 1943 to March 1944, a number of men of the Royal Artillery operated a wireless which was hidden in the bunk of Regimental Sergeant Major Mannion's bunk. The headphones and batteries for this small set, which fitted into a water bottle, were hidden in the bunk of Company Sergeant Major Angus Collie of the Gordon Highlanders. The wireless was not discovered in any of the many searches conducted by the Japanese and the set was later moved down to Tamuang where it was operated again.

---

311. AWM, 54, 554/5/1.
312. Sherwood and Doe, p.124.

On 25 October, Dunlop moved to Tarsao hospital camp. A small hospital continued to be maintained at Kinsaiyok until 1945, serving the groups maintaining the railway. By then Kinsaiyok had three cemeteries with around 400 graves.

Bhatona 174 Kilo
Also known as Matoma

Another of the Kinsaiyok satellite camps was Bhatona at about the 173 km to 175 km mark, just a few kilometres past Kinsaiyok Station before Lin Thin. It was only a small camp of predominantly Dutch and British POWs, which became effective in April 1943. It was really a hospital camp with two jungle camps under it to which prisoners were sent to work. The camp consisted only of old Indian tents of which the side walls had been taken away by the Korean guards, with the result that during the monsoon the rain 'lashed in' on the unfortunate occupants. It was described by Captain Roy Fewell of the 5th Battalion, Suffolk Regiment as 'a fever ridden jungle swamp continually under water.' Because of the swampy condition, when POWs died it was only possible to dig graves thirty inches deep.

During the monsoon, the camp, which was comprised only of tents, was also small, and, as a consequence, was quickly churned into a quagmire. In July 1943 there was also a party of Tamils employed at Bhatona. The job the men had to undertake was to build seven wooden bridges leading up to Rin Tin.

Major Guy Mayes, also of the 5th Battalion, Suffolk Regiment, was in charge of the work parties at one of these satellite camps, which the men called Bridge Camp, situated around three kilometres to the north of the main camp. He described the old tents where the men had to sleep as utterly incapable of keeping out the rain and, at first, there were no boards which meant the men had to sleep in the mud on the ground. No blankets were issued, and the prisoners had less that thirty-six inches of space to lie upon. Living conditions were 'disgusting'. Only the really severely sick were allowed to remain in the camp (a maximum of 5 per cent of the workforce regardless of their physical condition) along with two or three officers and the cooks. This meant the officers had to dig the latrines, collect the food from the main Bhatona camp, and run errands for the Japanese. In just a few weeks these latrines became fouled, as did the whole camp through sickness and disease.[313]

---

313. TNA, WO 235/857.

Occasionally crates of Red cross supplies were received but the Japanese took most of the items leaving about 20 per cent for the POWs for whom the packages were intended.

Getting supplies upriver to Bhatona by boat towards the end of the dry season in April proved challenging. The water level became so low that sometimes two boats had to pull each other up stream and everyone had to get into the water and push the boat.

The Japanese soldier in charge of the building work, the infamous Lieutenant Tarumoto, believed that: 'For us and probably for the POWs as well, the work at Bhatona was the most wretched of all the construction work done on the railway.' The Allied commander there, Lieutenant Colonel Baker, though clearly 'worn out' went into the jungle every day to carry wood back to the camp to keep the fires going as there were no other even partially fit men left in the camp. When the 'speedo' order was given, more native labour was sent to the camp, as well as an elephant and ten men from a Japanese construction unit, but this increase was offset by the rise in the number of sick and dead.[314]

When that native labour – in the form of Tamils – arrived in July 1943 cholera spread from there to the British camp almost immediately. This was because there was just one small stream which was used by both the Tamils and the prisoners. One day during this period, the senior Korean guard, a private Kanioka, pulled three men out of the hospital tent who were clearly suffering from cholera and dragged them into the rain. He stood them up and then knocked them down with his fist. The men died.[315]

Dysentery, as in all the camps, affected many of the men. When they were at work, such sufferers could do nothing other than rush into the bush. This, inevitably, meant the areas around the work stations became very unpleasant and very unhealthy. So, the men made simple toilets by the work sites.

One day, the person responsible for the supply of medicines to the camp, a Korean private named Myama, approached the British medical officer, Captain Forde Cayley, and tried to take away the latter's medical equipment. When Cayley objected, the Korean 'took off his clogs and proceeded to hit me all over the face and body until I was black and blue,' Cayley later wrote, 'and having done that, he commenced to kick me, mainly in the stomach.'[316]

In another incident, reported by Captain Peter Clarke another member of the 5th Battalion, Suffolk Regiment, an angry Tarumoto ordered every man out to work, including all those in hospital. Even though they were suffering

---
314. Tamayama, pp.59-67.
315. TNA, WO 235/857.
316. TNA, WO 235/857.

from dysentery, malaria, beriberi and tropical ulcers, they were marched two to three miles to the work area, with the exception of those who were so ill they collapsed.[317]

By the time work finished at Bhatona, fifty-two British and thirteen Dutch prisoners had died.

Rin Tin   181 Kilo
Also known as Rinten, Lin Tin, or Lin Thin

Rin Tin was principally a Dutch camp, where there had been so many deaths it was abandoned as a work camp and kept open only as a transit camp. John Coast passed through the Dutch camp of Rin Tin in May 1943: 'It was the eeriest and foulest place we had seen in Thailand and two things struck us immediately about it; first the acrid stink of dirt and decay, and something worse; and secondly, an uncanny stillness. Built and cleared on the top of the riverbank, it was entirely enclosed by a ring of high trees; not a bird sang, not a twig rustled … There was something evil, something ominous about the place; we wanted to clear out of it as quickly as we could.

'There were the shells of only three huts in the camp and there was one Dutch officer in charge, with a total command of about eight cooks for the parties going through. In the huts there were no slats; the roofs were full of huge lizards, and everywhere were bugs, lice, and bloated fat flies.'[318]

The camp, which John Wyatt described as 'a filthy hell hole' where the Dutch prisoners were living in 'foul and dangerous conditions' was also infested with large red ants – many of them up to an inch in length.

It was while he was working from Rin Tin that Wyatt saw one of the worst sights he witnessed during his time in Thailand. A POW was sat under a tree staring as if in a traz`nce with testicles the size of grapefruits – a severe case of beriberi. 'A bucket was placed in front of him to catch the drips and even today, more than sixty years later,' Wyatt wrote in 2008, 'I still carry this awful picture of the poor man around in my mind.'[319]

Towards the end of July there was an outbreak at Rin Tin of an undiagnosed illness, which manifested itself in spots on the face and body. It was not known if this was smallpox, typhus or plague, and it remained undiagnosed.

There was a native camp nearby and a report from a Royal Artillery bombardier stated that both dead and very sick ('helpless') natives were being carried and

---

317. TNA, WO 235/857.
318. Coast, pp.115-6.
319. Wyatt & Lowry, pp.82-3.

dumped in the POW cemetery to rot or die. The prisoners were not permitted to help these unfortunates in any way.[320]

Gunner Winch Percival of the Royal Artillery was at Rin Tin where he saw fellow gunner G.W. Clayton 'kicked, bashed and laid unconscious' for not moving quickly enough. Clayton did not recover from these injuries and later died.

While at Rin Tin Lieutenant Tarumoto employed Signalman Wainwright as his batman. One day, Staff Sergeant Leech was able to check on Wainwright and found him in very poor condition. Leech reported this to Tarumoto whose response was to kick the NCO and then rush out to Wainwright, kick the signalman and push him down a crevasse into a jungle stream. Fortunately, Tarumoto left Rin Tin the following morning to visit another camp and Leech, with three other British NCOs, was able to recover Wainwright and they carried him on a stretcher all the way to Kinsaiyok hospital, some ten kilometres or more. Three days later Wainwright died of cerebral malaria.[321]

In another incident on 8 September 1943, Captain Daneil McPherson was unable to find enough fit men for that day's work party and one of the guards made up the required number from the sick, as happened up and down the line. On this occasion, one of those chosen by the Korean Tokuyama was Private Feeny who was suffering severely from cerebral malaria and in no condition at all to work. Despite McPherson's protests, Feeny was sent out. During the rest period in the afternoon, Feeny, delirious and unaware of his surroundings, wandered off from the work party. He was attacked by some of the Japanese engineers with sticks and fists and was knocked unconscious. He was not taken back to camp until the end of the shift that evening, being carried by his comrades on an improvised stretcher. When McPherson examined him, Feeny's chest, arms and head were covered in bruises. In addition, he had eighteen bamboo wealds on his chest, fourteen on his arms and two on his head. Feeny died never having fully recovered from his beating.[322]

There were other reported incidents involving Tokuyama, one of which took place in September 1943. He accused the cookhouse staff of stealing a spade. Driver Wilfrid Adshead tried to explain that this was not the case. Tokuyama angrily hit Adshead with his fist and then picked up the spade in question and was about to hit the prisoner over the head. Lieutenant Denis Bluett grabbed the spade from behind. Tokuyama turned and tried to hit Bluett with the spade. Bluett prevented him from striking him, so Tokuyama threw aside the spade and started hitting Bluett with his fists until Captain E.T. Moss intervened.

---

320. Hardie, p.109.
321. TNA, WO 235/857.
322. TNA, WO 234/918.

Tokuyama turned his anger back on the cooks and poor Driver Adshead who all were subjected to further beatings.[323]

Kui Yae 186 Kilo
Also known as Kuii or Kui Mang, or simply Kui,

This camp was close to the railway and around four kilometres from the western banks of the Khwae Noi. This attap camp was built by Dutch POWs who were joined by Australians including 'D' Force V Battalion, Group 6, in August 1943, where they remained until 18 December of that year. It is believed that eventually the camp consisted of around 100 Dutch, 100 Australians and 100 British.

According to one source, only seven Australians made it out of Kui Yae, though cholera never made its appearance at this camp. A total of twenty-six POWs were killed here in an Allied bombing raid on 8 December 1944. So many trees had been felled during the construction of the railway it was not difficult for the Allied airmen to see and bomb the line.

Hindaine and Hindaine West 198 Kilo
Also known as Hindat

Hindaine camp was deep in the jungle close to Hindato village on a small tributary of the Khwae. There were some hot springs here and the prisoners built bamboo bath huts for the Japanese. This was another camp where the men were housed in wholly inadequate, rotting, leaking, tents. Twenty men were crammed into these tiny tents and the prisoners were so packed together that when one man rolled over all the others also had to roll over.

Major Alf Cough was Commanding Officer of 'D' Force's V Battalion which moved to Hindaine: 'This camp is just hell, the whole area a sea of black stinking mud, very little food; and men dying every day. For the last three weeks we have eaten nothing but rice and dried fish; for three weeks prior to that we had rice and dried cabbage at the rate of one cupful of rice plus a dessert spoon of fish or cabbage. The men cannot last much longer unless we get some decent food and medical supplies. I am tired of reading burial services and watching my men die without being able to lift a hand to help them; they are full of courage and keep their chins up until the last moment.'[324]

---

323. TNA, WO 235/918.
324. 2/4th Machine Gun Battalion, 2nd4thmgb.com.au.

Nearly all the men at Hindaine were suffering from ulcers, believed Lieutenant Leslie Riches 'these required frequent bandaging if they were to be properly looked after, but there was no treatment available for those ulcers at all.' When cholera broke out no attempt was made to supress the disease other than an order that all water was to be boiled.[325]

Corporal Leonard Roach served in the cookhouse and was able to provide an accurate summary of the food at Hindaine/Hindato. He also said that he was in a good position to see how the prisoners' rations were 'robbed left and right' by the Japanese guards. On one occasion 30,000 eggs were received at the camp. Of these 5,000 were given to the approximately 3,000 prisoners and the remaining 25,000 were kept by the approximately seventy-five Japanese. Another time 400 chickens arrived. Not one was given to the POWs.[326]

The camp's medical officer, Captain Ean Duncan, received no medical supplies at all. When the prisoners were struck down with an outbreak of dysentery, Major Cough collected money from all the officers to purchase opium which was the only substance they could buy from the locals which had some effect upon the illness. Food improved a little in July with the addition of some meat. The prisoners were also able to supplement their rations with a type of lily root found in the jungle which they were able to eat after it had been boiled. Hindaine was occupied from the end of May to 31 August 1943.

The latrines were about thirty yards from the tent lines and during heavy rain the latrines overflowed into the tent area. There were so many maggots swarming all around and on top of the latrine it became usual for the prisoners to take a piece of bush with them to brush the maggots away to prevent them crawling over their legs and bodies as they sat there.

At one point during the monsoon the river overflowed its banks and the water poured onto the land all around. The ground where the camp was located became a little island about the size of a football pitch. No supplies could get in but, at the same time, the prisoners had a rest as they could not get to work. The Japanese became very worried about being cut off and got the prisoners to build bamboo rafts. The prisoners were made to swim the rafts, which were about two metres square, across the flooded river, a distance of around 300 yards, backwards and forwards all day with supplies – most of which were, of course, for the Japanese.[327]

Two Dutch prisoners tried to escape, or were alleged to have done so, yet, being in the jungle, there was no marked boundary around the camp. Nevertheless,

---

325. AWM, 54 1010/4/122.
326. TNA, WO 235/963.
327. Wright, p.111-2.

they were sentenced to death. What happened to them was witnessed by Lance Corporal A. Prime of the Royal Corps of Signals. One of them was beheaded with a sword and the other Dutch soldier, having witnessed the beheading, 'ran amok and was bayonetted.'[328]

Around a kilometre away from Hindato station was Hindato West which was formed next to the Khwae Noi to receive supplies sent up the river.

Linson Wood Camp   203 Kilo

Dutch and British prisoners were held at this location. The camp had just a bunk for officers, but they did have their own mess. The camp had a canteen and a hospital as well as the unavoidably disgusting latrines.

As its name implies, this was a camp for the cutting of timber. According to Rod Beattie it was set up in December 1944.

Brankassi   208 Kilo
Also known as Prang Kasi, Branchali or Bang Kasi

Brankassi was a largely Dutch-occupied camp situated by the Khwae. The prisoners were accommodated in attap huts and tents which were adequate in the first few weeks as the weather was dry. The Japanese had three huts for themselves with the camp commander having one for himself alone. The prisoners built a cookhouse out of bamboo close to the river so that the cooks had a ready supply of water. At this time of the year the Khwae Noi was at its lowest level, but when the monsoon began the river started to rise. In one night alone it rose 20 feet and the men had to move the cookhouse in the dark. This happened three times as the river rose to a height of around 50 feet. The tents afforded little protection from the rains and conditions deteriorated rapidly as the camp became surrounded by a sea of mud. Eventually there was a railway repair shop erected which was built of wood and corrugated iron.[329]

Though some considered food to be in short supply at Brankassi was the food centre for the area and so was generally better off than many other camps. The guards here, on the other hand, were particularly sadistic, the prisoners being randomly beaten for no reason. On one occasion, Private F.E. Cox of 1/5 Sherwood Foresters, the camp bugler, blew 'lights out' at 22.00 hours instead of 22.20 hours which he had done the previous night, having been instructed to do so by both the Japanese and the British camp commanders.

---

328. TNA, WO 235/963.
329. TNA, WO 208/1925.

The following morning, at 08.30 he was called into the Japanese office. As punishment for his supposed error, the Korean guard, Morimoto, slapped Cox in the face. He then 'punched me in the face several times and put his leg behind me, pushing me onto the ground. He then kicked me in the stomach, ribs and face. And another Korean soldier came along a stuck his bayonet into my arm.' Cox still carried the scar from the bayonet wound after the war.[330]

With the arrival of the monsoon came cholera and men began to die in large numbers. One Australian claimed that so many of the Dutch troops died at Brankassi during the cholera outbreak because of their poor hygiene. Driver Merv Cox said the Dutch used to wash their backsides with water held in their dixies which they also used for their food.[331]

As part of 'F' Force, Idris James Barwick spent a short time at Brankassi, which he called Branchali, on his way to Nieke (see below). This he wrote, was called 'Hitler's Camp' or Regimental Camp' because everything was run very strictly to time in a highly regimented manner by the Japanese NCO in charge who, seemingly, looked surprisingly like Hitler.[332]

The 'F' Force men were employed on camp duties, which included general housekeeping, woodcutting, cookhouse fatigues and latrine digging. Idris was on the latrine party. They worked in gangs of eight with four in the trench at a time working for fifteen minutes while the other four rested, before swapping over.

There was one surprising story to tell of Brankassi concerning Private Jimmy Scott of the Gordon Highlanders. He was being treated for what was thought to be a septic throat. Fortunately for Scott, he was examined by s Japanese doctor who used to have a practice in Australia. Not only did he correctly identify Scott's illness as diphtheria he also arranged for the Highlander to be sent to Roberts Hospital in Singapore. Jimmy Scott readily acknowledges that the doctor saved his life.[333]

After completing twelve kilometres of track, the men at Brankassi were moved to Hindaine. The only POWs maintained here were employed as lorry drivers who were paid 1 Tical a day plus rice. The men of 'F' Force marched out of Brankassi whistling *Colonel Bogey*, glad to be moving on, though blissfully unaware of the horrors they were to endure in the camps further north.

---

330. TNA, WO 235/918.
331. Wright, p.116.
332. Idris Barwick, *In the Shadow of Death, The Story of a Medic on the Burma Railway 1942-45* (Pen & Sword, Barnsley, 2005), 121-5.
333. Mitchell, p.122.

Yongthi   213 Kilo

Yongthi was occupied by two small groups, one Australians from 'D' Force and the other Dutch. Accommodation consisted of one hut and a couple of large tents. When the monsoons began, the POWs constructed bamboo platforms to sleep on above the sodden ground. For around four or five months the prisoners worked along a 5-kilometre stretch of the railway, building bridges, carving cuttings out of hillsides and building embankments.

Onte and Bangan   214 Kilo

After the completion of the work at Brankassi, a party from 'D' Force's V Battalion was transferred to a place called Onte where they built a bridge across the Khwae Noi. They were joined by U Battalion, their work being on a five kilometre stretch of the railway, creating cuttings, embankments and building three bridges over small creeks.

The 'horrible little place' of Onte consisted of just one hut and a couple of big tents. The tents gradually rotted away and the prisoners had to sleep on the ground, but when the monsoon arrived they built bamboo platforms to sleep on. Four men died at Onte of cholera and their bodies were taken the two kilometres to Bangan for burial which the POWs had to carry through waist-deep water.

The Japanese did not allow any music or singing in the camp. Work began at 05.00 hours every morning and if the prisoners had not finished their rice breakfast by that time, the food was kicked out of their hands.[334]

Henry 'Harry' Surman, a driver of Australian 2/2nd Reserve Motor Transport Company, recounted one particularly unsavoury incident when the prisoners were accused of sabotage. The Japanese took ten of the prisoners and, at bayonet point, stood them over the campfire. Just when the other prisoners were about to put a stop to this, the Japanese allowed them to step out of the fire and, in the strange but not untypical Japanese fashion, then gave them pineapples and bananas![335]

After the completion of the bridge over the Khwae Noi, the party, under Warrant Officer Glen Blyden, moved on to Bangan. Classified by the Japanese as No.3 Detached Camp[336], Bangan was used to store supplies for the Japanese and as a base where they would bring in sick men who were then sent either by boat or train down to the base hospitals. According to Japanese records a total

---
334. 2nd4thmgb.com.au/camp/onte-yongthi.
335. Wright, p.121.
336. POWresearch.jp/en/archive/camplist.

of 936 POWs were at Bangan[337], and that 250 men were working at Bangan at any one time.[338] When the railway was finished those left at Bangan were transported to Kinsaiyok – not on a cramped barge, or on foot, but by truck, much to the delight of the exhausted prisoners.

Takanun   218 Kilo
Also known as Tha Kha-Nun, Tha Kanun, Takunun, Dha Kahnun, or Tarkanoon

A collection of camps was situated some three kilometres from the large Thai town of Takunun. John Coast was one of the prisoners in one of these camps on 14 May 1943, the clearings for the camps having been made about a month earlier by prisoners using 'parangs' which were tools used for cutting grass and bamboo. 'The area cleared had rapidly dried out and inches of dust lay everywhere. Nearest the river bank was a straight row of huge trees and below them was a little wooden house for the Nip commander and a row of neat, new Nip tents with wooden floors raised about a foot above the ground, carpeted with matting. Halfway down the river bank was their cookhouse. Separating the Nip area from us was about an acre of level ground to be dug up and made a vegetable garden; and on another flank of our area was a fair-sized Thai house surrounded by a small piece of cultivated ground …

'Our own area was roughly a square of open dusty land covering an acre of sloping ground. In a camp for about 1,200 men, there was tent accommodation for just over half – bad tents – and for the rest there was precisely nothing,'[339] According to B.N. Smith Laing, when the main body arrived there was no accommodation, no latrines, no cooking facilities and no hospital. The reason being that when the advance party arrived the men were immediately seized by the Japanese engineers and put to work on the railway.[340]

The next day, Dr Robert Hardie, who arrived at Takanun on 5 May, wrote that the men, mostly from the 5th Norfolks, were: 'living under appalling conditions, crowded in ragged leaking tents, with terrible food – nothing but rice and a modicum of what the Japanese say is dried vegetable but looks like dried seaweed.'[341] The only liquid the men received was half a pint of tea at each of the three meals of the day. As elsewhere, with the men being worked hard on such an inadequate diet, their resistance to illness rapidly diminished and soon of the 400 men in the camp, 240 were sick. Hardie found the hospital

---
337. ibid.
338. 2nd4thmgb.com.au/camp/bangan-camp.
339. Coast, pp.120-1.
340. TNA, WO 25/957.
341. Hardie, p.91.

consisted of five Japanese tents with mosquito nets but no floorboards, some twelve feet wide and fifteen feet long. There were a number of Dutch troops at Takanun, most of whom were Eurasians whose sanitary habits filled Hardie with 'dismay'. The only medicine available was some quinine.

The Japanese provided no tools or allowed any fit men for the building of accommodation huts, hospital huts or the cookhouse. Tools from the railway were allowed for the digging of latrines. Other than a single supply of candles, no lighting was provided for nighttime.

The latrines were dug on an isthmus which projected out into the river. Unfortunately, when the monsoon arrived, the water level rose in the river and the maggots which were living on top of the latrines were swept onto those prisoners sleeping nearby. Eventually, the entire isthmus was swept away.[342]

During 'Speedo' the Japanese drove almost anyone who could move out to work, launching 'furious tirades' against the Allied officers for so many being sick. The medical men left in the camp were so few they could scarcely look after all their patients in what passed for a hospital and there was no one to dig fresh latrines as the existing ones filled up. Conditions became 'frightful', with the patients crammed together in the leaky huts where the stench and squalor were 'shocking'. The few medical orderlies left to look after the sick were often called to work in the Japanese area of the camp, meaning the hospital deteriorated even further. For those sent out to work, the repeated calls of 'speedo' were usually accompanied by hefty kicks or clubbing with clenched fists or rifle butts.

The camp was so heavily infested with flies that when food was being served it was covered over with leaves and men were selected at each meal to fan away the flies with banana leaves.

There were instances of the very sick trying to commit suicide rather than face any more suffering. Though the medical teams would always try to save them, there was, as Hardie accepted, little point as, by that stage, they were most likely going to die anyway.

When cholera struck Takanun in the middle of May 1943, the first step the Japanese took was to erect a bamboo fence between their area of the camp and that of the prisoners. Anyone entering the Japanese area had to wipe their feet on a disinfectant-soaked sack which was held in a box at the gate. They then had to wash their hands in an adjacent bowl of disinfectant.

A cholera isolation area was created separated from the main camp by a small ravine. Captain Hugh de Wardener was one of those tasked with setting up the cholera area: 'We had to dig on the side of the ravine to make several, three

---

342. Wright, p.163.

or four, flats places to put the tents ... all we had were the tents, there were no ground sheets, there were no wooden things ... patients lay on the wet earth.'[343]

The Japanese were so fearful of cholera, if one prisoner in a hut contracted the disease, they allowed the doctors to quarantine all the other men from that hut. Though these men were not sent to work on the railway, they were free to move around a small area of the camp. This meant, at last, there were fit men available to dig new latrines.[344]

John Tidey caught cholera at Takanun but survived. He recalled 'most vividly' during his time in the isolation ward that 'a fellow would be taken ... being helped by two others, obviously going to the latrine. When they brought him back, he was just like a monkey, he was drained, the bodies were literally drained, and that is cholera.'[345]

A funeral pyre was erected a few hundred yards along the river and a regimental sergeant mjor was given responsibility for ensuring enough wood was collected to keep the pyre burning. He also had the sad task of arranging for the bodies to be collected and their remains to be disposed of.

Hugh de Wardener's memory of Takanun during the cholera epidemic was 'the incessant' playing of the *Last Post*: 'they used to burn the corpses and then there were the burials of the non-cholera [victims]. So the Last Post was ringing out at frequent intervals, it was sort of background music.'[346] As it transpired within just a couple of days, the Japanese provided a vaccine which meant that there were only about 100 cholera victims out of a camp of 2,500 men.

The men had to build a bridge at Takanun and. at the end of the working day, the prisoners often had to get back to camp over high, narrow beams above the Khwae Noi. At first, Signaller Bob Christie recalled, the men would slide along the beams on their backsides, but this added as much as an hour onto the journey. So the men, weak and exhausted as they were, accepted the risk of falling into the fast-flowing river and walked along the beams.[347]

As mentioned elsewhere, the medical orderlies performed heroics in many of the camps. De Wardner paid tribute to their work in Takanun: 'during the cholera epidemic, for instance, they had to empty the faeces away. A pit had been dug for the faeces. Well at night they had to move along the side of a ravine to put it in. Well, it needs one bloke to hold the fellow who had the pan, another bloke had to hold the light, and sometimes the whole slipped. And one time one bloke slipped into the pit.'[348]

---

343. Gill and Parkes, p.180.
344. Hardie, pp.94-5.
345. Gill and Parkes, p.183.
346. Gill and Parkes, p.183.
347. Wright, p.137.
348. Gill and Parkes, p.184.

Interestingly, the Dutch area of the camp was located between the cholera isolation zone and the main part of the camp, yet the Dutch did not have a single case of the disease. This was because it was standard practice in their army in the East Indies to be inoculated every two months.

In June 1943 the fit men were moved to a new camp built half-a-kilometre or so away from the existing camp which was left purely as a hospital camp. A proper attap and bamboo hut was built for the hospital in the middle of June and, towards the end of the month, the evacuation of the severely sick began. The selection process for those deemed so incapacitated they would be unfit for work for a considerable time, was undertaken by the so-called Japanese camp 'doctor', Nobusawa. The patients would be lined up each morning before dawn, many of them carried out on stretchers or helped along by the stronger men. After Nobusawa had made his selection, the 'melancholy procession' of these 'human wrecks' would make its way down to the riverbank to be packed into barges and sent down to Chungkai. Not all of them survived the three-or-four-day's journey.[349]

Lieutenant Colonel S.F. Pond's Party was moved with all its equipment to Takanun from Konkoita 3 July 1943. This was a terrible forty-mile journey for the men who were already in a very weakened state. The only way they could march this distance was by forming a shuttle system, in which the few fit and nearly fit, marched to each camp in turn where they put up tents, dug latrines and prepared the cookhouse, and then returned to the previous camp to carry the sick men and their equipment to the new camp. Those few fit men also had to help push the ox-carts carrying all the stores of the Japanese guards when they became bogged down in mud. These efforts would see the prisoners struggling along the road until well into the early hours of the following morning, only for the whole process to have to be repeated at 08.00 hours.

When Pond's Battalion finally reached Takanun the men pitched camp on a hill near to a creek, where there were no huts or latrines. They were told that they would be there for two months, but rumours were rife that all the Allied prisoners would be out of Thailand by the end of the month and the railway completed by Asiatic labour.

Nevertheless, after the fit and light duty men were sent out to work the 'No duty' men were ordered to build a fence around the site and to attend to camp hygiene. Early on 7 July the fit men started to dig the latrines before being sent out to the railway at midday. Work on the latrines had to be continued by the sick men as best they could.

---

349. Hardie, pp.103-5.

Cholera reared its head once again on 12 July and the camp was placed in quarantine. The only people allowed out of the camp were those working on the railway just outside the camp boundary. The Japanese guards supervised from a cautiously safe distance.

Two days later Lieutenant, later, Captain Maruyama at last accepted that the camp was in such an unhygienic condition that work on the railway was stopped and all the prisoners were tasked with completing the latrines, finishing a drainage area for the camp and collecting bamboo for flooring for the tents. The latrines were made as well as could be expected in the circumstances. 'we used slit trench latrines covered with bamboo, with earth over the bamboo' explained Captain B.A. Barnett. 'We left a little square opening over which you squatted. We made lids to cover that.'[350]

Maruyama would not let any men capable of light duties go into the cholera area for fear of spreading the illness and because all those light duty men were needed on the railway. Such was his fear of the disease he would not even allow the men suffering from cholera to receive materials to help construct any form of accommodation. This meant that tents in the cholera area were not erected, and huts were left unfinished.

On 17 July Maruyama ordered that the sick prisoners who remained in camp would only receive three-quarters of a mug of dry rice per day. Though the medical officers declared only sixty-four out of 570 prisoners fit for work, Maruyama took 150 men, regardless of their physical condition. 'It is pitiful to see skeletons dressed in boots and shorts slithering out in the mud,' wrote Adrian Curlewis in his diary for 19 July, and during that night thirty-seven prisoners died.[351]

The Japanese decided to reorganise the camp on 21 July, causing unnecessary suffering to the critically ill patients – fit on one side, unfit in the middle and the hospital at the end. So few men were fit for work, Maruyama punished the sick by not allowing them a midday meal form 25 July onwards. The unfit men were slowly starving to death.

On 27 July Captain Barnett was beaten up by two Korean guards, simply because he called them 'Koreans'. Though Captain W.B. Bowring believed it was to show their status over the prisoners.

During August some yak meat became available to the prisoners, with an average of six pieces of meat per meal, but work times had increased to anything from eleven to eighteen hours a day. 'Hewing rock and carrying baskets of spoil by moon and bamboo firelight through clay slime over the ankles is not a

---

350. TNA, WO 235/1034.
351. TNA, WO 235/1034.

pleasure,' Curlewis wrote in his diary. 'Tempers are frayed, pains are many and at times a hopelessness overcomes one and I wonder if all the suffering is all worthwhile. Our deaths are up to 68 and the future black. Struggling home on a greasy night, falling full length in mud that sticks, balancing on slippery boots across the scaffolding of three railway bridges 30ft above water level carrying pick/or shovel – hell, why go on recording misery. If I get out of this I want to forget it all, not remember.'[352] Despite his despair. Adrian Curlewis continued with his diary which was one of the documents used in the persecution of the Japanese for war crimes.

As the railway was rapidly reaching Takunun, Maruyama was desperate to make sure the line for which he was responsible for supplying the workforce was ready in time. By 3 August only three officers and ninety men were fit for work but Maruyama demanded that even those suffering severely from malaria, diarrhoea, beriberi and ulcers must work and the following day he took men from the hospital to bring the working party up to a strength of 200.[353] The prisoners were made to work through the night until the early hours of the morning, the men not returning to camp until 04.00 hours. Even though meat was available in the form of yaks, as punishment for so few men being fit for work, Maruyama would not allow the yaks to be slaughtered.

Adrian Curlewis recorded a memorable scene of the nationalities working together on the railway one night in August: '500 Tamils, 50 of us, 20 Nips working with picks, shovels, baskets, in railway cutting, 3 acetylene lamps, 6 big bamboo fires, every Tamil talking at the top of [his] voice at the same time, all men shoulder to shoulder, black bodies clad in loin cloth only, spitting and couching until finally a bellow above all "*Yasami*", and then a ten minutes smoke.'[354]

The tents had all perished by late August and when it rained the prisoners rolled up their bedding and sat on it to try and keep it dry. Despair had set in: 'My day is amongst foul-mouthed animals who have lost self-respect and decency,' Curlewis wrote of his fellow prisoners, 'who rob their mates, who cry to me for help on all occasions and then let me down by lying. Razors have been sold for food, brushes and combs gone, soap almost unobtainable, clothes in rags and dirty, tempers on edge and all hope gone … or if they have hope they are past fighting for health to get them home; blasphemy, flies, dirt. God, how I hate it all.'[355]

Padre Vellacott used to arrange talks in the hospital on various topics to try and maintain morale and on one occasion organised a 'concert' for them. During

---

352. TNA, WO 235/1034.
353. TNA, WO 235/1034.
354. TNA, WO 235/1034.
355. TNA, WO 235/1034.

this event a number of the patients began to sing which offended Maruyama. He had the offending singers lined up. He then went along the line smacking them across the face with his right hand. He turned round and went back along the line smacking the prisoners with his left hand. Maruyama said 'One more' and repeated the punishment up and back along the line of sick prisoners.[356]

By the middle of October 1943, with the seriously ill men having been evacuated, the hospital orderlies were sent to work on the railway and most camp duties were reduced or stopped. However, as soon as the railway had been completed, Maruyama was transferred elsewhere (believed to be Borneo) and a Sergeant Aoki was left in charge of the camp, the situation improved, and the guards actively helped to increase the supply of food. Aoki even sent one of his guards fifty kilometres down the line to purchase canteen items on three occasions.

On 20 November memorial services were held by order of the Japanese for the men who had 'co-operated' with the forces of Nippon in building the railway and lost their lives at all camps in Burma and Thailand. The camp commander at Takanun agreed to allow the POWs to make their own arrangements for the service, little realising what the prisoners had in mind. On the day of the service, the troops turned out in as smart a uniform as they could manage, even wearing their medals if the still possessed any, and formed up in true parade ground fashion. It was a display of military pride which the Japanese had unwittingly permitted the prisoners to present. Nevertheless, the ceremony went ahead, with the Japanese commander paying due respect to the dead.[357]

For those who remained at Takanun, Christmas of 1943 was a special day indeed. The cooks had been saving up items for a long time and were able to produce what were, under the circumstances, some very good meals. The prisoners even put on a pantomime – *The Babes in Thailand*.

Nam Chon Yai   229 Kilo

Captain Barry Baker wrote that Nam Chon Yai was marked ss '211 kilo Camp', though he knew that this was incorrect, and he estimated that it was 221 kilometres from the start of the line. His estimation was only seven kilometres out, the camp later being known as 228 Kilo camp. He arrived there in the spring of 1943 with approximately thirty-five of his sixty-eight men as part of a large group of prisoners. 'When we reached the site of 211 it was, as usual, raining,' Baker wrote, 'and there were no preparations at all, in particular there

---

356. TNA, WO 235/1034.
357. Peacock, pp.210-11.

were no huts or latrines or cookhouses. Our Jap OC … pointed out a heap of green tents which were to be our homes for the next few weeks.' The next day, the men were assembled for a *tenko* and were told that almost all the men were required for work parties leaving very few to try and construct some form of more habitable camp.

The tents, fifteen in all, were in fact merely inner or outer covers only. They were all torn and provided virtually no protection from the monsoon rains. The prisoners had almost no tools with which to build huts so many men had to sleep on the open ground. In spite of the torrential rain, no further accommodation was provided until 25 June, when an additional thirty-nine equally rotten or torn inner and outer covers were issued. The Japanese, by contrast, were accommodated in 'fine' bamboo and attap huts which were built for them by the POWs.[358]

J.R. Hill's party reached 211 Camp on 7 May 1943. To him the valley in which the camp was located and the sparse camp itself, was 'filled with an atmosphere of hopelessness and death'.

According to Harold Skinner, of 3rd (Indian) Corps Signals, the prisoners were ordered to catch and kill – with home-made fly swats – 100 flies per person per day. The daily 'catch' was checked by the guards each evening and then destroyed.[359]

As there was no barge traffic up to Nam Chon Yai, rice had to be carried on the men's backs or pulled along on hand carts. As the men were severely weakened, they could not move large quantities of rice to the camp, which meant that rations were small, and resulted in the men becoming weaker and the rations that could be carried, as a consequence, became even less. Then cholera struck and the death rate was so high that it became impossible to bury all the bodies and instead the bodies were burned in a pit.

It became the job of the prisoners to collect the dead bodies as they returned from their work on the railway each evening and put them into the burning pit. The fire was kept burning continuously by a small duty party which placed bodies in the pit, and, as Barry Baker noted, 'they never ran out of bodies to fuel the fire.'[360] So frequent were the deaths the playing of the *Last Post* was stopped because of the detrimental effect of hearing that music had on the prisoners.

There was one bright spot for the prisoners at 211/228 Kilo camp when a herd of wild pigs attempted to cross the river near where the men were working. The POWs set about them with spades and pickaxes and a few were killed and

---

358. TNA, WO 235/913.
359. Harold A. Skinner, *'Guest' of the Imperial Japanese Army 1941–45* (Privately published, Littlehampton, 1993), p.12.
360. Hilary Green, pp.121-3.

eaten.³⁶¹ A few clams were found in the river to supplement the meagre rations and a wild fig tree was discovered by the POWs. The figs were boiled with the prisoners adding their daily spoonful of sugar to the brew.³⁶²

Tha Mayo Wood   239 Kilo

This camp was built by Indian workers, but later it was occupied by POWs who cut wood as fuel for the Japanese steam engines.³⁶³

Tamajao   241 Kilo
Also known as Namajo, Tamaryo, or Namajon

Ernest Warwick arrived at Tamajao on 4 May 1943. The camp was well guarded on three sides – with Japanese machine-gunners positioned in tall bamboo posts – and the Khwae Noi forming the fourth side. The prisoners halted in a 'vast, dusty parade ground, along one side of which stood the specially constructed and well built officers' huts. In front of these was the inevitable Japanese camp commandant's platform complete with hand rail and a bamboo pole. Atop of this fluttered the Japanese flag.'³⁶⁴

The monsoon struck shortly after the troops arrived at Tamajao and, much to the surprise of the prisoners, they were issued with British Army style gas capes, taken, no doubt from stores seized in Malaya. These were given only to those who went out to work. The Japanese and Koreans were well fitted out with waterproofs and rubber boots. At the same time, fourteen waterproofed tents were erected for the guards.

Lieutenant Gerard Veitch ran the hospital at Tamajao, which was 'in a deserted paddock … with a few bits of old canvas put over the sick … that was our camp … there was nothing there; no signposts or anything like that.' There were just two tents, one for the cholera victims, the other for every other illness, with no possibility of isolating the cholera tent. There were two Japanese guards to watch over the area, but they stayed well-away, erecting a fence around the prisoners' area to keep the POWs away from them.

A Japanese doctor did visit occasionally, but there was little he could do as he expected all the prisoners would die.³⁶⁵ When the camp commander, Captain

---
361. AWM, 54 554/2/1A.
362. Hill, pp.89-90.
363. britain-at-war.org.uk/ww2/Death_Railway.
364. Ernest Warwick, *Tamajao 241: Prisoner of War Camp on the River Kwai* (Paul-Leagas, Ashingdon, 1987), p.65.
365. Wright, pp.144-5.

Suzuki, was approached for medicines, his response was that none were available for the prisoners as every item 'must be sent to the brave Nippon troops fighting in Burma.'[366]

More prisoners were herded into Tamajao until there was around 14,000 men in the camp, mostly British and Australian. The hospital was then run by Major Ray Boone, who was obliged to perform many operations, including amputations, in his little operating theatre. There he had a bamboo table on a solid timber frame. Across the upper end of the operating table was fitted a small teak handrail for patients to grip as minor procedures had to be conducted without anaesthetic.

There was a Tamil camp nearby, also with several thousand workers and their families, and two further camps were established about a mile down the track.

During their work on the railway, beatings became so frequent that the other prisoners took no notice. It was only when someone had a limb broken or was knocked unconscious that the men bothered to take note of the incident, and, if they were courageous enough, try to render the poor unfortunate some assistance.

At lunchtime four prisoners were selected to collect the food. Escorted by two guards, the hot boiled rice was carried from the cookhouse in huge metal dixies which were hung from poles carried on the shoulders of the struggling prisoners.

The first indication that the men at Tamajao had of the cholera outbreak was when a party of prisoners was marched towards the Tamil camp. In a small stream which ran out of the side of the camp were five dead bodies. With the Korean guards keeping well out of the way, the prisoners were ordered to dig a large grave. The POWs shovelled the bodies into the grave but before they could cover the pit they were ordered to search the surrounding jungle.

A short distance away they found three more Tamils on the ground, two of whom were still alive. These were carried back to the pit and laid on top of the other bodies. To the consternation of the burial party the two live Tamils began to struggle to pull themselves upright. The guards ordered the prisoners to fill in the pit. When they refused one of the guards snatched a spade from one of the prisoners and smashed in the skulls of the unfortunate Tamils.

Two days later cholera reared its head in Tamajao itself, carried into the camp among a recently-arrived party of 500 Dutch prisoners. Following the first Dutch death, British, Australians and Americans soon succumbed. Near the cemetery an area of jungle was cleared for the cremation of the bodies. 'There were no bugle calls or burial rites,' commented Ernest Warwick. 'The pitiful bodies were just picked up and hurled into the flames like bundles.' Several of

---

366. Warwick, p.72.

the prisoners who had to perform this task became victims themselves, suffering the same ignominious fate.[367]

Conditions at the camp became so desperate that disturbing numbers of prisoners took their own lives as the only escape from the pain and suffering they were forced to endure. One such incident was noted by Ernest Warwick. A young man who was suffering acutely from leg ulcers hobbled towards a large bonfire and threw himself into the flames.[368]

The prisoners were informed by a Thai trader that a convoy of barges carrying ammunition for the Japanese troops in Burma was due to pass Tamajao the following night. This was an opportunity Ernest Warwick and his friends could not let pass. Because of the work they had been undertaking they knew where the Japanese stored explosives and they knew how to handle them. They stole four slabs of gun cotton and detonators from the Japanese store and waited in the shallow cold water. The information proved accurate and as the convoy drew level to where the prisoners were standing, they threw the explosives onto four barges. The detonations set off a chain reaction, igniting the ammunition. The motor boat and all the barges it was towing blew up and sank. All the ammunition was lost and forty-three Japanese soldiers were killed with a further four missing. Remarkably, the Japanese ascribed the loss to the 'carelessness of a Nippon soldier'.[369]

Perhaps indicative of life in Tamajao as in other camps, is an incident described by Ernest Warwick during the last days of the camp. As the prisoners were eating their midday meal, there was a sudden wail like the howl of a dog, and the 'wreckage of a human being' ran out of the hospital hut, hastily followed by two orderlies. The prisoner tripped and fell over and was picked up by the orderlies and forcibly taken back inside the hut. The rest of the prisoners carried on eating as if nothing had happened, so inured were they to such scenes. The man in question had cerebral malaria. Within two hours he had 'mercifully' died.[370]

At the beginning of August almost everyone in the camp came down with either dysentery or malaria and on 16th of that month around 600 Tamil workers were brought in who established their camp between the POW camp and the access road, making a mess as was usually the case with the *rōmusha*.

A number of prisoners were removed to Takanun on 26 August. The night before the prisoners were transferred out to Takanun a heavy thunderstorm with strong winds ripped the tents to shreds and soaked everyone and everything.[371]

---

367. Warwick, p.76.
368. Warwick, p.68.
369. This wonderful story is told in detail in Warwick, pp.80-88.
370. Warwick, p.102.
371. Wright, p.146.

Some POWs remained at Tamajao after the line had been laid to and beyond the camp to carry out maintenance and repair of the track. But, on 16 October 1943, the very sick and disabled prisoners were despatched by barge and open railway truck down to the base hospitals of Chungkai, Kanburi and Tamuang. These men, many of whom were stretcher cases, were given one mess tin of rice and one army bottle of boiled water for the journey. It took the POWs three days to move these very ill men the half mile down to the railway. They were packed forty to fifty per truck. The train had to make frequent stops to offload the dead.

One of the tasks the prisoners had to perform was that of shielding three Tamil camps from the eyes of the senior Japanese officers who would be passing through on their way to the official joining ceremony at Konkuita on 17 October 1943. That morning the prisoners had to cut bamboo with deep green foliage to form screens to hide the 'squalid evil-smelling' camps where they were within sight of the track.

Swinton's Camp   249 Kilo

This camp was opened on 1 September 1943, and closed around the middle of December of that year. The prisoners had been force-marched from Nam Chon Yai, arriving at what would be referred to as 'Swinton's Camp' after Lieutenant Colonel George Edward Swinton, the senior officer at the camp. The Japanese officer in charge of the camp was Lieutenant Kokubo.

According to Colonel Swinton, the camp was situated on two narrow ledges alongside the river, each of which was about fifty yards wide and 150 yards long. The lower ledge was subject to flooding.

For the first six weeks the prisoners had to sleep in old army tents which had previously been classed as unserviceable. The canvas of these had either perished or had large rents and holes. 'The monsoon was still raging on our arrival,' wrote Captain Thomas Ellis, 'The ground was nothing but a mud swamp. After the worst march I have ever witnessed when completely under-nourished, weak, and many of them completely unfit men for such an undertaking, left 211 Kilo Camp at 0900 hours on September 1st, to march to 248 Kilo camp, half the force had no boots whatever, those who had had soles kept on by wire. Those without boots had been for the most part, been without boots for months, their feet were in an appalling condition from sores. The Japanese issued to those without footwear a pair of brown canvas P.T. After less than half an hour after leaving 211 Kilo Camp, these men had lost these canvas shoes, having had them sucked off by the mud which came well up over the ankles and often nearly to the knees.'[372]

---

372.   TNA, WO 235/913.

On arrival, the prisoners were given just one day to erect the tents, make a cookhouse, and erect bamboo platforms to sleep on, which entailed going out into the jungle to fell the bamboos, cut them and then split them. All this was simply impossible in the time they were given, especially in the tired and weakened condition of the men. Consequently, the first meal was not prepared for the prisoners until around fourteen hours after the leading group had reached the camp site. The prisoners were not given the opportunity to dig trenches round the tents for many weeks which meant that when it rained water 'streamed through them like a river'. The lower of the two ledges was completely submerged for two weeks in September 1943.

According to Thomas Ellis, who served as the camp's adjutant, a Korean guard called Fumimoto told one of the British officers whom he beat up: 'I am only a poor yellow coolie, you are haughty British officers, but you are now my prisoners and I can do just what I like with you.'[373]

All the officers were forced to go out to work and those officers and other ranks who were too ill to be driven out to work, were ordered to kill 100 flies a day. 'The sick were paraded at 18.30 hours every night on the Parade Ground,' Ellis later testified, 'and then made to file past [the] Japanese Medical Orderly to hand in their 100 flies which were checked.' The guards were ordered to patrol round the tents, and later the huts when they had eventually been built, to make sure the sick were killing flies. Anyone, of whatever rank, caught not killing flies or found lying down was beaten or taken out of the hospital and made to stand to attention in the sun or the rain.

The Japanese also took around fifteen sick POWs from the hospital each day to work in the Japanese area of the camp. They were expected to cut wood and carry water for the Japanese cookhouse, carry out maintenance on the Japanese buildings and work in the Japanese garden. This work was tough for the sick men who often broke down mentally with the work they were expected to perform – which often led to a beating.

The camp's medical officer, Captain Robson, used to battle with the Japanese and when one day he refused to pick out twenty-five men from the sick to join the working party he was slapped in the face for ten minutes 'as hard as it was humanly possible'. After this, Robson was left weeping and was no longer permitted to function as a doctor in the camp.[374]

In mid-1943, Red Cross parcels were received at this camp but were not distributed to the prisoners. Instead, they were given to certain prisoners as rewards 'for good work on the railway'. None were given to the sick. After dark, these stores were collected by the POWs and redistributed equitably.[375]

---

373. TNA, WO 235/924.
374. TNA, WO 235/924.
375. Kratoska, p.67.

At around the beginning of September a party of British prisoners joined the camp, consisting of approximately fifty officers and 150 other ranks. The day after their arrival they were all sent out to work except for seven men who were ill with malaria and three officers, two of the latter for medical reasons and the third, Lieutenant Colonel Lincoln Gordon, because of his age. Gordon was over fifty years old. Lieutenant Kokubo took the sick from Ellis' battalion to show the ten new arrivals what, in his view, real sick men looked like. Ellis' men were covered in 'huge, black, stinking ulcers' or were suffering badly from beriberi. Kokubo then let his Sergeant Noro beat the seven malaria suffers with bamboo sticks. Next, Kokubo hit Lincoln Gordon, telling him if he was not too old enough to fight the Japanese then he was not too old to work, and sent him out to the railway.

In November 1943, the first of the evacuations of the worst of the sick cases to a base hospital was due to take place. The sick were lined up for the Japanese Medical Officer to assess which individuals should be evacuated. Among the patients, one of them, Lieutenant T. Miles, had badly scalded feet and had great difficulty standing. Ellis told him to remain in his hut. During the inspection, Ellis told the Japanese MO about Miles. The Japanese MO demanded Miles should come out to be inspected. Miles hobbled out on a pair of rough wooden crutches. The Japanese MO, an NCO, asked if Miles was an officer, to which the latter replied that he was. He was then ordered to remove the rags which were round his feet acting as bandages. The bandages were stuck to his feet and pulling them off was causing Miles a great deal of pain.

Thomas Ellis takes up the story: 'The Medical Sergeant caught hold of the rags, pulled them off, kicked Miles in the stomach, hit him over the head and in the face until eventually he fell backwards several yards from the MO on the ground.' This was more than Ellis could stand and he intervened to explain that Miles had only been obeying his instructions. 'The Medical Sergeant saw I was mad with rage and he then set on me [and] hit me in the face.' The Japanese MO then said that not a single man, however sick he might be, would be evacuated. It was weeks before the first of the sick were sent down to a base hospital, during which time men died who could have been saved had they been evacuated earlier.[376]

Krian Kri   250 Kilo
Also known as Kriankri, Krieng Krai or Kroeng Krai

Q Battalion, consisting mainly of men from the 2/40th Battalion, 2nd AIF, were initially placed at Kinsaiyok camp in mid-March. The men were later moved

---
376. TNA, WO 235/924.

to a satellite jungle camp, a few kilometres down river. Their final move was to Krian Kri on 24 July 1943 where they remained until the line was completed.[377] In charge of the camp was a Korean called Tetsuichi Fumimoto who spoke very good English. The senior prisoner was Lieutenant Colonel Pine Coffin. The camp was situated on a long incline rising from a bluff above the Khwae Noi.

When they left Kinsaiyok, one of the prisoners, Lieutenant Geoffery Adams, was ordered to assemble a team to collect 100 head of cattle to be driven to Krian Kri. The native cattle –yaks – provided meat on the hoof for the prisoners and guards alike and nothing could be more important than to get this food to the new camp. Along with nineteen other prisoners, Adams herded the yaks for ten days through more than 120 kilometres of 'swamp, jungle mountain and stream' to bring this vital supplement to the meagre diet of the men. One of Adam's herders caught cholera from drinking from a stream and died; another had to drop out after developing an ulcer on his feet and not all the cattle made it to Krian Kri.

With just one Korean guard, Takeda, Adams' men considered killing him in the jungle and, with the cattle as food, escape to the hills. But the cattle they were driving meant an increased food supply for their comrades and a better chance of survival in camp than trying to escape.[378]

After they had reached Krian Kri it became Adams' job to look after the herd and to slaughter one yak every second day. In this, the meat was divided according to a strict rule. One quarter of the animal, plus liver and heart, went to the twenty-three guards and the remainder to the 900 prisoners.[379]

One of the jobs at Krian Kri was the cutting down of trees for bridges, the larger ones of which were transported downstream. This was a much sought-after task as the prisoners could float on the logs to guide them down the river.

The Japanese placed Lance Corporal William Walker in charge of the stores of a *rōmusha* camp which was situated around 100 yards from the POW camp. One day towards the end of August 1943 he was in the stores with two of the guards when one of the native labourers entered to give the guards a shave. After those two had been shaved, one of them suggested Walker should also receive a shave. As he had his shaving kit with him he accepted the offer.

This was reported to Fumimoto who told Walker to come into his tent. He told Walker he was a prisoner and if he wanted to have a servant he should wait until he was free. Fumimoto then hit Walker twenty-five times with his fists on each ear, causing them both to bleed. Walker was barely able to stand

---
377. Wright, p.146.
378. G.P. Adams, pp.90-107.
379. G.P. Adams, p.108.

after this treatment and began to stagger about. This encouraged the Korean to start kicking Walker's legs. It took ten days for Walker to recover his hearing.[380]

The usual daily battle between the medical officer and the Japanese over which prisoners were too unwell to go out to work was the same here as elsewhere. Fumimoto would only permit two patients to remain in hospital each day, regardless of the physical condition of the men. On one occasion, a corporal of the Royal Corps of Signals whose septic and ulcerated feet were so bad he was unable to stand, was made to crawl on his hands and feet to the cliff face where the prisoners were working, which was about a mile away. The other prisoners were not allowed to help him in any way and when he finally reached his workstation, he was beaten for being late. The smell of the stinking ulcers became so bad, however, the Japanese engineers sent the worst cases back to camp.[381]

At the height of the 'speedo', one party of thirty-four prisoners assigned to the Japanese engineers had to work from 08.30 hours until 14.00 without a break of any sort. They would then have a break of forty-five minutes when they would eat their meal of rice and burnt fish. No water or tea was given to the workers who were expected to drink from the streams flowing through the jungle. They then worked to 18.30 before their next break of thirty minutes. Work continued until 02.00 hours the following morning when the prisoners had to walk back to camp, a distance of about six kilometres.[382]

Lice and bedbugs 'bedevilled' the men as hygiene was hard to maintain. One man, who had simply given up on trying to keep himself clean and had become a breeding ground for vermin, was 'force-washed' by his mates.[383]

A stream ran between the camp and the railway. During the monsoon period, the stream became so full, the prisoners had to swim thirty or forty yards across to reach their work stations. A chain was formed for those who could not swim.

Kurikonta   258 Kilo

Kurikonta became 'H' Force's No 1 Camp. 'H' Force which, like 'F' Force, was under Malayan prisoner of war administration which had no jurisdiction in Thailand and was therefore less able to procure supplies for the prisoners under its control. Consequently, mortality rates were high.

This food shortage manifested from the moment 'H' Force arrived at Kurikonta due to the monsoon cutting off communications. 'The jungle trail which it had

---

380. TNA, WO 235/924.
381. TNA, WO 325/924.
382. TNA, WO 325/918.
383. Skinner, p.12.

been the intention to use for motor transport became waterlogged, bogged, and for long stretches totally non-existent,' ran the 'H' Force report, 'and the whole of the jungle path became a silent testimony to the important influence of weather in the affairs of men at war – all along the trail at intervals could be seen ditched, overturned and crashed vehicles which had tried but failed in efforts to get through with food and essentials. Meanwhile the misery and semi-starvation continued.'

Rations were so limited that they were at near starvation levels (usually twelve ounces of rice and two or three ounces of fish or other foodstuffs). The obvious solution to the road transport problem was the river, but all the available barges had been allocated to specific Japanese units in the forward areas and, despite the repeated representations of Colonel Humphries and his fellow officers, no barges could be acquired by the camp guards who had no authority in Thailand. The same reply was offered each time, the Japanese claiming that they were suffering the same privations as the prisoners which was, Humphries admitted 'palpably true'.

Eventually, after being permitted an interview with the IJA's Colonel Fuskase on a visit to Kurikonta, meat on the hoof was provided in the form of yaks, and a distribution was made to all six 'H' Force camps on a pro rata basis. Some of the camps were able to supplement their meat ration by 'assuming possession' of sundry stray yaks that had become separated from the herd as they were being driven through the jungle.

Humphries was able to arrange for communication between the six 'H' Force camps, with selected individuals being given armbands which allowed them to move up and down the line. In this way, 'H' Force headquarters was able to record death and sick rates and the issues of supplies from the IJA, as well as distribute officers' and other ranks' pay.

The latrines, which were no more than open, shallow pits with bamboo foot supports, had to be dug by medical officers as no other fit men were available, nor were any tools or materials provided for fly-proofing. Rain made these places fly-infested mud baths. The widespread prevalence of dysentery and diarrhoea resulted in the approaches and entrances to the latrines being fouled by men who simply could not reach the latrines in time.

The men were housed in leaking tents with up to twenty-eight men in each one. There were never enough blankets to go round and, because of the monsoon, the blankets that were available were perpetually sodden. Because of the long hours of work, the exhausted prisoners had neither the time nor energy to devote to personal hygiene which, in turn, was a factor in the spread of disease.

Konkuita   263 Kilo

Also known as Koncoita, Konkoita, Konikita, and even Conquita

When 'F' Force reached Konkuita on 10 May 1943, around 700 men of Parties Nos. 1 and 2, under Colonel, were detached from the I.J.A. Administration of 'F' Force and for all practical purposes came under the control of the engineers until they rejoined the force at Nieke in December.

All that Pond's men found were un-roofed huts occupied by Tamils and Burmese workers with only a small number of tents were provided for the POWs. The area was covered with 'vomitus and excreta,' wrote Colonel Kappe. 'Everywhere there was evidence of the effects of an epidemic, natives were lying about in various stages of death.'[384]

Assistant-Surgeon P. Wolfe reached Konkuita from Neike in late May 1943: 'On arrival there I saw a horrible scene. In one tent on the bank of the river fifteen patients were lying helpless. Eight of these were suffering from Cholera with nobody to attend to them. The whole area was polluted with infected stools and vomit, and full of flies.'[385]

Lieutenant Colonel Dillon wrote a report on Konkuita ('F' Force's No.4 Camp) on 3 June 1943 to the Japanese commander of 'F' Force, Colonel Banno: 'A very bad site; water runs into camp from all sides and lies there. There is no drainage. Cholera: There has been one death and there are now two cases. No building exists for segregation, and the two cases are in the hut with the rest of the men. There is no medicine or medical equipment to deal with the sick … It is reported that the coolies' cholera hospital is using as a latrine a small stream which flows into the one used by the prisoners for washing … In addition to a building for cholera patients, more accommodation is required for the main party. There are now 9 men to each bay on each side of the hut. There are 8 officers who are paying a large sum for this accommodation. More attap is urgently required to roof more huts.

'Mosquito nets, mats and blankets. None have yet been issued. As a result, malaria is rife.

'Clothing. Many men are without boots with soles. 150 pairs are required at once, and 200 more pairs within a month. Shorts and socks are now beyond repair.' All fit or unfit men except 11 cooks and duty men, 4 cowmen, the commanding officer, all other combatant and non-combatant men go out to work daily.' Dillion concluded that unless immediate action was taken to remedy

---

384. Kappe, p.26.
385. John Grehan, *Medical Officers on the Infamous Burma Railway: Accounts of Life, Death & War Crimes by Those Who Were There* (Frontline, Barnsley, 2021), p.103.

these problems, especially with regards to segregating the cholera cases, no men at all would be fit to work in just a matter of days.[386]

Hal Thirlwell, of 2/29 Battalion AIF, was one of those admitted to the cholera ward who survived. He ascribes his recovery from the illness to the large quantity of food he received. This, he said, was because so many of the patients were too ill to eat which meant extra rations for the others.[387]

Colonel Kappe saw Konkuita towards the end of July where the huts were 'indescribably' filthy and unavailing protests against being placed in such conditions made him realise that in the eyes of the Japanese the prisoners were 'on the same level' as the native labourers. The latter 'walked through the huts, spat, defaecated, and vomited … yaks were taken through the huts and dropped their excreta where the rice bags were stored.'

Corporal Thomas Thompson of the Royal Northumberland Fusiliers, arrived at Konkuita camp on 10 August 1943, along with 650 British and 300 Dutch prisoners. Already there were twelve British prisoners which had been sent as an advance party. It was still monsoon time, and the site was deep in mud and filth from which emanated a terrible 'stench'. There were just three dilapidated tents, one of which was used for stores and the other two for the worst of the sick.

The men were roused at 06.30 hours for breakfast of soft, boiled rice. Work normally began at 07.00 and finished anytime between 22.00 and 03.00 the following morning. Lunch was at 13.30 hours and again consisted of rice with a piece of dried fish about one cubic inch in size. The prisoners' last meal was when they arrived back in camp and to the usual rice was added a quantity of dried vegetable soup. Occasionally, they received a spoonful of peanuts and a sprinkling of salt. Once a week the POWs were given a spoonful of sugar and on every fourth or fifth day a fried rice ball.[388]

As this camp fell within Lieutenant Tarumoto's jurisdiction, maltreatment of prisoners working on the railway was commonplace. On one occasion, Thomas Thompson and seven others were 'beaten and bludgeoned' for one and a half hours because they misinterpreted an instruction regarding the work they were supposed to do. 'All of us received cuts, wounds and bruises all over our heads and bodies,' Thompson complained. When Captain Gennis tried to intervene by explaining the men had simply not understood the orders they were given, he too was beaten.

Beatings were also given out if a prisoner failed to stand to attention if any Japanese or Korean guard passed by, regardless of his rank. On one occasion

---

386. Grehan, pp.83-5.
387. Wright, p.158.
388. TNA, WO 235/857.

a party with Royal Artillery Lieutenant Burton did not see a Korean guard walking up to the group and so none of them stood to attention. The guard immediately started beating the men with his sword stick. Burton, who was a big man, took the sword stick off the guard. The guard reported this to the camp commandant. Four or five guards then seized Burton and dragged him off into the jungle. After a 'considerable' time, the guards returned without the British officer. Some of the prisoners went to find Burton who was 'a mass of blood and wounds'. Burton had been so badly beaten he had to be sent to a base hospital.[389]

Adrian Curlewis was at Konkuita in late 1943 and placed in a hut: 'in which there was human excreta, lice and filth. Outside there was a latrine filled with water and maggots. In the latrines you even had to sit decide a coolie and get some of his issue of disease. In addition, it was right beside the food … All night long coolies three feet from my head would be spitting and coughing all over me.'[390]

Konkuita was notable for being the place where the line being built northwards from Ban Pong met the line from Thanbyuzayat on 17 October 1943. The Japanese made the British rail laying party race the last kilometre against a Japanese party on the same work but cheated to allow the Japanese team to win.[391] 'The final frantic effort was made on 16 October,' remembered Roy Whitecross. 'From 6 am on Saturday we worked right through until 3 pm Sunday – 33 hours without a break, when the two ends of the line were joined at the 157 kilometre peg. We had linked Burma with Siam. Roughly we counted the cost, and reckoned that for every three men who had worked on the line, one now lay in lonely jungle graves.'[392]

A simple ceremony took place, in which the commanders of the two railway regiments each drove a symbolic golden spike into the final sleeper. In reality these were gold-coloured ebony spikes pushed into a prepared hole. (One legend has it that an enterprising Australian prisoner levered out the 'gold' spikes and sold them for a considerable sum to a greedy-eyed Thai who had witnessed the event).[393]

Another account described quite an elaborate event which was the subject of a Japanese propaganda film, the climax of which was the laying of the last section of track and the hammering home of that last spike. For this concluding scene, the producers needed happy, healthy prisoners showing their pride in

---

389. TNA, WO 235/857.
390. TNA, WO 235/1034.
391. TNA, WO 325/157.
392. Beattie, Rod, *The Thai-Burma Railway*, p.33.
393. IWM, Escritt Collection, *Beyond The Three Pagodas Pass*, p.22.

assisting in the great accomplishment on behalf of the Emperor. A few men, who did not look as ill-nourished or sick as the majority, were picked out and fitted with Japanese shirts, shorts and shoes.

After a rehearsal, all was ready. The cameras rolled, the prisoners dutifully manhandled the last section of rail into place and drove home the spikes: 'As the last spike was ready to be driven a most important but self-conscious looking senior and overweight officer of the Japanese Army came forward to perform the symbolic driving of the last spike. Panting with the weight of the hammer this portly dignitary aimed a feeble blow at the head of the spike which he missed completely and gave the rail a resounding clang instead. Bracing himself and looking quite dismayed at his own clumsiness, the officer took a much shorter grip of the hammer and managed to drive the spike in a fraction into the sleeper to be finished off by a lithe engineer who leaped to his assistance.' After the event, the film-star prisoners had to give back their new clothes and shoes.[394]

To celebrate, a holiday was announced for the 25th when a 'gaily festooned' train brought extra food rations for the Japanese along the line who also gave a special issue of rations to the prisoners. This was a quarter of a pound of ox tongue, and half a pomelo (a citrus fruit similar to a sweet grapefruit), per man. Officers also received six biscuits, a piece of peanut toffee and forty-five cigarettes.[395] The Japanese general officers attending the ceremony were carried in two Toyota diesel-engine boarded flatcars coupled together on top of which two attap-thatched roofs had been built.

After the line had been completed, a party of men was retained at Konkuita to conduct maintenance on the railway. During that time, Jim Kerr saw an incident he later recalled. As Konkoita was in the hills it was cold at night during the winter and he and his fellow Australians were sitting around a fire when they heard some Australians being marched passed the camp. Two of the prisoners went to see if there were any of the men from their regiment among the passers-by. Seeing this, the Japanese guards grabbed the two POWs and, at bayonet point, pushed them back into the fire. Both men were badly burnt with one of them dying.[396]

Nevertheless, the ill treatment of prisoners diminished after the completion of the railway as did living conditions in many of the camps. One consequence of this was the reduction in stealing among the prisoners, the men no longer having to compete with each other for survival.

---

394. Clarke, pp.60-1.
395. TNA, WO 235/1034.
396. Wright, p.81.

THE JOINING POINT FROM NORTH AND SOUTH

Thingomtha 273 Kilo
Also known as Thimongtha, Tiamonta, or Taimonta

It was at Thingomtha that a party of Australians of 'F' Force under Colonel Pond was sent to build a large bridge. It was clearly not a good camp and was described by Private Glen Skewes in his diary: 'May 23, 1943. We passed through the worst camp. Roofless huts.' Likewise, one prisoner wrote that Thingomtha consisted of: 'Two huts in a dense jungle about 100 yards from the railway line … It was a very small camp, often overlooked in food shipments.'[397] At times the food ration was reduced to seven and a half ounces a day per man.

On 24 May, Pond's men were addressed by 'F' Force's Australian commander, Lieutenant Colonel Kappe on the futility of escape and the dire consequences the prisoners would face at the hands of the Japanese if they were caught trying to escape. But then, two days later, all work on the railway was stopped due to a suspected case of cholera. No work meant the food ration was reduced. It was most probably this which prompted one of the prisoners to attempt to steal uncooked rice on 28 May. He was spotted by the IJA guards making off with a bag of rice, but the guards were unable to see who he was. The Japanese said that no meals would be permitted for any prisoners until the culprit came forward. It was not until 15.00 hours that the man admitted his guilt. The camp was lifted out of quarantine and work on the railway recommenced on 3 June.[398]

Working hours were from 07.00 hours to 21.00 hours with just one forty-five-minute break for lunch – if the guards were in a good mood. If the guards were in a sour mood, lunch time would be considerably shortened.

During the monsoon there were times when the prisoners were never dry, recalled Paddy O'Toole of 2/29th Battalion AIF. 'At nights you were curled up on the wet ground with a wet blanket … All your clothes were wet, you were wet and would stay that way.'[399] It was during the height of the monsoon, on 15 June, that Captain Adrian Curlewis was ordered to take a draft of 100 men north to Neike camp. Throughout the journey men were repeatedly 'bashed' by the Japanese sentries for failing to keep up the pace they demanded. 'Men frequently fell with their heavy burdens,' Curlewis later wrote, 'and were bashed until they were on their feet again'.

---

397. pacyfik.net.
398. Barnett Diary in Charles Kappe, *The Death Railway: The Personal Account of Lieutenant Colonel Kappe* (Frontline, Barnsley, 2022), pp.147-8.
399. Wright, p.165.

When Curlewis and the other two accompanying officers tried to intervene to protect the men they too were beaten by the Japanese. When they reached a small unnamed camp south of Nieke, they were informed that the party they were supposed to join was returning to Thingomtha the next day. Curlewis pointed out to the Japanese there was no point in the men continuing to Nieke only for them to be marched back to Thingomtha. But the Japanese insisted that they carry out their orders. As a result, the men, many of whom were ill and all of who were in poor condition, marched all the way to Nieke and then back to Thingomtha for no reason.[400]

As every prisoner was expected to work, the sick – the very worst cases – were housed in one of the accommodation huts. On one night in September 1943, after the evening meal, a few of the prisoners decided to go to the hospital to cheer up the sick with a sing-song. When he heard the noise, the camp commander, Captain Naoetsu Muriama, sent his sergeant to investigate. The Japanese NCO took the four men who were singing and lined them up outside Muriama's quarters. 'You are prisoners of war,' Muriama told them. 'You will not sing. Japanese soldiers do not sing and this is a military camp'. He then went up and down the line hitting the prisoners' heads and faces.[401]

At one stage meat on the hoof became readily available with a yak being slaughtered every day. The distribution of the meat, though, did not favour the prisoners. The approximately twenty guards would take what they wanted first. Then some would be given to the *rōmusha* who were working nearby, and the POWs would get the remainder, usually the same amount that was given to the twenty guards was left for the 300 or so prisoners.

Nieke and Shimo Nieke   282 Kilo
Also known as Nikhe, Niki, Niki-Niki, Neekey, Ni Thea, Niike or Nike

The Japanese Colonel Banno arrived at Shimo (Lower) Nieke by lorry on 10 May 1943, Lieutenant Colonel S.W. Harris in command of 'F' Force being the only POW. with him. This was to be the H.Q. camp for the 'F' Force area. It consisted of two partially roofed huts and seven large unroofed huts in a partly cleared hollow in the jungle. There was a small natural stream to provide water for all purposes. The camp had previously been occupied by 'coolie' labour.

During the next few days some I.J.A. stores arrived from Ban Pong and a small hut was roofed for Colonel Banno and his office. The other roofed huts

---
400. TNA, WO 235/1034.
401. AWM, 54 1010/4/64 Part 1.

were occupied by the I.J.A. guards. No shelter whatever was supplied for POWs – not even for a hospital, or a cookhouse.

The first batch of troops arrived on 13 May and thereafter continued to arrive daily. Some 400 seriously sick gradually accumulated at Lower Nieke. Some tents were issued, with I.J.A. instructions to use them to cover the unroofed huts instead of attap. However, most of them were old British tents, badly perished, and the pitch of the roof was, in any case, too flat for tents to be used as roofing and they were completely ineffective at keeping out the rain. This became all too apparent when the monsoon broke on 17 May as Shimo Nieke. Accordingly, they were removed by the prisoners and set up inside the hut frames, in which way they gave reasonable protection. The I.J.A., however, insisted on them being put back on the roofs. This stupidity was later repeated at Nieke, in spite of visual demonstration of rain pouring through, just as if no cover was there at all. From the start of the monsoon until well into September it was rare for the rain to stop for longer than four hours. There was one break of 24 hours in June and another in July.

Colonel Harris protested to Colonel Banno against the conditions the men had to endure, particularly regarding the roofing situation. No satisfactory answer was received. The most obvious necessity was for a hospital for the growing number of sick. It was already clear that after the long march from Ban Pong the force was heavily infected with malaria, dysentery, diarrhoea, and with septic sores on feet and legs. Banno explained that only the H.Q. would remain at Shimo Nieke. It was, therefore never used as a work camp.

The remainder of the force (excluding the 700 A.I.F. left at Konkuita which was to be known as No. 4 Camp) would be distributed to other camps which, he stated were all roofed. This was, of course, not true. When cholera was first diagnosed at Shimo Nieke Harris asked Banno if all this movement could be stopped to prevent the disease from spreading. Banno refused and, inevitably, the disease was carried to the other 'F' Force camps.

Nieke was one of the main points on the railway, where there were branch lines and camouflaged sidings. Kappe described the POW camp: 'Situated in a depression, the site was a bad one from the hygienic point of view and heavy rains made the area a quagmire, but viewed as a whole the camp cannot be said to be one that suffered badly from sickness.' Kappe suggested that the low incidence of sickness might have been due to the constant changes of personnel, although dysentery, malaria, beriberi and severe diarrhoea all took their toll.

Lieutenant Arthur Godman, though part of 'H' Force, was at Nieke: 'The accommodation at Nikki into which I was sent consisted of old, torn Indian Army tents. My particular tent was the outer cover of a tent and had several tears in the canvas through which the rain came. Inside the tent were two changs, one on each side, about three feet off the ground. When it rained – as it seemed to do every day – the ground was muddy and sometimes flowed through the tent … We were crowded into the tents, with each person having about eighteen inches of chang on which to sleep. It was impossible to lie on your back … We slept alternately head to foot so your head was between two pairs of feet. Before going to sleep you had to decide which was the least dirty pair of feet.'[402]

Large fires were kept going day and night in the central gangway of the huts during the monsoon. When the men came back to camp at night after a day working on the railway, they were able to dry their clothes – if they were not too exhausted. These fires were the only means of illumination at night.[403]

The prisoners were permitted to swim in the river and it was believed that it was because of this that the first cases of cholera were contracted at Lower Nieke. Not only did the native labourers use the river as a 'toilet', elephants used on the construction work also splashed around in the river at the same time the prisoners were in the water, stirring up the mud and muck which had accumulated on the bottom.[404]

Fortunately, infection rates were low, and the Japanese were quick to provide a small hut about half a mile from camp and an isolation hospital. This proved effective at stopping the spread of the disease, although the distance from the camp meant it was difficult to supply the isolation hospital with food and water. Cases, contacts, and suspects, were all segregated and Assistant Surgeon Wolfe bravely took charge and lived there. One day without warning two Tamil workers suffering from cholera were dumped at the isolation hut and left there for Wolfe and his men to look after. Five *rōmusha* cases in all were delt with, two of whom recovered.

There was what Harris called a 'minor horror' when a party of twenty prisoners on their way from Shimo Nieke to Nieke were intercepted by Japanese engineers and put to work pile-driving in the Khwae Noi. Fourteen days later, Lieutenant Colonel Dillon came across them, and found they had been pile-driving near Nieke daily from first light until 22.00 hours up to their armpits in cold, swift running water the whole time except for half an hour for lunch and 'driven with blows and sticks'. They were, by the time Dillon discovered them, in a terrible state and only three were fit for any work at all. Dillon managed to rescue them, but the men were 'too far gone', and all of them died.[405]

Dillon, though, was appalled at the conduct of some of the prisoners at Nieke. As elsewhere, theft among POWs was common. 'Elementary notions

---
402. Godman, p.93.
403. Barwick, p147.
404. Wright, p.173.
405. Grehan, p.18.

of solidarity and mutual help had largely vanished,' Corporal John Stewart Ullmann, the camp's interpreter saw. 'Survival was equated with theft.'[406] This led Lieutenant Colonel Dillion to address the men in the strongest terms: 'Dogs! ... You complain of being treated like dogs by your own officers! Well, it may be so, but I didn't imagine that British soldiers could behave the way you do. Yes, you'll probably say the Japs are responsible. But I'll let you have it straight out: I've never seen such scum of the earth as I see here assembled in Nikki. I never thought that such scoundrels could come out of England.

'And I hate to think that I deliberately sacrificed my freedom in Sumatra for the likes of you! ... Now, you tell me, are we going to let these bastards think that the white man, even in defeat, behaves like an animal?'[407] The reference to the prisoners' feelings about their officers clearly shows that, as elsewhere, there was a degree if resentment regarding the superior conditions the officers experienced.

As Nieke was a key centre of the railway, supplies of food were plentiful compared to other camps. The demand for labour was also very moderate, with only 150 of the 1000 plus men were being sent to work each day. This is in stark contrast to the other 'F' Force camps.

When the railway was complete, Nieke became a 'feeding' camp for those parties of prisoners coming down the line from the northern camps. As each trainload came in rice would be cooked and carried up to the station. One of those who helped with this was John Roxborough of 2/29th Battalion AIF who, even after all he had endured over the months, was still shocked with what he saw among those passing through the camp: 'Men who had once been healthy, robust being were now just walking skeletons, with a vacant stare of horror in their eyes.' Some of them who had legs amputated could only lie helplessly, their stumps seething with maggots.[408]

Little Nikhe 284 Kilo
Also known as Little Nikhe, Little Ni Thea or Little Nikke

Little Nikhe was No.1 Mobile Force's most southerly camp, was generally known by that force as 131 Kilo camp. The sick bay there (referred to by Rowley Richards as being a Regimental Aid Post rather than a hospital) was housed in one end of an accommodation hut. There were eight sleeping spaces in the sick bay, allowing two feet per patient. Dr Richards, the Regimental Medical Officer of 2/15 Australian Field Regiment, was with No.2 Battalion

---
406. John Stewart, *To the River Kwai: Two Journeys, 1943, 1979* (Bloomsbury, London, 1988), p.90.
407. ibid, p.91.
408. Wright, p.133.

of Lieutenant Colonel Charles Groves Wright Anderson's Force, noted that those with tropical ulcers, beriberi and pellagra were kept apart from those with dysentery and malaria. There were but a few mosquito nets which were reserved for the most severely ill patients.[409]

The men washed in a stream in a gully that had been dammed by the prisoners. They shaved using razors made from bits of metal that had been stolen from Japanese trucks by the POW drivers.

Rowley Richards relates an interesting conversation with Major John Chalmers at 131 Kilo camp. They were discussing, in October 1943, the recent demands of the Japanese for more workers from the ranks of the sick prisoners which put pressure on the senior officer, Colonel Anderson: 'He'll protect any man who is genuinely sick,' said Chalmers, 'but he can't let the malingerers get away with it or everyone suffers. Hell, Rowley, you know there are a lot of malingerers. The tricks they think up to toss the doc.' Richards took a different view of this, pointing out that a man has to either be knocked unconscious by the Japanese or be visibly rotting with ulcers or passing blood before he was allowed to be hospitalised. 'A man isn't sick [in Japanese eyes] until he is seen to be sick by the most medically ignorant [Japanese].' Though there were some who feigned illness to avoid being sent out to work, it was also the case that others were branded as malingers unfairly.[410]

It was also the case that men too sick to walk to the railway to work were carried on stretchers to the line as it was considered that, even lying down, they were capable of breaking boulders.[411]

It was also in October 1943, that Brigadier Varley visited Anderson's camp. 'This is a very rough camp,' Varley wrote in his diary, 'huts close together, roofs not by any means watertight, rough floors of split bamboo. Many men have not blankets and, without same or mats, they have no comfort.' Even Lieutenant Colonel Yoshitida Nagatoma (also spelt Nagatomo), in command of Number 3 Branch of the Thailand Prisoner of War Administration, admitted it was 'the worst camp of all' under his command and that improvements would be made, though he said that he considered the food ration to be adequate, which it very clearly was not.

All those prisoners like Varley who wrote diaries did so at great risk and they went to considerable lengths to keep them concealed. Beatings were given out to those who were found with a notebook, even the possession of a pencil could result in a bashing.[412]

---

409. Richards, pp.15-6.
410. ibid, pp.20-1.
411. Hardie, p.125.
412. Henderson, p.41.

Nikhe Camp 284 Kilo
Also known as Ni Thea

Another of the wood cutting camps, Nikhe, or 133 Kilo camp, was situated on hilly ground and proved to be cold at night. It was through the hills that the prisoners had to excavate numerous cuttings in the autumn of 1943. The camp was later occupied by William's Mobile Force, from 26 December 1943 to 11 January 1944.[413]

Shimo Songkurai 288 Kilo

On the night 14/15th May 1,000 men of the A.I.F. marched out from Lower Nieke to their permanent camp at Shimo, or Lower, Songkurai 'F' Force No.1 Camp, a distance of 7.5 miles. This party was to be joined by a further 800 A.I.F. men two days' later. Sergeant Erwin Heckendorf, of 2/30 Battalion, was one of those arrivals: 'We knew that we were going into not very good conditions. But even then, when we got to the final camp – Shimo Sonkurai, which was to be our headquarters, we were absolutely staggered. There was about three or four huts. One hut had a small portion of attap cover on it. The rest had no roof, no floor. Just the poles up, and a framework. The latrines were right beside the huts, and they were crawling with millions, and millions, and millions of flies – greenflies and maggots. Just one mass of flies and maggots. So we began to realise just how serious the situation was.'[414]

Initially, the senior Allied officer was Major N. Johnstone until Lieutenant Colonel Kappe took over command, who was equally as appalled with what he saw when he first arrived there: 'To call this place a camp at the time of arrival of our troops is a misnomer. Accommodation consisted of two lines of bamboo huts running parallel to the road at the foot of a steep hill covered with bamboo and the debris from the construction of the huts obviously several months previously.

'Except for 8 tents to cover the officers' quarters, no protection overhead had been provided. The exposure of the unroofed huts to tropical weather had put them in such a condition that in most cases they were almost in need of demolition and reconstruction.

'Latrines had been dug on the hillside above the huts and consisted of only two banks of wide shallow trenches, obviously a menace to health.'

---

413. 2/4th Machine Gun Battalion, 2nd4thmgb.com.au.
414. Edited from AWM NX36791, Heckendorf, Erwin Ernest (Sergeant).

'Kitchen accommodation did not exist, and the water supply was so meagre that ablution was impossible. No hospital accommodation had been provided for. The huts comprised … 18 or 20 bays each measuring 10 feet x 12 feet in which 10 men had to sleep. It was obvious that it would be impossible to accommodate the 2,500 A.I.F. destined for this camp.'[415]

It was the largest camp for Australians of 'F' Force. As it happened, for the first few weeks there was not much work undertaken on the railway, the focus of the prisoners' efforts was in improving and maintaining the road which ran roughly parallel to the proposed rail line. This allowed for the passage of Japanese troops and supplies to reach their forces in Burma.

There was quite a lot of ill-feeling in the camp regarding the better conditions experienced by the officers. According to Erwin Heckendorf, officers got 'first go at the rations' and when initially there was only one small portion with a roof in the huts 'the officers took that and kicked the men out of it. And when they put the new attap on some of the other huts the officers kicked the men out of that and went in there.'

Ted Whitmore, of 2/29th Battalion AIF, also believed that 'not a lot of representation from our officers' as one of the reasons why so many men died – along with all the other factors, of course.[416] The death rate in 'F' Force as a whole was 44 percent, but only 1 percent of Australian officers died and between 2 and 2.5 percent of British officers.[417]

On the other hand, Heckendorf was quick to praise some of the officers. One of the latter was the camp's senior medical officer, Major Hunt. Heckendorf made a point in his testimony to explained how Hunt put all the people in the hospital capable of any kind of labour to work on dealing with the latrines: 'We used to put earth over the top of them, cover them up and leave them there for about ten days, or fourteen days, opening up a new one in the meantime. … and they made wooden lids over the top of them, that would close up, and makes it flyproof to a certain extent. It took three periods of fourteen days to be sure that no maggots – no flies survived'.[418]

The crowded conditions and, of course, the terrible weather, meant that disease spread quickly and on 17 May cholera broke out. It had been brought with the prisoners from Nikke where the first case had been diagnosed the previous day. Five died before cholera vaccine was obtained, but by 25 May all troops had been inoculated. The soldiers of 'F' Force had been inoculated at Changi before they left for Thailand. But their hurried departure had meant there had

---

415. Kappe, p.31.
416. Write, p.161.
417. McCormack and Nelson, p.101.
418. AWM NX36791, Heckendorf.

not been enough time for them to receive their second injection which would have provided them with much greater protection.

To further exacerbate the problem First Lieutenant Tsuneo Fukuda, the camp commander, did not understand the principles of isolation. The cholera isolation area was separated from the main camp by a fence, but the latrine was shared by all. To make matters worse, because cholera is a waterborne disease, the creek in the camp was placed out of bounds. This meant that no water was available for washing, making it difficult for the hospital staff to maintain good hygiene standards.

Stan Arneil recalled in his diary: 'I just saw a cove carried from one of the huts, grey of face and limp of body. The ground is becoming covered in slime where these have bogged or vomited ... Two poor chaps were carted out on three poles and wrapped in a blanket or ground sheet were tossed on to a roaring fire five yards from the cemetery. It was a horrible sight and I pray I will not finish that way.'[419]

In reality, Fukuda took little interest in the operation of the camp at all 'except to lie on his back' and leave the running of the whole place to a Korean guard called Toyoyama. The suggestion was that this was because the pair had an intimate relationship.[420] Fukuda stated that he would not feed the sick as he believed that the Australian doctors were deliberately keeping men in hospital to sabotage the construction of the railway. As a punishment for this perceived crime all officers were denied food for twenty-four hours.

When he was further challenged over this, he apparently answered: 'The Geneva Convention and the principles of humanity have no bearing in your case. The railway must go through and if British and Australian POWs lose their lives, that is of no concern to us, and the conditions under which you are working must NOT be allowed to come into conflict with the aims of TENNO HEIKA [the Emperor]'[421]

There was a second occasion when Fukuda stopped all rations for twenty-four hours for the entire camp. This was due to the loss of a shovel. Anyone seen eating during this period was to be starved for a week.[422]

Toyoyama told the POW officers that they would get a beating if they did not have their parade states ready at the appointed time. He would then often turn up three or four minutes early, accuse the officer or NCO of not being ready in time, and would them give them the beating he had promised.[423]

---

419. Stan Arneil, *One Man's War* (Alternative Publishing Co, 1980), pp.96 & 99.
420. This was Major Cyril Wild's assertion, see TNA, WO 235/1034.
421. TNA, WO 235/1034.
422. TNA, WO 235/1034.
423. TNA, WO 235/1034.

By 24 May cholera appeared to be under control but on that day a secondary wave of infections manifested itself. As Yoshihiko Futamatsu explained, 'watercourses in the jungle were dirtied by rotted vegetation [and] animal excrement ... In particular there were times when bacteria abounded in water causing terrible contagious diseases ... even rainwater could become bacterial ... Into the Kwai Noi fed mountain streams and along them any people there soiled the water with their sewage.'[424]

The ground between the latrines and the nearest huts was frequently contaminated with faeces and the vomit of men unable to reach the latrines in time. According to Kappe, the incessant rain swept this infected matter under the huts and along the drains which passed through them. (At one point in August, the rain was so heavy that one of the latrines burst its bank and the 'filthy stream oozed through the camp area' and under the huts of the hospital.) As Kappe explained: 'Contact with boots, with patients direct, flies and the lack of covers for food, all played a part in spreading the infection.'[425]

Fukuda would not allow any fit men who would be needed on the railway to go into the cholera area. All duties, apart from nursing, had to be performed by those already in isolation. Those that did go out to work were treated badly, as reported by Chaplain George Polain: 'I saw them there with logs that elephants could not pull. They [the Japanese] forced our men to carry them and if they could not lift them, bashed them with shovels and sticks over the head, across the kidneys, and across the back, and so on. Also, they made them kneel across the logs and hold up bars, shovels and things. On another occasion, they were forced to bridge a creek with their bodies, their hands on one side and feet on the other. If they sagged at all they were bashed with spades.'[426]

Heckendorf related a distressful scene regarding the adjacent Asian labour camp at this time: 'The coolies got cholera badly, and they were dying, and you'd hear men being taken out to be burnt, when they weren't even dead, they'd still be groaning, or crying out in anguish, trying to get away. They became very frightened, and they used to try to crawl into our camp ...

'The camp was on sloping ground, and we were about four feet off the ground on the lower end ... and they used to crawl under there, and we had to poke them out with poles, to try and protect ourselves from getting a new outbreak of cholera. It was ruthless and cruel, it was like poking rabbits out of a log.'[427]

Before the disease was brought under control 101 prisoners had died which was just less than 50 percent of the 209 patients who had contracted cholera.

---

424. Futamatsu, pp.147-8.
425. Kappe, pp.34-5.
426. TNA, WO 235/1034.
427. AWM, NX36791, Heckendorf.

Of this number twenty-three were men who had helped tend to the cholera patients. Only three of these were members of the Australian Army Medical Corps, the remainder were volunteers.[428]

Sickness rates accelerated with the passing of every day, and it was estimated that within a month only 250 men out of the camp strength of 2,000 would be fit for work. As the number of workers decreased, so the working hours increased to seventeen or eighteen hours each day and, as only those who went to work received full rations, the food situation became increasingly desperate. The senior officers, including Major Hunt, demanded that, as the medical situation was so grave, that not only should all work be stopped, but that as soon as the men were fit enough to move, the entire area should be evacuated. A similar written protest was made concerning conditions at Upper Songkurai, and both letters were delivered by Colonel Kappe to Colonel Banno.

Surprisingly, on 4 June, Banno announced that work should cease indefinitely. Unsurprisingly, this period of relief lasted only four days. In what the prisoners viewed as a 'war' between the Japanese POW Administration and the IJA engineers, the latter insisted workers were required, at whatever cost.

Rations continued at starvation levels. The food ration was set at 16 oz of rice for those that worked outside the camp; 9 oz for those that worked in the camp; and just 6 oz for the sick. Part of the problem was that the rice supplied by the IJA was transported in 200lb bags, but sometimes these had holes torn in them in transit through which much of the contents were lost before they reached the camp or rats had eaten their way into the bags.[429]

When the roads collapsed during the monsoon, and the truck which had been supplied to transport the rations was transferred elsewhere, fifty of the fittest men were required each day to carry the rations on 60lb man-packs from other camps, mainly No. 2 camp. William Bowring said that that these men had to carry between 80 and 90lb each through mud which varied from six inches to three feet. In almost every instance, Bowring claimed, the men were simply unable to struggle back to camp and further parties of sick officers had to be sent out to help them.

With so many men occupied in transporting the food it meant there were less men available to work on the railway. So, Fukuda tried an alternative method. He ordered the rations to be transported in ox carts, which the men had to pull. But the road was in such a deplorable condition and as the prisoners had to drag the carts twenty-six miles from No.5 Camp, they arrived back at 02.00 hours the next day in a state of complete exhaustion. This method was not tried

---

428. Walker, *Australia in the War of 1939–1945*, p.598.
429. AWM, NX36791, Heckendorf.

again, but the problem of ration supply remained unresolved.[430] Fukuda said that he would only allow fit men to be employed in the collection of rations when there were less sick in hospital. It seems there was no need for the rations to be collected by the prisoners themselves as the camps on either side of Shimo Songkurai received their rations by Japanese motor vehicle, indeed the vehicles actually passed by Shimo Songkurai. Why Fukuda did not address this issue does not seem to have been satisfactorily explained.[431]

Of the food that did arrive at the camp, it was distributed by the Japanese on a sliding scale: six ounces for those in hospital, nine ounces for those working in the camp, and sixteen ounces for those working on the road and the railway. While the working men were paid, for most of the time there was nothing for the men to buy to supplement these meagre rations.

As with other camps there was a dire shortage of medical supplies. The Allied officers told Fukuda that if the Japanese would or could not supply the prisoners with such supplies, they would be willing to buy whatever might be available. This Fukuda was willing to agree to. The officers raised 1,500 dollars but all they received was 138 yards of muslin buttercloth for which Fukuda charged a dollar per yard.[432]

Adjacent to the POW camp/hospital was a *rōmusha* camp of Malay, Tamil and Chinese workers. Their camp was situated close to the Japanese quarters, and it was the habit of the Asiatic workers to throw their refuse, namely scraps of food, into the adjoining Japanese area, even using the ground as a latrine. The Japanese ordered Australian prisoners to guard the fence at night to stop this practice. 'I was a member of the guard on one occasion,' recalled Corporal Stanley Bryant-Smith. 'On this particular night the guard was drawn from malaria and dysentery patients. We performed our duties as required and to the best of our knowledge no Asiatic had entered the area, and no refuse had been thrown over the fence. However, on the following morning, Toyoyama discovered a small quantity of scrap food lying near the fence in the Japanese area, [he] also found that someone had used the area as a latrine.' He ordered every member of that night's guard to be brought to him and interrogated. Each prisoner stated they believed they had done their best but that they were all very sick men and it had been a dark and cold night. They also argued that if any Tamils had managed to get into the Japanese area it was because the guard was too small in number to cover the entire fence adequately.

---

430. Kappe, p.38.
431. TNA, WO 235/1034.
432. TNA, WO 235/1034.

Not satisfied with this, Toyoyama then tried to get each of the guards to admit it was they who has soiled the ground under threat of punishment with a large log of wood if they denied being guilty. When all remined defiant that they were not responsible, Toyoyama got a large Japanese guard to punch each of the prisoners in the face. Two of the prisoners, one of whom was Bryant-Smith, were knocked unconscious.

As this had still not resulted in an admission of guilt, Toyoyama selected a large, closely knotted bamboo rod and placed it on an open patch of ground close to the Asiatic quarters. He then ordered all eight of the POWs involved to 'kneel on this bamboo pole, in such a manner that their bodies and heads were erect and the full weight of their bodies was applied to their knees against the bamboo.' The men were forced to remain in that position for two days in the sun with nothing covering their heads or bodies.[433]

On 29 June every fit prisoner was sent out to work even though a party was needed to collect rations from No.2 camp (Songkurai). This meant that those so ill they were classed as 'no-duty' men had to walk the two kilometres to pick up the rations. On the way back, each one had to carry at least sixty-six pounds (thirty kilos).

Fukuda tried everything he could to send as many men out to work as possible, often resulting in the Japanese lieutenant undertaking extreme action. He allowed no fit men to undertake camp duties, leaving such tasks, including the digging of latrines and the carrying all rations to the hospital and isolation camps, to be done by officers. On two occasions he forbade the officers from eating for twenty-four hours, posting sentries to make sure those orders were carried out. Major Roderick Anderson claimed that Fukuda threatened to send the sick out of the camp into the jungle to fend for themselves if more men were not made available for work to make room for *rŏmusha* who would work. According to the Australian official history, the threat was to throw *all* the prisoners out of the camp to make room for the arrival of a group of Asians which was due to arrive. Colonel Harris managed to reach an agreement whereby a third of the camp would be handed over to the *rŏmusha*. 'It is a grim recollection,' wrote Harris, 'that we were able to make available a third of our accommodation only by taking into consideration the number of deaths which would inevitably occur in the next few weeks.'[434]

On 4 July, a pick went missing. This resulted in Lieutenant Fukuda announcing that none of the prisoners would receive any food until the pick was found, though, after protests, he allowed the workers and the sick to be fed. The next

---

433. TNA, WO 235/1034.
434. TNA, WO 235/1034 & 325/16.

morning the pick re-appeared, but this was not good enough for Fukuda who demanded that the culprit be found, or the camp would starve. Fukuda eventually relented and at 16.00 hours the prisoners were allowed to eat for the first time that day. At the war crimes trails in 1946, Fukuda was one of those sentenced to death, commuted to life imprisonment.

Working conditions in July became dreadful. Just getting to work involved a trek of up to two hours through rain and mud. Parties of men then had to carry fifteen-foot-long logs through the slush and mud for a distance of a kilometre, in one instance being beaten with a stick by a Japanese engineer every few yards. On another occasion, a sergeant who collapsed to the ground through exhaustion, was flogged and then forced to carry on working. Prisoners who became ill with an attack of malaria while out working on the railway, reported Major Anderson, were made to stand holding a pick at full arm's length above their heads until they collapsed. The prisoners then had the long struggle back to camp in the dark.

By 19 July some 1,350 men of a total camp population of 1,850 were sick. Major Noel Johnston, who had been left in charge of No. 1 Camp when Colonel Kappe left to command No. 3 Camp, decided to move the seriously ill to No. 3 Camp. This move was recorded in Kappe's report: 'The additional stretcher carry of 3 kilometres over slippery and hilly country placed an added strain on the semi-fit stretcher bearers and on the patients of the second party, which was made up of seven officers and 209 other ranks. Of the latter only 100 were fit to carry loads and these had to be detailed to carry the 16 stretcher cases and to assist the 94 men who were just fit to walk (stumble or crawl would better express their condition).

'As the party was assembling it was found that three of the stretcher cases were too ill to make the trip and they had to be re-admitted to hospital.

One died within a few minutes and another a day or two later. One of the men carried to No. 3 Camp died of exhaustion within a day of his arrival and many of the others who made the journey died subsequently.

'On this journey there was hardly a man, fit or otherwise, who was not burdened with a load of camp stores. The ordeal would have tested men in the best physical condition and it is no wonder, therefore, that even many of the fit became casualties and subsequently died through being forced out to work without an opportunity of resting after their ordeal. Of this party 109 were admitted to hospital directly on arrival.'[435] Some five hundred of the sick remained in Shimo Songkurai after the departure of the more serious cases and the distribution of some of the remaining prisoners to other 'F' Force camps.

---

435. Kappe, pp.71-2.

Indian labourers, including women and children were moved and put into one of the empty huts. They brought with them cholera.

It was in late September, when 277 were transported to the base hospital at Thanbaya, Burma, when the camp was closed. The rest embarked on a chaotically organised five-day trip by trains to Kanchanaburi. Most of the men were very sick with dysentery, beriberi and tropical ulcers. 'Conditions under which the train was loaded were terrible,' Noel Johnston recorded. There was one case of smallpox, the man being taken off the train to die. 'On the way down we lost in all 14 men,' continued Johnston in his report. 'You could not lie down on the whole trip. Men with dysentery were in a mess ... because they had up to 30 or 40 motions a day.' Ten men who had died on the journey were buried at Brankasi but the corpses of the others that died had to stay on the train until the party reached Kanburi.[436]

Songkurai   294 Kilo
Also known as Sonkuri or Songkla

Songkurai was 'F' Force's No.2 Camp. Some 900 all ranks arrived there on the morning of 20 May 1943 after a march of 315 kilometres. 'The sight that confronted us almost broke our hearts,' wrote Lionel de Rosario. 'The entire ground within the camp was covered with a thick carpet of black smelly mud.'

The camp was built on the side of a hill between two deep gullies down which flowed fast moving streams. It consisted of three huts, approximately 150, 200 and 250 feet long. The Japanese guards, POW officers and warrant officers were quartered in the smallest hut; the other two, which were roofless, being occupied by other ranks. Adequate latrines were already in existence, as was also a cookhouse. Water for the camp came from a small stream which ran through the jungle behind the camp. This was channelled into the camp along a bamboo trough. Due to a lack of metal containers, food was served in bamboo containers lined with large leaves from the jungle.

Lionel de Rosario described the huts in which they were to sleep: 'The huts were 100 metres long and six metres wide, constructed of bamboo with attap panels in the walls. There was an opening in each wall but no roof, and the floor, as outside, was a mud bath ... there was no rendering on the floor and the muddy water flowed through the hut.'[437] As the huts were without roofs, rigging up some form over overhead cover was a priority. They tried joining their groundsheets together and spread them over lengths of bamboo to form a kind of marquee. Then came the rain. So torrential was the downpour, the water

---
436. TNA, WO 235/1034.
437. Rosario, pp.109 & 111.

accumulated in the makeshift roof and its weight pulled the whole structure down, drenching the men underneath. The day after their arrival, the prisoners cleaned up the camp and the following day those that could were sent out to work on the railway.

Eventually, the prisoners found time to dig drainage trenches around the huts and the floors inside dried out. Also attap roofs were added, though those these only became the home of anopheles mosquitoes. Lice also infected the huts which crawled all over the prisoners' bodies at night.

On 23 May, Lieutenant Colonel Pope arrived with 700 men bringing the camp strength up to 1,600. Colonel Pope assumed command of the camp, but on 6 June relinquished it owing to ill health to Lieutenant Colonel A.T. Hingston. Colonel Pope subsequently died in Burma.

Regardless of the local time, the time maintained by the Japanese was always Tokyo time. This meant that the prisoners were always woken up in the dark, when it was already daylight in the land of the rising sun.

Rain fell every day and it was not until two weeks after the prisoners had reached Songkurai before the Burmese labourers finished roofing the two large huts. This meant that the prisoners were unable to dry their soaked clothing and this constant living and sleeping in wet clothes and bedding reduced their resistance to illness. Even when finished, the roofs proved inadequate, and the prisoners took the attap from the sides of the huts to reinforce that above them. Few prisoners had any form of groundsheet or spare blanket which they could lay on and the rough bamboo slats of their sleeping platforms scratched and tore their skin.

Padre J.N. Duckworth called Songkurai, run by Captain Muruyama, 'the horror hell' of prison camps: 'Our accommodation consisted of bamboo huts without rooves. The monsoon had begun and the rain beat down. Work – slave work – piling earth and stones in little skips on to a railway embankment began immediately. It began at 5 o'clock in the morning and finished at 9 o'clock at night and even later than that. Exhausted, starved and benumbed in spirit we toiled, because if we did not, we and our sick would starve. As it was the sick had half rations because the Japanese said, "No work, no food." Then came cholera. This turns a full-grown man into an emaciated skeleton overnight. 20, 30, 40, and 50 deaths were the order of the day … The Japanese still laughed and asked, "How many dead men?" We still had to work, and work harder. Presently, come dysentery and Beri-Beri disease bred of malnutrition and starvation. Tropical ulcers, diphtheria, mumps, small-pox, all added to the misery and squalor of the camp on the hillside where water flowed unceasingly through the huts at the bottom.'[438]

---

438. From Padre J.N. Duckworth "A Japanese Holiday", which was broadcast from Singapore to London on 12 September 1945. See britain-at-war.org.uk/ww2/Death_Railway/html/songkurai.htm.

The work at Songkurai was the construction of a wooden bridge over the river adjacent to the camp. For this the men had to carry tree trunks, up to twenty feet long and over foot in diameter, which Major Charles Humphrey of the Manchester Regiment said would require fifteen to twenty men to move but had to be done by just eight to ten men. They had to carry these a distance of 800 yards, often through mud up to their knees. During the building of the bridge a number of the prisoners were knocked into the river thirty feet below. The workers were frequently whipped by the engineers, using strands of fencing wire. For about a fortnight at the end of July 1943, the men worked from 09.00 hours in the morning until 03.00 hours the following morning and then back out to work again at 09.00 hours. Lunch break was an hour or less.[439]

'Men had been, and continued to be, beaten (until the completion of the bridge on August 20) with wire whips and bamboo sticks, and unfit men were punched and kicked, not for disciplinary reasons, but to drive them to make efforts beyond their strength,' wrote Colonel Kappe, who complained that the then camp commander, Lieutenant Hiroshi Abe, made no attempt whatsoever to stop this brutal treatment by his men.

Even though the area around Songkurai was virtually uninhabited, it was not long before a number of Thai and Burmese traders appeared looking for business. They were all males who made their way upriver on paddle boats. They could not openly trade with the POWs and so had to hide in the bulrushes at the edge of the river. They attracted the attention of the prisoners by making bird calls. Among the items they had for sale to those who could afford them were native biscuits, bananas, dried fish, eggs and cigarettes.[440]

As mentioned above, cholera had broken out on 23 May and by the end of the month sixty-three deaths had occurred. The Japanese provided a small hut for the cholera patients on the other side of the railway about a quarter of a mile from the main camp. It was staffed by a Dr Turner who was a lieutenant in the Federated Malay States Volunteer Force and two or three orderlies. Food was taken to them and left at a safe distance for the orderlies to collect. Dr Turner contracted cholera himself, but this did not stop him looking after his patients. He treated himself and recovered.[441]

The cholera hut was only partly roofed and the holes in the roof were so large that the rainwater poured down on the patients below. As there was no lighting, none of those men that had died during the night could be removed until daybreak. No accommodation was provided for the hospital orderlies tending to the patients and they had to sleep in the huts among the dead and the dying.

---

439. TNA, WO 235/1034.
440. Rosario, p. 144.
441. Laird, p. 98.

Dr Turner also operated a wireless set. The Japanese were terrified of cholera and would not go anywhere near the isolation ward, which meant it was the safest place to conceal the wireless. The greatest problem associated with the functioning of the radio was with re-charging the battery. This was overcome by certain AIF men who drove lorries along the road which ran alongside the railway, as explained by Captain Richard Laird: 'Originally, a spare battery was "won" by one of the drivers who complained that the battery on his truck was "*sudah habis*" (finished); the Nips produced a replacement and the "dud" was thrown out, but subsequently recovered. Thereafter batteries needing re-charging were swapped over under cover of spurious breakdowns. The batteries, covered with rice, were carried to and from the trucks by ration parties in the large containers used for cooking the rice. Various diversionary activities were mounted to distract the attention of the Nips while the batteries were being changed. With a covering of rice over it the good battery was then taken over to the cholera "hospital"'.[442]

Another doctor, Captain Peter Henry, 2/10th Field Ambulance, remarked on the speed at which cholera developed in men at Songkurai who were so weak from the lack of nutrition: 'Beri-beri was the worst disease up there and it was dreadful in itself, but if you contracted that, it often became easy to get cholera or dysentery. I saw one fellow this particular day who had beri-beri and he was very bloated, then the next day he was emaciated with cholera – he was like a skeleton within twenty-four hours. Cholera was that quick and lethal and there was little to nothing we could do to stop it.'[443]

The Japanese also made another hut available for the POWs suffering from dysentery. The Japanese used to test all prisoners for dysentery by putting either a piece of bamboo or a piece of wire or a glass tube up the rectum. This was a painful experience for fit men but was especially hard on those who were extremely ill, who would be pulled out of their hut to be tested and it undoubtedly precipitated the death of a number of them.[444]

In many respects the unsung heroes of the camps were the medical orderlies. Often these were just ordinary combat soldiers with no medical experience who volunteered to look after the sick men in shocking conditions and at risk each day of catching the diseases they were helping to treat. Among these was Reginald Thomas Jarman. He left us an account of an average day for him and his fellow orderlies in Songkurai No.2 Camp: 'Up before daybreak to collect the "half ration" of food for those not working, i.e., the sick and dying; feed

---

442. Laid, p.99.
443. Wright, pp.187-8.
444. TNA, WO 235/1034.

those who couldn't feed themselves; clean up all the mishaps of the night from dysentery patients who tried but couldn't make it to the latrines.

'The Japanese guard would then arrive to do a head count of all the sick while all the orderlies paraded outside. With this over, two orderlies would then go through both hospitals and remove all who had died during the night to an area outside. The daily average death rate was 4+. (I can remember one day when the death count was 10.)

'Each body was then carried on a makeshift stretcher to a guard post to be recorded, then to the burial ground away from the camp site. They would then dig the grave, remove any clothing before burial, complete the job, then return for the next body, and so on, until all the dead had been buried. This process could take most of the day as we only had one well-worn shovel to work with. Any clothing kept from those who died would be washed and, if not utilized as bandages, would be given to the those in the greatest need as, by this time, almost everybody's clothing had rotted off our backs from humidity, perspiration, mud and slush.'[445]

Apart from such clothing, the orderlies had nothing to dress wounds with for many months other than banana leaves wrapped round with puttees, sleeves cut from shirts, legs cut from trousers and officers' mosquito nets.

This all proved too much for a number of the men, who decided to risk all and escape. The first to do so at Songkuri was a group of eight who escaped on 5 July 1943, details of which were recorded in the following translation of 'Japanese Court Martial Case and Summary of Evidence' selected from a file of Court Martial Records belonging to the Legal Department of 18 Area Army:

Accused:	Ian O'Brian Poston Bradley, British Army Sgt
	Peter Richard Jackson, British Army Sgt
	Bernard Bradley, British Army, L/Cpl
	Frederick John 'Urado', British Other Rank
	Jack Ivor Evans, British Army Cpl
	William Henry Dawkins, British Army L/Cpl
Unit:	2 Detached Station, 4 Section, Malay PW Camp
Offence:	Acts contrary to PW Camp Penal Laws
Sentence:	Penal Servitude for Life
Date of Sentence:	18 November 1943

---

445. See the website Prisoners of War of the Japanese, www.POWs-of-japan.net/articles/83.htm.

The accused were captured in Singapore and were sent to 2 Detached Station for work on the Burma-Siam Railway. There was an outbreak of Cholera in early June 1943 and the accused felt unhappy and longed to return home.

Among the PWs was a man called Medley who had been in Siam before and knew the language and topography. On 5 June the accused got together and planned to escape to China or India and so return home. The accused men and another PW called Singleton sold various articles through Medley to Siamese who were working on the railway, and also got some food from the PW in charge of the cookhouse. Bradley got a lodestone from another PW and four maps were made.

Preparations for the escape were then complete, and on 6 June the accused and Singleton escaped under Medley's guidance (a total of 8 men).

In the middle of July, the party had reached a cave in the jungle near 'Chiyenaboe', 12 Km East of 'Nonaipon' (Siam) but it was the rainy season and free movement was impossible.

During their concealment, Singleton died on 13 September. On 2 October Evans, Dawkins and Medley went out to buy food and the other four were captured by the Kempeitai. Medley continued to do his utmost to escape but, on the 7th October Evans and Dawkins gave themselves up to Japanese officials of the Mitsubishi Mining Co. at 'Daibu' and they were handed over to the Moulmein Kempei on 14 October.

Signed:
Lt Col Shitamura Chikara, President of the Court
Lt Ishihashi Tsuki, Court Member
Lt Koyama, Mayata, Court Member

Another escape was attempted from Songkurai the following month, July 1943. Lieutenant J.B. Bradley RE was isolated in the cholera ward outside the main part of the of the camp where his job was to incinerate the corpses of cholera victims. This was a place the Japanese stayed well clear of, which allowed Bradley to wander around a little and he found a way through the jungle to the bank of a small river, the Huai Song Kalia. Along with Lieutenant Colonel Wilkinson RE, he planned to escape to tell the world what was happening to the prisoners of 'F' Force. They aimed to travel down the Huai Song Kalia, through the mountainous jungles to reach the Ye River and from there to the Andaman Sea.

Joining the two men were captains W.H. Anker, RASC, J. Feathers, RASC, lieutenants Robinson, RASC, I.M. Moffat, RE, G.A. Machade, SSVF, T.P.D.

Jones, Malay Regiment, Corporal Brown, SSVF, and Nur Mohammed, an Indian fisherman who had been taken prisoner by the Japanese.

They successfully escaped on 5 July 1943 and made their way along the river but found the dense jungle on the slopes of the mountains so thick that progress was pitifully slow. Their rations dwindled until, on 28 July, they ate the last of their rice. During the night Corporal Brown walked out into the jungle to die, not wanting to be a burden upon the rest. Others developed injuries from hacking their way through the undergrowth and Lieutenant Moffat's legs had become covered in tropical ulcers. On 2 August, Captain Feathers died during the night and three days later Colonel Wilkinson died from heart failure. On 9 August Lieutenant Jones collapsed unconscious and had to be carried to a hut next to a tributary of the Ye. In the hut Lieutenant Robinson died from septicaemia and dysentery, and the same night Jones begged them to carry on without him as he was virtually unable to move.

On 14 August, after six weeks, the last two of which were without food, the survivors reached the Ye and built a raft. This took three days, and on 17 August they set off down the Ye. They did not get far before the raft broke up in rapids. Three managed to reach the shore where they were found by Burmese hunters. They were taken to the native village and eventually arrested by the Japanese and taken back to the camp.

One of the officers left a note explaining why they had sought to escape: 'Food is short, health is failing, sickness such as Beri-Beri, Cholera, Malaria, Small Pox, Dysentery and Diphtheria is prevalent. Some 220 officers and men have died since our arrival here about five weeks ago ... therefore, I consider, with some of my fellow companions, that the risk we are about to take, be it life or death, is to some purpose if only to get away from here.'[446]

Thanks to the efforts of the British and Australian officers, particularly Major Cyril Wild, the Japanese were persuaded to drop the death sentences and the men went back to work on the railway.[447] This was a relief to the Korean guards who believed that their conduct had caused the food shortages which the escapees said was one of the reasons they tried to get away: 'Those on guard duty thought they would be decapitated; all realised that they had been helping the escapees by selling them tinned food and changing, at a nice profit, Thai money for Burmese,' recalled interpreter John Stewart Ullmann.[448]

Lieutenant Colonel John Williams first visited what he called Songkrei on 3 August 1943: 'I went first to a very large hut accommodating about seven

---

446. Quoted in Barwick, p.158.
447. Kratoska, pp.288-90. See also James Bradley's own account, *Towards the Setting Sun, An Escape from the Thailand-Burma Railway, 1943* (J.M.L. Fuller, Wellington, 1982), p.53.
448. John Stewart, *To the River Kwai: Two Journeys, 1943, 1979* (Bloomsbury, London, 1988), p.111.

hundred men. The hut was of the usual pattern. On each side of an earthen gangway there was a twelve feet wide sleeping platform made of split bamboo.

'The roof was inadequately made with an insufficient quantity of palm leaves which let the rain through everywhere. There were no walls, and a stream of water was running down the earthen gangway. The framework of the hut was bamboo tied with creeper. In this hut were seven hundred sick men. They were lying two deep along each side of the hut on the split bamboo platform. Their bodies were touching one another down the whole length of the hut. They were all very thin and practically naked. In the middle of the hut were about a hundred and fifty men suffering from tropical ulcers. These commonly stripped the whole of the flesh from a man's leg from the knee to the ankle. There was an almost overwhelming smell of putrefaction. The only dressings available were banana leaves tied around with puttees, and the only medicine was hot water.

'There was another hut further up the hill of similar design in which so-called fit men were kept and one well-roofed and better constructed hut occupied by the Japanese guards.

As more and more men fell sick in Songkurai from cholera, dysentery, beriberi, fever, and a form of trench foot, it became increasingly difficult to find the number demanded by the I.J.A. for working parties. As the weeks passed an increasing number of sick men had to be turned out to work until finally 65 to 70 per cent of working parties consisted of sick men. The cookhouse was a quarter of a mile from the camp, and as the sick figures rose there were no efficient means of carrying food thence 800 yards to the main hospital and the cholera isolation hospital another 400 yards further on.

'Through the never-ending rain,' ran the words of a report on the 'F' Force camps written in June 1943, 'parts of meals were ferried all day by parties of officers and convalescents in the few buckets and containers available. No containers would be spared for use in the hospital for boiling water for sterilisation of utensils anywhere in camp, thus further ensuring the spread of disease.'[449]

Those desperately sick men who were driven mercilessly to work sometimes never returned. Sergeant Stan Arneil wrote of this: 'If they [the Japanese engineers] wanted 200 men they had to have 200 men. The guards would deliver 200 men even if perhaps thirty of them might be on the backs of their mates. We would carry them back at night. Usually one would die during the day.'[450]

These sick prisoners were inevitably much slower than their healthier comrades which led, just as inevitably, to a beating. 'The ultimate result,' wrote Lionel de

---

449. TNA, WO 325/16.
450. Quoted in Hank Nelson, *Prisoners of War: Australians under Nippon* (ABC, Sydney, 1985), p.48.

Rosario, 'would be a senseless crumpled body left lying helplessly on the muddy ground. No one, not even our officer, could help him. He lay there all day in the rain or sun. In the evening, the subdued guard would allow the battered man to be carried by his colleagues back to the camp. The chance of an emaciated victim recovering was very slim ... The unlucky ones were pushed from the uncompleted bridge into the river to be swept away by its fast-flowing water.'[451]

During the cholera outbreak a man, suspected of having the disease, collapsed and Idris Barwick, a Regimental Nursing Orderly of the Royal Army Service Corps, helped carry the man to the cholera ward. There men were already dead or dying and the stench was dreadful. 'It was a smell that stayed with me for a long time,' he later wrote, it was 'the smell of death'. He was told by the Medical Officer to simply lay the man on the ground and then to rub his hands in lime before leaving.[452]

To his dismay, Barwick was himself admitted to the cholera ward as a patient. The men there, 'were covered in the bile and mess they had vomited over themselves, or by the men who lay beside them. They suffered from uncontrollable and unrestrained attacks of the most violent vomiting, which was always accompanied by "hair raising" screaming and groaning ... To make matters worse, they would probably be lying in their own excreta.'

De Rosario noted that cholera victims discharged all their bodily fluids through their mouths or their anus at frequent intervals. Within just a few hours the individuals became so dehydrated they died – usually within twenty-four hours of the first signs of the illness.

The hospital was divided into separate wards for fever, dysentery, cholera and later an 'Ulcer Ward' was added. During the height of the monsoon, one of the latrines which had filled up with rainwater, broke apart and a 'filthy stream oozed through the camp' and passed under the floors of the hospital huts and many of the sick bays collapsed.[453]

The cholera ward was close to the cemetery, which told its own story. When men were admitted to this ward they knew there was little chance of leaving it alive. Because most of the men had died of infectious diseases, the bodies were burned. As the Japanese refused to give the prisoners any tools with which to cut wood, collecting enough fuel for the pyres was a perpetual problem, made worse during the monsoon, the rains of which frequently extinguished the fires. As the daily death count reached more than thirty, the cremations continued day and night. The bodies were laid in rows, thirty or forty at a time, waiting

---

451. Rosario, p.127.
452. Barwick, p.137.
453. Walker, *Australia in the War of 1939–1945*, p.579.

for daylight to be cremated.[454] The cholera outbreak was brought under control after about three weeks, but during that time around 600 prisoners had died.[455]

Although the officers were not forced to work on the bridge, so many of them were in hospital that it was impossible for them to organise hygiene squads in the camp. This was remarked on by Major Tracey, when he arrived at the head of 866 Australians on 7 August 1943: "hygiene had been completely neglected, food containers were covered with flies and not washed between meals, all food was left uncovered and the floors of the kitchen were inches deep in mud and waste food. The Other Ranks' huts and hospital (they were all one) beggared description. Both the inside and outside of the huts were fouled and the excreta had not been cleaned up for days.

'No facilities existed for the sterilization of cooking and eating utensils, or for washing or bathing those too ill to make their way to the adjacent creek. The latrines were in close proximity to the sleeping quarters and were full to the brim, while maggots covered the surrounding earth."[456]

James Bradley remembered those latrines well during the monsoon period of 1943: 'The latrine pits were overflowing, because of the constant use and the now almost permanent rains, and the approach to them from the huts was fouled by men whose dysentery was so intense that they just could not reach the latrines in time.'[457]

As elsewhere, if the POWs were not perceived to be working hard enough, regardless of their physical condition, they were beaten, or worse. Idris Barwick described one incident where a worker was beaten and fell face down in the mud. His torturer then put his foot on the prisoner's head and pushed it deeper into the mud. His life was only saved by the courage of two of his comrades who took the risk of incurring similar treatment and pulled the man up before he suffocated.[458]

There was another incident at Songkurai involving an elephant similar to that at Wampo. The elephant in question was called Elphie. One day Elphie was struggling to shift her load. A visiting Japanese officer believed he could deal with the situation in the usual manner – by giving her a bash on the head with her driver's prodding iron. Elphie was enraged and tried to charge her assailant but was held back by her chains and the weight of her load.

A few weeks later, the Japanese officer returned to Songkurai and was recognised by Elphie. This time her load was not too heavy and, with a fierce

---

454. Barwick, p.157.
455. Rosario, p.126.
456. Kappe, p.93.
457. Bradley, p.51.
458. Barwick, p.160.

trumpet call, charged after the officer, dragging her load behind her. The officer ran for his life with Elphie in hot pursuit. As it happened, Elphie's logs became entangled in a tree which brought the elephant to a halt and her quarry escaped. It was the officer's last visit to Songkurai.[459]

Things began to improve somewhat at Songkurai in September with the laying of the track and the arrival of trains carrying supplies pulled by converted road trucks as engines. Wood-Higgs noted this in his diary for 22 September 1943: 'Canteen goods are trickling in, and we have been issued with one pair of socks, grey cotton and wool, and one pair of shorts elastic white cotton both of very inferior quality to make up some of our clothing deficiencies. Most of us are literally in rags.'[460]

At what Corporal Andrew Grundie called 'Sancry camp', he witnessed Private Dugan being forced to work even though he had become 'mentally unbalanced' due to suffering beriberi, dysentery, malaria and general malnutrition. One day he failed to arrive at his work station. At the end of the day an investigation was undertaken to find out what had happened to Dugan who was still missing. As none of the POWs could provide an answer they were made to stand to attention until around 02.00 hours the following morning before being allowed to return to camp (reaching there about 03.45 hours) and prepare themselves for the coming day's work. After four days Dugan was found. The inevitable punishment beatings began. After twenty-four hours of interrogation and beatings, Dugan was sentenced to twenty-eight days detention during which for eighteen hours each day he was tied by his arms and legs to two posts in a standing position outside the Japanese guardhouse. After just two days of such treatment Dugan was very close to death. He was taken to the river and pushed in, the Japanese throwing mud at him. He was then given a spade and a hoe and made to dig his own grave before being bayonetted to death by six of the guards.[461]

Altogether of the 1,600 prisoners at Songkurai, 1,100 or 1,200 died and the bridge over the Khwae Noi at Songkuria became known as the Bridge of 600, because 600 prisoners died during its construction. It is believed that this bridge, rather than the bridge at Tamarkan, is really the bridge which inspired the book of the *Bridge on the River Kwai*.

No.1 Mobile Force Camp   299 Kilo

On 17 September No.1 Mobile Force from the Burma end of the railway, whose function was to lay the rails, moved to this camp a short distance from the

---

459. Rosario, p.124.
460. Stanley Wood-Higgs, *Bamboo and Barbed Wire* (Roman Press, Bournemouth, 1988), p.87.
461. AWM, 54 1010/4/63, Part 1.

Burma-Thailand border. Measured from the northern start point of the railway at Thanbyuzayat this camp was 116 Kilo Camp, and this is the name given to it by the prisoners. It was 'the worst yet occupied' by any of the men of the force.

Situated about 200 yards from the access road it was 'a shockingly filthy area where one hut, hastily cleared of its cholera-stricken occupants to make way for the new arrivals, housed the entire force. Another four or five huts were used to house native labour.' The hut could accommodate only half the force at one time, but this was not a problem because the men were working in twenty-four hour shifts so only half the number were in the camp at any one time.[462]

Major 'Jim' Jacobs agreed that 116 Kilo camp was a terrible place, saying that it 'defied adequate description'. In at least one of the huts the prisoners had to share with Tamils who occupied one end. The huts were 'double deckers' with a second sleeping platform built five or six feet above the lower one.[463]

Kami Songkurai   300 Kilo

Located only short distance from Three Pagodas Pass and the border with Burma, Kami (Upper) Songkurai ('F' Force's No. 3 camp) was one of the most remote camps on the Burma-Thailand railway. This camp was occupied by a party of 386 A.I.F. (another figure of 393 has also been given) on the evening of 25th May. It continued as a working camp from that date until the suspension of work in November. According to Charles Kappe, the accommodation 'comprised two long rows of huts placed close together at the foot of three steep hills which formed a rough semi-circle enclosing the camp in rear. The area between the huts and the river which flowed parallel to and about 200 yards from the road at the foot of the other range of hills forming the valley was low-lying and swampy. During the wet season this swamp became a filthy quagmire of green mud, no attempt having been made to drain the area.

'The water supply comprised a well, two springs in the hills which later ceased to flow, and a small creek which became a veritable trickle of water an inch or so deep in the dry weather. In wet weather the well became fouled by refuse etc., washed down by the rain waters and by the leakage of contaminated water. The river was too far away for its waters to be drawn for cooking purposes and as a place for ablution it was placed out of bounds by the I.J.A.'[464]

Astonishingly, the creek was the only place where the Japanese would allow bathing. This flowed through the middle of the camp. It drained into the general seepage of the area and was always, as Kappe said, 'most foul'.

---

462. Walker, *Australia in the War of 1939–1945*, p.556.
463. Wright, p.202.
464. Kappe, pp.42-3.

When the Australians arrived, some Asian labourers were already in occupation. They were already suffering from cholera, which broke out in all the camps in this region of the railway in mid-May 1943. No arrangements existed for the isolation of cholera patients and all that the prisoners could do was collect the suffers together in one part of the accommodation huts.

An open latrine used by the *rōmusha* was situated just ten yards from the Allied officers' hut. With the men being forced to work as much as eighteen hours a day, seven days a week, sickness rates rocketed. Of the original 386, which had arrived on 25/26 May, 107 were already sick by the end of the month and one man had died already.

By 8 June 1943 there were more men sick (193) than were fit enough to work (182). Eighteen others were retained for camp duties (including eleven cooks and duty men and four cowmen and the commanding officer). Seven prisoners had died, all from cholera. Being so remote, few supplies reached the camp, medical equipment was almost non-existent and cooking equipment was extremely limited, though the water supply from the well, the cookhouse and the sleeping quarters were close to each other. It was also the case that rations were at first issued to the Tamil workers who cooked both for themselves and the prisoners. Although this practice was soon stopped, it allowed cholera to spread into the ranks of the Australians.

In late July and early August the numbers at Kami Songkurai were increased to 1685 as prisoners were moved from Ni Thea, Shimo Songkurai and Changaraya. One of those men was Stan Arneil, who had been at Shimo Songkurai. He was placed in the camp hospital where there were fourteen men to the bay which measured 3 by 3.5 metres: 'Scabies are rife and lice are making sporadic appearances,' he wrote, 'they burn the bed pans in the fire inside the huts, the smell being particularly vile. The latrines are on a slight rise about thirty yards from the wards and being open have filled so much with water that the seepage has burst from the ground and flows in the general direction of the English ward, next to this one.'[465]

Stan Arneil was also highly critical of the officers in the camp who were 'all well, have neither ulcers nor itch and are well shod,' and they had 'sugar, four tins of fish, tins of milk and as much soap tobacco and oil as they wanted.' That the officers kept so much for themselves when their men were struggling to stay alive was, Arneil wrote, 'was a wicked thing for the officers to do.'[466]

Cyril Wild joined Kami Songkurai as its interpreter on or about 3 August 1943. The strength of the camp at that time was around 1,100 of whom

---

465. Arneil, p.119.
466. ibid, pp.130 & 133.

approximately 700 were lying in a desperately ill or dying condition 'with their bodies crammed together touching one another on split bamboo slats. There was a leaky palm-leaf roof to this hut and no walls. As this hut was built on a hill, and the monsoon was at its height, streams of water ran continually under the bamboo sleeping platforms and along the earthen gangway.'

For a week or more, the Japanese engineers blasted stone in a quarry which was closely adjacent to the camp hospital. Showers of rock invariably fell in the hospital after each blast, and through the attap roof onto the prostrate bodies of hundreds of patients. 'The sick were consequently in a state of panic, verging on hysteria,' wrote Cyril Wild, 'and seriously ill men were sitting upright for hours at a time holding straw mats above their heads and waiting for the next shower of rocks. One patient had his arm broken by flying rock and, being already in very poor condition, died shortly afterwards from shock. Another had his wrist broken and he too died shortly after. Some of the patients dragged themselves onto the ground to hide under their beds which reduced their prospects of recovery.[467]

This was also described in detail by Captain Ronald Maston, who explained that on average twenty 'shots' a day were carried out at the quarry, with each shot comprising of about twelve charges: 'Following a shot being fired the metal from the quarry would be thrown right over the camp area and jagged pieces of metal, weighing up to six pounds, would crash onto the roof, breaking through the thin atap and onto the sick men.'[468]

During this period two British prisoners felt too ill to eat all the unappetising plain rice and were spotted throwing some scraps away. The Japanese used this to counter complains that the food ration was insufficient and actually reduced the rice issue by one-third, though this was later restored in part a few days later.

'We found [Kami Songkurai] to be a pigsty compared with the comparatively well-drained camp at Shimo Songkurei,' wrote one Australian. 'The ground here was practically flat and received the seepage from the hill at the rear of the camp. It was ankle-deep in mud, and the first thought that struck all of us was how the [earlier] occupants could have lived in such a place without doing something about cleaning it up.'[469]

Just how bad it had become was experienced by Reverend George Polain, one of the chaplains of 'F' Force: 'It was often very trying to conduct a service in a hut with 300 men with the nauseous stench of the awful ulcer cases all around & having often four or six dysentery cases squatting on their bamboo pans around one through the prayers, scripture readings & so on.'[470]

---

467. TNA, WO 235/1034.
468. TNA, WO 235/1034.
469. James Boye, *Railroad to Burma* (Allen & Unwin, Sydney, 1990), p.111.
470. George Polain, 'Report on the Work of Chaplains with "F" Force', AWM 54, 554/7/4.

Due to incurable tropical ulcers Major Roy Stevens of 2/12 Field Ambulance, A.I.F., had to undertake twelve amputations with just a hacksaw on a bamboo table in the bush.[471]

Roy Stevens also related an undated incident after the cholera outbreak had run its course in 1943, and the patients were due to move from the isolation ward to the main hospital. At the evening *tenko*, the Japanese said the count was out by one man. The Korean, Toyoyama, made all the men from the isolation ward, many of whom had dysentery and others with tropical ulcers, stand in the monsoon rain from 16.30 hours until 23.30 hours. One prisoner died during that time and another three or four died over the course of the following two days.[472]

Captain Swartz reorganised the camp, establishing a hospital at the end of one of the huts. He also formed a defined boundary between the prison camp and that of the native labourers. After these improvements Kami Songukrai was considered the best camp in the group. A supply of blankets and large mosquito nets was also received in June. Even so, throughout June and July there was, on average, less than 100 men well enough to work on the railway. It is said that, by and large, work conditions here were better than in many of the camps. Working hours were normally from 08.45 to approximately 19.30 hours.

In late July and early August, the Japanese increased the numbers at Kami Songkurai to 1685 by bringing in prisoners from Ni Thea, Shimo Songkurai and Changaraya. Many of the new arrivals were already seriously ill and utterly exhausted by being forced to march to Kami Songkurai through thick mud, while carrying their remaining gear.

On 19 August a line of huts had to be evacuated by the prisoners to make room for the arrival of a large body of native labourers. To accommodate the displaced prisoners an upper deck had to be built in the remaining huts. A fence was erected between the native area and the POW camp. Between the native huts and the fence, the natives threw scraps of rice and defecated and urinated. 'The stench was indescribable,' wrote Charles Kappe, 'as was the noise emanating from the huts for 24 hours of the day ... a particularly obnoxious latrine had been dug within 10 yards of the point from which the camp had to draw its water.'[473]

One day in the late summer of 1943, Private D.S. Pickard of 2/30 Australian Infantry Battalion saw two British POWs washing in the guards' area of the creek. This was upstream of the POW area and was divided from the POW area by a log. Toyoyama came along and saw the two prisoners. 'He became

---

471. TNA, WO 235/1034.
472. TNA WO 235/1034.
473. Kappe, p.82.

enraged,' recalled Pickard, 'stood them to attention, picked up a handful of mud and made them eat it. The mud was full of maggots and rotten rice due to all the camp food containers being washed un this area.'[474] Toyoyama was later handed a death sentence, commuted to life imprisonment, after the war.

In September 1943 the ludicrous situation developed where seriously ill men who were incapable of any meaningful work were sent from the camp to make up the numbers demanded by the engineers. Only the commanding officer, eleven cooks and assistants, plus four cowmen to look after the few valuable yaks which provided meat mostly for the Japanese, were allowed to remain in the camp. But all that happened was that many of the sick men were so ill they were sent back to camp by the Japanese engineers who threatened them with 'thrashings' if they appeared at work again. As the work was pushed on at a relentless pace without a break, the prisoners were promised three days' rest when they had finished their work here. But that became reduced to just one day, 19 September. Between 1 August and 28 November, when the camp was finally evacuated, a total of 490 men had died.

Around 100 of these deaths were a direct result of the seriously ill patients being forced to work. They were made to do a full twelve-hour shift with a single thirty-minute lunch break. Usually, they could only keep this up for four days. By day five they were completely incapable of getting out of bed and shortly afterwards they died.[475]

When the camp was evacuated in November, Roy Stevens was left with just 100 fit men to get 1,000 sick patients onto the train which would take them all down to Kanburi. 'One train pulled in and we commenced loading,' Stevens described, 'with the Japanese shrieking and screaming all over the place. Within a minute and a half, while the stretchers were being passed onto the trucks – the stretchers were fairly heavy ones that we had made of bamboo – the train pulled out without any warning. The result was that men fell back on the line. Some of them were pulled into the trucks. All of these were extremely sick men … One fellow who had been operated on and who had his leg amputated was left hanging from the truck and had to be hauled in by other people.' This happened with every train that stopped for them. They would only be able to get fifty or sixty men on board before the train would pull out without warning. Seventeen men died on the journey to Kanburi.[476]

---

474. TNA, WO 235/1034.
475. TNA, WO 235/1034.
476. TNA WO 235/1034.

Changaraya, 301 Kilo
Also known as Chaunggahla-ya

Major Gairdner was the Commanding officer of 'F' Force's No. 5 Camp which was even closer to the Burmese border near the Three Pagodas Pass. He described the camp in a report on 7 June 1943: 'On the evening of 27 May, the first party – 'A' Group (383) under the command of Major [blank] reached the camp and were housed in No.1 Hut, with the officers in a small room in the I.J.A. N.C.O.s hut next door. These huts were fully roofed.

'At 2100 hrs 'B' Group (318) under my command arrived in the pitch dark, having been held up for one hour at No.1 Camp. Accommodation was eventually found under what roofing existed by putting 200 men into 7 bays 12 feet by 15 feet, and the remaining 110 with 'A' Group. Cookhouse – This was found to be in use by 500 Burmese coolies with whom we were expected to share – which turned out to mean that we were allowed to use it when the Burmese did not want it, the natural result being that the mid-day meal on the first day was eventually served at 1700 hrs.'

Gairdner was shocked at the state of the place: 'The general sanitation of the camp when we arrived was nothing short of unbelievable filth. The Burmese had thrown all their unwanted rice and other food all over the camp and particularly near their own huts. Incidentally, there were parties of Burmese in every hut in our area, including those occupied by my own men, and had "shat" indiscriminately everywhere. The flies were a menace; remains of slaughtered animals and skins were in the undergrowth all around the cookhouse in every degree of decomposition.'

Gardiner continued with his description of conditions at Changaraya: 'Rations – These were drawn from the I.J.A. NCO i/c of the Burmese cookhouse, and it was found that both our own and the Burmese rations were issued in bulk to this cookhouse, so that we were given what they did not want.

'Cooking utensils – No utensils of any sort were issued to us on arrival and all our cooking had to be done in the Burmese containers and rice "qualies". There are two wells, the one near the cookhouse containing very dirty water fit only for washing the body and clothes. This was being used by the Burmese cookhouse for cooking water. The other is some 500 yards away by a very bad track, but excellent water.

'Containers – only 4 x 6 gallon containers managed to arrive in camp with the two parties and these were the only means of drawing water and cooking stews.'[477]

---
477. Grehan, p.74-5.

Around 80 percent of the men arrived in the camp with diarrhoea. 'This resulted in a further menace of the men following the example of the Burmese and shitting indiscriminately in the undergrowth,' complained Gardner, who had little sympathy for these sufferers, going on to write, 'Some undoubtedly could not get to the latrines in time, others were just lazy, as they have been throughout this crisis.' It must be noted that the latrines were some distance from the accommodation huts with paths to them through the jungle which made them difficult to get to in the dark nights.

Just over two weeks later Colonel Harris wrote to Colonel Banno about the state of Changaraya when he visited on 24 June 1943: 'Conditions in this camp are deplorable. British POW are living in close proximity to Burman labourers and camp hygiene is impossible. The ground is waterlogged, and it is not possible to construct adequate latrines and refuse pits. The I.J.A. Engineers insist on every available man going out on working parties. There are insufficient men for carrying out hygiene and sanitation. The water carry in this camp is a long one and there are NO buckets or water containers available ... There is a high incidence of sickness, disease and death in this camp. This high incidence of disease will continue until conditions are improved.'[478]

Conditions did not improve, and Harris' prediction proved only too accurate, and when cholera struck, the death rate was shocking. As at Kami-Songkurai, no arrangements existed for the isolation of cholera patients. Similarly, the only practical measure was to collect them together into one part of one of the prisoners' huts. It was not until June that separate accommodation was provided at Changaraya even though the outbreak began in mid-May. Captain Harry Silman, a Medical Officer with the 9th Northumberland Fusiliers, saw the cholera ward on 3 June: 'I have been over to the cholera centre. It looks like a scene from a film, completely unreal. There is a long, dark, attap hut, with over a hundred thin skeleton-like beings, writhing on the long platform, vomiting and passing motions where they lie. Groans and cries are the only noises to break the silence. Two or three orderlies with masks over their mouths were giving intravenous injections of saline, using Heath Robinson contraptions. About nine corpses lay outside covered with blankets and groundsheets, and a little distance away, the smoke of the pyre where the corpses are burning could be seen.'[479]

As in the other camps there was almost no medical equipment for the hospital. Everything had to be improvised – biscuit tins were made into miniature charcoal stoves for sterilising equipment, bedpans from largo bamboos, cannulas (for intravenous saline injections) from bamboo tips, tables from split bamboo,

---

478. ibid, pp.50 & 76.
479. war-experience.org/events/the-thaiburma-railroad.

water containers from long bamboos, buckets from bamboo strips, bandages and dressings from shirtsleeves, trouser legs, mosquito nets or from banana leaves tied on by witheys, stretchers from bamboo and sacks.

Major Bruce Hunt, one of the Australian doctors with 'F' Force, submitted a report concerning an incident at Changaraya involving Major Cyril Wild, the camp's interpreter. The Japanese corporal acting as the camp commander insisted on inspecting the thirty-seven prisoners who Hunt and Wild had said were too sick to go out to work: 'At the time scheduled for parade I fell in the thirty-seven men apart from the main parade, and Major Wild and I stood in front of them. The corporal approached with a large bamboo in his hand and spoke menacingly to Major Wild who answered in a placatory fashion. The corporal's only reply was to hit Major Wild in the face. Another guard followed suit and as Major Wild staggered back the corporal thrust at the Major's genitals with his bamboo. I was left standing in front of the patients and was immediately set upon by the Corporal and two other guards – one tripped me while the two others pushed me to the ground. The three then set about me with bamboos, causing extensive bruising of scull, back, hands and arms, and a fractured left 5th metacarpal bone. This episode took place in front of the whole parade of troops. After I was disposed of the corporal then made the majority of the sick men march with the rest of the troops.'[480]

Richard Laird passed through Changaraya on his way to Tanbaya Hospital and considered it to be 'the most depressing of all the camps I saw. Morale was bad; there was very little food and deep mud everywhere.'[481]

On 30 September 1943, No.1 Mobile Force moved to Changaraya to continue its line laying. At one point the following month, in a final push to get the Burmese end of the line finished, the men worked for thirty-three hours without a rest.

It would seem that remnants of the British Sumatra Battalion (see below) were moved to what they called 'Chaungena' or, 114 Kilo camp as measured from Thanbyuzayat, in November 1943, after it had been abandoned by 'F' Force. It was the worst camp the men had encountered: 'It was not even a working camp,' according to one report. 'The POWs were too sick to work and Japanese efforts to get maintenance parties met with little success. Huts were situated on the side of a hill. Some were without roofs and all were under the trees which dripped continuously.'[482]

They had to share accommodation with the native labourers separated by just an eight-foot attap screen. The conditions these labourers lived in were

---

480. TNA, WO 325/16.
481. Laird, p.103.
482. www.cofePOW.org.uk/armed-forces-stories-list/the-british-battalion.

even more cramped and squalid than those of the POWs. Their dead and dying were just pushed under the sleeping platforms, the bodies attracting millions of disease-bearing flies.

Local knowledge, though, proved highly valuable. The Eurasian soldiers from Sumatra knew which plants found in the bush were edible and even some that had medicinal value. It was also the case, reported in a number of camps, that the doctors with the Dutch troops who had lived in southeast Asia for a long time were able to indicate which plants had the most nutritional value.

One day a number of the prisoners were taken by Japanese guards wearing face masks to what had been the cholera hospital of the 'F' Force contingent at Changaraya. It made, A.A. Apthorpe, wrote, a sad spectacle: 'Pieces of equipment lay around as if the occupants had suddenly fled in the face of disaster. In the centre of the camp were a number of funeral pyres, with half-burned bodies and limbs protruding from among the charred bamboo.' Apthorpe and his comrades were tasked with burying the dead. It was, the men agreed, 'by far the most sickening and heart breaking job we had encountered on the railway.'[483]

Red Cross supplies occasionally reached the camps. In one instance in 1944, the Japanese commandant seized the supply of lint from an American Red Cross delivery from which he made, or had made for him, three pairs of pyjamas and a set of curtains for his hut.[484]

By the end of 1943 Changaraya had become so bad, the camp was closed down by the Japanese in January 1944. The bulk of the prisoners were transported to Kanburi, leaving around 200 British to continue maintenance work on the railway.

THREE PAGODAS PASS

Payatonzu 108 Kilo
Also known as Paya Thanzutaung or Paya-thonzu Taung

Payatonzu camp was just half a kilometre inside the Burmese border near the Three Pagodas Pass. It was first occupied in March 1943 by around 2,500 Dutch prisoners under Colonel Platte, who became the camp commander. The Japanese commander at Payatonzu was Lieutenant Osada (or Osoda).

On 15 April, Brigadier Arthur Varley, the senior POW was summoned to a meeting at Japanese No. 3 Branch of the 5th Railway Headquarters and was told that the line had to be completed up to the Thai border by the end of May, regardless of what this might entail and how impractical such

---
483. Apthorpe, p.116.
484. Hardie, p.149.

a target was. This meant the prisoners were forced to work from 09.00 until 04.00 hours the following day. Those weak men marked for 'light duties' were forced to work until 22.00 hours each day, and the sick who were supposed to undertake no work at all had to work from 21.00 to 04.30 and after that from 08.30 to 17.30 hours.

Being at the farthest point from Rangoon, food supplies were scanty and conditions dreadful at Payatonzu. The onset of the monsoon at the beginning of April made matters even worse: 'The downpour soon turns the camp into one big quagmire,' wrote Otto Kreefft, 'latrines are overflowing, food supplies dwindle even further and the sick and death rates increase. Because of the incessant rains the embankments have subsided and the work is getting behind schedule.'[485]

The Dutch prisoners were joined by No. 1 Mobile Force from 17 September 1943 to 26 September 1943, before moving onto Kami Sonkurai. In November 1943, the total number of men in the camp was 2,600. Even after the completion of the railway there was no respite for the prisoners who were fit to work. As there was limited coal available to power the locomotives, the engines had been adapted to burn wood. For this, the men had to cut down teak trees on a 'job and finish' basis. Divided into teams of six, the men had to fell the trees and then cut them into logs averaging eighteen inches long. Each team was expected to produce six cubic metres of wood per day. Over time, the guards demanded the prisoners produced first six-and-a-half metres a day and then seven. The men, unseen by the lackadaisical Korean guards, started collecting logs from the previous day to add to that day's total. Eventually, of course, the shortfall became apparent, but, as the quantity had been measured and signed off each day by the guards, no one was able to explain what had gone wrong. In the usual Japanese way, someone had to receive a good bashing for this error, and on this occasion, much to the delight of the prisoners, it was the Koreans.[486]

At the end of January 1944, the logging operation at Payatonzu came an end, the POWs being sent to Tamarkan.

Aungganaung 105 Kilo
Also known as Anganan, Auganang or Aunggonaung

Men from Ramsay, Black and Green forces worked from here from 11 May to December 1943. When they arrived here, after marching thirty kilometres for two days from Meiloe camp, the prisoners found that the camp had earlier

---
485. Kreeff, p.50.
486. Reed and Peeke, pp.78-9.

been occupied by *rōmusha* and that they had left behind some sixty of their dead cholera victims. The POWs had to bury them and clean up the site before they could move in. There were already many of these native labourers buried in the nearby jungle and many more unburied that were only found later. These were discovered further away from the camp where they had perished as they tried to escape the disease. Initially, there was no hospital hut or tent and the sick just had to lie in their bunks.

There were also still Burmese workers at this camp whose sanitation was 'deplorable'. When the Japanese built a new road through the camp it passed through the Burmese latrines which, therefore, had to be filled in and closed. No new latrine was dug for the Burmese in that area and the nearest one they could use was a distance away. Rather than walk to the latrines, the Burmese fouled all the area around the Australian huts. The area became filthy in the extreme with excreta. Inevitably, it was not long before the Australians began to suffer from dysentery and diarrhoea. Nevertheless, compared with other camps, Lloyd Harding of 2/40th Battalion AIF, considered Aungganaung to be fairly good, as there was more space in the huts and the food was 'reasonable'.[487] According to Sergeant Chris Guerin, there was no water supply in the camp and the prisoners had to form a bucket chain half a mile long from the river.[488]

Guerin also recalled steaks they enjoyed when an elephant died. In stark contrast to this memorable event was the punishment of two local Thais when the Japanese discovered that they had been buying tools from the prisoners. The two men in question were buried up to their necks with only their heads above ground. They were slowly eaten to death by ants but the prisoners who sold the tools to them were never identified as the transactions took place in the dead of night. Guerin also stated that the prisoners at Aungganaung had to build a special hut for a 'team of harlots' transported in for the pleasure of the Japanese.[489]

The work was particularly strenuous for the POWs and during the 'speedo' period the men were so exhausted, and the hours were so long, that rather than trudge all the way back to camp at the end of their shift, most of the men went to sleep by their workstations. The cooks took food out to them. Those sick prisoners who worked a half-day because they were too ill to work a full day received only half rations. Those that worked a full day had to move four metres of earth a day, regardless of their physical condition, and often had to march three or four kilometres to reach their workstation. The workers were granted a ten-minute tea break morning and afternoon, and an hour for lunch.[490]

---

487. Wright, p.212.
488. Newton and McGuinness, p.508.
489. Newton and McGuinness, p.510.
490. AWM, 54 1010/4/63, Part 1.

Aungganaung became the largest POW hospital camp on the Burma side of the railway. Its Japanese commander, Captain Hoshi, concerned with the plight of the prisoners, went into the local town to personally buy food for them. He was, it was said, 'rather proud' of the food he was able to get. He also organised a party of twenty men to gather edible grasses or vegetables in the jungle and things like bamboo sprouts and a form of mushrooms. He also claimed that he asked for seeds and attempted to start a vegetable garden, but it did not prove a success in the time available.[491]

Rations, though, were never sufficient and one night Sapper Iles was caught trying to steal food in the Japanese kitchen. He was taken and tied to the upright of the guard hut. 'His legs and arms were tied and his body was tied round the post,' Keith George Griffith wrote in his affidavit to the War Crimes Commission. 'He was being continually bashed by the guards, mostly with split bamboos ... Sapper Iles was still tied to the guard house during the day and all the night, being beaten at intervals. The following day he was still there. He finally became so ill he had to be taken to hospital.' Sapper Iles subsequently died.[492]

It was not uncommon for supplies of boxed meat for the prisoners to be green and full of maggots. At 105 Kilo camp several boxes of meat arrived in so bad a state that the Japanese commandant complained of the smell and demanded that the meat be eaten immediately. The Australian commander said that the meat could not be eaten as it was not fit for human consumption. The Japanese commander then ordered it to be buried for he could not stand the smell – even though his hut was 300 yards away. In the end, much of the meat was eaten by the hungry prisoners.[493]

For the men suffering from tropical ulcers the only truly effective medication was iodoform. Hoshi had a supply of this which he used to sell to patients suffering from this terrible illness in return for their few valued possessions, such as watches and rings.[494]

In late 1943, an extra issue of supplies was made by the Japanese. At Aungganaung this amounted to three small packets of cigarettes per man, an issue of margarine (which went straight to the hospital), and a small tin of condensed milk which had to be shared between eleven men.[495] Most of the prisoners smoked which meant those who did not smoke could barter their allowance with the smokers for extra food. It was remarked on by one non-

---
491. AWM, 54 1010/3/10.
492. AWM, 54 1010/4/63, Part 1.
493. Lionel Wigmore, *Australia in the War of 1939–1945, Volume IV – The Japanese Thrust, Part III - Prisoners of the Japanese* (AWM, 1957), p.550.
494. John Gilbert 'Tom' Morris, *A Soldier's Reflections Forty Years On*, AWM, PR 83/068.
495.   Kinvig, p.91.

smoker, that even those in extremely poor condition who needed food for their very survival, if they were heavily addicted would still be keen to exchange rations for cigarettes.[496]

The Japanese decided to make a propaganda film to show how well the POWs were being treated, choosing Aungganaung for the filming. The camp was cleaned up, tables were brought in and adorned with tablecloths and vases of flowers. Good quality crockery was laid out on the tables and heaped with fruit and cakes. The prisoners selected to appear in the film were given fresh clothes and were filmed singing happily as they marched off on a supposed work detail. The clothes, food and tables disappeared as soon as the filming ended.[497]

At the cemetery at 105 Kilo camp the prisoners had erected a large wooden cross made of railway sleepers. Into this was burnt the words: 'In honour of Australian, Dutch, British, American 3 & 5 branch prisoners-of-war who died in Burma'.[498]

As at Payatonzu, after the completion of the railway, a woodcutting party of several hundred men was retained to fuel the steam locomotives. The camp suffered an Allied bombing raid in January 1944. The camp was close to the railway line, which was machine-gunned, resulting in the death of one prisoner and the wounding of another. On 22 March 1944 the camp was attacked again, being machine gunned by two B24 Liberator bombers. Two days later, as a result of this, the remaining men were moved south into Thailand to Kanchanaburi.

Anganan 100 Kilo
Also known as Apalon or Regue camp

Before the arrival of men of No 5 Group on 29 May 1943, Anganan 2, which was located in a low mountain valley, was another which had previously been occupied by native workers and was dirty and badly constructed, and wholly inadequate for the Allied prisoners. It did, though, have its own water supply in the form of a stream nearby and a well, but the ground became a 'swamp' during the monsoon and a stream ran through two of the huts reaching a depth of up to one foot. The water was so deep the prisoners caught and ate lungfish that swam under the huts.

Lance Corporal Thomas Smith of 2/40th Battalion, wrote that conditions were so bad 'you didn't live there, you existed'. Some of the sleeping huts had three tiers of beds and when men went out to the latrine at night, they would

---
496. Wyatt & Lowry, p.82.
497. Brigginshaw, pp.74-5.
498. Kreeff, p.56.

crawl up to their bed carrying dirt and excrement back on their feet. There were snakes and rats in the roofs.[499]

This deplorable camp was notable for the large number of American dead (fifty-two[500]), which included crewmen from the USS *Houston* which was sunk in the Battle of Sunda Strait on 1 March 1942. One of the Americans was Max Offerle who wrote the following about conditions at the camp during the monsoon period: 'Actually, creeks and rivers form, and you can almost watch vegetation grow. The rainy or monsoon season turned everything to soup or mud, and they couldn't get supplies up there easily. Then the speedup on work came … Well, the men's health broke down. We started getting lots of malaria, beriberi, dysentery, and tropical ulcers because it seemed that the germ that causes tropical ulcers was more prevalent in the rainy season.'[501]

In June 1943, there was a break in a bridge on the line around the seventy-five-kilometre mark and no food could get through. Rations had to be reduced with those on outside work receiving two-thirds of the normal allowance and the sick remaining in the camp receiving just half the normal amount. The prisoners ate anything they could to survive. This included snakes and lizards which lived around the camp – monkeys were too fast to catch – and another of the Texans, Eddie Fung (the only Chinese-American soldier captured by Imperial Japanese forces during the Second World War), recalled a veritable feast when a large, engorged python was killed and cooked.[502] Efforts were made to create a vegetable garden here, the ground cleared and the garden maintained by the sick prisoners.

As well as Americans, there were a large number of Australians and Dutch prisoners at 100 kilo camp. A few of the Australians risked a severe beating by slipping out of camp at night to trade with locals. On one occasion, Colin Hamley, of 2/2nd Pioneers AIF, brought some Thai whiskey into the camp. This was sold to some of the prisoners who became extremely drunk. They made such a noise that it was feared the guards would be roused. If the Japanese saw alcohol had been taken into the camp, there was no knowing how serious the consequences might be. Luckily, the men soon passed out.[503]

Another feature of this camp was the conduct of a senior Korean guard the prisoners called 'snake eyes'. Not only did he relish beating the prisoners, often

---

499. Wright, p.223.
500. Kelly E. Crager, *Hell Under the Rising Sun: Texan POWs and the Building of the Burma-Thailand Death Railway* (Texan A&M University Press, 2008), p.101.
501. Robert S. La Forte and Ronald E. Marcello, *Building the Death Railway: The Ordeal of American POWS in Burma, 1942-1945* (Rowman & Littlefield, 1993), p.172.
502. Crager, p.106.
503. Wright, pp.217-8.

knocking them unconscious resulting in them being hospitalised, he also urged the other guards to behave in the same manner.

There were also what the Australians called 'bludgers'. These were men who simply could not be made to do work of any sort. They had become so dispirited with conditions that they gave up trying. They refused even to help with camp duties. They would not help maintain the accommodation huts or assist with camp hygiene. Their number included some officers. A few of deaths at 100 Kilo camp were attributable to this, the men feeling so depressed with the damp, unhealthy conditions and with the food, which was so unappetising, they stopped eating, which meant they did not have the strength to fight of disease.[504]

Lance Corporal Tom Fagan, of 2/4th Machine Gun Battalion, saw 100 Kilo camp at this time: 'Hundred are just lying on their bed-spaces, unable to move or fend for themselves. Dysentery, malaria, pellagra and malnutrition are making inroads upon so many already weakened and crippled … Very few have footwear, our legs filthy masses of tropical ulcers that run from knee to ankle. The only treatment is boiling water packs. The greatest fear is gangrene.'[505]

Between the middle of June and the end of September 1943, 226 prisoners were buried in the 100 Kilo cemetery. The camp's hospital accommodation was so limited the majority of the deaths occurred in the prisoners' sleeping huts.

After this period, conditions began to improve. The monsoon rains started to peter out, and food became more abundant. On 12 November the camp received its first batch of mail and, following completion of the railway, maintenance work required of the prisoners was done on a day-on-day-off basis. On 27 November the evacuation of light duty and hospital cases to base camps in Thailand began and in January 1944 most of the remaining prisoners were moved to Aungganaung.

Kyondaw 95 Kilo
Also known as Kyando, Kyindaw or Kyondan

Kyondaw was used as a transit camp for the sick prisoners of 'F' Force being moved to Tanbaya hospital camp (see below). During their stay the men were accommodated in huts previously occupied by *rōmusha*.

Owen Heron of 2/2nd Pioneers spent some time at 95 Kilo camp as well as being moved up and down the line with part of William's No.1 Mobile Force which arrived at Kyondaw on 3 September 1943. As at some of the other camos, it was felt that the officers did not provide the support the other ranks

---

504. Walker, *Australia in the War of 1939–1945*, p.559.
505. 2nd4thmgb.com.au/story/29927.

working on the railway should have received, as the former stayed mainly in camp. There was one officer, however, who gained Owen's respect, Lieutenant Lamb Hamilton. Sadly, the lieutenant died of dysentery.[506]

Lawa   85 Kilo

On 19 March 1943. Group 5 moved to a new camp at Lawa which was located in what was described in the Australian Official History as an area of rugged, heavily forested hills around eighty-five kilometres from Thanbyuzayat. The jungle had been partially cleared from the site and accommodation huts had been recently built of saplings with bamboo and attap roofs.

The group remained at 85 Kilo camp engaged in 'clearing, cutting and filling tasks' until the end of the month when it began moving to Apalaine. This camp was finally abandoned on 6 April.

Apalaine   80 Kilo
Also known as Apparon or Aparon or Apalon

No 5 Group arrived at Apalaine at the beginning of April 1943. The camp was in bamboo-encrusted hollow, set in thick jungle which prevented any breeze through the camp.[507] In June 100 Dutch prisoners were moved to Apalaine to clear the ground for a garden. They had to share accommodation with Burmese workers

No 1 Mobile Force moved to Apalaine in August 1943. Here No 5 Base Hospital was established, with Major Totaro Mizutani as camp commandant. He was 'a monster of inhumanity which raged unchecked down the line, leaving pain, suffering, and death in its wake.' At Apalaine thirty Australians died between 6 August and 7 December 1943, because of Mizutani's 'inhuman sadism'.[508]

Captain B.H.A. Graham reported one incident which took place at Apalaine during the winter of 1943. Mizutani, 'made a brutal attack on seventy-two sick men who were paraded. He struck them with his fist, he hit them with his sword and scabbard and he kicked them. Six of them fell and were unable to rise. The rest were forced to march twenty-five kilometres through mud (to Anganan Camp) which was knee deep for many miles. The majority of these men died, only four of cholera, the rest through malnutrition aggravated by disease.'[509]

---

506. Wright, pp.220-1.
507. Walker, *Australia in the War of 1939–1945*, p.559.
508. *Cessnock Eagle and South Maitland Recorder*, Friday 24 May 1946, page 8, recorded in 2nd4thmgb.com.au/camp/apalon-apalaine-337k-burma.
509. TNA, WO 325/157.

'80 Kilo Camp was a horrible place,' remembered Signalman Campbell Ian James. 'So many died and were buried there. The position of the camp was badly chosen, as it was divided by a wide, steep gully. When a man died he was wrapped in a mat, we could not afford to use a blanket, and carried from the hospital, down one side of the gully, and up the other, making numerous stops as the bearers were too weak from sickness and malnutrition, to make it in one go.'[510]

The hospital camp quickly acquired a reputation as a 'death' camp. The sick were virtually abandoned to their fate. Aid was non-existent, and men died in their own filth and lay unburied for days. About half the prisoners failed to survive, and many lost limbs. Clark Taylor, a member of the U.S. 2nd Battalion, 131st Field Artillery Regiment, had lost so much weight, he was down to little more than six stones due to malnutrition which also caused him to lose his sight for a number of weeks. Even though he also contracted dysentery and malaria made worse by tropical ulcers, he forced himself to join the working party at 105 Kilo camp rather than stay at 80 Kilo hospital where he knew he would die.

Another Texan, Max Offerle, watched his brother Oscar, who had worked at cookhouse then on the wood detail, die at 80 Kilo hospital: 'This ulcer had spread all up and down his leg, between his knee and his ankle. In fact, it started eating around the bone of his leg. Right before he died, there were two inches of bone showing. Blood, pus, mucous, or whatever it was, dropped down on his ankle and the top of his foot, and another large ulcer was there. I went over … and Oscar was semi-conscious, and he was hot. I put his head in my lap, and he died.'[511]

Of the Americans who worked on the line, 30 per cent of those that died succumbed to tropical ulcers – more than any other illness. Forty-seven Americans died at 80 Kilo camp during the 'speed' period alone.

It was during 'Speedo' that some men simply lost the will to live. Working on the railway meant only hunger, pain and unrelenting misery, whereas death meant an end to such suffering. 'You could usually tell,' Kelly Bob Bramlett observed. 'I think a lot of them died just because they gave up. I think maybe if they'd hung on, they could have made it, but there wasn't much for them to hang for at that time.' At times Quarry Gordon saw those who gave up the struggle as 'shirkers' for dying: 'Hell, he'd wind up and die, and that put more work on somebody else. Sometimes you'd think it was an "out" for a

---

510. www.POWs-of-japan.net.
511. Crager, p.97.

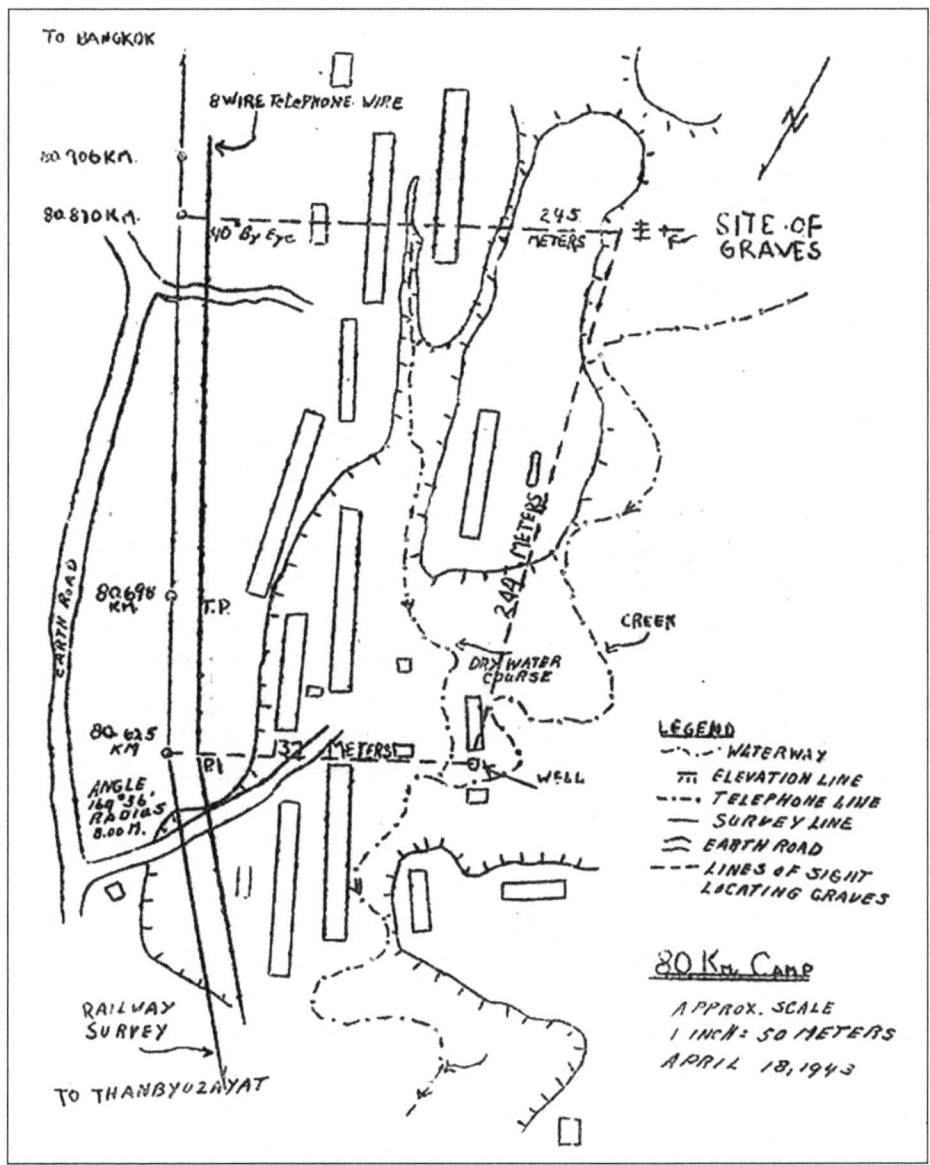

A plan of 80 Kilo Camp, from a report on camps by John Slaughter, Royal Norfolk Regiment. (*Roger Mansell, Palo Alto, CA.*)

man to die, because it was no problem to die; and you'd die and you'd be through with it.'[512]

A plan of 80 Kilo Camp, from a report on camps by John Slaughter, Royal Norfolk Regiment. (Roger Mansell, Palo Alto, CA.)

---

512. ibid, pp.101-2 & 104.

Meiloe 75 Kilo
Also known as Milo

Black Green and Ramsay forces arrived at Meiloe on 18 March 1943. They found the bodies of around twenty *rōmusha* in the huts who had died of cholera and had just been left behind when the Asiatic workers abandoned the camp. The prisoners had to carry them out and burn them.[513]

The greatest part of the camp was in a valley surrounded by thick jungle. The huts were good, and a river ran alongside the camp. The hospital, however, could only accommodate forty patients.[514] Mosquitoes and sandflies were the main pests.

The doctor at Meiloe was Lieutenant Colonel Sir Albert 'Bertie' Ernest Coates OBE, FRCS who became one of the most notable of all the doctors on the railway. He worked as the only doctor at 75 Kilo camp. In April 1943, 2,000 native workers moved into camps placed either side of the POW camp within just thirty to sixty yards. Soon they began defecating everywhere, even just a few yards from the POW huts. Inevitably this resulted in a sharp increase in sickness rates, particularly among the natives, and it was not uncommon to see bodies lying around untended. However, the camp was far from being the worst and it was situated near the River Mezali where, occasionally, the prisoners were allowed to swim. During the monsoon, however, the huts became flooded. Private Keith Griffith declared that in his fourteen feet by ten feet hut, which held sixteen men, the water in the centre rose to three feet.[515]

Dr Coates had to undertake numerous amputations at Meiloe. This was done with a 14-tooth-per-inch saw also used by the cooks to cut up animal bones. Fortunately, a Dutch chemist at the camp, Captain Van Boxhal, was able to extract Novocaine from local cocoa plants for use as a spinal anaesthetic. It was found that the Novocaine worked upwards through the body. The method which had to be adopted, therefore, was to strap the patient to a stretcher, turn the stretcher upside down so that the patients head was to the ground. They would then lay the stretcher down for the operation. The doctor then had just ten minutes to perform the amputation before the anaesthetic wore off.[516]

Coates contracted scrub-typhus and many of the men thought he would die. Although he could not stand, the Japanese sent him to run a new hospital

---

513. Wright, p.270.
514. AWM, 54, 1010/4/63 Part 1.
515. AWM, 54, 1010/4/63 Part 1.
516. Wright, p.242.

camp – 55 Kilo at Kohn Kuhn – where the main body of sick and injured were to be taken.[517]

After a visit by Major General Sasa, the camp commander, Lieutenant Hoshi, read out the following to all the sick patients: 'Major General Sasa has visited [the] camp and expressed himself very satisfied with it, its cleanliness and conditions. But one thing he was not satisfied with was the number of sick who are far too many. There should be no sick here – all sick men were left behind; if men become sick here they should not exceed 20 per cent – a total of 380, this has been much exceeded. Some men who are sick I am trying to send to Thanbyuzayat, but there is no transport and I am considering making them walk … it is very difficult to get food up here even for the Japanese and accordingly you should not grumble if you do not get food … You lack the will to work – if you are sick and can go to work, you must go; if you die you are soldiers and dying is part of your job … you are sick only because you don't try … men should work a full day even if sick …

'If you are sick you only lie down all day and if you lie down you don't need food. In future the sick will not get food, even rice – the workers only will be fed. You will be also forced to go to work.'[518]

Hoshi also declared that the prisoners had just one week to get the total sick down to 20 per cent and he said that any above this amount would receive no food regardless of their condition and be forced to work anyway. A large part of the problem was that the Japanese engineers responsible for the construction of the railway often sent men who were too unwell to work back to camp. But the camp authorities would simply send them back out again the following day. This, no doubt, was to shift the blame should the railway not be completed in the designated time.

In May 1943 the working hours of the prisoners was increased, with men leaving camp at 09.00 hours and not returning until 04.00 the following day. The men were moved from Meiloe later that month, but not before they were driven on at a punishing rate for the few days before they departed. The Japanese engineers marked out the area to be excavated and this had to be completed before the prisoners were allowed to return to camp. It is said that 'often' this meant the men had to work for up to thirty-six hours at a stretch.[519] The light duty men worked a 'half-day' from 09.00 on the morning until 22.00 at night, being joined by the no-duty men from 14.00. 'Light duty' to Hoshi meant prisoners suffering from malaria, dysentery and tropical ulcers. Even those so ill

---

517. POWs-of-japan.net.
518. AWM, 2019.22.101.
519. Brigginshaw, p.66.

they could barely rise from their beds were carried out to the work stations where they had to light and maintain fires so that the workers could continue their efforts through the night. These really very ill patients were kept out until work finished at 04.00 hours.[520]

John Henry Schurmann of 2/4 Machine Gun Battalion worked along with elephants at one stage during the building of one of the larger bridges built in the vicinity of Meiloe. That was until one day one of the Japanese hit one of the elephants. The elephant responded by simply nudging his tormentor over the bridge and into the water: 'Next day as the mahout was taking his charge to the bridge he was stopped, ordered down and as the Japanese party prepared to shoot the elephant the mahout tried to save the elephant's life. End result a party of Aussies had to bury both elephant and mahout, to balance an outraged Japanese ego.' Shortly after this Schurmann heard the call: 'One elephant has died – send us 20 Australians' as a replacement.[521]

Corporal Tom Morris regarded the Japanese engineers at Meiloe to be among the most incompetent. 'This inefficiency led to a considerable duplication of work for the hard-pressed POWs. It was not uncommon to build an embankment and then remove half of it, dig a cutting and then fill in a portion of it, all because of incorrect survey levels.'[522]

Meiloe was at the start of a range of mountains and when the line had been completed up to this point, according to Keneth Darwin, the engines struggled to cope with the gradient. The Japanese would call out the whole camp to help push the train up the slope. Often this would happen twice a night.[523]

On 11 May 1943, the whole camp, except those too ill to travel, moved to 105 kilo camp. Shortly afterwards cholera broke out in 75 Kilo camp. Fortunately, disaster was averted as a few weeks earlier the men had been given cholera shots. After a visit by Brigadier Varley and Lieutenant Colonel Nagatoma, it was decided to move all those who remained at the camp to the base hospital at 55 Kilo camp, Khonkan.

Mezali   70 Kilo
Also known as Masali, Masalé or Mizale

No. 1 Mobile Force moved to Mezali from Taungzun in July 1943. The place had been previously occupied by Burmese and it was in a filthy condition with

---

520. AWM, 54 1010/4/63 Part 1.
521. J.H. Sherman, *Random Recollections*, www.POWs-of-japan.net.
522. Morris, op. cit.
523. Wright, pp.240-1.

deep mud everywhere, and a complete clean-up had to be carried out by the POWs before they could move in.[524] The men, mostly Dutch prisoners with a few British and Australians, worked generally in workshops as labourers.[525] During the 'Speedo' period the men were forced to work from 08.30 to as late as 05.30 the following day.

In the autumn of 1943, after the completion of the railway, rations were still inadequate and of 884 men in the Mobile Force at this stage, only twenty-four were classified as fit, including Colonel Williams.

Kami Mezali 65 Kilo

Kami, or Upper, Mezali was a sub-camp of Mezali. It became the headquarters of 3 Group.

Ronshi 62 Kilo
Also known as Lonshi

Ronshi was the final staging camp for the men of 'F' Force on their way to Thanbaya. The move to Ronshi was carried out by route march and motor transport. The march – fourteen kilometres – began at 04.30 hours in the pouring rain and pitch darkness. Eventually Ronshi was reached by the first of the prisoners who stayed for thirty-six hours and were occupied in repairing a hut, which was to house the patients in transit.

Taungzun 60 Kilo
Also known as Tanzum or Taunzan

On 13 May, Anderson's and William's forces (No.1 Mobile Force) arrived at Taungzun on which marked the start of a period of 'abject misery'. Even before reaching Taungzun the prisoners could smell the stench of rotting human bodies and excrement. On entering Taungzun Captain C.R.B. Richards found the camp, previously occupied by native labour, to be 'inexpressibly filthy', with piled up filth and where there were *rōmusha* lying around dying and around eighty to ninety bodies buried in shallow graves of these workers who had died from an unknown illness. This illness was soon revealed as cholera.

---

524. mansell.com/POW_resources/camplists.
525. 2nd4thmgb.com.au/camp/mezali-70-kiilometerm-amp-burma.

A major clean-up operation was ordered by Colonel Williams. He organised burial parties and a clearing of the ground as the *rōmusha* with dysentery had just squatted wherever 'the call of nature came to them'.[526]

Though the senior medical officer, Dr Rowley Richards, strictly enforced quarantine regulations regarding the cholera isolation hut, two men broke the rules which Richards turned a blind eye to. The first of these was the Catholic padre, Peter Smith, who would sneak in to offer prayers to the patients or help in any way he could. The other, remarkably, was Colonel Williams. He would crawl through the grass to avoid detection. He would go in to shave the men or talk to them to try and lift their spirits and encourage them to fight on.[527]

As at other camps, those that were able to work and receive pay, contributed a portion of the money to the camp hospital for food for those unable to work. Here one of the officers along with the Red Cross representative kept a note of all the money each man handed over, to be repaid by the Army at the end of the war. Officers were only permitted to receive, after the Japanese had taken their share for board, the same amount as the maximum any of the other ranks received. The balance went into a bank account controlled by Brigadier Varley at Thanbyuayat.

The British Sumatra Battalion took over from No.1 Mobile Force on 17 May. Major Dudley Apthorpe was the battalion commander: 'Taunzun was a large camp with the railway station 2 kilometres up the line from the camp, to reach the station a large timber bridge, 70 yards long, further upstream was a road bridge. The monsoons had caused the river to rise and be very fast. The road bridge collapsed and then the rail bridge started to do the same. The build-up of fallen trees and debris on the rail bridge did not help, then the extra wood from the fallen road bridge also built up, the Japanese had the men working throughout the night clearing away these obstructions. The next day elephants were brought in to help. The bridge took 10 days to rebuild under horrendous conditions with the prisoners waist deep in the surging water, yet within 12 hours of its completion it collapsed again.

'By this time the toilet pits had overflowed and its effluent was running into the camp. Despair was causing many deaths, but the prisoners rebuilt both road and rail bridges.'[528] Taungzun became 'a reeking bog'.

It is said that one of the jobs the prisoners were made to do here[529] was dig tunnels about thirty to forty feet long into the sides of sandy cliffs. The Japanese let the prisoners know that, when the war was over the POWs would be herded into the tunnels where they would be shot and the entrances covered over.

---

526. Richards, p.143.
527. Wright, p.246.
528. Apthorpe, p.107.
529. Wright, p.200.

Khonkan   55 Kilo

Also known as Khn Kuhn or Khoukan

Khonkan was a base hospital for the northern part of the line. It was an abandoned work camp, being 'a cluster of filthy bamboo huts they called a hospital camp but really nothing more than a dump for the worst sick of the railroad.'[530] There were, in fact, eight large huts and one small one small isolation hut which held 100 dysentery patients. No beds or bedding were provided.

It was notable for being the camp where Lieutenant Colonel Coates conducted his most remarkable work caring for hundreds of men under the most deplorable circumstances. In an address in Melbourne in 1946, he described Khonkan: 'In 1943, 1,800 of the worst casualties of the railway work were concentrated at Kohn Kuhn, the 55 kilo camp, and there I was sent on a stretcher [he was suffering from scrub-typhus, see above] to take charge of the medical work Lieutenant Colonel Gottschall, a Dutch officer, was in charge of discipline, roll-calls, etc. … The "hospital" consisted of bamboo huts, with no equipment of any kind. Even tins for carrying water, such as petrol drums of which there were many at the local siding, could not be got. In that region, fortunately, bamboo grew to a great size and the bamboo water container came into universal use.'[531] Bedpans were also made out of old mess tins and half coconut shells. The large leaves from nearby trees became the toilet paper.

Coates had a helper, a Dutch captain, C.J. van Boxtel who was a 'genius at chemistry'. He made emetine from an extract of ipecacuanha plants which was used to cure dysentery with 'complete success'.[532] Boxtel also had a small bottle of dental cocaine tablets with which he found a way to make the cocaine up into a 2 per cent solution. This was injected into the patients' as a spinal anaesthetic which meant they felt less pain as their legs were being amputated.

It is said that around a quarter of the patients at Khonkan were suffering from tropical ulcers. These were housed exclusively in one long hut, the stench from which was 'unbearable' even at a distance. In the first few weeks, Coates wrote, 120 legs 'came off', with as many as four operations per day. All he had to operate with was one knife, two pairs of artery forceps and the use of the one and only camp saw which was shared with the carpenters and the camp butcher.

On top of this, many toes were removed without anaesthetic and often only using scissors. A cloth or a piece of paper was held over the eyes of the patient

---

530. Gavan Daws, *Prisoners of the Japanese* (Simon & Schuster, London, 2006), p.199.
531. Reproduced in 2nd4thmgb.com.au/camp/khonkan-360k-burma.
532. Walker, *Australia in the War of 1939–1945*, p.589.

so they couldn't see the dreadful amputation of their leg or foot.[533] Socks were used to cover the stumps.

The survival rates from these operations, however, were not great. To be specific, Coates performed 114 leg amputations, all but thirty-five of them above the knee. About 10 per cent of patients died directly after the operation and a couple of months later only approximately half of the remainder were still alive. Of course, it cannot be known how many would have died if Coates had not performed the operations.[534] In total, there were more than 500 patients treated for tropical ulcers at Khonkan.

Where it was hoped that patients could be treated for their ulcers without amputation, the affected matter would be scraped from the limb with a spoon as in other camps. Major Peter Campbell watched some of these procedures where four men would have to hold the patient down, the screams of the poor patients being 'nothing less than hair-raising'.[535]

Corporal Tom Morris volunteered to act as an orderly at Khonkan. He worked in the dysentery 'death house', where there was a 'thunder box' in the centre aisle, but few patients were capable of making their way to this 'offensive-smelling container'. To help alleviate the pain amputees were in, lying on the hard bamboo platforms, the orderlies slung rice bags between bamboo poles to create a kind of hammock.

As it was primarily a non-working camp, the prisoners were on half rations. To determine the level of food to be given out, the Japanese weighed each of the prisoners every month and their combined weight was used to calculate the rations for the following weeks. Unbelievably, the less the POWs weighed, they less food they received.[536]

As at the other camps, on 20 November a memorial service was held at 55 Kilo camp. Large, inscribed crosses were erected at the cemeteries in the camps, and a letter of condolence was read by Colonel Nagatoma to the assembled prisoners at Khonkan camp and by his representatives at other camps. Two days' rest was granted. Afterwards, the railway line having been completed, the Japanese announced that that fit men would remain in the jungle to maintain the line.[537] This was to fell trees for fuel for the steam locomotives and producing ballast for the line but mostly it was to repair the bridges and embankments damaged by the attacks of the Allied bombers. The 'light sick' were to go to Ban Pong, and 'heavy sick' to a hospital near Bangkok. The food in most camps

---

533. Wright, p.251.
534. Daws, p.201.
535. TNA WO 235/867.
536. Morris, op. cit.
537. Walker, *Australia in the War of 1939–1945*, p.556.

was now so poor that, although the major work was completed, the death rate began again to rise, particularly in the Kilo 55 hospital camp.[538]

As the Burma camps were dismantled the men, including Coates, were moved down to Nakhon Pathom which was a new hospital camp built some fifty miles from Bangkok to accommodate 10,000 patients. In July 1944, the sick from all the Burma railway hospital camps were transferred to the Nakhon Pathom where Coates had been appointed Chief Medical Officer.

Tanbaya Hospital Camp   53 Kilo
Also known as Thanbaya or Tambaya

Lieutenant Colonel C.T. Hutchinson, the Administrative Commander of 'F' Force, wrote the following in December 1943: 'At the end of June a project for the establishment of a hospital in some locality where food was readily available was put to the I.J.A. This was examined and a reconnaissance in Burma was carried out by the I.J.A. Medical Officer. However, nothing materialised and the project was shelved indefinitely. Nevertheless, at the end of July it was suddenly resuscitated and became a fait accompli almost immediately.' Orders were issued for the evacuation of a staff and 1,700 patients to the camp at Tanbaya by road and rail through three staging camps to be established at Changaraya (No.5 Camp), Kyondaw/Kando/Kamdaw, and Ronshi The move was to be carried out by motor transport in flights of 250 with nightly stages at Changaraya, Kyondaw and Ronshi.

The move began on 30 July with an advance party, consisting of administrative staff and eight officers and thirty-six other ranks of the medical staff drawn from all the 'F' Force camps, which reached Tanbaya at the beginning of August 1943. The camp, which was adjacent to the railway, had been an old coolie camp which had been allowed to fall into a bad state of disrepair. No tools were provided to improve the camp other than a single axe which had been carried from Thailand by one of the men. The *rōmusha* living in the camp fouled the whole area but requests to have the *rōmusha* moved to one end of the camp were ignored.

Indeed, with Tanbaya not being a work camp, the Japanese scarcely intervened at all with the running of the camp, leaving the prisoners to their own devices. It was unusual to even see a Japanese walking round the camp.

The first patients began arriving on 8 August. Patients were herded into closed or open trucks and as many as fifty-four in one closed truck was recorded. As the majority of these cases were suffering from tropical ulcers and/or dysentery

---

538. ibid.

the atmosphere in the trucks was dreadful. Deaths en route were not infrequent and as many as eight in one party were found to be dead on arrival. Altogether forty-three out of the 1,700 patients died on the journey.[539]

Colonel Hutchinson gave his description of described Tanbaya: 'The hospital was to accommodate twelve hundred and fifty patients who were to be drawn from two categories (i) men who would not recover from their present illness within two months, and (ii) old men with a permanent disability or unsuited for heavy work on the road …

'Secondary jungle had grown up all around. The actual site itself was dry considering it was in the middle of the monsoon. One hut and the cookhouse were roofed in, the remaining huts were in the process of being roofed and otherwise repaired. In the roofed huts the advance party, together with the I.J.A. guards, were housed. Other huts were occupied by coolies employed on the railway and on the repair of huts.

'The camp consisted of seven huts each a hundred metres long, with attap sides and roof and a wide bamboo platform to take two men, with a gangway along one side. Each of the huts were scheduled to take two hundred patients. In addition, there was a smaller hut to hold eighty patients and this had two platforms with a gangway down the centre. Later, when the establishment of the hospital was increased, a small camp the other side of the railway line and occupied by I.J.A. railway personnel and coolies was made available. Here there were two big huts, a smaller hut, and in addition, a small hut which was used as an operating theatre and chapel.

'When the hospital was finally established, the layout was:
'Ward I Administrative personnel
'Ward II Malaria and beri-beri patients
'Ward III Dysentery patients
'Ward IV Malaria and beri-beri patients
'Ward V' Malaria and beri-beri patients
'Ward VI Dysentery patients
'Ward VII (Medical (non-dysentery) patients
'Ward VIII HQ officers and stores (Q.M. dispensary etc.)
'Ward IX Tropical ulcer patients
'Ward X Tropical ulcer patients
'Ward XI Officer patients

'Latrines were the usual open trench type, and the majority were the old existing ones, only two new ones being provided. The camp lay on either side of the railway line and about a hundred yards from it. The actual precincts of

---

539. TNA WO 325/16.

the camp were fairly clear of trees, though the jungle was quickly reached. It did not, however, have that confined feeling prevalent in the working camps. An outcrop of low hills a mile and a half to two miles away made a pleasant view. The camp was bounded on three sides by two small streams, which eventually joined at the north-east corner of the camp. One flowed almost past the cookhouse and provided the water supply for the camp. The fourth side of the camp was bounded by the Thailand-Moulmein road. Towards the outcrop of hills and a thousand yards from the camp was a largish stream flowing in a north-westerly direction.'[540]

Water soon became a major problem at Tanbaya. The stream at the south-east corner of the camp was originally allotted for all purposes. On 13 October the supply suddenly dried up and the cookhouse had to be moved, this time to the other stream to the north of the camp. This source of supply also failed a week later and again the cookhouse had to be moved, this time to the large stream. Each move meant the water had to be carried increasingly longer distances. To save the long carry of water to the wards two wells were brought into use, but for these the I.J.A. provided neither buckets nor ropes. Prisoner ingenuity had to be employed again, using local materials.

At Tanbaya, which Albert Coates called 'a dirty depot for depositing the dying,'[541] amputations were conducted almost daily in the ulcer ward. Few amputees survived for long after the horrific ordeal of amputation, carried out by the surgeon with nothing but a wood-cutting saw borrowed from the Japanese. There was at least one confirmed death of a POW who hung himself after he had both legs amputated.

One of the more notable characters at Tanbaya was the English padre, Noel Duckworth. He gave away all his clothes apart from a pair of 'holey' shorts and used to keep back some of his rice ration in case another man was in greater need.[542]

Idris Barwick was one of the medical orderlies who accompanied the patients to Tanbaya. Much to his surprise, when he arrived there in early September 1943, he found everything 'tidy, no filth about, roofs were covered, the latrines were situated in convenient places, and the huts seemed to be orderly and clean.' All this he ascribed to Major Hunt who was a fierce, but fair, disciplinarian, whose word, at Tanbaya, was 'law'.[543]

Despite Hunt's fierce discipline he could not halt the decline in the health of the camp as a whole, which he wrote in that same month, September, was

---

540. Grehan, pp.81-4.
541. Coates, p.116.
542. Wright, p.255.
543. Barwick, pp.193-4.

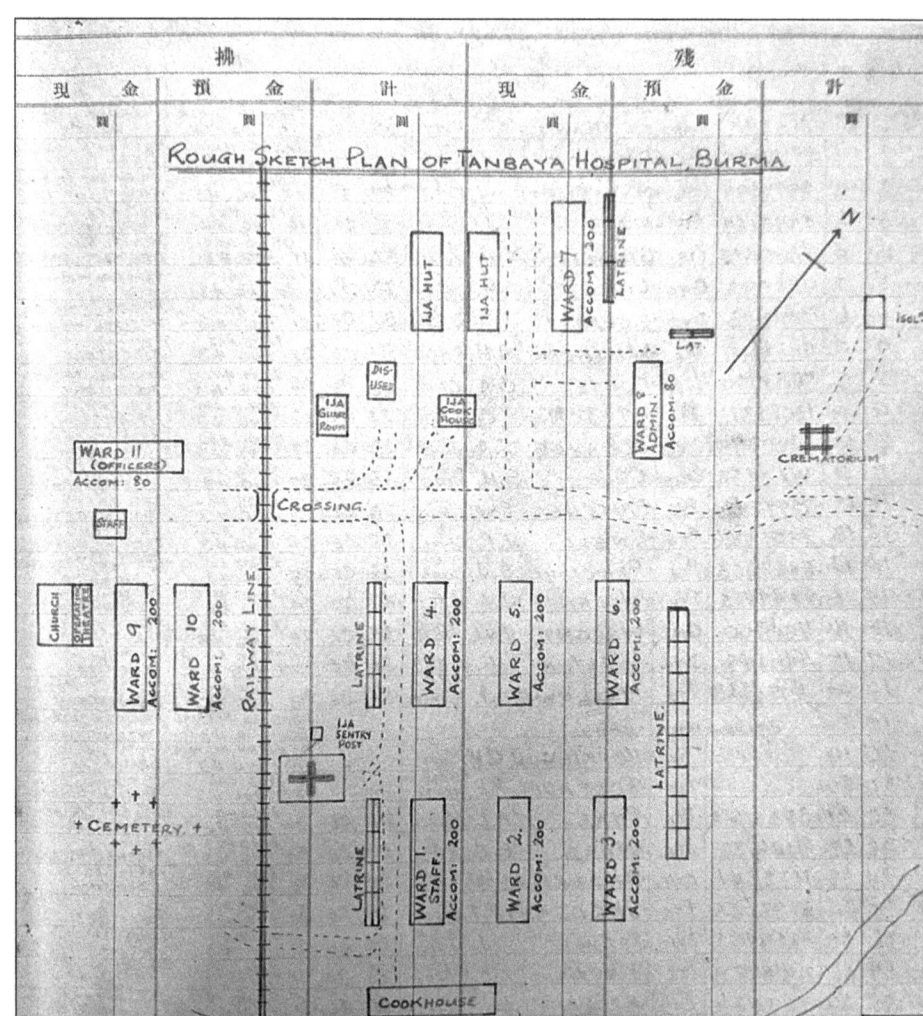

A sketch of Tanbaya Hospital camp taken from the diary of Lieutenant Colonel C.T. Hutchinson.

'getting worse, not better, every day… In 20 years of medical practice and extensive experience of 2 wars, I have never seen men in a more pitiable condition than the men in this camp. The real tragedy lies in the fact that much of the disease is really curable if proper vitamin-containing foodstuffs … were made available in sufficient quantity … men are dying in their hundreds and will continue to die until help comes.'[544]

Being a hospital camp there was no external work required, but there were the usual camp duties to be performed, and the patients were graded for their capacity

---

544. Quoted in Beattie, *The Death Railway*, p.81.

to undertake the various necessary tasks. That, of course, included cremating the many who died. One patient there, Lieutenant Frank Pantridge, wrote about this: 'As the bodies on the bonfire incinerated, the skulls made explosive noises. Every morning I could hear the repeated banging of exploding skulls.'[545]

When permitted to buy canteen supplies from the locals, the items were shared between the wards according to the number of men in each. Such foods included eggs, fruit, lady's finger, beans, sweet potatoes, and some meat to add to the rice ration. This fair distribution of goods applied to all ranks but officers, much to the resentment of the other ranks, were able to buy additional foodstuffs with their higher pay (the pay for privates was about enough to buy one duck egg per day along the Burma section of the railway[546]) Sick officers also each had an orderly to attend to their 'every want', whereas there was only one orderly between fifty or 100 other patients.[547]

As at Tamarkan, patients with septic scabies and sores and were encouraged to bath in the river to allow the fish to nibble away at their affected skin. Men would lie in shallow water for hours while the fish swam around them.

Despite the endeavours of Hunt and his team, approximately 750 men died, or approximately 45 percent of the total number of patients, in the two-and-a-half months from early September 1943 until the first of the patients were removed to Kanburi in late November. This outcome was a bitter disappointment, but at least the remaining 55 percent were saved from inevitable death in the working camps. During the move to Kanburi – a journey of five days in which they were not allowed off the train – the prisoners only received three meals. Some of the men were transported in horse boxes where the floors were covered in manure. In his final report from Tanbaya, in October 1943, Hunt pointed out that in five months 30 percent of the men in 'F' Force had already died from disease, that was 2,000 men.

A sketch of Tanbaya Hospital camp taken from the diary of Lieutenant Colonel C.T. Hutchinson.

Anankwin 45 Kilo
Also known as Anarkwan

Anderson and Williams Forces (No.1 Mobile Force) were sent to Anankwin 45 kilo camp on 24 April 1943 to lay rails and sleepers. They departed on 13 May 1943 to Taungzun.

---

545. Cecil Lowry, *Frank Pantridge MC: Japanese Prisoner of War and Inventor of the Portable Defibrillator* (Pen & Sword, Barnsley, 2020), p.73.
546. Kinvig, p.94.
547. Barwick, pp.201-2.

Anankwin became an important station on the railway with a locomotive depot and engine sheds with sidings[548] and an overhead locomotive replenishment water tank. It also became a base hospital, but it was understaffed and had little medicine or equipment. Even though it was then a hospital camp, the patients were required to maintain the road in the area. The Allied doctors were instructed to always treat the Japanese who needed medical attention before any prisoners or native workers. Yet, when Brigadier Varley visited in June 1943, he regarded the accommodation as being ample and the food 'fair'.

Beke Taung   40 Kilo
Also known as Bekitan or Beketaung

Lieutenant Colonel Chris Black led a force which included 610 Australians 190 Americans & 111 Dutch that arrived at Thanbyuzayat on 30 October 1942 and moved to Beke Taung. It was situated in a malaria-infested area and this, and dysentery, were prevalent throughout the camp. 'The 40 Kilo Camp was almost our undoing,' wrote American POW Tom 'Slug' Wright.[549]

It was ironic that initially there was no water in the camp which had to be brought from a creek about a kilometre away, but when the monsoons came the hospital hut was in a gully and almost surrounded by water.[550] Later a well was dug.

One American prisoner, Corporal H.R. Charles, described the kitchen which was like many in the camps along the railway: 'a roof of atap supported on four poles, a shield of bamboo and atap leaves lining the sides wait-high to keep the rain from blowing in on whatever provisions they had. There were four large black cauldrons, one filled with plain water, one with a watery soup, and two with rice.'[551]

Beke Taung's Medical Officer was Australian Captain John Higgins, assisted by Dutchman Dr Henri Hekking. Hekking was a herbalist who knew the jungle, and the diseases of the region, well and, in the absence of medicines, was able to find many plants that could help the sick. With permission from Lieutenant Yamada, Hekking was allowed to leave the camp accompanied by two guards, each carrying a rice sack. They returned with quantities of a plant called *cephaelis ipecacuanha* which was a cure for dysentery.[552] He also used

---

548. 2nd4thmgb.com.au/camp/anankwin-45-km-camp-burma.
549. La Forte and Marcello, p.187.
550. 2nd4thmgb.com.au/camp/beketaung-374k-burma.
551. H. Robert Charles, *Last Man Out, Surviving the Burma-Thailand Death Railway* (Zenith Press, St Paul, 2006), p.129.
552. Charles, ibid, pp.132-5.

leaves to heal cuts and beans to make a bitter tonic that reduced fever, and he instructed the prisoners on which herbs to gather when they were in the jungle. On his nightly forages he even treated sick or injured Thais in local villages. Dr Hekking is credited with having saved hundreds of lives.[553]

Unusually, Black's second-in-command, Major George Kiernan, stated that the Japanese camp commander 'tried to help us all he in the way of food for those who were ill'. Despite such efforts, no quinine was supplied by the Japanese sergeant in charge for four weeks during the height of the cholera outbreak.

The prisoners here laid the railbed with ballast behind a force of native labours which had cleared the jungle along the track and at first the work was not too strenuous.[554]

In November the water supply failed and what became known as 'Black Force' moved to Kun Knit Kway, 26 kilo camp, joining Ramsay Force.[555] Of the 138 men of Black Force who worked at Beke Taung, sixteen died at the camp and a further eighty later.[556]

Tanyin 35 Kilo
Also known as Tan Yin

In late October 1942, a body of 884 Australians from Java under Lieutenant Colonel Williams, 2/2nd Pioneers, AIF, was moved from Thanbyuzayat to Tanyin (Tan Yin) by lorry. The camp had two attap huts that were open on one side. There was a native well about 500 yards from the camp and a stream about the same distance away.[557] They were told that they had until 16.00 hours to clear a parade ground. No food would be issued until the task was complete. All they had to clear virgin jungle covered in thick bamboo were crosscut saws, axes, picks, shovels and machetes. It was at 18.30 hours that the ground was adequately prepared for the first parade to be held.

Williams Force was joined by Anderson Force in January 1943 to become No. 1 Mobile Force. This title was well-earned, as in the space of six months it was moved from 40 Kilo camp to 26 Kilo to 35 Kilo to 14 Kilo to 26 Kilo to 45 Kilo to 18 Kilo.[558]

Its job was to lay the rails on track bed prepared by the other forces. However, the operational use of the force was very inefficient, as Colonel Anderson

---

553. Crager, p.79.
554. Kinvig, p.66.
555. 2nd4thmgb.com.au/camp/beketaung-374k-burma.
556. Walker, *Australia in the War of 1939–1945*, p.553.
557. 2nd4thmgb.com.au/camp/tanyin-35-kilo-camp-burma.
558. Daws, p.189.

explained: 'As we were constructing the railway, there would be about ten kilos between the different camps; when we had got halfway, we would have to go to the next camp and retrace our steps instead of proceeding onwards. The simple thing would have been to take the line to the next camp, where the sick and gear would be carried, but no, the Japs decided we all would have to go back to the starting point, and then take the gear and the sick, with sick men carrying sick, right forward again. We would be carrying 10 per cent of our sick.'[559] Then, at the end of May 1943, the prisoners of No.1 Mobile Force were made to move camp at night so as not to disrupt work during the daytime. This meant they had to match after working all day.

Colonel Williams explained that at these camps the prisoners were given a time limit to build the huts, kitchen and latrines and all they could do was their best in that time: 'So far as the structure is concerned we could finish it with the materials we could get nearby, but as to the walling and roofing we had to wait for the supplies from other places and … we could not complete the walls and the roofing, and before we could put up our roofs and walls they [the Japanese] sent up men to live in such quarters.'[560]

It was also claimed by the other ranks at Tanyin, that there was some resentment by the other ranks with their own officers allowing sick men to be forced to work on the railway while they remained in camp. There was also an issue with prisoners intentionally seeking to avoid working on the railway. Men would buy salt which they would swallow in a large quantity with their food followed by a big drink of water. This would cause oedema – the swelling of parts of the body – mimicking beriberi. This was certain to result in a precautionary period of rest in hospital.

Through whatever causes, on 23 January, only ninety-nine out of 500 prisoners were sent to work. This led to a confrontation with camp commandant, Lieutenant Yamada, Colonel Anderson explained that because of the inadequate diet there was an outbreak of pellagra. If Yamada wanted more workers better food would have to be supplied. Yamada agreed to this, but still demanded more workers until the ration issue could be addressed.

This meant that many sick men were driven out to work. Rowley Richards tried to mitigate the effects of a hard day's labour on the severely undernourished prisoners by reaching an agreement with Yamada that the men could be rotated, working only on alternate days. Richards also managed to persuade Yamada that the sick workers should only do the equivalent of half-a-day's work, i.e., shift 0.8 metres of material.[561] He described his dealing with the Japanese as

---

559. TNA, WO 235/963.
560. AWM, 54 1010/3/10.
561. Richards, pp.122-7.

like playing 'God'. He had to decide who could stay in camp, who would get extra nutritious food and then he would have to barter with the Japanese to allow these things. These decisions could mean, quite literally, the difference between life and death. Often his attempts at keeping men in camp would result in him being beaten.

Despite all the hardships they endured, the POWs were treated reasonably well at Tanyin, and actually received an issue of clothing in early 1943, thanks to the conduct of Yamada: 'In appearance rather grim and forbidding ... he nevertheless exercised intelligence and tolerance in his camp administration. He rather stretched the rules of the Imperial Japanese Army in regard to prisoners to ensure that Lieut-Colonel Williams received treatment in accordance with his rank. When once he did complain that he himself was not being saluted as he moved about the camp, it was as if to say: "Look here fellows, after all I am the boss here; the least you can do is pay me a little respect occasionally."'[562] Ultimately, all this did Yamada no good, as he was relieved of his command, for, presumably, not getting enough work out of the prisoners he was responsible for.

The food ration here was better than in the more remote camps, with one cow killed each day, allowing, after the Japanese had taken their share, for every prisoner to have four or five ounces of meat. There was also a self-imposed rule that none of the limited rations should ever be allowed to go to waste. This, however, had possibly unforeseen consequences. Men who were very sick often could not face eating anything. This meant their rations were given to others, resulting in some men allegedly getting 'fat' while others starved.[563]

Reptu　　　　　　　　　　　　　　　　　　　　　　　　　　　　　　30 Kilo
Also known as Retphaw, Rephaw or Repo

The first prisoners arrived at Reptu on 26 December 1942, and were tasked to lay 15 kilometres of railway to Anankwin. Its sickness rates were alarming. In February 1943, 431 Dutch were on 'No Duty' and 385 were in hospital, making a total of 816 sick. Washing had to be taken to a stream 2.5 kilometres away.[564]

The inventiveness of the prisoners resulted in the erection of a new hospital building on 14 February 1943, which included a dispensary, an operating theatre, and a dental clinic. A pipeline was run into the building where the water supply could be regulated.

---

562. F. Aitken, *The Story of the 2/2 Australian Pioneer Battalion* (The Battalion Association, Melbourne, 1953), p.157.
563. Wright, p.263.
564. AWM, 1010/4/63 Part 1.

It was announced at the beginning of March that Reptu would be converted into a hospital camp. According to Captain Higuchi, at Reptu, 'a separation room and an operations room, and a medicine store was built after the camp was converted into the hospital.' This, though, may have been the existing building opened in February. The prisoners received a supply of loin cloths from the Japanese. While even this scanty clothing was appreciated, each man had to sign a receipt acknowledging that they had received 'one uniform complete, issued by the Japanese Imperial Army'.[565]

The new hospital camp, or casualty clearing station, opened with around 1,600 patients for a short time under Lieutenant Colonel Coates, assisted by Major Sidney Krantz as surgeon, before being closed down. Coates wrote of what it took to survive during his time at 30 Kilo camp: 'The route home is inscribed in the bottom of every man's dixie. Every time it is filled with rice, eat it. If you vomit it up again, eat some more; even if it comes up again some good will remain. If you get a bad egg, eat it no matter how bad it may appear. An egg is only bad when the stomach will not hold it.'[566]

Coates also faced the insoluble dilemma of the camp administration sending out men to work who were clearly unwell, for them to be returned by the Japanese engineers as they so sick as to be no use to them, only for the whole process to be repeated the following day.

Brigadier Varley visited Reptu in June 1943. The work the men had to undertake was that of unloading goods and materials from steam trains onto diesel trains which took the loads further up the line. Varley wrote that the accommodation here was 'ample' and the food 'sufficient'. By contrast, the Australian Official History stated that Reptu's sanitary arrangements were so bad that the latrines were 'physically dangerous'. Those men who were supposed to be convalescing had little opportunity for rest as they were continually engaged in boiling water and sterilising equipment. The camp was within walking distance of the Khwae, however, and the Japanese permitted the patients to swim and fish.[567] As well as the latrines, bamboo pipes were sunk into the ground around the camp. The men urinated into these and the urine was absorbed into the ground. These featured in an unusual incident when one POW, a Sergeant Coombes, was urinating into one of the pipes one night when he was spotted by the intoxicated camp commandant, Lieutenant Naito, who assumed Coombes was trying to escape. Naito caught and beat Coombes and then walked him away towards the cemetery with a Korean guard at bayonet point. Naito ordered

---

565. Brigginshaw, pp.64-5.
566. Brune, p.604.
567. Walker, *Australia in the War of 1939–1945*, p.546.

the guard to bayonet Coombes, but the Korean refused. Naito then ordered the guard to trip Coombes so that the prisoner fell to the ground. Naito took the rifle and fired at Coombes who quickly rolled over and the bullet missed him. Just as Coombes was raising to his feet, Naito fired again and the bullet went through Coombes left side but, in the darkness, the sergeant managed to get away and reach the Australian officers' quarters. An inquest into the subject took place, during which a Japanese guard who witnessed the incident, supported Coombes' version of events. Naito, who was more often drunk than sober, was removed from the camp.[568]

The British Sumatra Battalion moved to Reptu around halfway through May 1943 during 'Speedo': 'By now the rain was almost continuous,' recorded the battalion's officers. 'The sick rate started to go up and it was increasingly difficult to find working parties. Loading and unloading [rails and sleepers] went on throughout the twenty-four hours and the sound of the drumming rain, the creak of the bullfrogs and the curious clang as rails slid off the trucks was quite unforgettable.'[569]

Reptu was shut down because Major General Sasaki (or Sassa) of the Thai POW Administration 'halved' the sick figures in the Burma camps at a stroke by shutting down Reptu and sending all bar twenty patients out to work.[570] The men were sent to work camps while those few patients utterly incapable of any physical effort were transferred to Thanbyuzayat. Rather than having all the sick in one hospital site the Japanese decided to allow a hospital at each camp, as we have read. Though, as we also know, circumstances soon forced the Japanese to allow dedicated hospital camps. Sasaki also claimed that he had flown to Singapore and procured 10,000 pairs of boots, shorts, hats and blankets for the POWs at the beginning of 1943, but all the boots and hats were lost when one of the two ships carrying the items crashed and sunk.

Reptu was re-opened on 4 July 1943 under the command of Major Ted Fisher when Allied bombing raids rendered Thanbyuzayat camp unsafe. The bombing did bring the prisoners one unforeseen benefit. In the attack several cavalry horses were killed which had been shipped from Japan as mounts for IJA officers. The carcases were cut up and the meat sent down the line to Reptu in open railway wagons. By the time the meat reached Reptu it was crawling with maggots. But when the meat was boiled the maggots were driven out and the meat, the first in nineteen months for some men, was gratefully received. There was, as well, an occasional addition to the sparse ration for Jim Bolero

---

568. Brigginshaw, p.63; AWM, 54 1010/4/68, Part 1.
569. Apthorpe, p.100.
570. T. Hamilton, *Report on Conditions and Life and Work of P.O.W. in Burma and Siam, 1942-1945* (Medical Liaison Office Internee Camp, Bangkok, 12 September 1945).

of C Company 2/26 Battalion AIF. Unlike the work parties, there were no guards watching the water-carrying and wood-cutting details. This enabled Bolero to set traps in the jungle around Reptu to catch Burmese wildfowl. His traps, which sometimes also caught monkeys, were made from thread unpicked from webbing belts.[571]

On 16 August 1943, the camp commandant, Lieutenant Naito went out of the camp and returned in a drunken state. He beat up one of the guards and so three other guards ran to 55 Kilo camp to inform Colonel Nagatoma. The colonel went to Reptu to see for himself and found Naito still drunk and causing trouble. Nagatoma ordered the guards to throw Naito, in a truck along with all his gear. Naito was hated by the guards, and they were delighted to see the back of him.[572]

The medical staff prisoners received their first payments from the Japanese in October 1943, which were supposed to be the equivalent of those medical staff in the Japanese Army. This meant officers, warrant officers and senior sergeants received 30 rupees per month, sergeants 22 rupees, corporals 19 rupees, 12.5 for lance-corporals and 8 rupees for privates. The men did not receive anywhere near those amounts, with the Japanese taking back money for food and lodgings and claimed they were holding back money which they would bank on the prisoners' behalf.[573]

The camp was abandoned on 25 October 1943, according to Captain Higuchi, because it was thought that Allied forces might land on the nearby coast, and because railway construction had moved further south. The prisoners were moved up to 55 Kilo camp.

Kun Knit Kway   26 Kilo

Black's force was moved from 40 Kilo camp to 26 Kilo in November 1942. The camp had previously been occupied by *rŏmusha* and was in a shocking condition, where cholera had been rampant.

Lieutenant Colonel G.E. Ramsay's force arrived at Kun Knit Kway, Kun Kwit Kway or Kunhnitkway, on 20 December 1942, remaining there until 18 March 1943. The camp was situated at the end of a valley leading up to the mountains and dense jungle with the railway access road running through the middle. The camp hospital was on one side of the road with the work camp on the other. The camp guards were Korean, who were, one medical officer said: 'pure amoral coolie vermin, brutal by nature as well as orders'.[574]

---

571. Brigginshaw, p.62.
572. Wright, p.267.
573. Wright, p.267.
574. Newton and McGuinness, p.497.

The native labourers who had died of cholera had, seemingly, been buried where they laid as Jim Bodero recalled that after a particularly heavy downpour one night, the men woke up the next morning 'to see the rotting legs and arms of corpses sticking up stiffly out of the dirt floor under their sleeping platforms'.[575]

After being joined here by Black Force, the much-respected Colonel Ramsay gave a Christmas address to both parties – numbering around 1,500 men – in which he gave the prisoners an update on the progress of the war, hinting that the news came from a secret radio.[576] This may have raised the moral of the troops, but life there for the prisoners was not good, as one man recalled: 'Conditions were much worse than any we had so far experienced; the huts were only partly weather-proof, food was as bad as at Mergui, work was severe, being set on a piece-work basis. To make matters worse we came, for the first time, under the Korean guards, of whom the less said the better.'[577] By contrast, Alan Price of 2/3rd Motor Transport Company, who was part of Black Force, regarded Kun Knit Kway as one of the best camps and 'certainly the cleanest'.[578]

Being quite close to Thanbyuzayat the food situation was also comparatively reasonable at Kun Knit Kway. Rice was plentiful and was supplemented by a 'fair' quantity of green vegetables and about three ounces of meat a day.[579]

Stealing from fellow prisoners, nevertheless, was a constant problem and Len Stanfield, of 2/4th Casualty Clearing Station, saw how some American prisoners dealt with one man who had been caught in the act – by making him 'run the gauntlet'. Around forty of his comrades formed two lines which zig-zagged up a slope. Each man had a rag into which they had tied a stone in one corner, tying the other corner to a stick. The culprit had to run between the lines as his mates belted him with their makeshift weapons.[580]

When the line reached Kun Knit Kway, the prisoners were moved to 75 Kilo camp at Mieloe.

Hlepauk 18 Kilo
Also known as Alepauk or Rabao

A force under the command of Lieutenant Colonel C.G.W. Anderson arrived in Thanbyuzayat on the 5 October 1942. Five days later the 710 men of Anderson's Force marched to Hlepauk (and called 'The Gates of Hell', by Rowley

---

575. Brigginshaw, pp.53-4.
576. 2nd4thmgb.com.au/story/ramsay-force-no-1-battalion-force.
577. *Men May Smoke*, p.63, in Walker, *Australia in the War of 1939–1945*, p.449.
578. Wright, p.268.
579. TNA, WO 235/867.
580. Wright, pp.231-2.

Richards). This body was later reinforced by 200 British troops. The area around Thanbyuzayat was a level coastal plain of paddy fields, and the prisoners found construction work there relatively easy. But at Hlepauk the flat plains began to give way to ridges covered with thick jungle and the work became harder.

The camp itself was built in a valley with a range of hills on one side which reached to a height of 1,000 feet. The camp was beside the railway and the road, and on the other side the ground sloped gently upwards. In the valley was a small stream with clumps of bamboo and small 'scrubby' bushes.

There was an open square in the centre of the camp, with well-built wooden huts for the Japanese at one end and the prisoners' shabby bamboo huts forming two sides of the square. The cookhouse was in one corner and a guard room by the gate which, like many of the camps along the line, was marked by two large wooden posts.[581]

There was already a large number of native labourers at the camp as a consequence of which sanitary arrangements were very poor. Major Jim Jacobs of 18th Division Signals recalled upon arrival the disgusting condition the Tamils had left the huts in which they had only recently vacated to make room for the POWs: 'Piles of offal and human refuse were everywhere and the bamboo sleeping platforms were soiled with heaps of fermenting rice.'[582]

The latrines were open to flies and, as there was no disinfectant in the camp, they were described as being 'physically dangerous'. When Brigadier Varley visited the camp on 2 November 1942, he regarded it as 'a very rough camp, huts close together, roofs not by any means waterproof, rough floors of split bamboo.' In a second visit on 9 December, Varley saw no improvement, with numerous huts damaged by 'old age and wind', and portions of roofs having collapsed.

As the months passed conditions deteriorated further and the number of sick men began to increase. At the beginning of November one man in every three had been classified as too sick to work and in December this reached 50 per cent. Anderson's Force remained at Hlepauk until 3 January, when it moved to Tanyin where it joined Williams Force. Despite the conditions at Hlepauk only one man died of sickness in the period spent there by Anderson Force.

The Texan 2nd Battalion, 131st Field Artillery Regiment of the 36th Division, Texas National Guard (the so-called 'Lost Battalion') was sent to 18 Kilo camp where the men were shocked with the condition of the camp and the impoverished daily ration of a cup of steamed white rice, containing maggots and worms, and a half-canteen cup of watery vegetable stew. All water had to be hauled from nearby streams and two prisoners would carry a cut-off 55-gallon

---

581. Apthorpe, p.91.
582. Wright, p. 271.

drum from the river to the camp. Then the water had to be boiled before it could be used in the cookhouse. It was essential to keep the cookhouse fires going continuously, so other prisoners had to be constantly hauling wood into the camp.[583]

There was, though, one amusing situation at this camp. Bugle calls were Japanese Army ones which were blown by an American trumpeter who had been with a top band before the war, and he simply could not resist jazzing up the tunes. This, of course, brought repeated retribution from the Japanese, but must have made the prisoners smile.[584]

It was also from 18 Kilo camp on 20 November 1942 that Private Roy Pagani of the 18th Division Reconnaissance Corps made one of the few, if not the only, successful escapes from the Death Railway. Rather than wait until nightfall or carry as many provisions as he could. Pagani simply walked away in the middle of the day in bare feet with nothing but a loincloth round his waist. He believed he could adopt the customs of the locals and live as they lived: 'During my stay in the East, I found that a European would always be detected, no matter how good his disguise, due to the lack of sway in his posterior,' Pagani claimed. 'So, of course, this I had perfected whilst a POW, And I had hardened my feet by never wearing any footwear, as bad feet were the escaper's downfall.'[585] He was eventually taken into Japanese custody where, inevitably, he was treated badly. But he claimed to be a shot-down American airman and he was not returned to the railway where he would unquestionably have been executed. He survived but was not released until 1945.[586]

In total there had been thirteen escape attempts on the Burmese section of the line by the end of November 1942, including the above-mentioned Private Whitefield. On 8 October four Dutch, on 21 November three Dutch, and four days later a further four Dutch soldiers. All the Dutch escapees were Eurasians. It would seem that one of the Dutch prisoners was shot when surrounded by Burmese and three others were seized and handed back to the Japanese.

The shaky construction of the railway in general, not helped, of course, by the prisoners' efforts of subtle sabotage, was exemplified in how they dealt with problems encountered when building a bridge near Hlepauk. If one of the wooden piles to support the bridge could not be knocked deep enough into the riverbed because it had struck stone or some other impediment, instead of re-siting it, the Japanese simply sawed off the top to the required height.

---

583. Crager, p.77.
584. Apthorpe, p.91.
585. I. Morrison, *Grandfather Longlegs* (Faber & Faber, London, 1947), p.205.
586. See Philip Davies, *Lost Warriors - Seagrim and Pagani of Burma: The last great untold story of WWII* (Atlantic Publishing, 2017).

Sometimes, the piles were not driven straight and their way of correcting this was to get an elephant to pull it upright. This, according to Major Jim Jacobs, sometimes resulted in the pile snapping at the bottom. This did not seem to bother the Japanese, as long as the railway was built on time.[587]

Rowley Richards related an incident which occurred on Christmas Eve 1942. Captain Bill Drower sought to sell his silver cigarette case, but he could not bring himself to trade directly with the Japanese, So, the case was sold by another prisoner on Drower's behalf. It was bought by a Japanese officer who, in repeatedly 'fiddling' with it, broke the clasp. The Japanese officer found out on whose behalf the case had been sold and demanded his money back from Drower. He refused and was summoned to the guardhouse where he was beaten by ten Japanese. Drower fought back and yelled for help. His calls were heard throughout the camp and the entire body of prisoners was on the verge of mutiny. The senior Allied officers managed to keep a lid on the insurrection but Drower was saved, suffering no more than bruises and abrasions.[588]

The winter of 1942-3 was a cold one for the men at Hlepauk when the sun went down and they adopted the procedure of putting on all their clothes to go to bed and stripping down to their shorts, or G-strings to go to work in the daytime. It was also suspected that the Japanese were intercepting the Red Cross supplies of medicines sent to the prisoners and selling them off to the local Thais.

The local knowledge of the Dutch Eurasians proved invaluable. Parties were permitted to go into the jungle to search for edible plants. They gathered a type of wild spinach and the fruit of a shrub which they called 'wattle berry', which provided much-needed vitamin B to combat pellagra and beriberi. this was made into jam with melons and chindegar.[589]

The camp was in use until 19 March 1943.[590]

Thetkaw   14 Kilo

Green Force arrived here from Kandaw on 1 December 1942 by truck, remaining until 28 March 1943. Flies were a particular problem here to combat which the Japanese introduced a quota of flies which each prisoner had to kill each day, using whatever methods they could employ. Lice in the huts was an equally annoying problem, so much so, that many of the prisoners slept outside on the ground, even though it was bitterly cold at night and they risked punishment from the guards for being out of their huts.

---

587. Wright, pp.271-2.
588. Richards, pp.103-4.
589. Richards, p.101.
590. TNA, WO 203/6325.

On 12 February 1943, Major Alan Mull and two other Australian prisoners, Gunner Dickinson and Sapper Bell, escaped from Thetkaw camp. After about nine days Dickenson was recaptured. He said that after crossing hills, steep ridges and moving through heavy scrub, he had stopped for a rest as he was exhausted. By nightfall on that first day, he could go no further. He told the others to carry on without him, which they did, leaving him with food, water and some currency. He attempted to reach water in a gully and slipped off a cliff landing safely on a ledge where he remained for two nights. He moved off, and hid in a pump house and, when some Burmese boys passed by, he risked talking to them, asking them if there were any Japanese troops around. They said that there were indeed Japanese ahead and they took him to a mangrove thicket and told him to hide. A Burmese man arrived later and took Dickinson to the local village and handed over to the Japanese. Dickinson was taken to Thanbyuzayat cemetery and shot.[591]

Mull and Bell pressed on and had got as far as some 100 miles to the north where they were caught by Burmese police on the Salween River. On 10 March 1943, Major Mull was shot and killed resisting recapture; Bell was wounded in the arm and captured. It was difficult for white men to escape as the Japanese offered a 100 Rupee reward to the Burmese for each escapee they captured. Bell met the same fate as Dickinson. As he faced his executioners, Bell shook hands with Lieutenant Naito, who was in charge of the firing squad. He refused to kneel or sit in a tied position as was the Japanese custom, stating that he would die on his feet.[592]

On or about 3 May 1943, the camp was attacked by a party of about forty armed Burmese. They killed two Japanese guards and stole their rifles.

Wagale   8 Kilo

At Wagale, which was first occupied by Dutch prisoners, there was hardly a roof of any kind for a camp of 1,600 men. The three Dutch Eurasian escapees referred to above were from Wagale camp. After their capture they said that they had walked into Burma from Malay and did not speak English or Dutch. However, they were taken to Wagale where their identities were confirmed (Sergeant Van Haasen and privates Nelissen and Vredevoogd). They were confined to the guardhouse and on 27 December they were taken to the camp cemetery and shot.

---

591. AWM, 2019.22.101.
592. Walker, *Australia in the War of 1939–1945*, p 550.

Kandaw 4 Kilo
Also known as Kendaw or Kendau

A party of 1,026 Australian POWs under Major Charles Edward Green was the first to begin work on the Burma end of the railway. What became known as Green Force was split into two detachments for its move to Kandaw from Thanbyuzayat, the first under Major Green arrived on 1 October 1942, and the second (of 417 British, 590 and forty-seven Dutch) under Major J. Stringer which arrived on 24 October. These were the first Australians to start work on the line, the camp having been built by the Japanese 5th Railway Regiment and was filthy and infested with vermin having previously housed Burmese workers.

The camp was situated in a rubber plantation and was always damp and messy. In a report to the War Crimes Trials, Major Green submitted the following regarding 4 Kilo camp: 'The only latrines were those used by the natives. They were in a small gully, and were filled with water 6 inches of [i.e., from] the top and the whole area was covered in maggots. There was no kitchen at all and no hospital accommodation whatever. Immediate efforts were made to put the camp in order. Kitchens and latrines were built and an effort [was made] to improve the huts.'[593] Initially, 100 men were held back from work on the railway to clear a sports ground and a parade ground.

Being close to Thanbyuzayat rations were reasonable compared to those camps further south. In addition to the standard rice allowance, the POWs received meat every second day and a small quantity of vegetables.[594]

Lieutenant Colonel Nagatoma, commander of No. 3 Branch Thailand POW Administration, insisted that 'war prisoners' must sign a declaration stating that they would not attempt to escape. 'It is very necessary all soldiers sign parole,' he told Brigadier Varley. 'I cannot do my best for prisoners who have the intention to escape. All my orders must be obeyed. I will insist on this. I have the power to imprison or shoot for disobedience.'

Nagatoma made it clear that those who refused to sign such a declaration would be 'locked in'. That is exactly what happened to Major Green after he refused to sign the document which read: 'I the undersigned hereby solemnly swear on my honour that I will not under any circumstances attempt escape'. On 5 October 1942 he was taken back to Thanbyuzayat and placed in close confinement. Varley described the conditions Green endured: 'a plain cell, very dark, hard uneven floor. Not allowed anything to lieu [on] or take anything in with him. Not even lavatory paper. These later duties carried out in corner of

---
593. AWM, 54 1010/3/10.
594. AWM, 54 1010/4/63 Part1.

room through a trap door, excreta etc., depositing under floorboards. No water allowed for washing of body or hands. Food plain rice with salt sprinkled over it, making it unpalatable owing to quantity. Plain water to drink 3 times daily, sometimes weak tea. No blanket, bag or anything to lie on or rest head.'[595] Green was not alone in refusing to sign the declaration and Brigadier Varley had to explain to Nagatoma that it was every British and Australian's duty to try and escape. However, after two days confinement, the commander of the Dutch troops on the northern part of the railway, Major Hausenberg, did sign his parole and advised his men to do the same. Eventually, after Varley had made it clear that signing any such declaration under compulsion rendered it invalid, the prisoners complied.

As it happened there was an escape attempt made from Kandaw. On 10 November 1942, Private G.H. Whitefield slipped out of the camp. He gave himself up because he said that the natives, who were offered 100 rupees by the Japanese for each man they captured, knew of his whereabouts and movements.

According to his commanding officer, Whitefield had always behaved erratically and a hastily assembled medical board declared he was, 'Physically sound, but slightly deficient mentally, and a moral imbecile, not responsible for his actions'. Lieutenant Naito interviewed Whitefield himself and he agreed that the man was unbalanced and declared he would not be punished. That seemed to be the end of the matter until 14 December when he was taken to the camp cemetery and shot.[596]

Thanbyuzayat 0 Kilo
Also known as Thambuzyat

The first POWs arrived at Thanbyuzayat at the end of September 1942 under Brigadier Arthur Varley, where they established a base camp and hospital. Major Fisher was in charge of the hospital, and Lieutenant Colonel Thomas Hamilton was senior medical officer for all prisoners of war in Burma. Thanbyuzayat became the Japanese administrative terminus for the northern section of the railway where there was a large Japanese camp and vast dumps of materials for the railway construction. From the outset the possibility of attacks upon Thanbyuzayat by Allied bombers was considered and it was protected by anti-aircraft guns.

Upon their arrival, the prisoners were addressed by Lieutenant Colonel Nagatoma: 'We will build the railway if we have to build it over the white

---
595. Varley diary, p.47
596. Varley diary, pp.75-6.

man's body ... You are merely rubble ... If you want anything you will have to come through me for same and there will be many of you who will not see their homes again. Work cheerfully at my command.'[597]

From October 1942, Varley ordered the following deductions to be made from the prisoners' pay to help buy food for the hospitals in each camp: officers 20 percent, NCOs 15 percent and privates 5 percent. It was on 2 October, that Varley, as the senior Allied officer, was ordered to the Japanese headquarters where he met Colonel Nagatoma. He was informed that he would be permitted to have his own headquarters which would consist of a General Affairs Department of ten men, a Foodstuffs Department of seventeen, a Property Department, also of seventeen, plus a Medical Department of twelve.[598]

A small operating theatre was built at Thanbyuzayat in November 1942, in which emergency surgery could be carried out. It was in January 1943 that Thanbyuzayat became a base hospital for the northern part of the line with, initially 600 patients, the selected site being cleared by native labourers.

In his statement to the War Crimes court, the camp's Japanese Medical Officer, Lieutenant (Doctor) Higuchi, described the hospital at Thanbyuzayat: 'There was a separate ward for infectious diseases and a ward for the serious sick and an operation room and the medical store and there was a special separation ward for serious cases of infectious diseases [such as] dysentery and that kind, and the cook room and the laundry room, these were provided, of course, the latrine was also provided.'[599]

The Australian Official History describes Thanbyuzayat in somewhat different terms: 'Thanbyuzayat was a place of importance, where there were huge dumps of materials for the railway, and a large Japanese camp and headquarters, with anti-aircraft defences. The hospital consisted of shoddy huts of bamboos, with attap roof. Each hut was nearly 300 feet long with platforms 18 inches from the ground and one 6 feet alley way down the centre. They were overcrowded and infested with vermin. At the end of 1942 the Japanese built a new block with wooden floors and sound roofs. The provision of shuttered walls and mats for beds gave some degree of comfort, but only a yard of space per man was allowed, and the resultant overcrowding, together with the inevitable vermin drove the patients to sleep under the huts. Isolation was not provided except for dysentery.'[600] The vermin included 'dangerous' rats. The hospital, Brigadier Varley wrote, 'is about equal to a fowl shed, calf pen or machinery shed on a very poor farm.' It is also interesting to note that when the Japanese were asked

---

597. Crager, p.69.
598. Brune, p.593.
599. AWM, 54, 1010/3/10.
600. Walker, *Australia in the War of 1939–1945*, p.585.

if a Union Jack could be placed on the coffin of a British soldier during the burial, permission was refused. Lieutenant Colonel Nagatoma decreed that an Australian flag could be used but never a British one.[601]

Tom Hamilton also described Thanbyuzayat in unflattering terms, later writing that dysentery was the main 'death-dealing' disease: 'The dysentery ward was a crude bamboo and attap hut which looked and smelt inside like a charnel-hut. Emaciated skeletons of men lay dying in the stench of their own excreta … The medical orderlies had to clean the sick with scraps torn from mosquito nets and spare articles of clothing.'[602]

For the Emperor Hirohito's birthday on 3 November 1942, the men were granted a day off work and were even taken to a 'cinema show' that night. The show started at 21.00 hours and did not finish until 02.30. The prisoners were not permitted to leave until the end of the show. Concerts with a band were featured at Thanbyuzayat from time to time.[603]

There were other instances of reasonable conduct shown by some of the Japanese. On 30 November 1942, a Dutch prisoner went outside the camp, wearing only a sarong (a method adopted by Dutch Asian escapees to allow them to blend in with the native population), to buy food from the local Burmese. He was arrested and taken to the camp's guardhouse. The prisoner explained that he went to buy bananas and, as he did not have any money, he traded his shirt. The camp's temporary commander, Lieutenant Hosoda, did not punish the prisoner, instead he gave him some money to buy the bananas he wanted.[604]

On 7 December 1942, Nagatoma travelled to Rangoon and from there on to Singapore for a conference of camp commanders. On his return, he told Brigadier Varley that he had spent 20,000 yen while he was away on items for the prisoners. This included blankets, clothes, boots, hats, toothbrushes and tooth Powder, toilet paper and sporting equipment including footballs and table tennis, tennis, and baseball equipment.

In his idiosyncratic manner, Nagatoma wanted to provide for the welfare of the prisoners by building a tennis court and football field. But to clear the ground for these amenities, the light sick were kicked out of their huts.

A tennis tournament was held on 6 and 7 February, which included players from other camps, with a concert on the evening of the 6th. The prizes won were a towel, soap, toothbrush and tooth powder. A further tennis and a football tournament took place in March (Tanyin camp won the former and Reptu the latter).

---

601. Varley diary, p.66.
602. AWM, 541010/4/64.
603. AWM, 2019.22.101.
604. AWM, 2019.22.101.

At one sports tournament, some of the Australians dressed up as girls and caused 'many a laugh' when 'the girls chased a Japanese guard right to the guard house – about 200 yards – where he remained and did not return to the sports.' Film nights occasionally took place in the railway yard, which were often Japanese propaganda productions showing such footage as the sinking of HMS *Prince of Wales* and HMS *Repulse* and the attack on Pearl Harbor.[605]

The prisoners themselves also took part in a Japanese propaganda film, which included Dutch and Americans from outlying camps as well as the British and Australians. The purpose of the film was: 'to photograph the prisoners from all countries relaxing and recuperating after a hard day's labour at all kinds of work on the railway construction connecting Thailand and Burma and to show the working conditions and simple life under the kind and pleasant treatment of the Japanese Army.' Conferences between the Japanese and Allied officers were also filmed, as was a concert with an Australian brass band.

Tom Hamilton was also filmed undertaking a consultation with Lieutenant Higuchi, with both men examining a POW's chest. In fact, the only medical problem the patient had was piles![606]

The filming went on for days, portraying the Japanese in the best possible light. When it was noticed that some of the prisoners' clothes lacked buttons, these were issued and sewn on. After the filming, the buttons were taken back.[607]

Water was a major problem, practically all of it having to be carried from a well near the local village by men with buckets and tubs. In January 1943 the Japanese sent approximately forty men to deepen the well in the camp and to generally improve the water supply. When it was finished in February, the well was able to yield some 3,000 gallons a day which considerably relieved the water issue. Further wells were dug. In February an issue of clothing was received at Thanbyuzayat and was distributed to the camps as far south as Tanyin.

As in many of the camps, interpreters were not easily found, and the misunderstanding of instructions caused many difficulties. There were, though, a couple of amusing examples of this at Thanbyuzayat recorded by Brigadier Varley. Lieutenant Naito, who spoke English, asked an Australian driver what was wrong with a truck which would not start: 'The battery is flat,' explained the driver. 'What shape is it usually?' asked the lieutenant. On another occasion when Naito was told that there was 'a short' in a vehicle's electrical system, he ordered all shorts should be made longer.[608]

Thanbyuzayat became the base hospital for the northern end of the line to where the sick were transported from other Burmese camps. But, by early

---

605. AWM 2019.22.101.
606. AWM, 54 1010/4/64.
607. AWM, 2019.22.101.
608. Walker, *Australia in the War of 1939–1945*, op. cit., p.552.

February, the medical officer in charge of the hospital, Major Fisher, declared that the hospital was full. Despite this, the stream of patients continued. Brigadier Varley found his visits to the hospital very depressing: 'The constant contact with men in an emaciated condition, much underweight, crippled (some) with disease caused by deficiencies in diet, the constant toll of men by dysentery and diarrhoea, beri beri, pellagra, men covered with tropical ulcers, men losing their vision, numerous and recurrent malaria patients, men coughing up great worms, the cholera and smallpox threats, numerous rats in our quarters always reminding us of the possibilities of plague. The huts alive with bugs.'[609]

Much care was taken over the cemetery, where a garden was well-kept. This was planted with frangipani, bougainvillea and some shrubs. According to Major Dudley Apthorpe, all casualties were given a military funeral, with 'escort, pallbearers and bugler.'[610] Death certificates were produced and signed by the senior British Medical Officer, but these were later confiscated by the Japanese to conceal, no doubt, the true causes of death.

Thanbyuzayat was the target of Allied bombers aiming to destroy the railway line and its workshops. Varley had earlier sought permission to dig slit trenches for the prisoners to shelter in. This was approved – but only after they had dug trenches for the Japanese troops Varley also received permission to form a red cross on the ground at the hospital out of red soil and sand. When completed, the cross was 70 metres long and 70 metres wide.

In June 1943 it was subjected to two heavy raids. During the first of these, on 12 June, though no bombs struck the POW camp, some men were hit in the village at the water pump. According to Brigadier Varley, during the attack the Japanese 'became very excited, rushing around in all directions shouting, fixing bayonets, and loading rifles, and nobody was allowed outside the huts on penalty of being shot.'[611]

Three days later the bombers returned. The camp was surrounded on three sides by Japanese installations and the second attack was directed at these. As the bombers approached, Japanese soldiers and guards opened fire at them from inside the camp area. As a result, the camp was bombed and strafed.[612]

Though numbers vary, together the two raids resulted in the killing of a minimum of twenty-six prisoners and the wounding of at least a further thirty-four. Among those wounded was Varley himself. The day after the second of these raids the Japanese ordered the evacuation of the camp to Kandaw, Wagale, and Hlepauk camps which were no longer in use. No transport was provided

---

609. AWM, 2019.22.101.
610. Kinvig, p.85.
611. Walker, *Australia in the War of 1939–1945*, p.554.
612. Australian War Memorial, 54 554/2/1C.

and all the prisoners, regardless of their physical condition, had to make the journey on foot. Some were so ill they had scarcely left their beds for months and were expected not only to walk but to carry all their own bedding kit and mess gear into the jungle.[613] The men were in such poor condition it took eleven weeks to complete the move. On average two men died each day.

After the completion of the railway, 17,110 prisoners were sent back to Singapore and 10,770 were shipped to Japan and Formosa to continue to work on projects for the Japanese. The rest of those who had survived remained on the railway employed on maintenance duties until the Japanese surrender.[614]

---

613. Walker, *Australia in the War of 1939–1945*, p.555.
614. TNA, WO 203/6325.

Postscript

At the cost of 12,621 POW lives and possibly more than 200,000 Asian workers, the railway was built only a few weeks beyond the revised schedule. But it did the Japanese little good. They were already experiencing difficulties supplying the Southern Army due to the heavy attrition of their merchant marine at the hands of U.S. submariners. Then, when supplies did reach Thailand for transportation on the railway to Burma, more problems were encountered. The hurried nature of the construction, and the prisoners' efforts at sabotage meant that the track suffered from subsidence and buckling, and the shaky bridges were prone to collapse, on more than one occasion taking whole trains with them. According to one Japanese railway engineer, he and his fellow engineers knew that the new completion date demanded by Imperial Headquarters which brought about the 'speedo' period was unachievable. The result was 'many victims' and 'we ended up with an imperfectly-constructed railway with no prospect of maintaining transportation viability'.[1]

As we have seen, the railway was also the frequent target of Allied bombers. In November 1944 RAF and USAAF bombers undertook 697 sorties against the railway, dropping 1,000 tons of bombs. One particular raid, on 22 April 1945, involving forty B-24s, resulted in the destruction of thirty bridges and damage inflicted on a further six, in addition to which the approaches to a further seven bridges were blown apart. The famous bridge at Kanburi alone was subjected to seven major raids from the end of 1944 to June 1945.[2]

Due to the fact that it was a single-track line, it took just one accurate bomb, or a train to be damaged in a strafing attack, to cause major disruption along the entire railway. Eventually, movement along the line during daylight ceased, operations continuing only at night.

As a result of all this, the volume of traffic along the line was a fraction of the total that had been expected. This meant that the Japanese had to find alternative supply routes, with two divisions of reinforcements being forced to march on foot into Burma.

---

1. Futamatsu, p.97.
2. Kinvig, pp.81-2.

Finally, in perhaps one of the Second World Wars's greatest ironies, the railway which was to have propelled the Japanese into India became the main means of evacuation from Burma of Japanese casualties, sick as well as wounded, as the war began to turn decidedly in favour of the Allies. Many of these arrived in Thailand in conditions just as bad as those the prisoners had endured, suffering some of the same diseases and privations. I'm sure that this knowledge must have put a wry smile on many of the, by then, comparatively well-nourished a POWs' faces.

We began this book mentioning the War Crimes Trials that took place in 1946. It is only fitting that we conclude with a brief outline of the results of these proceedings.

A great many personal statements were submitted by the POWs in evidence of the inhuman treatment they had received at the hands of their captors, some of which have been included in the above stories of the camps. Added to these were the more structured reports of 'F' and 'H' forces, and that of Toosey and other officers.

In total 120 individuals were indicted. Of these 111 were found guilty and thirty-two were sentenced to death, including Captain Muruyama Hajime of Songkurai camp and Captain Noguchi who commanded the officers' camp at Kanburi.

Another who received the death sentence was Lieutenant Usuki of Konyu Camp. He was executed on 22 November 1946. He left behind a note which read, in part: 'I was put in a very thankless situation. Firstly, I was ordered to concentrate all my efforts on the early completion of the railway and hence the maximum labour force of POWs was required. Secondly the camps were completely surrounded by dense jungle, where the operation of transport was difficult, and where men fell sick one after another due to the hostile environment. Under these conditions, I proceeded to perform my duty with selfless devotion to my country.'[3] No doubt Usuki believed this and most of the Japanese who served on the building of the railway possibly believed it as well.

---

3. Tamayama, p.107.

Source Information

National Archives, Kew

WO 203/5823	South-East Asia Translation and Interrogation Centre Bulletins: 246 Burma-Siam Railway
WO 203/6325	Burma - Siam railway: history compiled by Canadian Intelligence Corps
WO 311/547	Burma-Siam Railway, Tamuang Camp: killing and ill-treatment of British POWs
WO 325/16	Burma-Siam Railway 'F' Force: account of events and war crimes against POWs working on railway
WO 325/17	Burma-Siam Railway Force H: war crimes against POWs working on railway
WO 325/18	Burma-Siam Railway Force H: affidavits relating to war crimes against POWs
WO 325/35	Report by Lt. Col. P.J.D. Toosey on Malay and Thailand Prisoner of War Camps
WO 325/157	Burma/Siam Railway: charges against Japanese high commanders
WO 325/90	Japanese Official Report.
WO 235/857	Judge Advocate General's Office: War Crimes Case Files, Second World War
WO 235/867	Judge Advocate General's Office: War Crimes Case Files, Second World War
WO 235/918	Judge Advocate General's Office: War Crimes Case Files, Second World War
WO 235/924	Judge Advocate General's Office: War Crimes Case Files, Second World War
WO 235/922	Judge Advocate General's Office: War Crimes Case Files, Second World War
WO 235/957	Judge Advocate General's Office: War Crimes Case Files, Second World War
WO 235/963	Judge Advocate General's Office: War Crimes Case Files, Second World War
WO 235/1034	Judge Advocate General's Office: War Crimes Case Files, Second World War

Australian War Memorial

AWM54 554/5/1 Dunlop, Lieutenant Colonel E.E., 'D' Force (Thailand): POW Camps, Thailand, Report on Kinsayok Camp and Hospital and Tarsau Base Hospital, 1943-1944

AWM54 554/2/1A	8th Division in Captivity – "A" Force (Burma): Reports on Conditions, Life and Work of Prisoners of War in Burma and Siam, by Brig C A McEachern, 1942-1945
AWM54 1010/3/10	War Crimes and Trials - Transcripts of Evidence
AWM54 1010/4/3	War Crimes and Trials - Affidavits and Sworn Statements
AWM54 1010/4/63	War Crimes and Trials - Affidavits and Sworn Statements
AWM54 1010/4/64	War Crimes and Trials - Affidavits and Sworn Statements
AWM54 1010/4/65	War Crimes and Trials - Affidavits and Sworn Statements
AWM54 1010/4/68	War Crimes and Trials - Affidavits and Sworn Statements
AWM54 1010//4/92	War Crimes and Trials - Affidavits and Sworn Statements
AWM 54 1010/4/122	War Crimes and Trials - Affidavits and Sworn Statements
AWM 2019.22.101	Transcript of the Diary of Arthur Leslie Varley, 1942-1944
AWM NX36791	Heckendorf, Erwin Ernest (Sergeant)
AWM 54 554/7/4	George Polain, 'Report on the Work of Chaplains with "F" Force'
AWM MSS 1037	R.F. Oakes, 'Work and be happy',
AWM PR 83/068	John Gilbert 'Tom' Morris, A Soldier's Reflections Forty Years On
AWM 2018.8.163	Report by Lieutenant Colonel G.E. Ramsay.

Imperial War Museum, London

Benford, E.S. *The Rising Sun on my Back, A Personal Account of War, 1939 – 1945*, Catalogue No. LBY K. 95 / 2303

Bishop, Richard William Noel, *Before the High King's Horses*, in private papers of Captain R.W.N. Bishop, Catalogue No. 3155.

Escritt, C.E. 'Note on the "V" Organisation', and *Beyond the Three Pagodas Pass*, as well as other documents in the Escritt Collection, Catalogue No. 2267

Published Books

Adams, Geoffrey Pharaoh, *No Time For Geishas* (Lee Cooper, London, 1973)

Adams, Kenneth, *Healing in Hell, The Memoirs of a Far Eastern POW Medic* (Pen & Sword, Barnsley, 2011)

Apthorpe, A.A., *The British Sumatra Battalion* (Book Guild, Lewes, 1988)

Arneil, Stan, *One Man's War* (Alternative Press, Sydney, 1980)

Aitken, F., *The Story of the 2/2 Australian Pioneer Battalion* (The Battalion Association, Melbourne, 1953)

Barwick, Idris James, *In the Shadow of Death: The Story of a Medic on the Burma Railway 1942-45* (Leo Cooper, Barnsley, 2005)

Beattie, Rod, *The Thai-Burma Railway, The True Story of The Bridge On The River Kwai* (T.B.R.C., Kanchanaburi, 2015)

Beattie, Rod, *The Death Railway – A Brief History of The Thailand-Burma Railway* (T.B.R.C. Kanchanaburi, 2015)

Best, Brian, [Ed.], *Secret Letters from the Railway, The Remarkable Record of Charles Steel – a Japanese POW* (Pen & Sword, Barnsley, 2004)

Brigginshaw, Jim, *Survival on the Death Railway and Nagasaki* (Pen & Sword, Barnsley, 2014)

Boye, James, *Railroad to Burma* (Allen & Unwin, Sydney, 1990)

Brune, Peter, *Descent into Hell, The Fall of Singapore – Pudu and Changi – The Thai-Burma Railway* (Allen & Unwin, London, 2014)

Burton, Reginald, *Railway of Hell, War, Captivity and Forced Labour at the Hands of the Japanese* (Pen & Sword, Barnsley, 2002)
Bradley, James, *Towards the Setting Sun, An Escape from the Thailand-Burma Railway, 1943* (J.M.L. Fuller, Wellington, 1982)
Coast, John, *Railroad of Death: The Original, Classic Account of the 'River Kwai' Railway* (Hyperon, London, 1946)
Crager, Kelly E., *Hell Under the Rising Sun: Texan POWs and the Building of the Burma-Thailand Death Railway* (Texan A&M University Press, 2008)
Davies, Peter N., *The Man behind the Bridge: Colonel Toosey and the River Kwai* (Athlone, London, 1991)
Davies. Philip *Lost Warriors - Seagrim and Pagani of Burma: The last great untold story of WWII* (Atlantic Publishing, 2017).
Daws, Gavan, *Prisoners of the Japanese* (Simon & Schuster, London, 2006)
Dunlop, E.E., *The War Diaries of Weary Dunlop* (Penguin, Harmondsworth, 1986)
Durnford, John, *Branch Line to Burma* (Four Square, London, 1966)
Charles, Robert H., *Last Man Out, Surviving the Burma-Thailand Death Railway* (Zenith Press, St Paul, 2006)
Clarke, Hugh, *A Life For Every Sleeper, A Pictorial Record of the Burma-Thailand Railway* (Allan & Unwin, Sydney, 1986)
Coates, Albert, and Rosenthal, Newman, *The Albert Coates Story, The Will that Found the Way* (Hyland House, Melbourne, 1977)
Ebury, Sue, *Weary, The Life of Sir Edward Dunlop of the Burma-Thailand Railway* (Viking, Harmondsworth, 1994)
Futamatsu, Yoshihiko, (Author), Davies, Peter N. (Editor), *Across the Three Pagodas Pass: The Story of the Thai-Burma Railway* (Renaissance Books, Folkstone, 2013)
Fyans, Peter, *Conjuror on the Kwai, The Incredible Life of Fergus Anckorn* (Pen & Sword, Barnsley, 2011)
Gill, Geoff and Parkes, Meg, *Burma Railway Medicine, Disease, Death and Survival on the Thai-Burma Railway 1942-1945* (Palatine, Lancaster, 2017).
Gillies, Midge, *The Barbed-Wire University, The Real Lives of Prisoners of War in the Second World War* (Aurum, London, 2011)
Godman, Arthur, *The Will to Survive* (Spellmount, Staplehurst, 2002)
Goode, Fred C., *No Surrender in Burma* (Pen & Sword, Barnsley, 2014)
Gordon, Ernest *Through the Valley of the Kwai* (Harper & Row, London, 1962)
Green, Hilary Custance, *Surviving the Death Railway* (Pen & Sword, Barnsley, 2016)
Grehan, John, *Medical Officers on the Infamous Burma Railway: Accounts of Life, Death & War Crimes by Those Who Were There* (Frontline, Barnsley, 2021)
Hardie, Robert, *The Burma-Siam Railway, The secret diary of Dr Robert Hardie 1943-45* (Imperial War Museum, London, 1983)
Henderson, Stan, *Comrades on the Kwai*, Socialist History Occasional Papers Series No.6 (Socialist History Society, 1997)
Kappe, Charles, *The Death Railway: The Personal Account of Lieutenant Colonel Kappe* (Frontline, Barnsley, 2022)
Hill, J.R., *Unknown to the Emperor*, (Zeebra, Manchester, 1998)
Kreefft, Otto, [Trans. Webb, John and Crombie, Netteke] Burma Railway, A Visual Recollection (Museum Bronbeck, 2008)
Kinvig, Clifford, *River Kwai Railway, The Story of the Burma-Siam Railroad* (Brassey's, London, 1992)

Knights, Alfred E, [Ed. Reginald Harland], *Singapore and the Thailand-Burma Railway* (Arena, Bury St. Edmunds, 2013)

Kratoska, Paul H., *The Thailand-Burma Railway, 1942-1946: Documents, and Selected Writings* (Routledge, New York, 2006)

Laird, Rory, *From Shanghai to the Burma Railway, The Memoirs & Letters of Richard Laird, A Japanese Prisoner of War* (Pen & Sword, Barnsley, 2020)

La Forte, Robert S. and Marcello, Ronald E., *Building the Death Railway: The Ordeal of American POWS in Burma, 1942-1945* (Rowman & Littlefield, 1993)

Lloyd, Stuart, *The Missing Years: A POW's Story from Changi to Hellfire Pass 1942–45* (Rosenberg Publishing, Dural, NSW, 2009)

Lomax, Eric *The Railway Man* (Vintage, London, 2014)

Lowry, Cecil, *Last Post Over the River Kwai, The 2nd East Surreys in the Far East 1938-1945* (Pen & Sword, Barnsley, 2018)

Lowry, Cecil, *Frank Pantridge MC, Japanese Prisoner of War and Inventor of the Portable Defibrillator* (Pen & Sword, Barnsley, 2020)

McCormack, Gavan, and Nelson, Hank [eds.], *The Burma-Thailand Railway: Memory and History* (Allen & Unwin, Sydney, 1993)

Marcello, Ronald, and Himmel, Richard, (eds) *With Only the Will to Live: Accounts of Americans in Japanese Prison Camps 1941-1945* (Rowman & Littlefield, Lanham, 1994)

Mitchell, Stewart, *Scattered Under The Sun, The Gordon Highlanders in the Far East 1941-1945* (Pen & Sword, Barnsley, 2012)

Morrison, I., *Grandfather Longlegs* (Faber & Faber, London, 1947)

Nelson, Hank, *Prisoners of War: Australians Under Nippon* (ABC, Sydney, 1985)

Newton, Reginald W.J. and McGuinness, Peter E.M., *The Grim glory of the 2/19 Battalion A.I.F*, (2/19 Battalion Association, Sydney, 1975)

Owtram, H.C., *1,000 Days on the River Kwai: The Secret Diary of a British Camp Commander* (Pen & Sword, Barnsley, 2017)

Parkes, Meg, *Captive Memories Far East POWs & Liverpool School of Tropical Medicine*, (Palatine, Lancaster, 2015)

Pavillard, Stanley S., *Bamboo Doctor, Saving Lives on the Railway of Death in World War Two* (Macmillan, London, 1960),

Peacock, Basil, *Prisoner on the Kwai* (London: William Blackwood & Sons, 1966)

Peek, Ian Denys, *One Fourteenth of an Elephant, A Memoir of Life and Death on the Burma-Thailand Railway* (Doubleday, London, 2004)

Reed, Bill, with Peeke, Mitch, *Lost Souls of the River Kwai, Experiences of a British Soldier on the Railway of Death* (Pen & Sword, Barnsley, 2004)

Richards, Rowley, and McEwan, Marcia, *The Survival Factor* (Costello, Tunbridge Wells, 1989)

Roberts, Ian, *Survival & Separation on the River Kwai, The Ordeal of a Japanese Prisoner of War and His Family* (Pen & Sword, Barnsley, 2023)

Rosario, Lionel de, *Nippon Slaves* (Janus Publishing, 1995)

Seiker, Fred, *Lest We Forget, The Railroad of Death* (Bevere Vivis Books, Worcester, 1996).

Sherwood, Johnny, and Doe, Michael, *Lucky Johnny: The Footballer who Survived the River Kwai Death Camps* (Hodder & Stoughton, London, 2014)

Shuttle, Jack, *Destination Kwai 'Reluctant Gypsy'* (Tucann, Heighington, 1994)

Skinner, Harold A., *'Guest' of the Imperial Japanese Army 1941-45* (Privately published, Littlehampton, 1993)

Steel, Charles, Secret *Letters from The Railway - The Remarkable Record of Charles Steel - A Japanese POW*, (Leo Cooper, Barnsley, 2004)
Stewart, John, *To the River Kwai: Two Journeys, 1943, 1979* (Bloomsbury, London, 1988)
Summers, Julie, *The Colonel of Tamarkan: Philip Toosey and the Bridge on the River Kwai* (Simon & Schuster, London, 2006)
Tamayama, Kazuo, *Building the Burma-Thailand Railway 1942-43, An Epic of World War II* (The World War II Remembrance Group, Japan, 2004)
Taylor, Ellie, *Faith, Hope and Rice* (Pen & Sword, Barnsley, 2015)
Twigg, Reg, *Survivor on the River Kwai, The Incredible Story of Life on the Burma Railway* (Viking, London, 2013)
Urquhart, Alistair, *The Forgotten Highlander, My Incredible Story of Survival During the War in the Far East* (Abacus, London, 2011)
Walker, Allan S. *Australia in the War of 1939–1945, Series Five, Medical, Volume II, Middle East and Far East*, (Australian War Memorial, Canberra, 1962)
Warwick, Ernest, *Tamajao 241: Prisoner of War Camps on the River Kwai* (Paul-Leagas Ashingdon, 1987)
Wigmore, Lionel, *Australia in the War of 1939–1945, Volume IV – The Japanese Thrust, Part III - Prisoners of the Japanese* (Australian War Memorial, Canberra, 1957)
Wood-Higgs, Stanley, *Bamboo and Barbed Wire* (Roman Press, Bournemouth, 1988)
Wright, Pattie, *The Men of the Line: Stories of the Thai-Burma Railway Survivors* (Miegunyah Press, Melbourne, 2008)
Wyatt, John, & Lowry, Cecil, *No Mercy from the Japanese, A Survivor's Account of the Burma Railway and the Hell Ships* (Pen & Sword, Barnsley, 2008)
Young, Stuart, *Life on the Death Railway* (Pen & Sword, Barnsley, 2013)

Internet Sources
2/4th Machine Gun Battalion, 2nd4thmgb.com.au.
Anzac Portal
BBC People's War
Colonel Harold Lilly: Far East POW Hero, spondonhistory.org.uk/archive document
far-eastern-heroes.org.uk
FEPOW Liberation Questionnaires lq-cofepow.org
cofepow.org.uk/armed-forces-stories-list/the-british-battalion
britain-at-war.org.uk/WW2/Death_Railway
legal-tools.org/doc
Center for Research Allied POWS Under the Japanese, mansell.com/pow_resources/camplists.
powresearch.jp/en/archive/camplist
pows-of-japan.net
mansell.com/pow_resources
sapiens.org/archaeology
secondtwentiethbattalionaif.wordpress.com/prisoner-of-war-POW
www.tweedewereldwereld.nl
routeyou.com
wartimememoriesproject.com
WW2today.com via pacificparatrooper.wordpress.com

Index

Abe, Lieutenant Hiroshi, 215
Adams, Lieutenant Geoffery, 192
Adams, Private Kenneth, 54, 62–63
Adshead, Driver Wilfrid Stanley, 172–173
Akester, Captain George, 98
Allingham, Private Alfred Arthur, 99
Anckorn, Gunner Fergus, 88–89, 104,
Apthorpe, Major Dudley, 77, 232, 246, 259, 262–263, 271
Anderson, Lieutenant Colonel C.G.W., 204, 255–256, 261
Anderson, Major Roderick, 51, 211–212
Anker, Captain W.H. 218
Arneil, Sergeant Stan, 207, 220, 225
Atherton, Sergeant Frederick, 78
Atkins, Lieutenant Alfred 'Tommy', 89
Austin, Lieutenant Richard, 148–149

Baker, Lieutenant Colonel, 170
Baker, Captain Barry Custance, 51, 93, 184–185
Banno, Lieutenant Colonel Hirateru, 195, 200–201, 209, 230
Barbour, Lieutenant Duncan, 163
Barnett, Captain B.A., 182
Barnard, Captain John, 38, 115
Barratt, Lieutenant Colonel Saint-Clair Edward John, 88
Barwick, Driver Idris James, 176, 202, 219, 221–222, 251, 253
Baynes, Sergeant Len (Snowie), 93, 95, 97
Bell, Sapper Alexander, 265
Bell, Lieutenant James, 83, 98
Benford, Lance Bombardier, E.S., 56, 142, 144,
Benson, Lieutenant Colonel H.C., 64
Bhumgara, Sergeant Joseph, 45
Bilyard, Lance Corporal William, 73
Black, Lieutenant Colonel C.M., 37, 72, 254–255, 260

Bluett, Lieutenant Denis, 172,
Blyden, Warrant Officer Glen, 177
Bolero, Jim, 75, 259–260
Boone, Major Ray, 187
Bouch, Captain T., 130
Bowring, Captain W.B., 182, 209
Boxtel, Captain, C.J. van, 247
Bradley, Lieutenant J.B., 218, 222
Bradley, Sergeant Ian O'Brian Poston Bradley, 217–218
Bramlett, Kelly Bob, 240
Britt, Corporal Leo, 90
Brown, Corporal, 219
Bryant-Smith, Corporal Stanley, 210–211
Bulled, Signalman Reg, 112
Burbridge, Sergeant Leslie, 102
Burton, Lieutenant Anthony, 197

Campbell, Major Peter, 248
Carlton, Private, 72
Cayley, Captain Forde, 170
Chalker, Bombardier Jack, 82
Chalmers, Major John, 204
Charles, Corporal H.R., 254
Cheda, Major, 110
Christie, Signaller Bob, 180
Clarke, Captain Peter, 170
Clarke, Hugh V., 138–139
Claydon, Private Thomas, 98
Clayton, Gunner G.W., 172
Coates, Lieutenant Colonel Albert Ernest, 65, 242, 247–249, 251, 258
Coast, Lieutenant John, 156, 167, 171, 178
Collie, Company Sergeant Major Angus, 168
Coombes, Sergeant, 258–259
Cough, Major Alfred, 173–174
Corlette, Major E.L., 156
Cornelis, Commander J.C., 130
Cox, Private F.E., 59, 175–176,

Curlewis, Captain Adrian, 182–183, 197, 199–200
Curtiss, Corporal Joseph, 82

Dawkins, Lance Corporal William Henry, 217–218
De Wardener, Captain Hugh Edward, 89, 113, 179
Dickinson, Gunner Keith Johnson, 265
Dickson, Captain Mathew Crawford, 82,
Dillon, Lieutenant Colonel F.J., 195,
Dooley, Company Sergeant Major, 49,
Driver, Captain J., 64
Drower, Captain W.M., 66–67, 70, 264,
Duncan, Captain Ean, 174
Duckworth, Padre, Noel, 214, 251,
Dunlop, Lieutenant Colonel Ernest Edward 'Weary', x–xi, 88, 90, 113–114, 116–118, 120, 136–138, 154–161, 164, 169
Dugan, Private, 223
Durnford, Lieutenant John, 76, 114–116, 119, 127–128
Dyer, Captain Donald, 63

Ellis, Captain Thomas, 189–191
English, Major Jeffrey, 65, 131, 153
Escritt, Captain Ewart, 46
Evans, Corporal Jack Ivor, 217–218

Fagan, Lance Corporal Tom, 238
Feathers, Captain J., 218–219
Feeny, Private, 172
Fewell, Captain Roy, 169
Field, Lawrence, 148
Fisher, Major Walter Edward, 259, 267, 271
Fitzgerald, Private Patrick, 99–100
Fukuda, First Lieutenant Tsuneo, 63 207–212
Fumimoto, Tetsuichi, 190, 192–193
Fung, Private Eddie, 237
Fuskase, Lieutenant Colonel, 194
Futamatsu, Yoshihiko, 104, 107, 208, 273,
Futamatu, Norihiko, 55

Gairdner, K.G., 44
Gairdner, Major K.D., 229
Gaskell, Major George, 152–153

Gennis, Captain, 196
Gerritsen, Captain D., 110
Gilbert, Company Sergeant Major Leslie, 84,
Gill, Major W.E, 43–46, 48, 50–51
Godman, Lieutenant Arthur, 60, 201
Gordon, Captain Ernest, 74, 80–82, 86–87
Gordon, Lieutenant Colonel Lincoln, 191
Goto, Captain, 84
Gottschall, Lieutenant Colonel, 247
Green, Major Charles Edward, 37, 266–267
Grenier, Major H. G., 135
Griffith, Private Keith George, 235, 242
Grundie, Corporal Andrew, 223
Guerin, Sergeant Chris, 234

Haasen, Sergeant Van, 265
Hachisuka, Captain, 133
Hajime, Captain Muruyama, 274
Hallam, Sergeant M., 156,
Hamilton, Lieutenant Lamb, 239
Hamilton, Lieutenant Colonel Thomas, 259, 267, 269–270
Hamley, Colin, 237
Hands, Captain John Lawrence, 154, 165
Hardie, Dr Robert, xi, 89, 95–96, 100–101, 167, 172, 178–181, 204, 232
Harding, Lloyd Francis, 234
Han-ne, Army Civilian Employee Lee, 163
Harrell, Chief Specialist J.A., 56
Harrison, Major H., 151
Harvey, Lieutenant Colonel W., 58, 110
Hausenberg, Major, 267
Headley, Reverend L.V., 64
Heekeren, Hendrik Robert van, 97,
Hekking, Dr Henri, 254–255
Henderson, Corporal Stan, 81
Henry, Captain Peter, 216
Heron, Owen, 238
Higgins, Captain John, 254
Higuchi, Captain Tomizo, 258, 260, 268, 270
Hill, J.R., 92, 99, 102, 186
Hilton, Private Eric Bertrand, 111–112
Hingston, Lieutenant Colonel A.T., 214
Hiramatsu, Staff Sergeant, 126–127
Hiroda, Lieutenant, 152, 154–155, 158

Hoskins, Frederick, 43
Howard, Lieutenant, 75
Humphries, Lieutenant Colonel H.R., 54, 64, 116, 120, 125, 132–133, 142, 146, 150, 194
Humphrey, Major Charles, 215
Hunt, Major Bruce, 111, 206, 209, 231, 251, 253
Hunt, Private G.V., 112
Hutchinson, Lieutenant Colonel C.T., 249–250, 252–253

Iles, Sapper, 235
Ishida, Major General, 12
Ishii, Lieutenant Colonel, 110

Jackson, Sergeant Peter Richard, 217
Jackson, Captain W.R., 62
Jacobs, Major Jim, 224, 262, 264
Jarman, Reginald Thomas, 216
Johnson, Lieutenant Colonel A.A., 98, 108
Johnston, Major Noel, 212–213
James, Signalman Campbell Ian, 240
Jones, Lieutenant T.P.D., 219
Jones, Sergeant H., 52, 126, 129
Jupp, Herbert, 105

Kappe, Lieutenant Colonel Charles, 54, 195–196, 199, 201, 205–206, 208–210, 212, 215, 222. 224, 227
Kelly, Sergeant Francis, 99
Kemp, Gunner George, 56
Kenneally, Fusilier Timothy, 99
Kerr, James, 141, 198
Kiernan, Major George, 255,
Knights, Lieutenant Colonel Alfred Ernest, 46, 109–112
Kosakata, Lieutenant, 71–74
Krantz, Major Sydney, 258
Kreefft, Otto, 233
Kuriyana, Second Lieutenant, 98

Laird, Captain Richard, 38, 216, 231
Laming, Lieutenant Colonel, 88
Lancaster, Bombardier G.R., 56
Leech, Staff Sergeant, 52, 85, 172
Lilley, Lieutenant Colonel Harold Hutchinson, 103

Lloyd, Major John, 68
Lloyd, Stuart 148
Lomax, Lieutenant Eric, 52, 60–61

Machade, Lieutenant G.A., 218
Mackie, Private William, 57
Malcolm, Lieutenant Colonel John Wright, 62,
Mannion, Regimental Sergeant Major, 168
Maruoka, Lieutenant, 110–111
Maruyama, Captain, 182–184
Marsden, Major E.A., 62
Maston, Captain Ronald, 226
Matsumoto, Lieutenant, 150
Mayes, Major Guy, 169
McEachern, Lieutenant Colonel C.A., 160, 162
McPherson, Captain Daneil, 172
Miles, Lieutenant T., 191
Milner, Lieutenant Colonel, 99
Mizutani, Major Totaro, 56–57, 239
Moate, Private Joseph, 156
Moffat, Lieutenant I.M., 218–219
Mohammed, Nur, 219
Moir-Byres, Captain George Francis, 98
Moon, Major A.A., 156
Morris, Corporal John Gilbert 'Tom', 77, 235, 244, 248
Moss, Captain E.T., 172
Motoyama, Kinzo, 57, 102
Mull, Major Alan, 265
Muriama, Captain Naoetsu, 200

Nabuswa, Lieutenant, 91
Nagataro, Lieutenant Kokubo, 99,
Nagatoma, Lieutenant Colonel Yoshitada, 204, 244, 248, 260, 266–269
Naito, Lieutenant, 258–260, 265, 267, 270
Nakamura, Colonel S., 62
Nelissen, Private,v 265
Nellis, Regimental Quartermaster Sergeant Alfred E., 103
Nevey, Lieutenant Colonel T.H., 161
Newton, Captain Reginald, 45, 59, 88, 133, 162
Noguchi, Lieutenant Hideji, 66–68, 78
Nobusawa, Lieutenant Hisashi, 85, 181

Oates, Lieutenant Colonel Roland, 147, 149
Offerle, Max and Oscar, 237, 240
Okada, Sergeant Seiichi, 57, 157, 160
Osada, Lieutenant, 232
Osborn, Colour Sergeant Valentine Thomas, 73
O'Toole, Patrick, 199
Owtram, Lieutenant Colonel Cary, 52, 66, 80–81, 84–89, 159

Padfield, John Edward, vii
Pagani, Private Roy, 263
Pantridge, Lieutenant Frank, 253
Parsons, Major John, 39, 65, 110
Pavillard, Dr Stanley, 38, 103–104, 106–107, 122–124, 140, 164
Peacock, Major Basil, 91, 96–97, 108–109, 116, 184
Peek, Lance Corporal Ian Denys, 102, 124–125, 140
Percival, Gunner Winch, 172
Pilkington, Captain, 150
Pine, Coffin, Lieutenant Colonel, 192
Platte, Lieutenant Colonel, 232
Polain, Reverend George, 208, 226
Pomeroy, Captain E.C., 74
Pond, Lieutenant Colonel S.A.F., 181, 195, 199
Pratt, Sergeant C.W.J., 49
Pickard, Private D.S., 227–228
Price, Alan, 261
Priestman, Sergeant George, 82, 105
Prime, Lance Corporal A., 175

Ramsay, Lieutenant Colonel George E., 37, 41, 65, 261
Raymond, Lieutenant Christopher, 100
Reay, Sergeant Edward, 99
Richards, Captain Charles Rowland Bromley 'Rowley', 71, 203–204, 245–246, 256, 262, 264,
Riches, Lieutenant Leslie Gordon, 174
Ridgwell, Richard, 113
Rivett, Rohan Deakin, 76
Percival, Gunner Winch, 172
Roach, Corporal Leonard, 174
Robinson, Lieutenant, 218–219

Roberts, Major, 70, 72
Roberts, Eric, 105
Robson, Captain, 190
Rosario, Lionel de, 139, 213, 215, 221–223
Ross, Chaplain Christopher, 46, 49

Sasa (Sasaki), Major General, 100, 243, 259
Sadler, Private Ronald, 82
Sanjionchi, Lieutenant, 125
Schurmann, Sergeant John Henry, 244
Scott, Private Jimmy, 176
Seiker, Sergeant Fred, 73–74
Sherwood, Sergeant Johnny, 114–115, 146, 168
Shimoda, Major General, 11
Shingyochi, Lieutenant, 130
Shuttle, Sergeant Jack 93–95, 99
Silman, Captain Harry, 230
Sirivejjabhandu, Boon Pong, 44, 75
Skewes, Private Glen, 55, 199
Skinner, Harold, 185, 193
Slaughter, Lance Corporal John, 50, 241
Smith, Ensign C.D., 66
Smith Laing, B.N., 178
Smith, Lance Corporal Thomas, 236
Smith, Padre, Peter, 246
Smith, Sergeant Fred, 61
Soldinoff, Major de, 68
Stanfield, Len, 261
Steel, Battery Sergeant Major Charles, 59, 141, 165–166
Stevens, Major Roy, 227–228
Stoten, Corporal Alfred, 81
Stringer, Major J., 266
Sugasawa, Lieutenant Colonel, 48
Surman, Henry, 177
Suzuki, Captain, 95, 187
Swartjes, Captain J., 110
Swartz, Captain R., 227
Swinton, Lieutenant Colonel George Edward, 93–95, 189
Sykes, Major R.S, 43–46

Takasaki, Major General, 11–12
Tanaka, Lieutenant, 46, 110, 127, 165
Tarumoto, Second Lieutenant Juji, 52, 80, 84–85, 98, 105, 170, 172

Taylor, Clark, 240
Taylor, Private C.F., 124
Thirlwell, Hal, 196
Thompson, Corporal Thomas, 196
Tidey, John, 180
Tillema, Captain Hendrik Anthonie, 71
Tomlinson, Gunner William, 61
Toosey, Lieutenant Colonel Philip, 44, 47–49, 54, 59, 66, 71–76, 78, 274
Tsuruta, Probationary Officer Masaru, 70
Toyoyama, Kisei, 51, 207, 210–211, 227–228
Twigg, Private Reg, ix-x, 101

Ullmann, Corporal John Stewart, 203, 219
Urado, Frederick John, 217
Urquhart, Corporal Alistair, 57, 142, 144
Usuki, Lieutenant Kishio, 274, 136, 159

Varley, Brigadier Arthur Leslie, 37, 40, 77, 204, 232, 244, 246, 254, 258, 262, 266–271
Veitch, Lieutenant Gerard, 186
Vellacott, Padre, 183
Vredevoogd, Private, 265

Wainwright, Signalman, 172
Walker, Lance Corporal William, 192–193
Wanty, Fusilier Leonard William, 56–57
Warwick, Ernest, 186–188
Weber, Captain Max, 68, 85
Weber, Donald, 85
Whitecross, Roy, 197
Whitefield, Private G.H., 263, 267
Wilkinson, Lieutenant Colonel, 218–219
Wild, Major Cyril, 111, 219, 225–226, 231
Williams, Lieutenant Colonel J. M., 219, 245–246, 255–257
Williamson, Lieutenant Colonel John Rowley, 83
Winchester, Captain M.K., 50, 116, 148
Wolfe, Assistant-Surgeon Patrick, 195, 202
Woods, Major F. A., 135
Wyatt, Lance Corporal John Augustine, 54, 96, 166, 171

Yabe, Major, viii
Yamada, Lieutenant, 254, 256–257
Yanagida, Lieutenant Colonel, 83
Young, Bombardier Stuart, 58, 125